Virtue Ethics and Contemporary Aristotelianism

Bloomsbury Studies in the Aristotelian Tradition

General Editor:
Marco Sgarbi, Università Ca' Foscari, Italy

Editorial Board:
Klaus Corcilius *(University of California, Berkeley, USA)*; Daniel Garber *(Princeton University, USA)*; Oliver Leaman *(University of Kentucky, USA)*; Anna Marmodoro *(University of Oxford, UK)*; Craig Martin *(Oakland University, USA)*; Carlo Natali *(Università Ca' Foscari, Italy)*; Riccardo Pozzo *(Consiglio Nazionale delle Ricerche, Rome, Italy)*; Renée Raphael *(University of California, Irvine, USA)*; Victor M. Salas *(Sacred Heart Major Seminary, USA)*; Leen Spruit *(Radboud University Nijmegen, The Netherlands)*.

Aristotle's influence throughout the history of philosophical thought has been immense and in recent years the study of Aristotelian philosophy has enjoyed a revival. However, Aristotelianism remains an incredibly polysemous concept, encapsulating many, often conflicting, definitions. *Bloomsbury Studies in the Aristotelian Tradition* responds to this need to define Aristotelianism and give rise to a clear characterization.

Investigating the influence and reception of Aristotle's thought from classical antiquity to contemporary philosophy from a wide range of perspectives, this series aims to reconstruct how philosophers have become acquainted with the tradition. The books in this series go beyond simply ascertaining that there are Aristotelian doctrines within the works of various thinkers in the history of philosophy, but seek to understand how they have received and elaborated Aristotle's thought, developing concepts into ideas that have become independent of him.

Bloomsbury Studies in the Aristotelian Tradition promotes new approaches to Aristotelian philosophy and its history. Giving special attention to the use of interdisciplinary methods and insights, books in this series will appeal to scholars working in the fields of philosophy, history and cultural studies.

Available titles:
Elijah Del Medigo and Paduan Aristotelianism, Michael Engel
Phantasia in Aristotle's Ethics, edited by Jakob Leth Fink
Pontano's Virtues, Matthias Roick
The Aftermath of Syllogism, edited by Marco Sgarbi, Matteo Cosci
A Political Philosophy of Conservatism, by Ferenc Hörcher

Virtue Ethics and Contemporary Aristotelianism

Modernity, Conflict and Politics

Edited by
Andrius Bielskis, Eleni Leontsini
and Kelvin Knight

BLOOMSBURY ACADEMIC
LONDON • NEW YORK • OXFORD • NEW DELHI • SYDNEY

BLOOMSBURY ACADEMIC
Bloomsbury Publishing Plc
50 Bedford Square, London, WC1B 3DP, UK
1385 Broadway, New York, NY 10018, USA
29 Earlsfort Terrace, Dublin 2, Ireland

BLOOMSBURY, BLOOMSBURY ACADEMIC and the Diana logo are trademarks of
Bloomsbury Publishing Plc

First published in Great Britain 2020
This paperback edition published in 2021

Copyright © Andrius Bielskis, Eleni Leontsini, Kelvin Knight and contributors, 2020

Andrius Bielskis, Eleni Leontsini & Kelvin Knight have asserted their right under the
Copyright, Designs and Patents Act, 1988, to be identified as Editor of this work.

Cover image: Depiction of Aristotle from the fresco of the forecourt, the propylaeum,
of the National and Kapodistrian University of Athens made by the Austrian painter
Karl Rahl (1812–1865) in 1859 and completed by the Polish painter Eduard Lebiedzky
(1862–1915) in 1889. © National and Kapodistrian University of Athens

All rights reserved. No part of this publication may be reproduced or transmitted in any form or by any
means, electronic or mechanical, including photocopying, recording, or any information storage or retrieval
system, without prior permission in writing from the publishers.

Bloomsbury Publishing Plc does not have any control over, or responsibility for, any
third-party websites referred to or in this book. All internet addresses given in this
book were correct at the time of going to press. The author and publisher regret any
inconvenience caused if addresses have changed or sites have ceased to exist,
but can accept no responsibility for any such changes.

Library of Congress Cataloging-in-Publication Data

Names: Bielskis, Andrius, 1973-editor. | Leontsini, Eleni, editor. | Knight, Kelvin, editor.
Title: Virtue ethics and contemporary Aristotelianism: modernity, conflict
and politics / edited by Andrius Bielskis, Eleni Leontsini, and Kelvin Knight.
Description: London; New York: Bloomsbury Academic, 2020. |
Series: Bloomsbury studies in the Aristotelian tradition |
Includes bibliographical references and index. | Summary: "This compelling and distinctive volume advances
Aristotelianism by bringing its traditional virtue ethics to bear upon characteristically modern issues, such as
the politics of economic power and egalitarian dispute. Clearly divided into three parts and featuring a
contribution from Alasdair MacIntyre, this volume bridges the gap between Aristotle's philosophy and the
multitude of contemporary Aristotelian theories that have been formulated in the twentieth and twenty-first
centuries. Part I draws on Aristotle's texts and Thomas Aquinas' Aristotelianism to examine the Aristotelian
tradition of virtues, with a chapter by Alasdair MacIntyre contextualising the different readings of Aristotle's
philosophy. Part II offers a critical engagement with MacIntyrean Aristotelianism, assessing MacIntyre's
development of Aristotelian themes and revealing their conflict with modernity. Firmly establishing the relevance
of Aristotle's thought today, Part III demonstrates the ongoing influence of Aristotelianism in contemporary
theoretical debates on governance and politics. Extensive in its historical scope, this is a valuable collection
relating the tradition of virtue to modernity, which will be of interest to all working in virtue ethics and
contemporary Aristotelian politics"– Provided by publisher.
Identifiers: LCCN 2020005710 (print) | LCCN 2020005711 (ebook) | ISBN 9781350122178 (hardback) |
ISBN 9781350122185 (ebook) | ISBN 9781350122192 (epub)
Subjects: LCSH: Aristotle. | Virtues. | Virtue. | Ethics.
Classification: LCC B485.V547 2020 (print) | LCC B485 (ebook) | DDC 171/.3–dc23

LC record available at https://lccn.loc.gov/2020005710
LC ebook record available at https://lccn.loc.gov/2020005711

A catalogue record for this book is available from the British Library.

A catalog record for this book is available from the Library of Congress.

ISBN: HB: 978-1-3501-2217-8
PB: 978-1-3502-5146-5
ePDF: 978-1-3501-2218-5
eBook: 978-1-3501-2219-2

Series: Bloomsbury Studies in the Aristotelian Tradition

Typeset by Deanta Global Publishing Services, Chennai, India

To find out more about our authors and books visit www.bloomsbury.com and sign up for our newsletters.

Contents

Notes on contributors — vi

Introduction — 1

Part 1 The Aristotelian tradition of virtues

1. Four – or more? – political Aristotles *Alasdair MacIntyre* — 11
2. Plato and Aristotle on nature and society *Richard Stalley* — 25
3. 'Managers would not need subordinates and masters would not need slaves': Aristotle's *Oikia* and *Oikonomia* reconsidered *Andrius Bielskis* — 40
4. Aristotle and two senses of happiness *Buket Korkut Raptis* — 58
5. 'Going through time together': Aristotelian friendship and the criterion of time *Eleni Leontsini* — 76
6. Byzantine Thomism: Aristotelianism and Thomas Aquinas' reception in Byzantium *Athanasia Glycofrydi-Leontsini* — 94

Part 2 Modernity, conflict and MacIntyrean Aristotelianism

7. Aristotelianism, Austinianism and the problem of the good *Kelvin Knight* — 111
8. Virtues and the common good: Alasdair MacIntyre reads Aristotle *Christof Rapp* — 126
9. Williams and MacIntyre on the human good and ethical objectivity *Apostolos Malakos* — 147
10. Alasdair MacIntyre's Nietzschean anti-modernism *Golfo Maggini* — 162

Part 3 Virtue ethics and modern social and political theory

11. From field to forest?: Exploring limits of virtue ethics *Joseph Dunne* — 175
12. Aristotle and the politics of recognition *Tony Burns* — 192
13. Human flourishing and labour: Aristotle, MacIntyre and Marx *Egidijus Mardosas* — 208
14. Alasdair MacIntyre's Aristotelianism: A Marxist critique *Paul Blackledge* — 222

Index — 237

Contributors

Andrius Bielskis (co-editor) is Professor of Political Philosophy and Director of the Centre of Aristotelian Studies and Critical Theory at Mykolas Romeris University, Vilnius, Lithuania. He is also Professor of Philosophy at Kaunas University of Technology, Lithuania. He is member of London Metropolitan University's Centre for Contemporary Aristotelian Studies in Ethics & Politics (CASEP), co-convenor of the Contemporary Aristotelian Studies Group of the PSA (CAS) and member of the steering committee for the International Society for MacIntyrean Enquiry (ISME). He is the author of four books, *Towards a Post-Modern Understanding of the Political* 2005), *The Unholy Sacrament. Ideology, Faith, and the Politics of Emancipation* (2014; in Lithuanian), *On the Meaning of Philosophy and Art* (2015; in Lithuanian and English), and *Existence, Meaning, Excellence: Aristotelian Reflection on the Meaning of Life* (2017), the co-editor of *Virtue and Economy* (with K. Knight, 2015), the editor of *Democracy without Labour Movement?* (2009; in Lithuanian), *Debating with the Lithuanian New Left: Terry Eagleton, Joel Bakan, Alex Demirovic, Urlich Brand* (with A. Pažėrė, 2013; in English), and the author of many scholarly papers in English, Lithuanian and Greek. He was the principle investigator of the research project 'Structures of Meaning' funded by the Research Council of Lithuania (2012–15). He was also an International Onassis Fellow affiliated with the National and Kapodistrian University of Athens (2017–18), conducting research on Aristotle's teleology and natural inequalities, especially focusing on Aristotle's notorious conception of natural slavery.

Paul Blackledge teaches at Northumbria and Shanxi universities. He is the author of *Friedrich Engels* (2019), *Marxism and Ethics* (2012), *Reflections on the Marxist Theory of History* (2006) and *Perry Anderson, Marxism and the New Left* (2004). He is also the co-editor of *Virtue and Politics: Alasdair MacIntyre's Revolutionary Aristotelianism* (2011), *Alasdair MacIntyre's Engagement with Marxism: Essays and Articles 1953-1974* (2008), *Revolutionary Aristotelianism: Ethics, Resistance and Utopia* (2008) and *Historical Materialism and Social Evolution* (2002).

Tony Burns is Professor of Political Theory at the School of Politics and International Relations at the University of Nottingham. He is Director of the Centre for the Study of Social and Global Justice (CSSGJ). He is a former chair of the Contemporary Aristotelian Studies Group of the PSA (CAS) and a former member of the steering committee for the International Society for MacIntyrean Enquiry (ISME). He is author of *Aristotle and Natural Law* (2011), and wrote the chapter on Aristotle in *Political Thinkers: From Socrates to the Present*. He will be contributing a chapter on Aristotle's social theory and the politics of recognition in the *Brill Companion to the Legacy of Ancient Greek Political Thought* (2020). He is currently working on a research project devoted to the politics of recognition in the history of political thought from the ancient Greeks to the present, which is to be published by Rowman & Littlefield International. *Social Institutions and the Politics of Recognition*, Vol. 1, *From the Ancient Greeks to the Reformation* (Rowman & Littlefield International, 2020); Vol. 2, *From the Reformation to the French Revolution* (Rowman & Littlefield International, 2020).

Joseph Dunne is Emeritus Professor of Philosophy and Education at Dublin City University and Senior Research Fellow at the Centre for Aristotelian Studies and Critical Theory at Mykolas Romeris University, Vilnius, Lithuania. For forty years he taught at St. Patrick's College Dublin, where he was founding head of the programme in Human Development. He has also taught at Duke University, the University of Oslo and at the University of British Columbia. His *Back to the Rough Ground: Phronesis and Techne in Modern Philosophy and in Aristotle* (1993) has been widely recognized as an important book in retrieving the philosophical significance of Aristotle's conception of practical wisdom and in demonstrating its pertinence to a range of contemporary professions, including teaching. He is the author of many articles in international journals, and has co-edited *Questioning Ireland: Debates in Political Philosophy and Public Policy* (2000); *Childhood and its Discontents: The First Seamus Heaney Lectures* (2002); and *Education and Practice: Upholding the Integrity of Teaching and Learning* (2004). He is at present completing work on a collection of essays, with the provisional title, *Persons in Practice: Essays between Education and Philosophy*.

Athanasia Glycofrydi-Leontsini is Emerita Professor of Modern European and Neohellenic Philosophy at the Department of Philosophy at the School of Philosophy of the National and Kapodistrian University of Athens, Greece. She is widely known both in Greece and abroad for her work on the Scottish enlightenment, neohellenic philosophy and aesthetics. She is a member and former vice-president of the Institut International de Philosophie (IIP) and a member of the European Academy of Sciences and Arts. She was Philosophy Erasmus Coordinator (2004–15). She is member of Greek and Foreign philosophical societies and has organized many international conferences at the University of Athens (on Adam Smith, J. J. Rousseau, P. Vrailas-Armenis, and neohellenic philosophy). She was a member of the Organizing Committee of the 23rd World Philosophy Conference (FISP, Athens, 2013). She has authored eight books in Greek: *The Epistemological Foundations of Thomas Reid's Aesthetics*, PhD thesis (1988), *Neohellenic Aesthetics and the European Enlightenment* (1989), *Neohellenic Philosophy: Persons and Problems* (1993), *Neohellenic Philosophy: Moral and Political Questions* (2001), *Systems of Fine Arts in Neohellenic Aesthetics* (2002), *Aesthetics and Art: Critical Reconsiderations* (2006), *An Introduction to Aesthetics* (Athens, 2008) and *An Anthology of Ancient Greek Philosophical Texts* (2009, secondary education textbook). She has also annotated and edited critical editions of Modern Greek philosophical works from fourteenth century onwards in the *Corpus Philosophorum Graecorum Recentiorum*, in which she is a joint general editor. In these critical editions are included four volumes of Petros Vrailas-Armenis *Philosophical Works* (1973, 1974, 1986, 2004) and three volumes of Demetrius Kydones, *Thomas Aquinas' Summa Theologiae in Greek* (1976, vol. 15; 2011, vol. 19; 2019, vol. 20). She has also published widely in international journals and in collected volumes in English, French, Italian and Greek. In 2004, she received an award from the Academy of Athens for her scientific work on the promotion of the research of modern Greek philosophy, and in 2011 she was the recipient of a DAAD scholarship.

Kelvin Knight (co-editor) is Reader in Ethics and Politics and Director of the Centre for Contemporary Aristotelian Studies in Ethics & Politics (CASEP) at London Metropolitan University. Elsewhere, he is General Secretary of the International Society for MacIntyrean Enquiry, co-Convenor of the Contemporary Aristotelian Studies Group of the PSA (CAS) and Senior Research Fellow at the Centre for Aristotelian Studies and Critical Theory, Mykolas Romeris University. He is author of *Aristotelian Philosophy: Ethics and Politics from Aristotle to MacIntyre* (2007), editor of *The MacIntyre Reader* (1998) and co-editor of three collections on contemporary Aristotelianism: *Revolutionary Aristotelianism: Ethics, Resistance and Utopia* (2008) and V*irtue and Politics: Alasdair MacIntyre's Revolutionary Aristotelianism* (2011) with Paul Blackledge, and *Virtue and Economy: Essays on Morality and Markets* (2015) with Andrius Bielskis. Having led a master's course in human rights since 2003, he is at last completing a book on the history of human rights and hoping to live long enough to compose one on their philosophy.

Eleni Leontsini (co-editor) is Tenured Assistant Professor of the History of Philosophy: Ancient Greek Philosophy, Modern Philosophy, Neohellenic at the Department of Philosophy, University of Ioannina, Greece, and International Research Fellow at Mykolas Romeris University's Centre for Aristotelian Studies and Critical Theory. She is also Adjunct Academic Staff at the Hellenic Open University, Visiting Researcher at the Department of Philosophy at the University of Glasgow, member of London Metropolitan University's Centre for Contemporary Aristotelian Studies in Ethics & Politics (CASEP), co-Convenor of the Contemporary Aristotelian Studies Group of the PSA (CAS) and member of the executive committee of the International Society for MacIntyrean Enquiry (ISME). Her research focuses on classical, modern and contemporary Aristotelianism, specializing in Aristotle's moral and political philosophy. She is the author of *The Appropriation of Aristotle in the Liberal-Communitarian Debate* (with a foreword by R. F. Stalley, 2007; in English). She has co-authored the philosophy textbook *Anthology of Ancient Greek Philosophical Texts* (2009), which is part of the Greek National Curriculum, and she has co-edited *Kythera: Myth and Reality*, vol. 4: *'Ekklesia, Education, Philosophy'* (2003; in Greek) and *States and Citizens: Identity, Community, Diversity* (2016; in Greek). So far, she has published over sixty papers (in English, Greek and Slovenian) in scholarly journals and edited volumes.

Alasdair MacIntyre is both the Rev. John A. O'Brien Senior Research Professor of Philosophy at the University of Notre Dame and Senior Research Fellow at the Centre for Contemporary Aristotelian Studies in Ethics & Politics (CASEP) at London Metropolitan University. He has written widely in philosophy since his first book, *Marxism: An Interpretation* (1953). His *After Virtue: A Study in Moral Theory* (2007) was the seminal critique of modern moral philosophy in the name of the virtues, and therefore provides an important reference point for those who wish to theorize a virtue ethics. He has made great contributions to the history of philosophy, to moral philosophy, to the philosophy of politics and of the social sciences, and, especially, to the renewal of Aristotelianism and its challenge to rival traditions. Since those other classics that are *Whose Justice? Which Rationality?*, *Three Rival Versions of Moral Enquiry* and *Dependent Rational Animals: Why Human Beings Need the Virtues*, he has produced an examination of the philosophical work of Edith Stein set against the background of early twentieth-century phenomenology (2005; 2006) and *God, Philosophy, Universities: A Selective History of the Catholic Philosophical Tradition* (2009). A few of his very many fine essays are collected in *The Tasks of Philosophy* and in *Ethics and Politics* (2006). His most recent book, *Ethics in the Conflicts of Modernity: An Essay on Desire, Practical Reasoning, and Narrative* (2016) has been the subject of conferences in the United States, United Kingdom and elsewhere, because it provides the fully Aristotelian argument to which *After Virtue* pointed.

Apostolos Malakos studied politics and philosophy at Harvard and McGill universities before receiving his PhD from the London School of Economics and becoming Lecturer in Political Theory at Queen Mary University of London. He is currently researching German idealism at the University of Luxembourg, while is also a visiting research fellow at the Centre for Contemporary Aristotelian Studies in Ethics & Politics (CASEP) in London Metropolitan University, where he has led a project on *Virtue and Truth: Dasein as ἀληθεύειν* and research collaborations on both Aristotle's *Metaphysics* and *Nicomachean Ethics*. Besides his many publications in politics and philosophy, Apostolos is author of a couple of books of poetry and has translated T. S. Eliot's *The Wasteland* into Greek.

Egidijus Mardosas is a researcher at the Centre for Aristotelian Studies and Critical Theory at Mykolas Romeris University, Lithuania. He defended his PhD thesis entitled *Alasdair MacIntyre's Revolutionary Aristotelianism: Politics of Emancipation, Community and the Good* (2017; in English) at Vytautas Magnus University, in which he argues for the emancipatory potential of the MacIntyrean politics of the common good. He is the author of several scholarly papers on Aristotelianism and Alasdair MacIntyre's political philosophy, including 'Marxism and Aristotelian Ethics' (2016). He participated in the Mykolas Romeris University's research project 'Structures of Meaning' funded by the Research Council of Lithuania. His current research focuses on the relation between Neo-Aristotelian thought and the Marxist critique of capitalism.

Golfo Maggini is Professor of Modern and Contemporary Philosophy at the Department of Philosophy, University of Ioannina, Greece, and Affiliated Professor at the School of Education, University of Warsaw, Poland. She has authored four books: *Habermas and the Neo-Aristotelians. The Ethics of Discourse in Jürgen Habermas and the Challenge of Neo-Aristotelianism* (2006; in Greek); *Towards a Hermeneutics of the Technological World: From Heidegger to Contemporary Technoscience* (2010; in Greek), *La justice de la pensée – La critique de la métaphysique de la subjectivité dans le* *différend heideggérien avec Nietzsche* (2011; in French) and *Bios-Kinēsis-kairos-technē-polis. Phenomenological Approaches: Martin Heidegger-Hannah Arendt-Jan Patočka-Michel Henry* (2017; in Greek). She has also edited in Greek Martin Heidegger's *Phenomenological Interpretations to Aristotle* (2011) and Françoise Dastur's *Heidegger et la question du temps* (2008); George Steiner's *Heidegger* (2009), and co-edited *States and Citizens: Community, Identity, Diversity* (2016; in Greek) as well as the two-volume *Philosophy and Crisis. Responding to Challenges to Ways of Life in the Contemporary World* (2017). She has also published over sixty papers in Hellenic and international philosophy journals. Her focus of research interest lies in phenomenology, philosophical hermeneutics, theory of modernity and postmodernism, contemporary practical philosophy and the continental philosophy of technology.

Buket Korkut Raptis is Associate Professor of Philosophy at the Department of Philosophy of Muğla Sıtkı Koçman University, Turkey. She received her PhD in philosophy from the University of Notre Dame where she also worked as a postdoctoral scholar. She has authored papers on the subject of ethics and philosophical anthropology with reference to Aristotle, Marx, Nietzsche, Scheler, Bourdieu, Deleuze, Badiou and MacIntyre. Her current work tries to unveil the philosophy of nomadic cultures based on anthropological, sociological and cultural studies. She also has a special interest in thinking through Turkish language by exploring etymological connections among certain concepts.

Christof Rapp is Professor and the Chair for Ancient Philosophy at Ludwig-Maximilians-University Munich. His main fields of research are ancient philosophy (especially Aristotle) and its relations to modern debates in ontology, ethics, action theory and the philosophy of mind. Since 2009, Christof Rapp has been appointed as academic director of the Center for Advanced Studies (CAS) at the Ludwig-Maximilians-University in Munich and is co-director of the Munich School of Ancient Philosophy (MUSAΦ). He is editor of the journal *Zeitschrift für philosophische Forschung* and was editor of *Phronesis. A Journal for Ancient Philosophy*. He is the author of over 200 scholarly publications, including monographs, co-edited volumes and scholarly papers with top academic journals and publishers.

Richard F. Stalley studied classics and philosophy at Oxford and spent a year as Frank Knox Memorial Fellow at Harvard University. He taught for many years at the University of Glasgow where he is now Emeritus Professor of Ancient Philosophy and Honorary Professorial Research Fellow. He has published widely in the fields of ancient philosophy and Scottish philosophy. He has a particular interest in the political philosophy of Plato and Aristotle. His publications in that field include *An Introduction to Plato's Laws* (1983), and he has edited *Aristotle's Politics* for the Oxford University Press, World's Classics series (1995).

Introduction

Andrius Bielskis, Eleni Leontsini and Kelvin Knight

Aristotelianism has become an increasingly distinctive and important philosophical paradigm since the 1980s. This has especially been the case in ethics. Alasdair MacIntyre built on the work of Elizabeth Anscombe, Philippa Foot, Hans-Georg Gadamer and Peter Geach in reviving an Aristotelian tradition of the virtues. His *After Virtue* opened the way for Rosalind Hursthouse, John McDowell, Michael Slote and others to theorize a 'virtue ethics', which innumerable textbook writers and editors then juxtaposed to deontology and utilitarianism in demonstrating the relativity of modern moral theories.

This book follows MacIntyre in putting the virtues in another context: that of the Aristotelian tradition of theoretical and practical reasoning. The essays it collects all contribute to the debate on the importance of Aristotelian practical philosophy, yet it attempts to situate Aristotelianism and the tradition of the virtues against the background of modernity and its moral and political conflicts from a novel perspective. Through its fourteen specially commissioned papers, the book discusses the various aspects of Aristotle's philosophy, Aristotelianism and their contemporary relevance today. In addition, one of the main parts of the volume focuses critically on MacIntyre's Aristotelianism, including his argument in his recent book *Ethics in the Conflicts of Modernity*. The book also aims to bridge the gap between Aristotle's philosophy and the multitude of contemporary Aristotelian philosophical theories that have been formulated in the twentieth and twenty-first centuries by discussing Aristotle's philosophy, its legacy and its influence on medieval, modern and contemporary philosophy.

The volume is divided in three parts entitled 'The Aristotelian tradition of virtues', 'Modernity, conflict and MacIntyrean Aristotelianism' and 'Virtue ethics and modern social and political theory'. The first part examines key topics relevant to the Aristotelian tradition of the virtues by engaging at large with Aristotle's text but also with Thomas Aquinas' Aristotelianism in ways that new arguments and textual research and interpretation are presented along with the relevance of Aristotle's thought to contemporary moral and political theory. The second part focuses on the discussion of some aspects of MacIntyre's philosophy, mostly in a critical way, revealing the conflict of capitalist modernity with MacIntyrean Aristotelianism, but also with Aristotelianism itself. Finally, in the third part, the chapters focus on topics relating contemporary Aristotelianism to contemporary moral and political philosophy, articulating new philosophical approaches that render Aristotle's thought relevant to contemporary theoretical debates about social and political practice. A key premise of this book is therefore that Aristotelianism rightly understood can provide us with the theoretical and ethical resources for a radical critique of contemporary moral and political order.

Aristotelianism was central to medieval philosophy, becoming decentred in the Renaissance and an object of critique in the Enlightenment. The so-called Battle of the Ancients and the Moderns expressed a deep conflict between the 'old' and the 'new', classical civilization and enlightened civil society, tradition and modernity. Since the seventeenth century, this conflict has been implicit in all areas of European culture (in both East and West) and, from the nineteenth century onwards, has been relocated into the domain of social and political philosophy. The 'Battle of the Ancients and the Moderns' became famous in Britain as Jonathan Swift's *The Battle of the Books*, published in 1704 in his *A Tale of a Tub*, but the contrast dates from the fifteenth and sixteenth centuries via texts of Dimitrius Doukas and Marcus Mousourous. Already, since the texts of Andronikos Kallistos and Vasilius Bessarion (titular Latin Patriarch of Constantinople), admiration of new fields of knowledge had been combined with respect for the ancients. Benjamin Constant later gave the distinction its most famous expression. Consequently, many modern philosophers and scientists identified Aristotelian practical philosophy with an antiquity from which they were determined to break. To this day, the 'Battle of the Ancients and the Moderns' extends beyond philosophy departments to everyday life.

All changed with the publication of Alasdair MacIntyre's *After Virtue*. This revitalized Aristotelianism without, however, rejecting the importance of modern science, and rightly argued that Aristotelianism was philosophically the most powerful of pre-modern modes of moral thought. Yet due to his and other people's work, Aristotelianism today is much more than a pre-modern mode of ethics: the revival of Aristotle's philosophy today has turned Aristotelianism into a distinct and powerful philosophical tradition. Our aim in this volume is to explore the various aspects of this tradition and to argue that Aristotelian virtue ethics and politics have radical implications for contemporary debates on the nature of social and political practice.

The revival of Aristotle's moral philosophy in the twentieth century gave birth to a new branch of normative moral philosophy, the so-called virtue ethics. This focuses on the human agent and on the characteristics that she should cultivate, if she is to fulfil her potential. The main question to ask when one makes moral decisions is not 'Which rules should I follow?' but 'What kind of person should I become?' in order to act morally. According to virtue theory, the basic judgements in ethics are judgements about character. The virtues are traits a human being must possess in order to flourish, to live a good life (*eudaimonia/eu zēn*). The right action is the one that a virtuous person would do, guided by the virtues. The concept of virtue is explanatorily prior to that of right action.

Since Aristotle's conception of virtues or excellences is intimately linked to political life, Aristotelian virtue ethics is relevant to modern political theory. This reveals that one should put Aristotelian moral and political virtues or excellences (*aretai*) back onto the political agenda. After all, to give just one example, Aristotle has set many of the principles that we now take for granted and are part of our communal European cultural heritage, such as the separation of powers (checks and balances), that is, the vesting of the legislative, executive and judiciary powers of government in separate bodies, a distinction that Montesquieu borrowed from Aristotle.

One of the tasks of this volume is to focus afresh on key aspects of Aristotle's thought, such as his notions of the common good, virtue (*aretē*, i.e. excellence), justice, equality and friendship in relation to the art of politics. For example, Aristotle in his *Politics* emphasizes the importance of good government by arguing that the politicians should always rule having only the common interest of their citizens in mind. As he says: 'Constitutions which aim at the common interest are correct and just without qualification, whereas those which aim only at the interest of the rulers are deviant and unjust, because they involve despotic rule which is inappropriate for a community of free persons' (*Pol.*1279a17–21). In addition, Aristotle's notion of civic friendship could be of great use to contemporary political discussion, since it can function as a social good. Friendship between fellow citizens is important because it contributes to the unity of both state and community by transmitting feelings of intimacy and solidarity. In that sense, it can be understood as an important relationship predicated on affection and generosity, virtues lacking from both contemporary politics and society that seem to be merely dominated by post-Enlightenment ideals. For Aristotle, friendship is important for society because it generates concord (*homonoia*), articulating thus a basis for social unity and political agreement. Aristotle's theory requires us to have concern for our fellow citizens; 'concern for others' as opposed to the mere 'respect for others' that contemporary liberalism advocates. As Aristotle puts it himself, 'friendship seems also to hold states together, and lawgivers to care more for it than for justice; for concord seems to be something like friendship, and this they aim at most of all, and expel faction as their worst enemy; and when people are friends they have no need of justice, while when they are just they need friendship as well, and the truest form of justice is thought to be a friendly quality' (*NE* 1155a22-28).

Yet although Aristotle's writings serve as a common source, contemporary Aristotelian theories are rarely based on a close analysis of Aristotle's texts. One of the central aims of this book is to reconsider Aristotelian theory and to pinpoint its legacy, relevance and importance to contemporary moral and political theory. What is needed is to go back to Aristotle's texts and examine his arguments afresh from both a scholarly and a philosophical perspective that would enable us to reconcile the ongoing debate between ancients and moderns, and to produce new philosophical ideas enabling us to solve contemporary philosophical questions.

Aristotelian ethical and political theory differs from many rival traditions in refusing to reduce its subject to one of rule-following. Ethics, on any Aristotelian account, aims at the good life for human beings. Politics also aims at the common good and the common *eudaimonia* for all the citizens of the state. Virtues, to emphasize it again, are those dispositions that lead individuals to actualize such goods. To make such assertions is not to propose that Aristotle can be our contemporary, addressing our concerns and answering the questions that we now ask. But, although he lived at the dawn of recorded history and of philosophical enquiry, his philosophical insights still have much to contribute to contemporary moral and political discussions.

At the end of the day, ancient philosophy would have no relevance if it had nothing to contribute to contemporary philosophical questions. There is no point in studying the past philosophical texts as if these were 'museum exhibits' or 'new archaeological findings' which we should only interpret in a careful and scholarly manner, maintaining or restoring all their likely historical peculiarities, using only the methodological tools that a classicist does. On the contrary, the philosophers of the past should be studied in such a way as to better understand the problems of the present, even if in this case we might find ourselves in a position where we have departed from 'the letter' of their arguments. This could not be more strongly true in the case of Aristotle and the Aristotelian tradition. As MacIntyre succinctly pointed out:

> No doctrine vindicated itself in so wide a variety of contexts as did Aristotelianism: Greek, Islamic, Jewish and Christian; and that when modernity made its assaults on an older world its most perceptive exponents understood that it was Aristotelianism that had to be overthrown. But all these historical truths, crucial as they are, are unimportant compared with the fact that Aristotelianism is *philosophically* the most powerful of pre-modern modes of moral thought. (*After Virtue*, 1985: 118)

MacIntyre's point is still relevant today – if not more so – since we are experiencing a notable revival of activity on various philosophical areas in Neo-Aristotelian philosophy as well as in the study of Aristotle's philosophy per se. Yet Aristotelianism today is far from only the most powerful of pre-modern modes of moral thought; it is now back at the mainstream philosophical agenda. This is very true if we consider the various contemporary interpretations of Aristotle, like those by Fred D. Miller who advocated that Aristotle is a libertarian by attempting to render the concept of rights central to his political theory, or the one by Martha Nussbaum who argued that Aristotle provides the basis for a certain sort of social democracy compatible with some forms of liberalism. In fact, we have a variety of interpretations of Aristotle and Aristotelianism. Hence, the chapters in this book are motivated by a shared belief that there is something in Aristotle's conception of goods and virtues to which we should attend even now.

The first chapter of the volume sets the scene. Its author, Alasdair MacIntyre, presents Aristotelianism as a distinct position in contemporary ethics. The chapter, which was presented at the founding conference of the UK Political Studies Association's Contemporary Aristotelian Studies group, provides a point of reference for most of those that follow, and a focus for several. MacIntyre engages in the discussion of four (at least) political Aristotles and argues that there are so many varieties of Aristotelianism today that to merely say that one is an 'Aristotelian' is not enough, since one would need to specify what 'kind' of Aristotelianism we are talking about and what its key presuppositions are. The point provided in his chapter here is that of disagreement within modern Aristotelianism, and this book is the scene of continuing disagreement within the parameters of Aristotelian ethics. But it should be pointed out that, despite *After Virtue*'s title, MacIntyre himself refuses to identify Aristotelianism with virtue ethics. Such identification would return Aristotle to a past of interest to classicists but hardly to philosophers. At most, Aristotle would be invoked to remind us that institutionalized rules should not crowd out concern for personal and political judgement and the moral virtues. Ethics textbooks could refer to him in passing in chapters devoted to virtue ethics, supplementing their central debate between deontology and consequentialism.

As MacIntyre's chapter acknowledges, Aristotle is available for rival interpretations and uses. Even interpreters within this volume, accepting that Aristotelian practical philosophy should not be limited to virtue ethics, differ as to whether an Aristotelian practical philosophy should be informed by any Aristotelian naturalism. MacIntyre's own rapid transition from denial to affirmation is famous. He has no doubt that Aristotle's greatest interpreter has been Thomas Aquinas, and he therefore presents himself within the tradition of a specifically Thomistic Aristotelianism. Athanasia Glycofrydi-Leontsini's chapter agrees with this interpretation and discusses the importance of the translation of Thomas Aquinas into Greek as well as its enormous influence on the Byzantine philosophical and theological scene in the fifteenth century, focusing on the reception of Thomas Aquinas in Byzantium and the contribution of Demetrius Cydones to the formation of the first Byzantine School of Thomism in the East. If other Aristotelianisms are available, it is nonetheless the case that Thomistic Aristotelianisms are the most comprehensive. On their account, Aristotle can be used to contribute far more than occasional thoughts for consideration by contemporary philosophers, and far more even than filling alleged gaps in modern philosophy. On the account of such Thomistic Aristotelians as MacIntyre, Aristotelianism is a self-supporting philosophical position in rivalry to those signifiable by such names as Kant, Bentham or Nietzsche.

Some chapters in this volume come close to such a position in bringing Aristotelianism into critical engagement with contemporary rivals. Kelvin Knight, for example, defends MacIntyre's Aristotelian uses of the term 'good' against J. L. Austin's cautions. Some such uses reveal much about ordinary ethical aspiration, motivation and action, and perhaps also about the scope for an Aristotelian politics. Others engage with Aristotelianism, especially that of MacIntyre, but from rival viewpoints. Golfo Maggini adopts Friedrich Nietzsche's genealogy and argues that MacIntyre's approach to understanding morality as historical has structural resemblances to Nietzsche's genealogical critique of Enlightenment morality, especially his criticism of the latter's claims to absolute norms and objectivity. Although she is critical of MacIntyre's Aristotelianism, especially his commitment to Aristotle's naturalism, she sees more convergence between MacIntyre and Nietzsche than it is usually acknowledged. Similarly, Apostolos Malakos engages with MacIntyrean Aristotelianism, and, by choosing as a point of his departure Bernard Williams' critique of an Aristotelian conception of the 'good', he questions an Aristotelian naturalism on the basis that the distinctive human good cannot be convincingly perceived as given in the form of our biological end. Christof Rapp critically challenges the use that MacIntyre makes of some Aristotelian theorems drawing on Aristotelian ideas and Aristotelian terminology via adopting a special view to the virtues' alleged dependence on the good of particular communities, by pointing out that Aristotle does indeed famously emphasizes the role of the city-state for the moral education of the youth since it is only through the support of parents, teachers and good laws that young people acquire the virtues. But, according to Rapp, the common good of the political community are indeed closely connected within the Aristotelian model of the virtues, but not in the way suggested by Alasdair MacIntyre, that is, as a close connection between a person's virtues and the community she lives in. MacIntyre's Aristotelianism is further challenged by Paul Blackledge's Marxist critique, which argues that there is a contradiction between the revolutionary implications of his historical-sociological conception of practices and more reactionary implications of his ahistorical account of human nature.

Andrius Bielskis, Tony Burns, Joseph Dunne, Buket Korkut Raptis, Eleni Leontsini, Egidijus Mardosas and Richard Stalley, all, in different ways, interpret Aristotle as an essential philosophical figure for us to conceptualize and pursue the human good today. What is distinctive and most valuable in Aristotelianism today is Aristotle's teleology, which, as Andrius Bielskis argues, should be rescued from his erroneous naturalism. He argues that Aristotle's claims about the natural inequalities between men and women, and masters and slaves, are inconsistent with his teleological account of nature and of the human good. This is so because, as MacIntyre argues in *Ethics in the Conflicts of Modernity*, all human beings have a capacity to act as rational agents in achieving their final end, and that human *ergon* – the essential function – must be the same for every human being.

Buket Korkut Raptis follows this line of argument and provides a fresh interpretation of an ongoing scholarly debate on the nature of happiness in Aristotle's writings. Instead of choosing either dominant or inclusivist interpretation of happiness, she argues that there are two sense of happiness in Aristotle's practical philosophy. Her comprehensive account of *eudaimonia* includes both interpretations: the blessedness of philosophical contemplation is impossible without the essential happiness which distinguishes us from a mere animal life. Eleni Leontsini emphasizes that living in the company of others (*suzēn*) is an important Aristotelian political notion, prominent in both his moral and political theory, since, as Aristotle points out, '*suzēn* is the result, the *ergon* of *philia*, since *philia* is the pursuit of a common social life' (*Pol.* III.9.1280b38-40). She focuses on the notion of *suzēn* in relation to personal *philia*, arguing that 'going through time together' is not an essential element of Aristotle's general definition of friendship, and that the 'criterion of time' should not be taken literally as 'living together' in a continuous and uninterrupted way, but that it should be understood in a much broader sense if Aristotle's account of *philia* is to have any standing at all.

Tony Burns' chapter aims to show how aspects of social theory, especially the Durkheimian tradition in the history of sociological thought, can shed light on our understanding of the politics of recognition. He connects this discussion to the writings of Aristotle, arguing that there is a clear recognitive dimension to Aristotle's thinking about justice, and that it is plausible to associate Aristotle's thought with the idea of a politics of recognition. Joseph Dunne's chapter questions Aristotle's theory of virtue from inside. Accepting the key premises of Aristotle's virtue ethics, he argues that to be truly ethical we need to move beyond our individual and collective concern to flourish. Borrowing the symbols of 'field' and 'forest' from Charles Taylor, he argues that beyond the 'field' of concern with living well in an Aristotelian sense, we must step into the 'forest' – an ethical space for a radical self-transformation through openness to the supreme good that goes beyond the demands of flourishing and moral duty. Although in a very different way, Dunne's line of argumentation resembles Richard

Stalley's outstanding comparison between Plato's and Aristotle's conceptions of nature and of political community. Stalley argues that despite important similarities between Plato and Aristotle, Plato's philosophical account of nature is based on his belief that humans live in a divinely ordered universe, and that the task of humans envisaged by Plato is to play our part within the ethically ordered universe.

In a similar way to Bielskis' attempt to critique Aristotle's 'natural' inequalities, Egidijus Mardosas' essay engages with Aristotle's arguments on why workers should be excluded from the *polis*, and argues that, although MacIntyre's conception of practices allows us to reconnect virtue with work, we need to supplement both Aristotle's and MacIntyre's accounts of human flourishing and politics with Karl Marx's problematization of the relationship between labour and human flourishing. Certainly, criteria of time and context must be borne in mind in interpreting any philosopher, especially those who are no longer around to answer for themselves. However, some contemporary philosophers argue that a lot of what Aristotle, or Marx, say of human flourishing, or even of politics, is of continuing philosophical significance, and that it rivals other, contemporary philosophical positions.

All of the chapters in this book are presented in the hope of advancing and provoking debate about Aristotelianism's contemporary philosophical significance and scope, both theoretical and practical, and to pinpoint the important research that has been done, especially in the field of Aristotelian moral and political theory, but also in virtue economy, virtue epistemology, logic and metaphysics, since Aristotelianism is nowadays one of the most dynamic paradigms in both moral and political philosophy, and not only. As one of our authors has argued, that a tradition is in good order is demonstrated by its ability to sustain argument about the goods and excellences that give it point and purpose.

Part 1

The Aristotelian tradition of virtues

1

Four – or more? – political Aristotles

Alasdair MacIntyre

The four political Aristotles whom I will discuss are Aristotle himself, Aristotle as understood in the thirteenth century by Aquinas, Aristotle as understood by some sixteenth-century renaissance Aristotelians, and the Aristotle of the present day, object of scholarly enquiry, subject of a huge and, even as we speak, ever-growing number of dissertations, invoked politically from time to time by protagonists of several alternative and rival points of view. So my first remarks are about Aristotle himself or rather about his text. I note immediately that a high proportion of the statements that scholarly commentators make about that text fall into one of two classes. Either they are presented as obvious truths, and so are scarcely worth repeating, or they are much disputed claims, only to be asserted if backed up by extensive interpretative argument. So what is someone to do if, as now, they need to provide a brief but accurate portrait of Aristotle as a political figure in less than five pages, so that what they say will unavoidably be highly contestable but shamelessly unargued? If they are shameless enough, they will simply proceed with the task. As I do now.

I

I begin by juxtaposing two aspects of Aristotle. He famously asserted that the human being is by nature a political animal (*Politics*, I.2.1253a2-3); an animal, that is, whose well-being requires citizenship in a *polis*. But he himself resided for part of his life in Macedonia, which was not a *polis*, and for an even longer period in Athens, where he was a *metic*, a resident alien and not a citizen. And his friends and allies among the Macedonian elite imposed on Greece a form of rule quite other than that of a *polis*. Yet, on Aristotle's view, someone without a *polis* must be either a beast or a god, and evidently Aristotle did not think himself to be either of these. What he did think of himself as was an enquirer, someone exemplifying another universal human trait, the desire to understand. So, as such an enquirer, how might he have conceived his political role and function? When Aristotle returned to Athens in 335, no longer a member of the Academy, but a teacher and researcher, presiding over other teachers and researchers at the Lyceum, he was nearly fifty years old. What political role would Aristotle have expected a man of his achievements and that age to play?

The relevant texts are from Book VII of the *Politics* and Book X of the *Nicomachean Ethics*. In the former, Aristotle dissents from Plato's view that soldiers should be one kind of person and rulers another. They should be the same people, but at different times in their lives, since 'younger men have *dynamis*, but older men have *phronēsis*' (*Politics* VII.8.1329a14-16). Aristotle thus seems to have envisaged the political life as proceeding through stages, beginning with a period of military service, then a period of undertaking those tasks of personal and political decision-making through which *phronēsis* is acquired – the *phronēsis* required for 'deliberation about what is expedient and judgment about what is just' (*Politics* VII.9.1329a4-5) – and finally the stage of holding those high offices in which *phronēsis* is exercised as a ruler. But if this is so, something has been left out, for in his discussion of political education at the close of the *Nicomachean Ethics* Aristotle makes it clear that for the acquisition of political *phronēsis* deliberative experience, although necessary, is not sufficient, since 'if anyone wants to become adept in a *technē* or in *theōria*, he must go to the universal' (*NE* X.9.1180b20-22). How is he to do that? What has been left out is just what Aristotle intended to supply in his teaching at the Lyceum. His political role and function is that of the educator, and that role can only be discharged by two different kinds of attention to the formation of moral habits.

First, attempts to instruct will be fruitless unless the students have already developed to some significant degree those moral and intellectual habits without which political learning cannot take place. Lacking such habits, the student will be guided by passions and immune to argument (*NE* X.9.1179b26-9). Second, the aim of instruction is to produce legislators who will know how to design, enact and administer laws that will inculcate those same habits, so that citizens may learn how to rule and how to be ruled for the common good of the *polis* (*NE* II.1.1103b3-6). Such political education does of course require more than good habits. It also requires a degree and kind of experience that is inevitably wanting in the young, but also missing from those whose upbringing has resulted in an inability to learn from experience (*NE* I.3.1095a2-6). Notice that these remarks all come from the *Nicomachean Ethics*, not the *Politics*, something not surprising if we follow Richard Bodéüs in understanding the former as just as much a political discourse as the latter.

Bodéüs's (1982) claims in *Le philosophe et la cité* are of course contentious (for measured criticism, see Francis Sparshott's 1997: 413–16). But I do not think that his critics have shown him to be mistaken in what he asserts, only in what he denies, in his giving too exclusively a political account of Aristotle's intentions. What critics have rightly emphasized – Sparshott is an excellent example – is not only that Aristotle's concern with moral and intellectual habits extends beyond the political, but also that, unless we give due weight to this, we shall not understand Aristotle's conception of politics. The good of the citizen *qua* citizen is the common good of the city. But the good of the citizen *qua* human being is more and other than his good *qua* citizen. And the moral and intellectual habits, the virtues, that the citizen needs are human virtues. Aristotle insists that the virtue of the citizen is not the same as the virtue of the human being, that one can be a good citizen without being a good human being (*Politics* III.4.1276b35-1277a5 and III.4.1277a12-25). But he also says that, when rule is exercised over free human beings, 'the good citizen must have the understanding and the ability to rule and to be ruled and this is the virtue of a citizen' (*Politics* III.4.1277b12-15). Yet one cannot have the understanding and ability to rule without *phronēsis*, and one cannot have *phronēsis* without also having the moral virtues, the virtues of the human being as such.

What then is the relationship between the achievement, together with one's fellow citizens, of the good of the *polis*, and the achievement by each citizen as an individual of his own final good as a human being? Aristotle poses this question in Book VII of the *Politics*, when he discusses the disagreement between those who hold that the best life for a human being is the life of political practice and those who hold, to the contrary, that it is the life devoted to philosophical enquiry. Aristotle's response is to argue that this is a badly framed set of alternatives. The activities of *dianoia* and *theōria*, the activities of philosophical enquiry, are as much or even more a part of the life of practice as are political activities (*Politics* VII.3.1325a16-1325b23). The plain inference is that the political life is by itself an incomplete life for a human being. It is indeed through developing and exercising the virtues in the life of the *polis* that we become rightly disposed and directed towards the achievement of our final end, but we will be politically in error if we believe that, or act as if it were the case that, there is not more to each life than politics. We will also of course be in error if we suppose that the pursuit of our ultimate end can, except in some exceptional cases, be an alternative to the pursuit of the ends of political life.

If so, one conclusion follows for us as interpreters and teachers. The *Nicomachean Ethics* and the *Politics* have to be taught together or not at all. Yet academic practice is such – and has been such for a very long time – that almost always the *Nicomachean Ethics* is taught in courses in moral philosophy to one set of students and the *Politics* in courses in political theory to quite another. The presupposition of such practice is that ethics is one thing, politics quite another, and that questions about the relationship between the two are to be raised only after each has been studied largely in isolation from the other. The lesson to be learnt is that the organization of the curriculum always has intellectual and sometimes moral and political presuppositions. And, if I am right, the presuppositions of our modern curriculum are and have been anti-Aristotelian. So that to teach students to read Aristotle's texts as they should be read is to teach against the cultural grain.

It is important that the thesis that the *Nicomachean Ethics* and the *Politics* must be read together can be held without a commitment to Bodéüs's interpretation of Aristotle's purposes. It was urged upon us in a 1984 article by A. W. H. Adkins (1991: 75–93), whose compellingly argued contention was that 'the relationship of *ergon* to *aretē* and *eudaimonia*, and the importance of all three to Aristotle's ethical and political thought' (Adkins 1991: 92) can only be understood when the *Ethics* and the *Politics* are read together. Adkins laid particular emphasis on the relationship between the *ergon* of a ruler and the *ergon* of a human being, and in this I would want to follow him. Why so? For two different and contrasting reasons.

First, there is the place that this relationship has in Aristotle's instructive accounts of what he takes to be cases of political failure, for example in what he says about Sparta and in his analysis of the danger to democratic constitutions posed by the characteristic democratic conception of freedom. The Spartans prized and praised virtue, but their almost exclusively military conception, or rather misconception, of the virtues resulted in a lack of ability to manage their own affairs. 'They find it necessary to undertake large wars, but there is never any money in the public treasury' (*Politics* II.9.1271b11-13), something to be remarked not only of the Spartans but also of contemporary, far from Laconic Americans. On Aristotle's view, it is because they – certainly the Spartans, and perhaps also the Americans – are defective in respect of the human *ergon* that they are defective in respect of the *ergon* of a ruler.

At first sight, a very different case is that of those democrats who undermine democratic constitutions because of their democratic misconception of liberty. On that democratic view, 'to be free is to do whatever one wants' (*Politics* V.9.1310a31-2); it is to be free from external interference that may frustrate one's desires. But, on Aristotle's view, this is a misconception of freedom. To be constrained by respect for the constitution is not to be unfree, but to live in security. Democracies thus become the victims of demagogues, and the bad political outcomes for both victims and victimizers have their source in failures to discipline and transform their desires. Once again, it is because rulers are defective in respect of the human *ergon* that they are defective in respect of the *ergon* of a ruler.

That human beings *qua* human beings, *qua* rational animals, have a distinctive *ergon* is then, so Adkins reminds us, a thesis indispensable for any genuinely Aristotelian politics and ethics. Yet just here is the great difficulty that Aristotle creates for himself. As Adkins puts it, it was Aristotle's view that 'in the case of other things that have *erga*, not all of them perform those *erga* excellently: not all sculptors are as good as Phidias, not all eyes have 20/20 vision. But all can and must perform the *ergon* to some extent ... However in the case of the *ergon* of man (*anthrōpos*), the function can be discharged, the task performed, by only a small fraction of mankind' (Adkins 1991: 90). And this suggests that Aristotle confronted a dilemma that he failed to recognize.

Let me therefore put it to Aristotle, albeit posthumously, that, if he continues to assert that only 'a limited number of adult male Greeks with a leisured way of life', as Adkins puts it, are capable of pursuing and achieving the ends of political activity, then he will have to accept that his use of *ergon*, his conception of *ergon*, is incoherent and so put in question the central theses of his ethics and politics. But, if he reforms his use of *ergon*, so that it is no longer incoherent, then women, productive workers, such as farmers, slaves and barbarians can no longer be excluded from the ranks of citizens. And there is no third way. Modern followers of Aristotle have of course often argued – I have been one of them – that these exclusions can be excised from Aristotle's political theory without damage to its overall structure. Here I am suggesting something much stronger, that, unless they are excised, the foundations of that theory are put seriously in question. I have used the verb 'suggest', for clearly further argument is needed, although some of it is supplied by Adkins in his article. Here all that I can do is to take note of Aristotle's dilemma and move on.

II

The movement is one of sixteen centuries, from fourth century BCE to thirteenth century CE. And at once an obvious question is posed. Must it not be absurd to try to find application for Aristotle's theory of the *polis* to the empire, or the kingdoms, duchies and city-states of thirteenth-century Western Europe? The events that led to the disappearance of the *polis* were after all set on foot in Aristotle's lifetime by his nasty pupil, Alexander, and the history of political change that separates Aristotle from his thirteenth-century followers surely makes any genuinely Aristotelian politics impossible and his theory irrelevant. R. G. Collingwood made the point once and for all: 'Can you say that the *Republic* gives one account of "the nature of the State" and the *Leviathan* another? No; because Plato's "State" is the Greek *polis*, and Hobbes's is the absolutist State of the seventeenth century' (Collingwood 1939: 61). And Collingwood's argument seems to hold as compellingly of Aristotle and Aquinas as it does of Plato and Hobbes. Is there any reply to it?

I begin by putting on one side Aquinas' *De Regimine Principum*, a puzzling text in a number of ways, as well as the unfinished commentary on the *Politics*, and what I have to say about Aquinas will focus largely, although not entirely, on his mature judgements in the *Summa Theologiae*. One of Aquinas's intentions in writing the *Summa* was to instruct those whose role it might be to give moral and political advice either to rulers or to ruled or to both, and also to those who were the teachers of those called upon to fill such advisory roles. There are two ways to read the *Summa*. One is to begin at the beginning and work through the text question by question until one reaches, not the end, but the point at which Aquinas broke off, leaving it to be finished by his Dominican colleagues. The other, which is pertinent to my present purposes, is to begin from one or more of the practical conclusions in the Second Part of the Second Part, that is, from the answers that he was providing to questions posed by his morally and politically puzzled contemporaries. Then we read backwards, first in order to identify the premises from which Aquinas had derived his conclusions, next in order to discover the justifications that he had advanced for taking those premises to be true, and so we proceed until we arrive at the relevant first principles, whether principles of natural reason concerning the moral and the political or revealed truths. If we read the text in this way, we learn something interesting about Aquinas's use of Aristotle. What Aquinas is doing is drawing upon Aristotle's concepts, theses and arguments – and also of course upon those of others, most notably of Augustine – in order to construct answers to thirteenth-century questions, some of which Aristotle himself could not have asked.

Aquinas's most important debts to Aristotle are in respect of his conception of human agency. Note at once that the problems that I posed earlier about Aristotle's use of *ergon* do not arise over Aquinas's use of *opus*, William of Moerbeke's translation of *ergon*. Every human being, in Aquinas's view, is actually or potentially capable of that exercise of reason which is the human *opus* (*Sententia libri ethicorum* I, lect.10, 122-6). And in exercising their practical reason in their everyday lives, human agents always presuppose some answer to the questions 'What is my final end?' and 'To what ends should my actions here and now be directed, if I am to be directed towards that final end?' Reflection upon those questions at once makes it plain that, whatever ends they are or should be pursuing, their progress towards them depends upon their relationships to and interactions with others, those with whom they share the lives of the family, workplace and political society, and together with whom they engage in a variety of projects. So agents come to pose questions not only about their individual goods but also about those common goods that they share with others and about the parts that the achievement of those common goods inescapably play in the achievement of their individual goods. It is in asking and answering those questions about common goods that they show themselves to be not only rational animals but also political animals.

What qualities must we have, if we are to act with others in achieving our and their common good? To answer this question, we must first consider what kinds of relationship we need to have with them. Aquinas contends that those relationships must be structured by their and our acknowledgement of the authority of law. But whose law and which law? A central political and legal problem for Western Europe in the thirteenth century was that of competing jurisdictions, of rival authorities and of rival claimants to authority. What falls to the church courts to decide and what to the secular courts? Within the church, who is accountable to the local bishop and who only to the pope? How is the administration of the king's law to take account of the courts in which local feudal landowners preside? Is this or that university to be subject to the authority of the city council, of the bishop, of the king or of the pope? Does customary law have the force of law? A prerequisite for giving an answer to these questions that is not dictated by the present distribution of power is that we are able to appeal to a shared conception of law. It is Aquinas's contention that we are able to appeal to such a conception, because we already possess such a conception, often without knowing that we do so.

What then is law? Aquinas's answer is that the precepts of law are precepts of reason directed towards the common good and promulgated by someone with the authority to promulgate them (*S.T.* Ia-IIae, 90). And each of us as a rational agent is potentially aware of the authority of those precepts without conformity to which we will be unable to deliberate rationally with those others with whom we share common goods and so be unable to achieve those common goods. For, if we are to be able to deliberate rationally with others, both we and they must be able to evaluate each other's practical reasoning as reasoning and respond to it as rational agents rather than trying to get our own way by force or the threat of force or deceit and fraud. But this is possible only if both we and they speak to each other truthfully, abstain from doing each other bodily harm, respect each other's legitimate property, keep our promises to each other, and so on. And to obey such injunctions and rules is to conform to the precepts of the natural law.

What the natural law provides is therefore twofold. It tells us what our relationships to others must be, if we are to be able to deliberate rationally with them about how to achieve their and our goods. And it provides a standard by which we may pass judgement on the various systems of positive law enacted in various societies, including our own. But practical knowledge of the natural law involves more than an ability to identify its precepts. It involves knowing how to judge which precepts are relevant in this or that set of circumstances and how to apply those precepts to particular cases, especially to difficult cases. What do we need if we are to be capable of this kind of knowing how? We need the virtue of *phronēsis*, Latinized as *prudentia*, defined as Aristotle defined it, that habit of mind and action that directs us towards our individual and common goods through the contingent particularities of our situation. But, and here again Aquinas follows Aristotle, no one can have the virtue of *prudentia* unless she or he has the other moral virtues to a significant degree. Aquinas recognizes that our moral development is characteristically uneven, so that someone who is generally just may still be inadequately courageous or temperate, but without a certain degree of courage, justice and temperateness, we will also be lacking in practical judgement, in *prudentia*.

For Aquinas, therefore, unlike some of our contemporaries, an ethics and politics of rules is not to be contrasted with an ethics and politics of virtues. Without the virtues we would be inept in our application of rules. And without rules, our understanding of the virtues would be incomplete, since the rules set limits to the kinds of action through which our good can be achieved. Consider the relationship of rules to virtues in the decision-making of legislators. It might seem that, since, as Aristotle and Aquinas agree, the aim of rulers is to legislate so that those who are ruled may become good, whatever the natural law enjoins should be enacted as positive law. But this is a mistake. Enacting prohibitions of certain types of bad act may well make matters worse rather than better: 'imperfect human beings, unable to tolerate such precepts, would break out into even worse evils' (*S.T.*, Ia-IIae,96 ad 2). What the ruler has to judge is the effect of this particular legislation as moral education on this particular population and such judgement requires the exercise of the virtue of *prudentia*.

What I have been trying to bring out is the way in which and the extent to which Aquinas puts Aristotle's conceptions of the deliberative rationality of the agent and of the virtue of *phronēsis* to work in discussions of political problems of the thirteenth century, so that it becomes clear that the charge of anachronism fails. I could have tried to meet this charge in other ways, by for example showing how Aquinas is able to find thirteenth-century applications for Aristotle's conceptions of justice, courage and temperateness, so spelling out those conceptions further. Had I pursued this line of argument systematically, it would have involved the claim that Aristotle's conceptions of deliberative rationality and of the virtues, although first advanced in the fourth century, are not only fourth-century conceptions but also conceptions that have so far withstood criticism from many standpoints in many times and places. To do so however would be to divert me from taking note of what is more relevant to my present purpose, namely, that Aquinas was only one of a number of Aristotelian writers on politics in the high and the late-middle ages, and that some of these were in some respects more faithful to Aristotle than he was. Here I take note of only one, Nicole Oresme, fourteenth-century translator of both the *Nicomachean Ethics* and the *Politics* into French.

Of him Jean Dunbabin wrote: 'When he misinterprets Aristotle, it is not because medieval political preconceptions blur his understanding, but because it suits his book to do so' (Dunbabin 1982: 730). She cites as an example Oresme's use of Aristotle's teaching that priestly offices ought not to be held by farmers or craftsmen to attack the Dominicans and the Franciscans for admitting to their ranks just such people. Oresme, as an aristocratic humanist, invokes Aristotle as an authority against the Dominican and Thomistic tradition, a tradition that as political and moral theory had no great influence beyond the Dominican order until the sixteenth century, when it was infused with new life by Francisco de Vitoria. For Vitoria, Aristotle's texts play a crucial part in his incisive critique of Spanish claims to exercise rightful authority over the indigenous inhabitants of the Americas. That critique was carried further by Bartolomé de las Casas, Dominican and bishop of Chiapas, in his insistence that the Spaniards were wholly without justification in making war upon and enslaving those inhabitants. In the great disputation on these matters at Valladolid in 1550, conducted before an audience of jurists, theologians and members of the royal council, Las Casas' antagonist was another aristocratic humanist, Juan Ginés de Sepúlveda, whose arguments against Las Casas invoked Aristotle's doctrine of the natural slave. So in these debates, two rival and antagonistic Aristotles confronted one another. We should note that Sepúlveda was, unlike Las Casas, a distinguished Aristotle scholar, at home with Aristotle's Greek and translator of several of Aristotle's works into Latin, including the *Politics*. He belongs to, even if a minor figure among, those renaissance Aristotelians for whom Aristotle is at once a fourth- and a sixteenth-century figure, a contemporary of both Demosthenes and Machiavelli.

III

A full history of the Aristotelianism of the Renaissance and more particularly of the moral and political Aristotelianism of that period still has to be written. When it is, it will be deeply indebted to such path-breaking scholarship as that of Charles B. Schmitt (1983a) and a number of others. But until it is, all generalizations have to be cautious. Yet some common themes are plainly of the first importance, especially when they appear in Aristotelian thinking in very different political contexts. Consider two contemporaries, the Englishman John Case (1539/46–99), who taught at Oxford, and the Sienese Francesco Piccolomini (1523–1607), who taught at Padua. Case published commentaries on several of Aristotle's works, including the *Nicomachean Ethics* and the *Politics*, while Piccolomini was the author of a treatise, *Universa philosophia de moribus*, in which, although he occasionally disagrees with Aristotle, his overall project is to present an Aristotelian account of the virtues. (For a fuller account of John Case, see Charles B. Schmitt (1983b) and my paper (MacIntyre 1999). For a fuller account of Piccolomini, see my paper (MacIntyre 2006). Some of what I say here repeats what I say in these essays). I begin with Piccolomini.

He addressed his book to the senators of the Venetian republic, urging upon them that sound instruction of Venetian young men concerning the virtues was necessary for the flourishing of the Venetian or any other republic. Virtue is that which renders a human being fit for *imperium* (X.110), and philosophical teaching about the virtues has an indispensable part in making the young virtuous. Such teaching is not of course the only thing necessary. Natural endowments and good habits are also essential. 'Nature forms appropriately what belongs to the body, habituation corrects desire, education forms reasoning' (X.33). What kind of education? 'The mistress of this education is civil philosophy: by forming prudence it prescribes laws to particular inclinations' (X.33). How then does philosophy carry out this task? It supplies a theoretical knowledge of the human good that enables the student of philosophy in particular situations to judge whether or not it would further the achievement of that good, if he were to act on this particular inclination. Prudence is just applied philosophy, and generally, although not necessarily, the lack of a philosophical education will be a source of imperfect prudence, especially of the kind of prudence required to manage the affairs of the Venetian republic.

The difference from Aristotle is striking, although unperceived by Piccolomini. Aristotle did indeed hold that a theoretical knowledge of the human good can and should inform practice on certain occasions, as I suggested earlier in this chapter and as I have argued elsewhere (MacIntyre 2006: 26–7). But, in order to make good use of this theoretical knowledge, one must already possess the virtue of prudence. The acquisition of prudence, on Aristotle's account, does not itself require theoretical study. An action is virtuous when it is the kind of action that a *phronimos* would perform in that particular type of situation, when the agent, knowing that what he does is the just or courageous or temperate thing to do, does it just because this is what justice or courage or temperateness requires, and when in so acting the agent acts from a settled and stable disposition (*NE* II.5.1105a31-33). To become prudent and virtuous, one needs teachers who both by example and by instruction will train one so that one becomes disposed to respond appropriately in each particular set of circumstances, while still unable to explain why one acts as one does, let alone to provide a theoretical account. At this stage what matters about one's teachers – older family members, friends, athletic trainers, whoever – is their possession of prudence and other moral virtues, and not their aptitude for theory.

With Piccolomini, by contrast, the key role is that of the philosopher as teacher, the philosopher as servant of the Venetian republic, playing a badly needed part in the life of that republic. Venice was, on Piccolomini's view, an example of that mixed form of government that Aristotle had commended, a city whose senators already exhibit the virtues that are needed for the political life. It never seems to have occurred to him either that Aristotle would have taken sixteenth-century Venice to be the type of commercial oligarchy that embodies a drastic misunderstanding of the point and purpose of a *polis* or that, if Venice's senators – who had not been educated in philosophy – already exhibited the virtues, his claims about the need for a philosophical education were put in question. Yet none of this makes his bold claim that it is through learning moral and political philosophy that one becomes prudent less interesting, especially because it is not only his claim, but one to be found in the writings of other renaissance Aristotelians.

In 1585, the Oxford University Press published its first book, John Case's *Speculum quaestionum moralium, in Universam Ethicen Aristotelis*, a detailed exposition of and commentary upon the *Nicomachean Ethics*. Case's preface addressed the students of both Oxford and Cambridge, telling them that moral philosophy is 'the norm of *mores*, the mistress of the virtues, the *gnōmon* of life, the rule of actions'. What then is the relationship between moral philosophy and *phronēsis, prudentia*? We are not simply to identify them, as we may be tempted to do, since 'moral philosophy treats these goods in terms of *genus, prudentia* in terms of *species*' (lib. VI, cap.5). The philosopher supplies the agent with a set of generalizations. The prudent agent applies them to particular types of situation. As with Piccolomini, prudence is taken to be applied moral philosophy. And, again as with Piccolomini, the university teacher of moral philosophy has been assigned an indispensable social and political role.

To anyone who cites Aristotle – as Shakespeare did (*Troilus and Cressida* II, ii, 16) – in order to argue that the students of such teachers are too young to benefit morally from their instruction, Case has two replies. The first is that what matters is not being young in years but being immature. The second is a response to the objection that, if a boy can obey the precepts of virtue, as on Case's view he can, then it must be that the precepts of virtue can be obeyed without prudence. Not so, says Case. Prudence must be already in the boy, even if inchoately (lib.VI, cap.13). So, contrary to Aristotle, the teaching of moral philosophy to the young can be effective by moving the young from inchoate prudence to the exercise of that heroic and general prudence which it is the end of moral education to inculcate. Why does this matter politically? In his unpublished *Apologia academiarum* (for a summary see Binns 1990) Case declared that 'without universities and men educated in letters great empires are nothing other than dens of wolves and tyrants.' So that, just as with Piccolomini, the teacher of Aristotelian moral philosophy is portrayed as an indispensable servant of the renaissance state.

It is important in more than one way that the Aristotle whose texts were given this kind of political importance, whether in Venice or in England, was of course Aristotle misunderstood. How typical this type of misunderstanding was certainly needs further enquiry. Yet, if the teaching of Aristotle was to win the regard and approval of those for whom the most urgent question was whether or not that teaching would foster respect for established authority, whether in Venice or in England, perhaps the only acceptable Aristotle was the Aristotle of Piccolomini and Case. And those of us who identify ourselves as Aristotelians can take comfort in this, that, when that Aristotle was not too long afterwards rejected as a political and moral teacher, the philosopher who was rejected was not in fact Aristotle, but an impostor.

IV

For two hundred years, from the early seventeenth to the early nineteenth century, no one made anything much of Aristotle, politically or otherwise. But then two things began to happen. Classical philology gradually provided better texts than anyone had had since Aristotle's ancient editors. And scholars provided commentaries of ever-increasing linguistic, historical and philosophical sophistication. A privileged minority of German, British and French schoolboys – and a few determined and intense girls – learnt at school and as undergraduates to be at home in classical Greek, even in Aristotle's crabbed Greek, in numbers that would have amazed their medieval and renaissance predecessors. And even the linguistically deprived Greekless students in moral philosophy and political theory classes found and find themselves provided with translation after translation. So it might seem that the twentieth and twenty-first centuries must be the age of Aristotle finally being understood, rescued from medieval and renaissance disagreement and partisanship by the objectivity of classical scholarship and by the excellence of historical and philosophical commentary. The objectivity and the excellence are real enough. But so too is the continuing depth of disagreement and partisanship. So that ours has become yet another age of a multiplicity of Aristotles, political and otherwise.

There is a foreshadowing of this in the nineteenth century, when Aristotle is invoked as a predecessor by thinkers of quite different philosophical and political views. Mill in *On Liberty* refers to Aristotle as a judicious utilitarian and, since this is what he took himself to be, this is more than a compliment. Marx remarkably often cites and praises Aristotle as having prepared the way for his own thought, and Heinz Lubasz (1977) and Patricia Springborg (1986) have brought out just how far Aristotle's influence on Marx extended. T.H. Green believed himself to be developing Aristotle's view in his discussion of the relationship of duties to rights, saying of Aristotle that he 'regards the state (*polis*) as a society of which the life is maintained by what its members do for the sake of maintaining it...and which in that sense imposes duties; and at the same time as a society from which its members derive the ability ... to fulfil their several functions and which in that sense confers rights' (Green 1986: 39). And A. C. Bradley argued in 1880 that, just because the ideals of modern civilization are so different from those of the Greek city, the spirit of Aristotle's conception of the Greek city is a valuable corrective to the errors and defects of modernity (Bradley 1991). Aristotle thus retains his place in our recent and contemporary conversations

Yet at this point, we cannot avoid asking whether what this narrative has provided are four – or more – perspectives on Aristotle, four – or more – different uses to which Aristotle can legitimately be put or, instead, four – or more – Aristotles. With all the gains provided by twentieth-century translation and commentary, questions of this kind remain to vex us, so that I cannot avoid returning to the account of Aristotle that I presented in the introductory section of this chapter, noting that each of its main contentions is an answer to a still disputed question. I begin with my assertion that Aristotle's exclusions of women and others from the political life rendered his use and understanding of the concept of the specific *ergon* of human beings incoherent, and that therefore a consistent Aristotelianism would require their excision from his political philosophy. Susan Moller Okin, whose scathingly effective feminist critiques made her untimely death even more lamentable than it would otherwise have been, argued that those exclusions cannot be excised from Aristotle's thought, unless we reject some of his central metaphysical concepts, notably that of form, since these too presuppose the inferiority of women. One does not have to be an antifeminist to disagree with Okin, as the example of Charlotte Witt shows. My point is simply that, in arguing as I did and do, I was and am taking up a position on a still highly disputed terrain.

Second, consider my claim that the *Politics* and the *Nicomachean Ethics* should be read together or not at all and set beside it what Carnes Lord has written in his 'Introduction': 'It is probably best to assume that the *Politics* was composed by Aristotle as an independent work intended to be intelligible in its own terms without depending essentially on the ethical writings' (Lord 1984: 19–20). So here again extensive argument is needed, but there is no reason to believe that it would, no matter how skilfully deployed, secure agreement. The same is true of a third claim that I made, when I presented as Aristotle's view the thesis that the philosophical life, the life that culminates in the achievement of *theōria*, is the completion of the political life and not an alternative to it. A very different view is argued powerfully by Richard Kraut. 'On my reading, Aristotle holds that there are two good ways of answering the question "What is happiness?" According to the best of these two answers, happiness consists in just one good, the virtuous exercise of the theoretical part of reason. ... According to the second best answer, happiness consists in virtuous practical activity' (Kraut 1989: 5), and Kraut goes on to speak of these as the best life and the second-best life.

I am, as of now, convinced of two things: first, that I will not be justified in continuing to hold the positions that I do, unless I am able to supply adequate argumentative responses to such arguments as those of Okin, Lord, Kraut and all those others whose positions are incompatible with mine *and*, second, that I can in fact supply such a response. But I would be foolish to suppose that by making it, I will secure agreement, if only because those with whom I disagree share those convictions with respect to their positions. How then should we proceed? Immediately, by reminding ourselves of how wide and deep the disagreements are, some of them wide-ranging and systematic, others concerning the translation of particular passages, yet others to do with both of these. As an example of the latter, I think of my own disagreements with the author of one of the more impressive late twentieth-century books about Aristotle's politics, Fred D. Miller, Jr. (1995), in which Miller ascribes to Aristotle the thesis that 'that constitution is best according to nature which is unqualifiedly just and which guarantees the rights of its citizens according to this standard', so making of Aristotle a precursor of modern theorists of rights.

The case for this thesis could not be made better than Miller makes it. Yet quite a number of us remain unconvinced. What do we quarrel with? In part, it is Miller's broad claim about the place that a Hohfeldian notion of a claim right has in Aristotle's thought; in part it is Miller's translations of such expressions as '*to dikaion*', '*to hautou*' and '*exousia*'. But these are closely related. Miller says, for example, that 'one important use of "*to dikaion*" is to refer to a right in the sense of a just claim' and he goes on to give examples of what he takes to be such uses. One problem for me is that in modern English, the expression 'right' never has the same sense as the expression 'just claim'. A right may well be cited in order to show that a particular claim is just. But just claims can have other grounds. So, if we translate '*to dikaion*' to mean 'just claim', this is enough to show that it cannot be translated by 'right' and the grounds that Aristotle might give for asserting that some particular claim is just would certainly not include the citation of some right. So Miller and I would translate such passages as NE V.3.1132a24-29 very differently. Do I think that in saying this I have given someone who takes Miller's view sufficient reason for changing her or his mind? Of course not. Yet this is only one among a set of apparently unresolvable disagreements, and no single political Aristotle emerges from contemporary debates, but rather a figure presented in very different guises. Tell me merely that you are an Aristotelian and I will not as yet know what you are telling me.

V

How then should we think about this condition that we find ourselves in? Very much, I suggest, as we already think about medieval and renaissance Aristotelians. With such figures as Aquinas and Oresme, Piccolomini and Case, we distinguish, so far as we can, between what they found in Aristotle's texts as they encountered them and what they brought to those texts as interpreters, and we further distinguish, so far as we can, between what they brought to those texts that was influenced by their culture and what they brought to those texts that was peculiarly their own. In putting these distinctions to work, we have to recognize that Aristotle's texts, even when we have learnt more from the philologists than was possible for our medieval and renaissance predecessors, underdetermine their interpretation at significant points. Learning to think about ourselves in this light is not an alternative to developing further and defending further the various accounts of Aristotle as a political thinker that some of us have advanced. But, if we do not so learn, we may be in danger of becoming the victims of our own unrecognized presuppositions.

Bibliography

Adkins, A. W. H. (1991), 'The Connection between Aristotle's *Ethics* and *Politics*', in David Keyt and Fred D. Miller, Jr. (eds), *A Companion to Aristotle's Politics*, 75–93, Oxford: Blackwell.
Aristotle (1957), *Politica*, ed. W. D. Ross, Oxford: Oxford University Press.
Aristotle (1991), *Ethica Eudemia*, ed. R. R. Walzer and J. M. Mingay, Oxford: Oxford University Press.
Aquinas, Thomas (1267), *De Regimine Principum* (any edition).
Aquinas, Thomas (1225-1274), *Aristotelis Libri. Sententia Libri Ethicorum* (any edition).
Aquinas, Thomas (1265-1274), *Summa Theologiae* (any edition).
Binns, J. W. (1990), 'Elizabeth I and the Universities', in J. Henry and S. Hutton (eds), *New Perspectives in Renaissance Thought: Essays in the History of Science, Education and Philosophy: In Memory of Charles B. Schmitt*, 244–52, London: Duckworth.
Bradley, A. C. (1991), 'Aristotle's Conception of the State', in D. Keyt and Fr. D. Miller (eds), *A Companion to Aristotle's Politics*, 13–56, Oxford: Blackwell.
Bodéüs, Richard (1982), *Le philosophe et la cite. Recherches sur les rapports entre morale et politique dans la pensée d'Aristote*, Liège: Presses universitaires de Liège, Les Belles Lettres (trans. in English Bodéüs, Richard (1993), *The Political Dimension of Aristotle's Ethics*, trans. Jan Garrett, Albany, NY: SUNY Press).
Case, John (1585), *Speculum quaestionum moralium, in Universam Ethicen Aristotelis*, Oxford: Oxford University Press.
Collingwood, R. G. (1939), *An Autobiography*, Oxford: Oxford University Press.
Dunbabin, Jean (1982), 'Politics: Reception and Interpretation', in N. Kretzmann, A. Kenny and J. Pinborg (eds), *The Cambridge History of Later Medieval Philosophy*, 723–37, Cambridge: Cambridge University Press.
Green, T. H. (1986), *Lectures on the Principles of Political Obligation*, Cambridge: Cambridge University Press.

Kraut, Richard (1989), *Aristotle on the Human Good*, Princeton: Princeton University Press.
Lord, Carnes (1984), *Aristotle: The Politics*, trans. Carnes Lord, Chicago: University of Chicago Press.
Lubasz, Heinz (1977), 'The Aristotelian Dimension in Marx'. *Times Higher Education Supplement* (1 April): 17.
MacIntyre, Alasdair (1999), 'John Case: An Example of Aristotelianism's Self-Subversion?', in T. Hibbs and J. O'Callaghan (eds), *Recovering Nature*, 71–82, Notre Dame: University of Notre Dame Press.
MacIntyre, Alasdair (2006), 'Rival Aristotles: Aristotle against some Renaissance Aristotelians', in Alasdair MacIntyre (ed.), *Ethics and Politics: Selected Essays*, 22–40, Cambridge: Cambridge University Press.
Mill, J. S. (1859), *On Liberty* (any edition).
Miller, Fr. D. (1995), *Nature, Justice, and Rights in Aristotle's Politics*, Oxford: Oxford University Press.
Piccolomini, Francesco (1583), *Universa philosophia de moribus*, Venezia: Tip Francesco De Franceschi.
Schmitt, Charles B. (1983a), *Aristotle and the Renaissance*, Cambridge, MA: Harvard University Press.
Schmitt, Charles B. (1983b), *John Case and Aristotelianism in Renaissance England*, Kingston and Montreal: McGill-Queen's University Press.
Shakespeare, William (1609), *Troilus and Cressida* (any edition).
Sparshott, Francis (1997), 'Review of The Political Dimensions of Aristotle's Ethics Richard Bodéüs' Translated by Jan Edward Garrett Albany: State University of New York Press, 1993, xiv + 250 pp, *Dialogue*, 36 (2): 410–13.
Springborg, Patricia (1986), 'Politics, Primordialism, and Orientalism: Marx, Aristotle, and the Myth of the Gemeinschaft', *American Political Science Review*, 80 (1): 185–211.

2

Plato and Aristotle on nature and society

Richard Stalley

I

Although Alasdair MacIntyre sees himself as belonging to 'the Aristotelian tradition', he makes it very clear that Aristotle himself can be seen as part of a larger tradition of Greek philosophy. In *Whose Justice? Which Rationality?* (*WJWR*), MacIntyre gives space to the Sophists and Pre-Socratics, to Socrates himself and above all to Plato. He emphasizes the continuities between Plato and Aristotle and suggests that Aristotle is 'trying to complete Plato's work, and to correct it precisely insofar as that was necessary to complete it'. He even claims that, in ethics and politics, at least, Aristotle 'is not so much opposing as redoing the work of the *Republic*' (MacIntyre 1988: 94).

In spite of this emphasis on the continuities between the two philosophers, MacIntyre recognizes important differences between them. He associates these differences partly with disagreements in metaphysics – they both use the language of Forms, but they understand this in very different ways – and partly with their different reaction to the political events of their times. Thus, MacIntyre writes:

> Plato contrasts the Form and the realm of particulars. Emphasising their disparity, Aristotle understands the form as confronted only in particulars, albeit often imperfectly so exemplified; where Plato contrasts the ideal of polity and the realm of actual *poleis*, emphasising their disparity, Aristotle understands the type of *polis* which is best at conforming to a standard which is already implicitly embodied and acknowledged, albeit in important ways, within the practices of actual Greek politics. And this is why the findings of political enquiry, as Aristotle understands them, can be brought to bear on the choices between Macedonian custom, Greek political practice, and Alexander's seduction by Persian despotism. (1988: 93–4)

MacIntyre also claims that in his last work, the *Laws*, Plato himself 'redid' the work of the *Republic*. He points to similarities between the *Laws* and Aristotle's *Politics*, and suggests that Plato may have changed his mind under the influence of Aristotle's critique. I believe that MacIntyre is right to emphasize the continuities between Plato and Aristotle, but it is important also to notice the ways in which they diverge. In this chapter, I shall explore the continuities and divergences between the accounts of human society found in various works of Plato and in Aristotle's *Politics*.

II

Plato's *Republic* has been interpreted in many different ways. At one extreme there is the view that Plato is presenting a blueprint for political action – that he really hoped to establish a city ruled by Platonic philosophers. Those who take this view have sometimes held that he hoped to implement the *Republic*'s proposals when he became involved in the politics of Syracuse and that his failure there led him to abandon that ideal. This change of heart was held to be embodied in his final dialogue, the *Laws*, which describes a more practical ideal city. Other lines of interpretation have emphasized that the *Republic* begins and ends as an investigation of justice in the individual soul. Socrates offers his account of an ideally just city as a means of illuminating justice in the individual. For that purpose, it does not matter whether the ideal city could ever come into existence. But, either way, the *Republic* is the natural place to start an examination of Plato's conception of human nature and society. So I shall begin by considering some of the key points which arise in the account of the city, which we find in the earlier parts of that dialogue.

1. Socrates starts the search for justice by asking his companions to join with him in imagining how a city might come into being. His first move in this investigation is to observe that human beings, as individuals, are not self-sufficient (369b). They have many needs that they cannot satisfy on their own. They therefore come together as helpers and associates, sharing (*koinōnein*) things with one another because they think that is in their own interests. The city is thus seen as a *koinōnia* (a sharing or partnership).[1] Our fundamental needs are for food, housing and clothing. The most basic community will therefore comprise a farmer, a builder and a weaver. Socrates refers to this community as a 'city' (*polis*), but it does not have much in common with the Greek *polis* of the fourth century. It looks as though Plato, at this stage, wants to examine the nature of human society as such without making any presuppositions about the form that society should take. In this sense, his approach foreshadows that of later political philosophers who started by postulating a state of nature.
2. A second point to notice is that, in order to satisfy these needs, the citizens must, not only co-operate but also work. So the basic city is situated in the real world of human experience, not in some imaginary golden age. This point is reinforced at 372a ff. where Socrates imagines the citizens living a simple rustic life. Glaucon objects that this community lacks all the advantages of civilized life. It is, he says, a 'city of pigs'. Socrates disagrees. He insists that it is the genuinely healthy city, but offers, nevertheless, to describe a luxurious or 'fevered' city. The implication here is that the citizens are subject to the potentially destructive passions and desires which come with embodiment as human beings.

3. At 370a ff., it is agreed that things will go best if each member of the community, instead of trying to do everything for himself, sticks to one role. One reason for this is simply that workers will do their tasks more efficiently if they can devote their whole time to their professions. But Socrates also argues that things will go better if each person sticks to the task for which he is best suited by nature (370a-c). This soon comes to be treated as the fundamental principle on which society ought to be organized. It presupposes two other assumptions. The first is that people differ in their natures (*phuseis*) (i.e. in their inborn characters and aptitudes). The second is that these natural differences fit them for different tasks. If they stick to these, they will each be acting *kata phusin* in accordance with nature.

4. Initially, the principle that everyone should specialize on one job for which they are suited by nature seems fairly innocuous, but it acquires a much greater significance when Socrates argues that the city should have an army. He insists that the soldiers, or 'guardians' as he calls them, should also be specialists, and discusses how those with appropriate natural aptitudes (*phuseis*) should be selected and trained (373a-374c). In doing so, he compares the selection and training of the guardians with the methods used in breeding and training guard dogs. Like guard dogs, they will need to be fierce towards their enemies but gentle towards their friends (375a-376c). For this they will need to develop a nature that is not only 'spirited' but also 'philosophical'. Socrates describes at great length the training in gymnastics, music and poetry which will be needed for this purpose (376c-412a).

5. There is a further application of the principle of specialization at 412b ff. There Socrates raises the question of which of the guardians should rule. He argues that this task should be given to those among the older guardians who show most wisdom and practical ability in the relevant matters (412b-c). This results in a system of three classes, which is explained in the so-called myth of the metals (415a-c). The citizens are to be told that they are all brothers and sisters, but that some (those fitted to be rulers) have gold in their nature, others (those who will be soldiers) have silver, while there is iron or bronze in the nature of those who will be farmers or artisans. This threefold division becomes the basis for Socrates' account of justice. The city will be just when those fitted to be rulers do rule and the other classes willingly obey. Where this is the case, the city will be established in accordance with nature (*kata phusin*) even though the class of rulers is naturally (*phusei*) less numerous than the others (428e). Socrates goes on to apply this conception of justice to the individual. He argues that, corresponding to the three classes in the city, there are three elements in the human soul: reason, spirit and desire. The soul will be just when reason rules and the other elements obey (434d-444e). So, a central claim made by Socrates in these books of the *Republic* is that both the city and the soul will be just when they are organized in accordance with nature.

This does not prevent Socrates from making some proposals which would have seemed decidedly unnatural to most of his contemporaries. One of these is that women, as well as men, should be guardians, that is, they should be eligible to become both soldiers and rulers (451b-457b). In making this point, Socrates emphatically rejects the argument of those who say that women differ from men in nature and should therefore have different roles. He acknowledges that there are things which men generally do better than women, but insists that there are no specifically masculine tasks for which all women are unsuited. He also points out that female dogs are expected to carry out the same tasks as males. Thus, he claims, it is not the idea that women should be guardians that is contrary to nature (*para phusin*), but rather the current practice of excluding them from such roles (456b-c).

Other features of Socrates' city which might have shocked his contemporaries include the requirements that guardians should have no private property and no families of their own. The abolition of private property for the guardians is initially proposed on the grounds that owning property would be incompatible with their role. They would become farmers and householders rather than guardians and would be tempted to exploit the other citizens rather than to be their protectors (417a-b). The replacement of the family by a system of matings organized by the rulers is first suggested as a form of selective breeding: mating the best male and female guardians will ensure that they produce the best offspring (458c-459e). But later another purpose is suggested for the abolition both of the family and of private property. At 462a ff., Socrates argues that the greatest evil that can befall a city is for it be pulled apart and become many instead of one. Correspondingly, the city's greatest good is whatever draws it together and makes it a unity. This should be the aim of all legislation. Socrates goes on to argue that cities tend to fall apart when their citizens feel pleasure and pain at different things. They are drawn together when they share the same pleasures and pains and call the same things 'mine' and not 'mine'. A system that ensures that they have no property or families of their own will bring this about. The relationship of the citizens to one another will then be like that of the parts of a single living body, which share the same pleasures and pains. At 466d, Socrates reaffirms that there is nothing contrary to nature (*para phusin*) in these proposals.

III

The account of the city in the *Republic* presupposes a distinctive, revisionary account of nature, one which is very different from anything that would have been recognized by most of Plato's contemporaries. It is also very different from that assumed by Aristotle in the *Politics*. Aristotle agrees with Plato that the *polis* is a *koinōnia*, a partnership or association, which comes into existence because human beings, by themselves, are not self-sufficient, but he develops this point in a very different way. In the first book of the *Politics* he argues that every kind of association (*koinōnia*) comes into being for the sake of some good. The city, which is the most sovereign association and includes all the rest, is directed to the most sovereign good (1252a1-7). He goes on to argue that the most basic element out of which the *polis* is formed is the household. This arises from two distinct unions. The first is that of male and female, which arises from the common desire of all living beings to reproduce. The second is that between the element which naturally rules and the element which is naturally ruled. The household thus comprises both the union of man and wife and that of master and slave (1252a24-b15). Aristotle is careful to distinguish these two unions. Nature, he claims, makes everything for a single purpose. So he criticizes 'barbarians' who treat the female and the slave in the same way. Later he clarifies this point by explaining that the rule of the free man over the (natural) slave is distinct from the rule of male over female. The natural slave lacks the power of deliberation, while the female has it, but not in an authoritative form (1260a9-13).

According to Aristotle, the next form of association, after the household, is the village. This is the first to comprise more than one household and to be concerned with more than the mere satisfaction of daily needs. Aristotle suggests that it originates most naturally (*kata phusin*) as a cluster of closely related families (1252b15-18). The final and perfect association is the *polis*, which is formed from a number of villages. At this stage, Aristotle claims, we have reached the height of self-sufficiency. The point here seems to be that the *polis* provides everything that is needed, not just if we are to survive in reasonable comfort, but if we are to lead truly human lives. So Aristotle claims that, while the *polis* may have come into being for the sake of mere life, it exists for the sake of the good life (1252b27-30).

Both Socrates in the *Republic* and Aristotle start from the assumption that human societies are associations which come into existence because human beings are not self-sufficient. Both also claim to be describing societies that are in accordance with nature. But the results they come up with are on many points radically opposed. Aristotle takes for granted the superiority of men over women and assumes that the household must be the fundamental unit of society. His city is thus an idealized version of the Greek *polis*. Socrates, on the other hand, denies the natural superiority of men and proposes to abolish the household. His city is thus very different from any *polis* that actually existed. It is not surprising, therefore, that, when he discusses Socrates' city in *Politics* Book II, Aristotle takes particular exception to the proposals for the abolition of the family and of private property. He argues, at some length that these measures would not achieve their intended purpose of unifying the city by creating friendship among the citizens (Stalley 1991: 182-99; Mayhew 1997). They would, he claims, be more likely to do the opposite. He also offers a more philosophical objection: that Socrates goes wrong in assuming that the greatest possible unity is the supreme good (Stalley 1999: 29-48). As Aristotle puts it, 'The city by its nature is some sort of plurality. If it becomes more of a unit, it will first become a household instead of a city, and then an individual instead of a household.' 'It follows that even if we could, we ought not to achieve this object: it would be the destruction of the city' (*Politics* 1261a19-22).

The disagreements between Plato and Aristotle result, to a large extent, from the fact that the two philosophers are assuming different conceptions of nature. Aristotle draws quite explicitly on accounts of nature and of human good, which he develops elsewhere. In the *Physics* he argues that everything which exists by nature has within it an inner principle or cause of movement and growth (192b20-3). Thus, the form of an animal, a cat for example, is incipiently present within the animal from the earliest stages of its development, but it is fully realized only in the adult animal. Nature is thus a tendency within the animal which moves it towards its natural end. Aristotle also holds that nature does nothing in vain. This means that every species must have a unique function. Human beings are distinguished from all other creatures by their possession of reason. We may infer, therefore, that human beings achieve their true end only if they are able to live a life of rational activity. This requires them to live in the distinctive form of social and political organization which is the Greek *polis*. So human beings are essentially *polis*-dwelling animals, and the *polis* may be seen as something which exists by nature. Indeed, a human being without a *polis* is like a hand without a body. Only within that form of society can one lead a truly human life (1253a1-29). So if, as MacIntyre suggests, Aristotle is seeking to defend the Greek *polis*, that defence is clearly founded on his metaphysics of nature.

Aristotle's account of nature is closely linked to the method of scientific investigation, which he calls *epagōgē*.[2] As MacIntyre describes this, it is a 'method of moving from a set of particulars to a universal, to the concept of the form which those particulars to different degrees exemplify' (91). This way of proceeding may well underlie much of what Aristotle has to say in later books of the *Politics*,[3] but it is very different from anything we find in the *Republic*. As we have seen, the early books of that dialogue make no real pretence to invoke the experience of existing communities, but rather rely on a conception, never fully explicit, of what is in accordance with nature. In *Republic* Book VIII, Plato compares the constitution of his ideal city to four other types. But these types are theoretical models that make no reference to the experience of real cities.[4]

IV

Socrates' procedure in the opening books of the *Republic* evidently raises questions about his concept of nature and of philosophical method. If we are to find answers to these, we need to look to the middle books of the dialogue from 471e onwards. There Socrates is challenged to show that the city he has been describing is possible. In reply he points out that he and his companions are seeking to discover 'what sort of thing justice is'. He points out that answering this question does not require them to show that a perfectly just man has ever existed. They need merely to find a model or pattern (*paradeigma*) of real justice. Similarly, when they look for justice in the city, it will suffice if they can show how a city most like the one they have described could come into existence (473a-b). Socrates claims that a city of this kind will be possible providing one condition is satisfied – that the city has philosophers for its rulers. Cities will have no rest from evils until philosophers become kings or kings become philosophers (473d). Accordingly, the middle sections of the *Republic* are largely occupied with an account of philosophers and of their education. This is based on the theory of Forms. The key point is that philosophers have turned away from the everyday realm of becoming to that of the Forms. They thus have genuine knowledge rather than mere belief.

Most modern interpreters have seen the idea of the philosopher ruler as central to Plato's political philosophy, but Aristotle does not seem to have seen it that way. At many points in his writings, he attacks the Platonist doctrine of the Forms and he specifically criticizes the idea that there is a Form of the Good.[5] But, in the *Politics*, he makes no mention of philosophers or of the Forms.⁶ This has led some to speculate that there was once a version of the *Republic* without its middle books. But, even within the *Republic*, as we have it, the connection between the city as described in the early books and the need for philosophers as rulers is not as clear as it might be. Socrates is evidently committed to the view that (a) if philosophers were rulers, they would establish a city along these lines, and (b) there are no other circumstances in which such a city could be established. But, insofar as he argues these points, he does so somewhat indirectly. The key passage is at 517b-521b, where Socrates interprets the simile of the Cave. The main point made there is that, although philosophers would prefer to spend their time contemplating the Forms, they must be compelled to return to the Cave, that is, to the earthly city, in order to act as rulers. One reason for this is that philosophers are not prey to the desires that come with our embodiment. They will not, therefore, be liable to the corruption that affects most human rulers. But Socrates' main point is that because philosophers have a grasp of the truth, they have a goal or target (*skopos*) at which to aim in everything they do (519c). The implication seems to be that only the philosopher has a clear conception of the good which is the proper end of all political activity.

If these arguments were sound, they would show that philosophers make the best rulers, but they do not, in themselves, explain why philosophers would choose to establish a city like the one which Socrates has been describing. Equally it is not obvious why Socrates' city could not come about in some other way. It needs wise rulers, but it is not clear that these must be Platonic philosophers. The accounts of the selection and training of the guardians in Books III and IV stipulate that they will need a 'philosophic' (i.e. wisdom-loving) disposition, but imply that this could be cultivated by a training in music and poetry (375e, 411e). This might suggest that there is no essential connection between the constitution described in the early parts of the *Republic* and the metaphysics of the middle books. But that would, I suggest, be a mistake. One obvious point here is that, in order to accomplish the main aim of the *Republic*, Socrates has to show that there are objective standards of good and evil, standards that are not simply the product of human wishes and desires. His account of the human soul implies that we all have a rational element in our souls which has some capacity to grasp these moral truths. Similarly, his account of the city, with its claim that some people are especially qualified to rule, implies that there are objective standards which some people understand better than others. The introduction of the philosopher rulers, and the account of the Forms which goes with it, provide this objectivity. While that account is in many ways very puzzling, it does, at least, constitute an affirmation of the idea that there are objective standards of good and bad, right and wrong. Without the Forms, Socrates would have no real answer to Thrasymachus.

More important, for the purposes of this chapter, is the way in which the theory of Forms, as that appears in the middle books of the *Republic*, serves to situate Socrates' account of the city and the soul within the framework of an orderly universe. This is particularly apparent in the similes of the Sun and the Cave. In the first of these, the sun is described, as 'most like' the good and also as its 'offspring' (*ekgonos*) (506e-507a). It is not only the source of light that makes vision possible but also the cause of 'nourishment and growth in living things'. Similarly, the Good not only makes the other Forms knowable but also is the source of their being and existence (509b). The language here is intentionally mysterious, but the simile clearly implies that the Good determines the structure of reality. In other words, the Universe is organized for the best, even if that is not apparent to us. The simile of the Cave conveys a similar message. The career of the philosopher who turns from the everyday changing world to the realm of the Forms is likened to that of a prisoner who escapes from the Cave in which he[7] has previously spent his entire life. When he reaches the sunlit upper world and finally comes to see the sun, he not only realizes that the sun causes and governs everything in the upper world but also understands that it is, in a way, the cause of everything he used to see down in the Cave (516b-c). The implication here is, again, that the Good is in some sense the ultimate cause of nature as we encounter it in our everyday world.

These similes imply a view of nature that differs in significant respects from Aristotle's. Things are intelligible only in so far as they can be seen to play a part in the larger structure of reality. The Forms are fully intelligible. Things in our 'visible' world are intelligible to the extent that they resemble the Forms. Nothing in the visible world is perfect, but some things display the order of the universe better than others. This is one reason why Socrates lists astronomy as one of the disciplines that philosophers must have studied. He claims that the heavens above are the most beautiful and most exact of the things which can be seen. They fall far short of truth, but we can still use them as models (*paradeigmata*) by which to study the true realities (529c-d). Towards the end of the *Republic*, a similar message is conveyed by the myth of Er (612a-621d). This tells how virtuous souls will be rewarded after death, while bad ones will be punished. It combines this with the idea that the motions of the heavens reveal the order and harmony of the universe (616b-617c). So the universe is a moral as well as a physical order (*kosmos*). We play our proper part in this to the extent that our souls and cities are organized in accordance with nature.

V

For a fuller account of Plato's conception of nature, we must look at the *Timaeus*. The greater part of that dialogue is taken up with a long discourse, put into the mouth of Timaeus who is 'an expert in astronomy and has made it his business to know the nature (*phusis*) of the universe'. His task is to deal first with the origin of the cosmos and then with the nature (*phusis*) of human beings (17c), but the opening sections of the dialogue recall the *Republic*'s account of human society. Socrates reminds his listeners of a conversation, supposed to have taken place on the previous day, in which he himself had described 'the kind of constitution which seemed ... likely to prove the best, and the character of its citizens' (17c).[8] This ideal constitution is largely identical with the one described in the early books of the *Republic* up to 471c, and is built on the same principles. In constructing it, Socrates and his companions 'followed nature in giving each person only one occupation, one craft for which he was well suited' (17c-d). But, strikingly, Socrates gives no hint of the claim that there should be philosopher rulers. This might be taken to imply that the political philosophy of the *Republic* can somehow be detached from the metaphysics of the Forms, but, in fact, the structure of the *Timaeus* and its incomplete companion dialogue, the *Critias*, suggests that Plato meant to indicate some kind of connection between political and cosmological themes.[9]

The opening sections of Timaeus' discourse recall the metaphysics and epistemology of the *Republic*. He begins by drawing a contrast between 'that which always is and has no becoming' and 'that which becomes but never is'. 'The former is grasped by understanding, which involves a reasoned account.' 'The latter is grasped by opinion which involves unreasoning sense perception' (27e-28a). Since Timaeus will be describing our changing visible world, the best he can do is to supply a 'likely story' (29d). According to this, the universe is the product of a beneficent craftsman, or Demiurge. The Demiurge was himself good, and desired that all things should resemble him in their goodness. He took over a world that was full of disorderly and discordant motion and brought it to order, since he judged 'that order was in every way better than disorder' (30a). He also recognized that, among the things which are visible by nature, what has reason or intelligence (*nous*) is always better than what is irrational. Since there cannot be reason without soul, he endowed the universe with a soul (the World Soul). So our world is a living creature with soul and reason. In constructing it, the Demiurge took as his model the eternal living creature which embraces within itself all other kinds of animal. He used this as an 'intelligible' model for bringing the visible world to order (30b-d). The universe is thus 'a single visible living thing which contains within itself all the living things whose nature it is to share its kind' (30d-31a). It is 'both divinely originated and a domain of natural beings working in natural ways' (Broadie 2011: 276).

When he comes to describe the origin and nature of human beings, Timaeus tells how the Demiurge took less pure fragments of the stuff from which he created the World Soul and handed them over to lesser 'created' gods to endow them with bodies (41d-42a). To go with the immortal rational element of the soul, these gods also created two mortal elements. One of these is characterized by courage (*andreia*) and spirit (*thumos*), and is ambitious for victory. The other is the source of appetites (69b-71a). Thus, on Timaeus' account, the human soul has three parts which correspond fairly closely to those identified by Socrates in the *Republic*.[10] On its first embodiment, the immortal rational soul is buffeted this way and that by impulses that come from the body. In this condition, the soul lacks intelligence but, as the bodily impulses subside, it gradually recovers its natural (*kata phusin*) motion and becomes rational. If it then receives the right kind of education, it will travel through life 'whole and healthy', but if it does not, it will 'limp its way through life and return to Hades uninitiated and unintelligent' (44b-c). Later Timaeus makes it clear that the fate of our souls depends partly on physiology and partly on the communities in which we live. Disorders in the body lead to folly and stupidity, which are seen as 'diseases' of the soul. These will be greatly aggravated if someone in this condition lives in a city with a bad constitution, where discourse, both public and private, is bad and where there is no proper education (87b).

Even among Plato's immediate successors there were disagreements as to whether Timaeus' account of creation is to be taken literally or is simply an expository device.

Either way, the underlying message is that the universe is an ordered system and that its orderliness must, in some sense, be the work of *nous* (mind or intelligence). Human beings, likewise, have some share of intelligence. Their primary task is to create order in their souls by ensuring that their rational element rules over the potentially subversive elements of spirit and appetite.[11] In presenting this picture, Timaeus uses the word *phusis* (nature) in at least two different ways. In many passages, it refers to the character or nature of the materials on which the Demiurge has to work. This suggests an analogy with the activities of craftsmen such as carpenters or stonemasons. These craftsmen take materials which exist in nature and exploit their natural characteristics in order to make something new, an artefact which does not exist in nature. But Timaeus also uses the word *phusis* in referring, not to the materials on which the Demiurge works, but to the products of his craftsmanship. In particular he talks about the *phusis* of the universe or cosmos and the *phusis* of mankind (27a, 29d, 30b, 42a, 68d, 77a, 90c). In this sense, both the regular movements of the heavenly bodies and properly ordered human soul may be described as 'according with nature'.

The conception of nature implicit in these passages is clearly different from that of Aristotle. Plato suggests that to discover what kind of life is truly natural for human beings, we have to reflect, not on any inbuilt tendencies to seek the good that is distinctive of our species, but on an understanding of our place in the universe at large.[12] MacIntyre at times seems not to recognize this point. For example he writes 'From the Platonic standpoint the nature of each kind of thing is to be specified in terms of the good towards which it moves, so that the adequate characterization of human nature and of the passions as part of that nature requires reference to that good' (MacIntyre 1988: 77). This attributes to Plato what is in fact the Aristotelian view.

VI

The *Laws* is Plato's last and longest dialogue. It is set in Crete and is thus the only one of Plato's dialogues that takes place away from Athens. It is also the only one in which Socrates plays no part. It depicts a long and leisurely conversation between an unnamed Athenian, a Spartan named 'Megillus' and a Cretan named 'Cleinias'. They are walking through the Cretan countryside towards a shrine of the god Zeus. At the beginning of the dialogue, the Athenian asks about the distinctive laws and institutions of Crete and Sparta. The main message of the first two books is that these are on the right lines, in the sense that their institutions are directed to making the citizens virtuous, but they fall short of that goal because they presuppose a defective conception of virtue. Book III is largely devoted to what purport to be historical accounts of the Dorians, of Athens and of Persia. These lead to the conclusion that no individual or group of individuals can be trusted with unrestricted power. Law, seen as the product of reason, must be supreme. At the end of Book III, Cleinias reveals that there are plans to establish a new city in Crete. This gives the Athenian the chance to describe what a city governed by laws, rather than by men, might look like in practice.

The city which the Athenian describes is radically different from that of the *Republic*. We may note, in particular, the following:

1. The city of the *Laws* is based on the principle that law should be sovereign. The constitution of the city is thus designed to ensure that every aspect of the citizens' lives must be guided by law. There is a complicated system of checks and balances to ensure that those in authority always act in accordance with law.
2. The *Laws* does not require a *Republic* style division of the citizens into three classes. All citizens play some part in the government of the city and are expected to fight in its defence. This means that there is no place for the philosopher rulers of the *Republic*.
3. There is no proposal for the abolition of property or of the family. Every citizen family is to have an allocation of land which will be inalienable. Regulations for marriage and the upbringing of children seem, if anything, to be designed to strengthen the family. Women are expected to take an active part in public life, though the detailed arrangements for this are somewhat obscure.
4. The *Laws* agrees with the *Republic* in demanding that reason rule both within the soul and within the city, but it understands these claims in what seems to be a very different way. There is no reference to the Forms, and the reason of the state is embodied, not in philosopher rulers, but in its system of laws. These are seen as the work of a wise legislator or legislators.[13]

The relation between the *Republic* and the *Laws* has long been a matter of debate. Some scholars have seen the points noted here as indicating that Plato had radically changed his political and/or his philosophical views. Others have argued that there is no real inconsistency. In support of this view, they have suggested that the *Republic* presents a theoretical ideal while the *Laws* offers a model which is more closely concerned with the practical necessities confronting cities in Greece in third century BCE.[14] I will not explore these issues here. Instead I will take a cue from MacIntyre who claims that in the *Laws*, and in some other late dialogues, Plato is correcting his earlier views and, in doing so, is moving in an Aristotelian direction. This view is attractive because the *Laws* must have been written during the period 367–47 when Aristotle was associated with Plato's Academy, and because there are some similarities between the city of the *Laws* and the ideal city described by Aristotle in *Politics* Books VII and VIII. The key question is whether the similarities are simply the consequence of the *Laws* having a more practical focus or whether they indicate that Plato has 'corrected' his position in significant ways. If he has changed his view, there is a further question whether his views have moved closer to Aristotle's.[15]

MacIntyre's treatment of these points in *WJWR* is strongly influenced by the work of G. E. L. Owen who had argued that some of Plato's later works, particularly the *Parmenides*, contain powerful criticisms of the theory of Forms, at least as that appears in dialogues like the *Republic*. These criticisms resemble arguments used by Aristotle (Owen 1965b). The conclusion drawn from this was that in his later works, Plato abandoned or, at least drastically modified, his theory of Forms. This would explain why the *Laws* contains no obvious reference to the Forms or to associated doctrines such as that rulers must have knowledge rather than mere belief. At the time when MacIntyre wrote *WJWR*, Owen's view was widely accepted, particularly among Anglophone scholars, but more recently, it has been undermined by stylistic analyses of Plato's works. These indicate very firmly that the *Timaeus* is among Plato's later writings.[16] As we have seen, the theory of Forms plays an important part in that dialogue, so a late dating for the *Timaeus* makes it very unlikely that Plato had altogether abandoned the theory of Forms when he wrote the *Laws*. This does not in itself undermine the claim that there is some convergence between the Plato of the *Laws* and the Aristotle of the *Politics*. However, I will argue that, so far as concerns questions about nature and society, there is little to suggest that Plato has moved in an Aristotelian direction.

The *Laws* is closer to the *Politics* than to the *Republic* to the extent that it uses arguments which appear to make claims based on experience and that it takes account of the fact that a community's laws and institutions must be adapted to the particular circumstances in which it is established. But the method by which it pursues these points is very different from that of Aristotle. The *Laws* is a dialogue in which the participants represent the 'mindset' of their different communities.[17] Crete and Sparta were conservative societies which were often admired for their stability. In the opening books the traditions and institutions of these societies are subjected to friendly and constructive criticism by the visitor from Athens, a more open and intellectually vigorous city. There is nothing like the Aristotelian *epagoge* and no systematic survey of different constitutions. Rather, tradition is seen as a source of wisdom, albeit one to be used critically. Moreover, in the supposedly historical sections of the dialogue, the Athenian's account of events is clearly shaped by the conclusions to which he wants to move rather than the other way around. This is particularly obvious in the accounts of Athens and of Persia (694a-702b). These are designed to convey the message that neither autocracies nor democracies can prosper if their rulers are not restrained by law. In making this point, the Athenian argues that Athens was able to defeat the Persian invasions because at that time its citizens were 'slaves to the law', but Athens collapsed when it was ruled not by laws, but by men. MacIntyre notes the difference between this account and that given in the *Gorgias*, where Socrates' condemnation of democracy includes those who led Athens against Persia as well as their less admirable successors. He sees this as marking a change in Plato's attitude to democracy. But a more plausible interpretation is that Plato tailors his history to the conclusions he seeks to draw.

The fundamental principle which the Athenian follows both in his criticisms of Crete and Sparta and in his constructive suggestions about the new Cretan city are expressed most clearly in Book I. There the Athenian claims that the object of their discussion is to investigate the natural correctness of laws (627d).[18] The criterion for deciding this is provided a few pages later by an account of what is naturally best for human beings. The main point there is that the virtues of wisdom, temperance, justice and courage constitute the divine goods. They are ranked by nature (*phusei*) ahead of the human goods (health, beauty, strength and wealth). The task of the lawgiver is to ensure that the citizens rank them in the same way. All legislation must be designed with this in mind (631b-d). The implication here is that genuine laws are natural but not in the sense that they exist by nature, or that there are laws which are common to all communities. The claim is rather that the good life is directed towards the divine goods, that is, the virtues of wisdom, temperance, justice and courage. A legal system accords with nature to the extent that it promotes these virtues. Consistently with this there are large number of passages where the Athenian suggests that the legislation he proposes would be in accordance with nature (*kata phusin*).[19]

The conception of nature here and the teleology that underlies it is made explicit in book X. There the Athenian argues that all wrongdoing stems from one or other of three false beliefs about the gods – the belief that there are no gods, the belief that the gods do not care about human affairs and the belief that they can be won over by prayer and sacrifice (884a-885c). He sees outright atheism as having its source in a false conception of nature. The atheists claim that most of what happens in the world is due to nature or chance. Only the small areas which fall under human control offer any scope for *technē* (art or skill). The Athenian, on the other hand, argues that *technē* has priority. He claims that the source of motion in the universe must be a soul or souls and that the soul that governs the universe must be rational and good. It has arranged things so that ultimately the just will be rewarded and the unjust punished (887c-907a). A key step in this argument is the claim that the circular movements of the heavens 'bear the closest possible relation and similarity, in every way, to the movement of reason (*nous*)' (898a-d). Thus, the order of the heavens shows that we live in a divinely ordered universe. Our task as human beings is to play our part within it. In doing so, we are acting in accordance with nature. For this reason, astronomy is given a prominent place in the education of all citizens (820d-822d) and is a required subject of study for the members of the Nocturnal Council (966d-967d).

The cosmology of *Laws* X differs from that of the *Timaeus* in some significant respects. In particular, there is no reference to the Demiurge. But the fundamental account of nature in Book X and in the *Laws* as a whole appears to be unchanged. It is difficult to discern any movement towards the Aristotelian conception.

VII

What emerges from all this is that MacIntyre is right to emphasize that the ethical and political theories of both Plato and Aristotle are founded on what might be called 'teleological' accounts of human nature. There are however important differences in the ways in which they understand this teleology. To put it crudely, Plato is strongly influenced by mathematics and favours a 'top-down' approach that understands human life as part of the larger order of the universe.[20] Aristotle is influenced by biology and understands human beings as animals with an inbuilt impulse towards the good distinctive of their species. These differences have a powerful effect on the ways in which the two philosophers theorize about human society. They are particularly conspicuous when we compare the early books of the *Republic* with the opening chapters of the *Politics*. On the other hand, they make less difference when it comes to practical matters. So, there are points of similarity between the city of the *Laws* and the one imagined by Aristotle in *Politics* VII and VIII, but these are underpinned by different conceptions of the universe at large and our place within it. They should not, therefore, be taken as signs that Plato's philosophical views have moved in an Aristotelian direction.

Notes

1. *Koinōnia* is the noun formed from *koinōnein* (to hold or act in common). In this context it might well be translated 'partnership' or 'community', but it is also used of quite casual forms of association (see, for example, *Republic* 343d).
2. This is often, though misleadingly, translated as 'induction'. For Aristotle's account see, for example, *Prior Analytics*, 81a38-b9, 99b15-100a17.
3. Aristotle's school is said to have compiled accounts of the constitutions of 158 Greek cities. It is widely accepted that the *Politics* draws on this material.
4. Aristotle criticizes this part of the *Republic* precisely because it makes claims which have no foundation in practice. See *Politics* 1315b40-1316a29.
5. See, in particular, *NE* 1106a14-1107a27.
6. It is also notable that in the *Timaeus*, as we shall see, Socrates himself recalls a discussion in which he had described an ideal city with a constitution very like that set out in the early books of the *Republic* but makes no mention of philosopher rulers.
7. In referring to the prisoners Plato uses masculine forms but, since he holds that the philosopher rulers may be women, he presumably means his readers to understand that the escaped prisoner may be either male or female.
8. I use the translation by Donald Zeyl in Cooper 1997 (1224-1291).
9. Critias has agreed to tell a story according to which Athens itself once had a constitution like that described by Socrates and was enabled by it to defeat an invasion of Greece by the mighty empire of Atlantis but, before that they will hear from Timaeus, who is an expert on astronomy and has made it his main business to know the nature (*phusis*) of the universe. His speech will begin with the origin of the *kosmos* and concludes with the nature of human beings (27a-b). Critias' story is begun in the dialogue named after him but that is left unfinished after a few pages. If it had been completed it would presumably have developed the political themes of the *Timaeus*, so it is reasonable to see the original plan of the *Timaeus* and *Critias* as an attempt to interweave political and cosmological themes.
10. The key difference is that, in the *Timaeus*, the parts of the soul are given bodily locations and their interactions are, at least partially explained in physiological terms.
11. Similarly, in *Philebus* 28c-30e 'the spectacle of the ordered universe (*kosmos*) the sun, the moon, the stars and all their regular motions' are taken as evidence that everything is under the direction of a rational soul, to which our own souls are akin.
12. Both Plato and Aristotle have been seen as offering teleological views of nature. So far as Plato is concerned this has been disputed by Brisson 2019: 104–23. He interprets 'teleology' as referring primarily to Aristotle's doctrine of causes and, in particular, to the final cause. Given that conception Brisson is correct but it may be that he understands 'teleology' in an unduly restricted sense.
13. Some have seen an indirect reference to the Forms in the description of the Nocturnal Council (961a-968a).
14. See, for example, Saunders 2002: xxxii–xxxiii. For a more nuanced view see Bartels 2017.
15. If there is Aristotelian influence in the *Laws*, it does not seem to have impressed Aristotle himself. His treatment of the laws in *Politics* II 6 is cursory and unsympathetic. In particular he plays down the differences between the constitutions described in the *Laws* and in the *Republic*.
16. See Julia Annas and Christopher Rowe, *New Perspectives on Plato, Modern and Ancient*, Cambridge MA. (2002), especially the chapters by Annas and Kahn.

17 See Schofield's introduction to Schofield and Griffith 2016: 3.
18 Literally 'correctness and error with regard to laws, what it is by nature'.
19 See, for example, 636c, 642a, 686d, 690c, 720c, 809d, 815b, 816b, 839c, 853a, 870e, 927a, 931c. Older translations, including that by Saunders, frequently obscure these points, for example, by translating *kata phusin* as 'correct'. The translation in Schofield and Griffith 2016 is more reliable in this and in many other respects.
20 Gerson (2005: 6) cites the late Neo-Platonist Simplicius, *On the Categories* 6, 19–32, who distinguishes two methods of explanation. One starts from sense-perception (*aesthēsis*) and the other from the intellect (*nous*). According to Simplicius, Aristotle prefers the former and Plato the latter. Simplicius is arguing for the overall harmony of Platonic and Aristotelian philosophy. I do not find that plausible, but Aristotle can certainly be seen as working within a Platonic tradition.

Bibliography

Annas, J. and C. Rowe (2002), *New Perspectives on Plato, Modern and Ancient*, Cambridge, MA: Harvard University Press.
Aristotle (1995), *The Politics*, trans. Ernest Barker, revised by R. F. Stalley, Oxford: Oxford University Press.
Bartels, M. L. (2017), *Plato's Pragmatic Project*, Stuttgart: Franz Steiner Verlag.
Brisson, L. (2019), 'Can One Speak of Teleology in Plato?' in Luca Pitteloud and Evan Keeling (eds), *Psychology and Ontology in Plato*, 104–23, Cham, Switzerland: Springer Nature.
Broadie, S. (2011), *Nature and Divinity in Plato's Timaeus*, Cambridge: Cambridge University Press.
Cooper, J., ed. (1997), *Plato: Complete Works*, Indianapolis: Hackett.
Gerson, L. (2005), *Aristotle and Other Platonists*, Ithaca and London: Cornell University Press.
MacIntyre, A. (1988), *Whose Justice? Which Rationality?* London: Duckworth.
Mayhew, R. (1997), *Aristotle's Criticisms of Plato's Republic*, Lanham: Rowman and Littlefield.
Owen, G. E. L. (1965a), 'A Proof in the *Peri Ideon*', in R. E. Allen (ed.), *Studies in Plato's Metaphysics*, 293–312, London: Routledge.
Owen, G. E. L. (1965b), 'The Place of the *Timaeus* in Plato's Dialogues', in R. E. Allen (ed.), *Studies in Plato's Metaphysics*, 313–38, London: Routledge.
Saunders, T. (2002), *Plato: The Laws*, revised edition, London: Penguin Books.
Schofield, M. and T. Griffith (2016), *Plato: The Laws, Cambridge Texts in Political Philosophy*, Cambridge: Cambridge University Press.
Stalley, R. F. (1983), *An Introduction to Plato's Laws*, Oxford: Blackwell.
Stalley, R. F. (1991), 'Aristotle's Criticism of Plato's *Republic*', in D. Keyt and F. Miller (eds), *A Companion to Aristotle's Politics*, 182–99, Oxford: Blackwell.
Stalley, R. F. (1999), 'Plato and Aristotle on Political Unity', in M. Vegetti and M. Abbate (eds), *La Repubblica di Platone Nella Tradizione Antica*, 29–48, Napoli: Bibliopolis.

3

'Managers would not need subordinates and masters would not need slaves'

Aristotle's *Oikia* and *Oikonomia* reconsidered

Andrius Bielskis

Introduction

Alasdair MacIntyre urged contemporary Aristotelians to rescue 'Aristotle from himself in understanding his ethics and politics' (2016: 86). MacIntyre's conceptions of human dependence and vulnerability provide us with philosophical and ethical tools to reinterpret Aristotle's notion of πολιτικόν ζῷον (*zōon politikon*) in a new and radical way.

We need to reinterpret Aristotle's argument that humans are by nature political animals against the background of his conceptions of *oikos* and *oikonomia*. Yet the account of *oikia* that we find in the *Politics* is disappointing. It is not surprising that republican political theorists such as Hannah Arendt (1998) interpreted Aristotle's distinction between the *polis* and the household in terms of the modern distinction between the public and the private. Conceptualizing it as the distinction between freedom and necessity, these political theorists reinforced the conservative reading of Aristotle's political philosophy. They argued that the political is the public sphere of freedom, equality and rational deliberation in pursuit of the common good, while *oikonomikē* is the despotic sphere of necessity where the owners of property command the process of production for the sake of their private interest. There are good reasons to question this dominant interpretation. The premise of contemporary left-wing Aristotelians as far as the relationship between the *polis* and the *oikos* is concerned should be Aristotle's claim (a proto-Marxist one) on automation (αὐτόματος) ('we can imagine a situation in which each instrument could do its own work, at the word of command or by intelligent anticipation, like that of Daedalus or the tripods made by Hephaestus. ... A shuttle would then weave of itself, and a plectrum would do its own harp-playing. In this situation *managers would not need subordinates and masters would not need slaves*' (Aristotle 1998: *Pol* I.4.1253b33-39, emphasis added). Indeed, we do not need to imagine this situation: it is (albeit partly) our reality today. Automation frees humans from tedious but necessary tasks, and potentially allows us to enjoy more creative activities that, at least for Aristotle, require free time. Thus we need an Aristotelian argument of extending the sphere of the political to the sphere of economy. Hence the importance of focusing on *oikos* and *oikonomia* rather than just on *polis* and *praxis*.

I will therefore attempt to do three things in this chapter. First, I will briefly discuss Aristotle's conception of nature in order to locate where the source of his 'natural' inequalities lies in his *Politics*. I will then go through Aristotle's key claims on the verticality of three types of relationships within the household to argue that the verticality of the first two are arbitrary and are not philosophically justified. To argue that the relationships of *oikia* should be politicized, the notion of political rule will be also discussed to argue that it should be extended to the spheres of production and reproduction. I will then spell out the importance of Aristotle's argument on the nature of *oikonomia*, *chrēmatistikē* and *kapilikē*. The chapter will conclude that a progressive reading of Aristotle ought to interpret the inequalities within *oikia* and *oikonomia* in conjuncture with Aristotle's critique of the unnaturalness of *chrēmatistikē* as the limitless generation of exchange-value.

Aristotle's account of *phusis*

To criticize Aristotle's claim that women are *by nature* inferior to men and that there are slaves by *nature*, we need first to understand what Aristotle meant by *phusis*. Although the conception of *phusis* in Aristotle's philosophy is a huge topic in its own right (Miller 1995; Annas 1993: 142–58, Lear 1998: 15–54; Kraut 2007), my primary task is to spell out the key characterizations of *phusis* in order to make his claims about the two vertical social relationships within the household – between master (*despotēs*) and slave (*doūlos*) and between *man* (*posis*) and *woman* (*alochos*) – intelligible. I will argue that Aristotle uses *phusis* loosely and inconsistently in the *Politics*, and that his account of *phusis* in the *Physics* and elsewhere (that is to say, the teleological conception of nature which is philosophically defensible today) does in no way entail the 'natural' inequalities between men and women and between masters and slaves.

Aristotle defines nature by saying that 'animals and their parts, plants, and simple bodies like earth, fire, air, and water' exist due to nature and that in each of these nature is 'in itself a source of change' (Aristotle 1996: *Ph*.II.192b11-14). Thus his definition of *phusis* is that the 'nature of a thing' is 'a certain principle and cause of change and stability in the thing, and it is directly present in it – which is to say that it is present in its own right and not coincidentally' (*Ph*.II.193b20-24). This definition immediately allows Aristotle to draw a sharp contrast between *phusis* and *technē*. In the case of arts, change comes from outside, from the artisan, while the source of change in nature is internal and is not, as it is the case in a doctor curing himself, coincidental. So change in animals – coming to be, growth, flourishing, procreating and passing away – is internal and is inscribed in its very being, whereas in art, change comes from outside and therefore is external. Furthermore, the efficient cause of an artefact is not of the same kind, that is to say, a bed is not produced by a bed but by a human being, a carpenter. The cause of coming to be of an animal or a plant is of the same kind. The cause of a lion cub's birth is the sexual intercourse of male and female lions[1] while the efficient cause of a portrait is an artist who is a human being.

Given that every and each thing that has a nature is a substance (*ousia*) (*Ph.* II.192b34), the next question Aristotle poses is what kind of natural change happens in substances. This leads him to the discussion with Antiphon whether the nature of a substance (or a thing) is only its matter. To prove that the nature of a bed is its matter, Antiphon argued that if a bed was buried and rotted, its shoot would grow into a tree, not into another bed. For Aristotle, however, to claim that the nature of a bed is wood is to fail to explain what the bed is. This is also the case with natural substances. To explain why an acorn grows into an oak, the concept of form, which defines what the thing is, is essential. Without the concept of 'form' (*eidos*), nature would have no direction, change would be chaotic and therefore unintelligible. Although it is an open question whether Aristotle fully committed himself to arguing for the existence of prime matter as a completely formless 'primary underlying thing' (*prōton hupokeimenon*) underneath all change, the matter of artefacts and of natural substances is not formless either. So, for example, the wood of a bed has a form, so does bronze in a sculpture; both wood and bronze have different natures which are explainable only by reference to their different forms not in the sense of their shapes but in the sense of what they are. Thus, Aristotle argues that 'the nature of a thing' is 'the shape and form of that which has in itself its own source of motion and change' (193b3-5) and concludes that 'form (*eidos*) is a more plausible candidate for being nature than matter is because we speak of a thing as what it actually is at the time, rather than what it then is potentially' (193b6-9).

Nature is therefore a process and growth from potentiality (*dunamis*) to actuality (*entelecheia*) or, as Aristotle puts it, nature 'is a passage towards nature' (193b12-13). The directedness towards itself means that growth is internal – towards the completion of a natural form – as opposed to art whose purpose is an external object (e.g. health in medicine). Nature as growth is directed towards the end (*telos*), towards the completion of the form of a natural being: 'The nature of a thing is its end and purpose' since change 'comes to an end' and 'this concluding point is also the purpose of the change' (194a29-31). Aristotle qualifies this claim by saying that 'not every final stage has a claim to be called an end; only the best is an end' (194a32). This assertion is also repeated in *Politics*, where Aristotle states that 'nature is an end' and that 'the end is the best' (φύσις τέλος ἐστίν and τὸ τέλος βέλτιστον [ἐστίν]) (Aristotle 1998: *Pol*.I.2. 1252b33 & 1253a1).

This claim and Aristotle's account of the four causes/explanations (*aitiai*) of change – material, efficient, formal and final – commit him to seeing *phusis* also in terms of *perfected nature*. The *phusis* of a natural being then is a process of growth from the potential state of being (that is to say, a natural predisposition or propensity for something in someone) to the actual state of being when, due to favourable conditions and circumstances, the form of life of a natural being is realized. The full realization of the form as a natural activity (rather than a static state of being) – that is, a flourishing life – is an end which is the best.[2] The perfected *phusis* is, of course, philosophically debatable (certainly, the dominant modern accounts of nature ever since Isaac Newton and Thomas Hobbes rejected Aristotelian teleology), but it is, I want to assert, the most essential aspect of Aristotle's account of nature. Its peculiarity lies in its *normative element*. The perfect exemplification of a particular form of an organic life (the life of an oak, of a wolf, of a dolphin or of a human being) is a standard or a norm.³ It is not a norm in the sense of Plato's *eidos* (although the difference between Plato's account of forms and that of Aristotle's may be slighter than is normally suggested, the issue which cannot be pursued here), even less so in the sense of such Kantian normativity as that proposed by Christine Korsgaard, but in the sense of the concrete and actual embodiment of the flourishing of that form of life.

From *Physics* to the *Generation of Animals*

Apart from Aristotle's assertion that 'the matter which does the desiring' is akin to a woman longing for a man (*Ph.* 192a33-34) and his claim that a father causes a child, there is nothing of philosophical significance in the *Physics* (or in *De Anima* for that matter) that would allow him to argue, as he does in *Politics*, for the superiority of men over women and the existence of natural slaves. Together with the claim in *Physics* that one 'might liken it to a woman longing for a man, or what is ugly longing for what is beautiful, if it were not for the fact that the matter is not in its own right something that is either ugly or female, except coincidentally' (192a24-27), both of these assertions should be dismissed as philosophically arbitrary and, therefore, irrelevant. What is relevant instead is Aristotle's argument throughout his written corpus that human nature and the essential human function (*ergon*) is reasoning – including practical deliberation – which sets humans apart from other animal species. Thus, *logos* is the highest functional part of the human *psychē* whose actualization constitutes the form of being a human. The logical conclusion, therefore, must be that the human form and its *telos* is and must be the same for every human being and that every human being has the potential to live a flourishing rational life, given favourable *social* conditions and *right* ethical choices.⁴

How then can we explain the gap between Aristotle's conception of nature (including human nature) in *Physics* and *De Anima*, where the same human form is presupposed and argued for, on the one hand, and his claims in favour of the 'natural' inequalities in *Politics*? A part of the answer lies in Aristotle's claims in the *Generation of Animals*. In Book I, Aristotle discusses maleness and femaleness, as the chief principles of generation, and asserts that maleness is an active while femaleness is a passive principle: 'The male as possessing the principle of movement and of generation, the female as possessing that of matter' (716a6-9). This claim is also repeated in Book II where Aristotle adds that 'the male is separate from the female, since it is something better and more divine in that it is the principle of movement for generated things, while the female serves as their matter' (732a7-10). In a similar fashion to what is stated in *Physics*, Aristotle also claims that while male semen is the efficient cause of biological generation, female menstrual blood is the material cause of generation. Furthermore, in Book IV, he links the form (or formal cause) to sperm ('semen possessing the principle of the form', 765b13), and claims that male animals are hotter than female ones and that marks the difference between males and females in terms of ability (*dunamia*) and inability (*adunamia*). The weakness of the female animals is seen as their inability to produce semen and cause form. Yet separation of the sexes is needed for the generation of the same natural kind to occur.

Thus, it seems that it is here that we find the source of Aristotle's mistaken belief that men are naturally superior to women by nature: men are active and their seed is the efficient cause of generation, while women are passive, less perfect, and akin to matter (*GA*. II.3.737a21-25). We know now from modern biology that both male and female reproductive parts contribute *equally*, although in different ways, to the *form* of a new life. Yet Aristotle also argues there that in 'all animals that move around, male and female are separate. While one animal is female and another male, they are *identical in species*. So, for instance, both [men and women] are human beings' (*GA* 730b33–731a1). This last claim therefore implies that Aristotle believed that the essential nature of men and women was one and the same.[5]

The relationships of *oikia* and political rule

To explain his claim that every association comes to being for some good and that the *polis* is the most authoritative (*kuriotate*) association that includes all others, Aristotle, in *Politics*, proceeds to locate the most elemental compound (*suntheton*) (*Pol*. I.1.1252a19). The first and the necessary union is that between man and woman 'who cannot exist without one another' (1252a27).[6] By immediately drawing another distinction between a 'naturally ruling element' (which is so by virtue of intelligence) and a ruled element, Aristotle introduces master and slave as a way of juxtaposing his conception of political community to Plato's. Although his critique of Plato is advanced in Book II, Aristotle introduces natural inequality between both master and slave and man and woman at the very outset of *Politics*. In this way, it allows him to advance the argument that even if *oikia* is an essential part of the *polis*, these associations are ontologically different. Not only do they serve different functions and aim at different goods, their relationships within them are different too. The polis is 'an association of equals' and it aims at 'the best and highest life possible' (*Pol*. VII.8. 36-37), while the good of *oikia* is reproduction and the satisfaction of (other) recurrent needs (1251b13-14) and the relationships within it are 'naturally' vertical. It is for this reason, according to Aristotle, that Plato's attempt to blur the distinction between family and the state is a mistake as it obliterates the difference between the despotic relationships of *oikonomia* and the relationships among free and equal citizens in the *polis*.

This juxtaposition – the horizontality of the *polis versus* the verticality of the household – became very important for political philosophers in the twentieth century. They saw politics as the sphere of equality and freedom, and juxtaposed it to the vertical command, hard toil and necessity of *oikonomia*. The most important of them was Hannah Arendt, who interpreted Aristotle precisely in these terms (1998: 22-78, 1961: 104, 234). For her, *oikia* was a private sphere, the sphere of animal-like necessity and despotic command, while she saw the ancient Greek *polis* as the paradigm of the public sphere, the sphere of freedom whose essential virtue was not *phronesis*, as Aristotle maintained, but courage. She argued that the '*raison d'être* of politics is freedom, and its field of experience is action' (Arendt 1961: 146). Her accounts of labour, work and action were also very close to what Aristotle meant by *douleia* (slaving and slavery), *poiesis* (making) and *praxis* (action). While being sympathetic to 'the great wealth of Marxian ideas', she criticized Marx and interpreted labour as a painful, repetitive and meaningless 'effort that leaves no traces, no monument, no great work of remembrance' (Arendt 1998: 79, 81). In so arguing, her account of labour came close to Aristotle's claim that *doulos* is 'a servant in the sphere of action' (and life), not in the sphere of production (*Pol.* I.4.1254a7). Arendt went as far as to wrongly claim that the Greeks, including Aristotle, despised labour so much that they subscribed to the 'theory of the non-human nature of the slave' (1998: 84). Work for Arendt was productive activity due to which humans create a variety of things – the human artifice. For her, work, rather than labour, is the source of property. She accused Marx, and classical political economists, for not being able to distinguish between labour and work, between necessity and utility, and exalted action as that which created and maintained the public sphere of politics whose meaning was freedom, equality, excellence and distinction. In so arguing, not only did she fail to question the exclusions and 'natural' inequalities in Aristotle's thought but she also relied on them to argue against Marx in order to applaud the sphere of the political for the courageous and civilized few.

This republican interpretation of Aristotle and his conception of *oikia* should be resisted. We should reject the temptation to compartmentalize *oikonomia* and *politikē* in the way Arendt (and others who followed her) did. This is so *not* because all that goes on in households is of public and therefore political importance (the sphere of intimacy, for example, should be private indeed), but because *oikia* and *oikonomia* are a part of communal life, and thus what kind of *relationships* are in the reproductive and productive spheres is of public and political importance. In short, we should interpret *oikia* – the sphere of biological and social reproduction – and *oikonomia* – the sphere of production, of *poiesis* – in the light of second-wave feminists' claim that the private (and personal) is political. In the rest of this chapter, I will argue that, once the inconsistencies of Aristotle's erroneous biologism are rejected, there are conceptual resources in his philosophy to substantiate this interpretation.

Aristotle's argument that the *polis* is ontologically prior (πρότερον) to *oikia* and to each of us (ἕκαστος) because the whole (ὅλον) is necessarily prior (πρότερον ἀναγκαῖον) to the part (μέρους) (*Pol*.I.2.1253a18-20) should not be understood in terms of his supposed political organicism. The analogy between the human body and the *polis*, which follows immediately as the explanation of this thesis, is a metaphor and nothing else. An *oikia* vis-à-vis the *polis* is not the same as a hand vis-à-vis the body, because even if the city is destroyed, its families can still survive. After all, Aristotle tells us that families and their households came to being chronologically before the city: they can and did exist independently from the state, which is clearly not the case with the parts of the body (a hand cannot *functionally* exist apart from the body, unless, of course, it is a hand of a white walker in *Game of Thrones*). We should understand the claim in teleological terms: the term *proteron* is linked to *proteros*, which also means superior and higher. Hence, the claim is that the life of the *polis* is higher, more authoritative and better than the life in an *oikia*: the function and the end of the *polis* is *eu zēn*, not just a mere satisfaction of ephemeral needs (Bielskis 2017: 88).

Yet there is more to it than that. It also means that *oikia* is an essential part of the *polis* in that the life of *oikia* is a more elemental version of the life of the *polis*. In this sense, we can say that *oikia* is the mirror of the *polis*. That the household is intimately linked to and is an integral part of the city is also evident from Aristotle's notion of *politeia*, whose meaning is both 'constitution' *and* the best constitution. I will turn to the issue of the best political constitution and the best *polis* in a moment. However, at this stage, it is worth emphasizing that rendering *politeia* as 'constitution' may be misleading (although it is indeed its usual translation) if we forget that for Aristotle it did not mean just an institutional structure of the political offices of a *polis*[7] or 'a way of organizing (τάξις) the inhabitants of a city' (*Pol*.III.1274b38). *Politeia* is also 'the way in which the city lives' (IV.2.1295a40). Thus, Aristotle, in a similar way to Plato, argued that there is an intimate link between the character of a typical citizen and that of the way of life of a city:

> All would agree that the legislator should make the education of the young his chief and foremost concern. After all, the constitution of the city will suffer if this does not happen. The form of education must relate to each form of constitution. The type of character appropriate to a constitution tends to sustain that constitution as well as bring it into being. The democratic type of character creates and sustains democracy; the oligarchical type creates and sustains oligarchy; and in every case the best type of character will always tend to produce a better form of constitution. What is more, every capacity, and every form of art, requires as a condition of its exercise some measure of previous training and some amount of preliminary habituation, so the same must clearly go for acts embodying goodness of character. (*Pol*.VIII.1.1337a11-20)

Although Aristotle claims that education should not be left to private enterprise (τέκνα ίδιος) and thus aims to neutralize the education of children within *oikia* (1337a25-27), he nonetheless stresses the importance of nurturing of children which initially takes place only within *oikia*. So, in the *Nicomachean Ethics*, he claims that it is natural for parents and children alike to relate to each other through *philia* (love and friendship) (1155a17-21). It is through nurturing, care and love that parents, as citizens of the *polis*, initially habituate children in virtues. In the same respect, vice versa is also true: the lack of nurturing, insufficient care and the absence of love initially contributes to bad habits and dysfunctional character traits of children as future citizens. However, Aristotle's strongest assertion to link the two is the claim that every 'household is a part of a city', and the relationships in the household and their goodness 'must be considered with reference to the goodness of the whole' (1260b13-14).

The goodness of the whole, of course, is the goodness of the *polis*. Although there is an ongoing debate as to which constitution is the best, I have argued that it is *politeia*, where citizens rule and are ruled in turns (Bielskis 2006: 16–31). Aristotle states in the *Nicomachean Ethics* that the best constitution is monarchy (*EN* VIII.10.1160a35-36). The same claim is made, although less emphatically, in *Politics* (III.18.1288a15-18). However, apart from saying that if a ruler (or a family) is greatly superior to other citizens in virtue he should permanently rule, Aristotle never explains why this is so.

For him, as for Plato, the principle of ruling is *aretē*: the best *polis* is the city ruled by the virtuous, by the wise (*phronimoi*). Now the normative definition (i.e. understood in teleological terms) of the state 'is an association of equals (τῶν ὁμοίων) for the sake of best life possible', while 'the best (τὸ ἄριστον) is happiness (εὐδαιμονία) and that consists in (moral) excellence (ἀρετῆς) and its perfect (τέλειος) actualization (ἐνέργεια) and its employment (χρῆσις)' (*Pol*.VII.1328a35-3). This definition presupposes that *ideally* the best *polis* would be the one in which all its citizens were virtuous human beings. It also means that the *polis* is an association of equal and free individuals. Although Aristotle makes it clear that 'it is impossible for a city to be composed entirely of good men' (*Pol* III.4.1276b40-1277a1), he, nonetheless, argues that at least in one case a good man and a good citizen coincide: in the case of political rule (πολιτικὴν ἀρχήν) (1277b9).

To put it briefly, the argument is as follows. A good citizen is not the same as a good man. The key *aretē* of the good man is *phronēsis*, practical wisdom, which is best exemplified in and most needed for ruling. Other virtues such as justice, temperance and courage are also needed since one cannot be fully *phronimos* without having acquired and without practising these virtues. The essential characteristic of a good human being then is his or her ability to be a good ruler ('the excellence of the good man is in ruling' (1277a28)) and *vice versa*, a good ruler is a good human being (1277a13-14). Thus, the good man is good 'in virtue of a single absolute excellence' (1277a33). This is not the case with a good citizen since the goodness of a citizen depends not only on different functions different citizens perform in a *polis* but also because citizenship and its excellence are relative to a particular constitution. A good citizen in a democracy, for example, will not be the same as a good citizen in an oligarchy. Thus, *the* excellence of citizens is to preserve their political association and its constitution (1276b29). Yet by defining a citizen in his usual teleological (that is, functional) terms – a citizen is someone 'who shares in the administration of justice and the holding of office' (1275a22-3) – Aristotle acknowledges that such definition is 'democratic'[8] because political participation is the key feature of a democracy. The difference between the goodness of a human being and that of a citizen is that the first is realized only in ruling, while the second is realized both in ruling and in being ruled. In as much as a citizen is someone who is good in being ruled and obeying, the excellence required of a citizen is right opinion (δόξα ἀληθής) (1277b25-9). Hence, the excellence of good men and the excellence of citizens coincide only when citizens rule – that is, in their capacity of political rule – rather than when they are being ruled.

It is obvious, then, why the excellence of the good man – the *phronimos* who is able to rule himself/herself and others and accomplish noble ends – is different from the excellence of a good citizen. In bad constitutions (i.e. tyranny, oligarchy and democracy), the excellence of citizens will serve to preserve constitutions which are based on force rather than on the common good. Now the only constitution in which (at least theoretically and by definition) the good man and the good citizen do not sharply diverge is *politeia*. This is so because the political rule of ruling in turns is fully practised only in *politeia*. Furthermore, only *politeia* – as the mixed form of government run by citizens in turns, with collective deliberation by the many rather than by the few – accommodates Aristotle's conception of a citizen as someone who takes part in political and judicial offices better. If citizenship is defined as an activity rather than as a status, the constitution of a city should be arranged in the way to accommodate the activity. Similarly, although with some caution, we can push this argument as far as the definition of the state is concerned: the *polis* is an association of similar persons, of equals and the political consequence of this similarity is that they all have an institutionalized opportunity to rule. In this respect, monarchies and aristocracies are *less political* because ordinary citizens and their rulers are separated from each other; certainly, they are not equal. Finally, given that Aristotle maintains that it is in ruling that *aretē* can be fully exercised, it is only *politeia* that gives a chance to rule and therefore exercise the excellence of *phronesis* to many rather than to a few (as it is the case in aristocracy) or to one (as it is the case in monarchy). Furthermore, political rule – the rule of the free and virtuous – is more *kalon* than the despotic rule of the unfree since it requires more excellence (*Pol.*VII.14.1333b27-29), and thus the practice of ruling of the free and equals makes those who rule more morally excellent as well. Aristotle himself suggests that *politeia* is the best constitution in the way of his conclusion in *Politics* Book IV, Chapter 11 where he explains why the 'middle class' as an ethical and political mean is essential for the well-being of the city (1296b2).

Now the relevance of this for our discussion on *oikia* and *oikonomia* is that the principle of *politeia* – the principle of rule and being ruled in turns for the sake of the common good – should be extended to the spheres of reproduction and production. This is not, of course, what Aristotle actually says. Yet there are enough conceptual resources in Aristotle's philosophy to substantiate this claim.

First, let us start with the relationship between man and woman within *oikia*. As stated earlier, there is nothing in Aristotle's philosophical account of *phusis* – that is, in the account that is philosophically defendable today – to argue for the natural superiority of men over women. Aristotle's belief in natural superiority of men, thus, is the result of his mistaken biology in the *Generation of Animals* and in the patriarchy he inherited from the general culture of ancient Greece.[9] Aristotle's realism and his *endoxic* method of taking into account existing reputable opinions made his arguments on the role and virtues of women in *oikia* much more in line with the institutions and culture of patriarchy than that of Plato's. Thus Aristotle's claim that the husband is responsible for acquiring property, while the responsibility of the wife is to use it, mirrors the customary Athenian practice whereby property belonged to men, while women's legal ownership to property was highly restricted and they were allowed to use and, occasionally, manage it when their husbands were away (Eidinow 2016: 293).

Aristotle's claims – that the female possesses the faculty of deliberation (*proairēsis*) but it lacks authority (*akuron*) (*Pol.*I.13.1260a13) *and that aretē* is not the same in a man and in a women (1260a20-23) – should be rejected on the grounds of it being inconsistent to Aristotle's account of human nature and to our interpretation of *politeia* as the principle of political rule and of acquiring virtues. Aristotle himself politicizes the relationship between man and woman in the household by saying that his rule over her is political (*politikon*) (1259b1) and, therefore, *politeia*-like. Yet by claiming that women are naturally inferior to men, he fails to recognize in the actually existing character traits of women (and slaves) the arbitrary habituating force of the existing institutions and conventions of patriarchy and slavery. In so doing, he wrongly conflates his sociological observations and his teleology; he fails on the grounds of his own account of human nature and of the human good:

> There are three ways through which people become good (ἀγαθός) and excellent (σπουδαῖος). These three are nature (φύσις), habit (ἔθος), and reason (λόγος). So far as nature is concerned, one must start by being a human (ἄνθρωπος) and not some other species of animal. Then one must have certain qualities of body and soul. But there are some qualities which it is no help to have had at the start. Habits cause them to change: implanted by nature in a neutral form, they can be modified by the force of habit either for better or worse. Animate beings other than men live mostly by natural impulse, though some are also guided to a slight extent by habit. A human lives by reason too; and he is unique in having this. It follows that these [three powers] must be turned to agree: humans are often led by reason not to follow habit and natural impulse, once they have been persuaded that some other course is better. (*Pol.*VII.13.1332a38–b8)[10]

The moral of this passage is clear: the imperfections of one's nature can be improved by habits; equally, they can make it worse; yet the only judge of both of them is reason, which, when used politically, can dismantle corrupt institutionalized habits and improve people's nature for better.

The end of the relationship between *posis* and *alochos*, and its activity of *gamikē*, among other things, is both for itself and for the reproduction of the same kind. Human existence then is ontologically marked by intersubjective cooperation: its coming to be is the consequence of the intercourse between a man and a woman, and its growth into a language using animal is possible through care, love, nurturing and teaching. It is the mutuality of these social relationships that creates the linguistically and ethically mediated milieu[11] – first of all the family and the household – in which a human being grows. Furthermore, Aristotle claims that parents love their children as themselves since children, although existentially separate, are their parents' other selves (*heteros autos*) (*NE* 8.12.1161b27-9). Thus to argue that women are by nature inferior to men and to treat women as if they were so is potentially to cripple the development of children by depriving them from learning from their mothers as intelligent and virtuous human beings.[12] In short, the equality of parents within family is good for children and their education. The supposed natural inferiority of women also contradicts Aristotle's claim that the purpose of education is to improve nature's deficiencies (*Pol.* VII.17.1337a1-3). By conveniently treating patriarchal practices, habits and institutions as natural, Aristotle fails to see the transformative power of education that he himself advocates.

While the relationships between parents (father) and children is indeed vertical – Aristotle's claim is that parental rule over children is like that of a king (*Pol.* I.12.1259b1) – their verticality is such that it makes parents responsible for their children in meeting their physical, emotional and intellectual needs for the sake of children's well-being now and for the sake of their future when they become independent practical reasoners. Alasdair MacIntyre (1999) is right when he argues that our success and our failures are partly the success and failures of our significant others. Yet this 'king-like' verticality should not be pushed too far. Numerous educational and psychology studies show that often (but not always) the best parents and teachers are those who treat and guide their children as if they were equal to them, and that the imposition of one's parental and educational authority, even for the sake of children's well-being, is detrimental to children's development and learning.

The case of slavery: A reconsideration

The issue of natural slavery and the relationship between *despotes* and *doulos* is an important topic that needs a separate and in-depth discussion.[13] For one thing, the issue of slaves – what Aristotle calls a slave by nature (*phusei doulos*) – is central to his argument in *Politics*. Its central problem is how to reconcile Socrates' idea that the only people who can legitimately rule are those who have *aretē* with Aristotle's realism of emphasizing the importance of, what he calls, the *phainomena* – the data of experience, something that is available to us through sense perception. Thus, his disagreement with Plato mentioned earlier goes much deeper than his disagreement of what he takes to be Socrates' view on family and private property.[14] It is this that makes *Politics* uneven: on the one hand, there is a very strong Platonic aspect of articulating the form of the *polis* centred around the ethical ideals of *aretē* and of the common good (Books I, III, VII and VIII) and, on the other hand, his methodological commitment to remain close to the empirical reality of existing practices and institutions (Books II, IV, V and VI).[15] The argument for *phusei doulos* is Aristotle's unsuccessful attempt to bridge this dualism – the dualism between the sociology of social and political institutions, one of which was slavery, *and* the notion of *aretē* as the principle of ruling – by employing the notion of *phusis*, which he was trying to account for not by appealing to the Platonic harmonious cosmic order above, so to speak, but by looking down to the biological reality of different animal species. In short, the source of Aristotle's erroneous naturalism was his attempt to glue the notion of *phusis* with the *phainomena* of existing institutions.

We should approach Aristotle's account of natural slaves from the aforementioned insight on automation. The latter idea, at least to a certain extent, is his redeeming feature. The passage on automation quoted in the introduction (*Pol*.I.4.1253b33-1254a1) follows immediately after Aristotle establishes that property (*ktesis*), as a part of the household, consists of a sum of instruments for the purpose of life. He then provides his first definition of *doulos* 'as an animate (*empsuxon*) article of property' (1253b33). The point he makes about the instruments moving on their own 'at the word of command or by intelligent anticipation' is incredible, given the technological culture of his time. Aristotle's claim that if this were true 'managers (*architecton* / ἀρχιτέκτων ἀρχιτέκτων) would not need subordinates (*hupēretēs* / ὑπηρέτης) and masters would not need slaves' suggests that he saw the institution of slavery as an economic and practical necessity. Hence his attempt to justify the existence of slaves by introducing the Socratic-Platonic notion of nature as ethical – something that permeates Aristotle's work – to distance himself from (but not to reject!) the conventional account of slavery promoted by the likes of Thrasymachus and Callicles.[16]

After Aristotle spells out the key elements of his account of natural slaves – (a) the existence of hierarchy between the ruler and the ruled among other animal species, which is also evident in arts and in human psyche; (b) the notion of an organic compound as one common entity, the existence of which is beneficial for the ruling element and a ruled, hence, the equality between the two is harmful; and (c) the animal-like appearance as very different from other humans – he provides his second definition of a slave:

> Someone is thus a slave by nature (*phusei doulos*) if he is capable (*dunamenos*) of becoming the property of another (and for this reason does actually becomes another's property) and if he participates in reason (*koinōnōn logon*) to the extent of apprehending (*aisthanesthai*) it in another, though destitute of it himself. (*Pol* I.1254b20–24)

There are two points of interest here. The first one is the ridiculous claim – the claim is both a philosophical nonsense *and* is empirically wrong, something which Aristotle must have had observed – that natural slaves and their bodies look physically different from the bodies of freemen, and that nature intended so but the contrary often happens (1254b27-33). These kinds of claims about nature – a similar one is his claim that the nature of tame animals is better than that of wild animals – show how different from *and* out of place the aforementioned claims are vis-à-vis the hylomorphic account of *phusis* in his *Physics*.

The second point has to do with the vagueness of Aristotle's claim that a natural slave is someone who is capable or has a potentiality to become a property of another, and for that reason does become so. It is not immediately clear what Aristotle means by it. How one becomes a slave *and* what it means to say that someone has a potentiality for becoming a slave are the questions Aristotle never addresses directly. A possible explanation of this is that Aristotle wants to distance his conception of natural slaves from the existing institution of slavery whose origin is forced captivity and its institutionalization through laws. Thus, not every actually existing slave is a natural slave. It follows therefore that all non-natural slaves are enslaved unjustly, the conclusion Aristotle never arrives at.

We find a clue to answer these questions in chapter six where Aristotle discusses conventional slavery. It is instructive that Aristotle engages with alternative views on slavery *after* he has explained his account of natural slaves. He wants to show that his opponents – jurists who see slavery as owing its existence to law – are unable to provide a better explanation to his, and that they (or at least some of them) rely on a rudimental conception of natural slave similar to his own. Yet Aristotle does not claim that their arguments are completely wrong or that they contradict his account of natural slaves[17]. His engagement with conventionalists may be read as an answer to the question of how one becomes a natural slave.

The crux of it is as follows. There are those who see the legally established institution of slavery as a consequence of victory in war when the victors, due to their superior power, vanquish the losers, enslave them and legalize their enslavement through laws as conventions. Some argue that these laws are illegal because it is detestable to subjugate others by force, while others think that it is not. Aristotle's answer to the dispute is his argument that *aretē*, when equipped with other resources, is most fitting to use force, and thus whenever something or someone is conquered, it is done so on the basis of some goodness in it. The disagreement between the two, according to Aristotle, is left to the disagreement as to what counts as justice. Some argue that it is goodwill or benevolence (*eunoia*/εὔνοια),[18] while others claim that justice is what is in the interest of the strong. Aristotle's conclusion is that the least convincing argument is that those who are superior over others in virtue should not rule and, therefore, by implication, the appeal to goodwill without strength and virtue is stupidity since it will always mean subjugation by the strong who are so by virtue of *aretē*. His answer to those[19] who defend slavery on the basis that it exists in law and that law is a sort of justice is that they would never agree with the enslavement of someone who does not deserve it, and thus they do not like to call them slaves but call them barbarians. According to Aristotle, in so doing, they seek to express the same idea of natural slaves he presented (thus assuming that barbarians, as a rule, are natural slaves).

What Aristotle's engagement with the proponents and critics of conventional slavery shows then is that Aristotle accepts the institution of slavery on the basis of implicit racism and Greek imperialism, which was inbuilt in the existing institution of slavery. It is a well-known fact that, as a rule, slaves were foreigners in Athens, 'barbarians' who were ignorant of the local life, its norms and political institutions (Garlan 1988: 46). Although reluctantly, Aristotle, nonetheless, justifies the original acquisition of slaves through force (war or otherwise) by adding *aretē*: power in a conquering action is never without some goodness. Therefore, people who were conquered and became enslaved were capable of becoming slaves, and so they are enslaved justly. He acknowledges that there is a divergence between his account of natural slaves and that of conventionalists' (who accept slavery 'merely on legal sanctions and superior power') (*Pol* I.6.1255b14-15), implying that it is not always the case that all existing slaves are natural slaves. Yet he never explicitly condemns the *institution* of slavery. His claim – when a natural slave is in an organic compound with a wise master they are in a relationship of friendship – is thus a propaganda-like window dressing for the monstrous institution of slavery.

In as much as Aristotle implies that the original acquisition of slaves by force is justified and that *eunoia* is *anoia* (ἄνοια),[20] he sharply departs from Socrates' claim that 'we have discovered that, in no instance, is it just to injure anybody' (Plato 1925: 335e). In so departing, he is closer to Thrasymachus' version of Realpolitik and Callicles' conception of nature than to Socrates' and Plato's ideal politics. Might is right, and if we, the Greeks, are able to conquer barbarians who are slavish anyway, our rule over them is just and natural. It is indeed an economic and practical necessity for us, the natural masters, to have slaves and, given that enslaved barbarians have no clue about our way of life and do not speak our language, they are incapable of deliberation and of political *aretē*, and thus they are truly natural slaves. If, however, we had self-moving instruments able to assist us in life and in production, we would not need our imprudent slaves.

Oikonomikē, chrēmatistikē, kapilikē and a concluding remark

Aristotle starts his discussion on the household management (*oikonomikē technē*), the art of acquisition (*chrēmatistikē*) and trade (*kapilikē*) by claiming that *oikonomikē* is not the same as *chrēmatistikē*, the art of acquiring property, and that the function of the second is to *provide*, while the function of the first is to *use* what *chrēmatistikē* has provided (*Pol* I.8.1256a10-13). He goes on to spell out the different natural ways of providing the means of subsistence necessary for both different species of animals and human beings alike. He lists pastoral, freebooting, fishing, hunting and farming as different ways of life and of acquiring what humans need in order to live. All of these ways of acquisition are *natural*. Following this reasoning, he also claims that 'the art of war is in some sense a natural mode of acquisition' and that hunting is a part of the art of war, which 'ought to be practiced, not only against wild animals, but also against human beings who are intended by nature to be ruled by others ... because this sort of war is naturally just' (1256b23-26). This last claim then substantiates our interpretation of Aristotle's understanding of the acquisition of slaves by force as just and natural. He concludes the discussion on the naturalness of *chrēmatistikē* by claiming that it is a natural part of *oikonomia*, and that all the things acquired and stored up as necessary and useful for the life in the city and the household constitute true wealth (ἀληθινὸς πλοῦτος). The important point he makes is that all wealth thus understood – food, instruments and other articles of property – is *limited*. It is so because it is useful – it serves our particular needs – and the number and size of things we can use is limited.

This is not the case with another kind of *chrēmatistikē*, which is limitless and therefore unnatural.[21] It is at this point that Aristotle articulates the difference between use-value and exchange-value (*Pol*.I.9.1257a5-19), which became so essential for modern economic theory. The primary and natural purpose of a sandal is to wear it (use-value), but at the same time, it can be used as a means of exchange (exchange-value). One can exchange the sandal in return for food or anything else (including money). Aristotle's point here is that even if in both cases the sandal is used as a sandal, yet the second way of using it, as a means of exchange, 'is not its proper and peculiar use' (1257a12-13). All pieces of property can be exchanged in this way, using them not for what they are but as a means of exchange. Yet the reason for such exchange is a natural fact that people need other things, which they have less of: they exchange what they have for what they do not have. This gives rise to *kapilikē* – retail trade – which, however, is not a natural part of *chrēmatistikē* as a way of acquiring use-values. Thus, *kapilikē*, as exchange for the sake of exchange or, to put it in Marx's terms, for the sake of more exchange-value, is not a part of natural acquisition of things, because its end is more exchange-value rather than use-value consumed in the household and the city.

Aristotle then provides a historical-genetic argument to show how the *chrēmatistikē* of use-value gradually grows into the *chrēmatistikē* of exchange-value. Even in a big household, the need to exchange things is minimal because all its goods are shared in common. When such a need arises barter is used: wine is exchanged for wheat, oil for meat, etc. Yet when the size and scope of an association grow, with it grows its reliance on foreign trade to meet its members' needs. Then currency is invented to aid merchants in their trade: valuable commodities such as gold, silver and other metals are used as a means of exchange. At first, they are measured by their weight and size. Later they are also stamped, and so money (*nomisma*) is invented. Its name is instructive since it comes from *nomos*: it is a convention and thus not a thing (certainly, it is not an Aristotelian substance). When money starts to dominate exchange, then *kapilikē* starts to dominate *chrēmatistikē*. The natural art of acquisition turns into the unnatural *chrēmatistikē* when the end of wealth creation mysteriously turns into generation of *nomisma*, a nonentity, the acquisition of which is limitless. Then *chrēmatistikē* takes the form of *kapilikē*, which seeks to generate the greatest profit possible. The result is that a *perception* emerges that the art of acquisition is about money-making, that wealth is identical to *nomisma*, and that to create wealth is to practice *kapilikē*.

This analysis – in its rudimental form of course – prefigures Marx. If we add to it (especially to the last claim) the notion of the objectification of labour power in commodities and the market driven system of exchange, then we will get something very close to what Marx meant by commodity fetishism.[22] *Chrēmatistikē* in the form of *kapilikē* does indeed alter our perception in the way that we start to think of wealth in the form of exchange-value. Yet Aristotle warns us that to look at wealth in this way is to miss that wealth, in its natural form, is a means for us to live well. The natural end of wealth is to use it so that our diverse needs are met. Wealth, therefore, has a natural limit. To live a flourishing life is to lead the life of moderation when the amount of wealth needed is also governed by the virtue of *sōphrosunē*. This is not the case when wealth is seen as money, which prompts people to increase it indefinitely: then their 'state of mind is concern about living, rather than living well (*eu zēn*)' (*Pol*.I.9.1257b41-1258a1). Thus, the life of the limitless acquisition of wealth reduces people to the life of the mere necessity of economic despotism in which, as Marx and those who follow his analysis argue, still live workers and capitalists alike under the capitalist mode of production.

The ridiculousness of our predicament is that, contrary to Aristotle who lived under the cruel shadow of natural necessity, we live in the midst of enormous wealth in the era of automation, and yet slavery in the form of wage labour still exists.

Notes

1. Aristotle's argument is that it is a male who is the efficient cause of a baby: 'A father causes a child' (*Ph.* II, 194b30). From the point of view of modern biology, we know that the cause of conception requires both male and female parts, the union of egg and sperm. Thus, the efficient cause of a child is both a father and a mother, not just a father. This will become important when we discuss Aristotle's sexism rooted in his erroneous biology of *On the Generation of Animals*.
2. Richard Kraut applies Aristotle's account of *phusis* to human nature and argues that there are 'three ways in which Aristotle talks about nature. As first nature, it is what is

already present in us prior to habituation. As second nature, it is what grows into us, as a result of a process of habituation. And, as perfected nature, it is the goal at which we should arrive when the process of habituation has worked well, and we achieve something that is good' (Kraut 2007: 213). I will come back to the issue of human nature in the discussion of *oikia*.

3. It is instructive that the etymology of 'norm', according to various etymology dictionaries, comes from Greek *gnomon* and Latin *norma* as 'carpenter's square'. Thus, 'norm' originally means pattern and rule through which an artisan gives form to its creation. By normativity here I do not mean, therefore, the Kantian notion of imposing a universal rule on our behaviour (which presupposes the contrast between inclinations and desires, on the one hand, and rational law as freely chosen, on the other hand), but the actualized form in its perfection given to an artefact through a concreate instance of perfect creation. It is therefore not an accident that Aristotle links *phusis* to *technē*: both nature and art are the processes of creation directed towards their perfect forms, although in the case of art the source of change, as stipulated above, is external while in the case of nature it is internal. Nature is the process of the creation of substances – the individual instances of natural kinds – whose normativity lies in their actualized form of natural flourishing. In short, normativity thus understood lies in the individual actualization (or its failure) of the natural form and thus normativity is functional through and through.

4. Alasdair MacIntyre makes a similar point by arguing that there is an incoherence in Aristotle's thought as far as his treatment of women, natural slaves and productive workers are concerned. He claims that all human beings have a capacity to act as rational agents in achieving their final end 'which is theirs by nature. But if this is human *ergon*, it must be the *ergon* of every human being' (MacIntyre 2016: 86). The same claim is argued by MacIntyre in the first chapter of this book.

5. For an outstanding discussion on women in the *Generation of Animals* see Sophia Connell (2016).

6. In different places in *Politics*, Aristotle uses *thēlus* (θῆλυς) and *arrhēn* (ἄρρεν) for female and male, but occasionally also *posis* (πόσις) and *alochos* (ἄλοχος) which is commonly translated as husband and wife, yet a more accurate translation is 'man' and a 'partner of his bed' while the activity uniting them is *gamikē* (γαμική), whose more accurate translation is 'love making' rather than 'marriage' as it is rendered in our Victorian and post-Victorian translations.

7. 'A *politeia* is an organization of offices in a city, by which the method of their distribution is fixed, the sovereign authority is determined, and the end to be pursued by the association and all its members is prescribed' (*Pol.* IV.2.1289a16-18) (this is a slightly modified translation of Aristotle 1998: 135).

8. 'We may thus conclude that the citizen of our definition is particularly and especially the citizen of a democracy' (*Pol.* III.1.1275b5-6).

9. It is a well-established fact that women in Athens did not have political rights. In addition, married women, apart from their dowries, were not allowed to accumulate personal possessions, let alone property, because legally property and personal possessions belonged to their husbands (Eidinow 2016: 294). Aristotle acknowledges this by claiming that sometimes women rule households but do so oligarchically since they are inheriting their wealth and property, as a rule, from their husbands (the word Aristotle uses is ἐπίκληρος which means 'heiress') (*EN* VIII.10.1161a1-3). However, he never considers that, despite their inherited wealth, they can also rule monarchically.

10. Again, here I modified the Barker and Stalley translation of Aristotle (1989: 282).

11 'A human being alone [due to language] possesses a perception of good and evil, of the just and the unjust …; and it is in association in these things which makes a *family* and a city' (*Pol*.I.2.1253a15-17) (italic added).
12 I am grateful to Alasdair MacIntyre for this insight brought up in one of the human rights seminars at London Metropolitan University.
13 I addressed this issue briefly in Bielskis (2017: 90–5). For an outstanding discussion on slavery in Aristotle see Schofield (2005: 91–119).
14 On difference between Plato's and Aristotle's accounts of nature and political society see chapter two of this volume.
15 Of course, the classification is preliminary because the tension between his normative-teleological claims and empirical ones are everywhere in *Politics*.
16 There is no direct reference to Thrasymachus and Callicles in *Politics*, book I. However, Aristotle's claim that 'some think that being just consists in stupidity/good will (*anoia/eunoia*) while others hold that the rule of the stronger is in itself justice' (*Pol* I.6.1255a17-19) may be plausibly read as Aristotle's reference to the discussion between Socrates and Thrasymachus in the *Republic*. This is how C. D. C. Reeve interprets it as well (see ft. 41 on p.10 of his translation of Aristotle (1998)). I have chosen both *anoia* and *eunoia* of both editions – David Ross's and Alois Dreizehnter's – because together they render what Aristotle seems to suggest in chapter 6 better than any of them alone. That is, goodwill on its own, without strength or any other positive quality (e.g. *aretē*), is not justice but stupidity because it will never be able to rule, thus it will always be subjugated to the rule of others. If this interpretation is correct, then Aristotle here (but also in his account of natural slaves) is closer to Thrasymachus than to Socrates.
17 '[Th]ose who hold an opposite view are also correct' (*Pol* I.6.1255a3-1). In my previous interpretation of Aristotle's account of natural slaves, I underestimated this point and the importance of chapter 6 (Bielskis 2017: 90–5). However, I still stand by my critique of Aristotle's conception of natural slave as inconsistent to his teleology. The fundamental contradiction is as follows: by saying that the end of a natural slave is to be ruled by a natural master, Aristotle is effectively claiming that it is good for someone to be incapable of practical deliberation, given his claims that a natural slave is someone who is incapable of deliberation and his claim (both in *Physics* and in *Politics*) that nature is the end and that the end is the best.
18 C. D. C. Reeve translates *eunoia* as benevolence (see Aristotle 1998: 10).
19 Presumably to sophists who believed that laws and justice are relative depending on a city one lived.
20 This last point, of course, is debatable.
21 Marx, in the comment on Aristotle's distinction between *oikonomia* and *chrēmatistikē*, calls the second use of the art of acquisition (i.e. the unlimited one) 'chrematistics' (see Marx 1990: 253).
22 I follow Ruth Groff's interpretation of commodity fetishism: '(1) In capitalism, the human labor power that is objectified in commodities is conflated with the natural properties of material objects, such that commodities appear to exchange in the ratios that they do in virtue of the latter rather than in virtue of the former; (2) even if we appreciate that it is the social phenomenon of value (rather than the natural properties of objects) that underwrites exchange-value, the system is one in which macro-level "decisions" about the allocation of total productive capacity are made by the market, rather than being made directly and intentionally by the members of society as a whole, i.e., by a collective human subject' (Groff 2015: 318).

Bibliography

Annas, J. (1993), *The Morality of Happiness*, Oxford: Oxford University Press.
Arendt, H. (1961), *Between Past and Future: Six Exercises in Political Thought*, New York: The Viking Press.
Arendt, H. (1998), *The Human Condition*, Chicago: Chicago University Press.
Aristotelis (1957), *Politica: Oxford Classical Texts*, ed. D. Ross, Oxford: Oxford University Press.
Aristotelis (1984), *Ethica Nicomachea: Oxford Classical Texts*, ed. I. Bywater, Oxford: Oxford University Press.
Aristotle (1953), *Generation of Animals*, trans. A. L. Peck, Harvard: Harvard University Press.
Aristotle (1980), *Nicomachean Ethics*, trans. D. Ross, Oxford: Oxford University Press.
Aristotle (1989), *Politics*, trans. E. Barker and ed. R. F. Stalley, Oxford: Oxford World's Classics.
Aristotle (1996), *Physics*, trans. R. Waterfield, Oxford: Oxford University Press.
Aristotle (1998), *Politics*, trans. C. D. C. Reeve, Cambridge, IN: Hackett.
Bielskis, A. (2006) 'Pilietija ir valstybė klasikinėje politinėje mintyje' ('Citizenry and the State in Ancient Political Thought'), in V. Laurėnas et al. (eds), *Pilietinė visuomenė: politikos įpilietinimo projekcijos*, 16–31, Klaipėda: Klaipėdos universiteto leidykla.
Bielskis, A. (2017), *Existence, Meaning, Excellence*, London & New York: Routledge.
Connell, S. M. (2016), *Aristotle on Female Animals: A Study of the Generation of Animals*, Cambridge: Cambridge University Press.
Eidinow, E. (2016), *Envy, Poison, and Death: Women on Trial in Classical Athens*, Oxford: Oxford University Press.
Garlan, Y. (1988), *Slavery in Ancient Greece*, trans. J. Lloyd, Ithaca & London: Cornell University Press.
Groff, R. (2015), 'On the Ethical Contours of Thin Aristotelian Marxism', in M. J. Thompson (ed.), *Constructing Marxist Ethics*, 313–35, Leiden: Brill.
Kraut, R. (2007), 'Nature in Aristotle's Ethics and Politics', *Social Philosophy & Policy Foundation*, 24 (2): 199–219.
Lear, J. (1988), *Aristotle: The Desire of Understanding*, Cambridge: Cambridge University Press.
MacIntyre, A. (1999), *Dependent Rational Animals*, London: Duckworth.
MacIntyre, A. (2016), *Ethics in the Conflicts of Modernity*, Cambridge: Cambridge University Press.
Marx, K. (1990), *Capital. Vol. I.*, trans. B. Fowkes, London: Penguin Classics.
Miller, F. D. (1995), *Nature, Justice, and Rights in Aristotle's Politics*, Oxford: Clarendon Press.
Plato (1925), *The Republic*, trans. J. L. Davies and D. J. Vaughan, London: Macmillan.
Schofield, M. (2005), 'Ideology and Philosophy in Aristotle's Theory of Slavery', in *Aristotle's Politics: Critical Essays*, 91–119, Lanham: Rowan & Littlefield Publishers.

4

Aristotle and two senses of happiness

Buket Korkut Raptis

Aristotle's account of happiness (*eudaimonia*) is one of the controversial topics of *Nicomachean Ethics*. In order to achieve a comprehensive view on Aristotle's account of happiness, we first need to uncover the questions Aristotle himself attempts to answer and, then, readdress the premises of our discussion on the basis of his answers. Concerning happiness, there are two main questions that Aristotle addresses: (a) What does happiness consist in? and (b) What kind of life is the happiest life? These are two *distinct* questions. We should not subsume them under the question (c) What is happiness? In *Nicomachean Ethics* (hereafter *NE*) Book I, Aristotle answers question (a), and in Book X, he gives an answer to question (b). If we seek an answer to question (c) by trying to reconcile Aristotle's claims in Books I and X, then we might end up with a debate based on misleading premises. I suspect that the current debate between the monist interpretation of happiness (the view that happiness consists exclusively in philosophical activity) and the inclusivist interpretation (the view that happiness also involves morally virtuous activities) is driven by just such premises.[1]

I What does happiness consist in?

In *NE* I 7, Aristotle claims that happiness (or the human good) consists in 'activity of soul in accordance with virtue, and if there are several virtues, in accordance with the best and most complete virtue' (*NE* 1098a16-18).[2] How shall we understand this claim? Is this a definition of happiness? If, by definition, we mean the explication of necessary and sufficient conditions, then Aristotle does not define happiness here. Rather he explains the *source* of happiness. According to Aristotle, some basic external goods are among the necessary conditions of happiness, but they do not constitute happiness. Since Aristotle does not give us a definition of happiness here, he does not answer the question of what happiness is. The question is rather: What does happiness consist in? This is a question about the source of happiness. The source is what functions as a *constitutive principle*, not merely as a necessary condition. As Aristotle explains:

> But perhaps it is quite wrong to be guided in our judgment by the chances of fortune, since true prosperity and adversity do not depend on fortune's favours,

although, as we said, our life require these in addition; but it is the active exercise of our faculties in conformity with virtue that causes happiness, and the opposite activities its opposite. (*NE* 1100b8-11)

What is then the source of happiness? Is it the activity of soul? What kind of activity? We should first clarify the ancient Greek notion of *energeia* which is translated as 'activity' here. *Energeia* is not the same as action (*praxis*). It is not *praxis*, but *energeia of soul in accordance with virtue* that is considered to be the source of happiness for Aristotle. In this context, the opposite of *energeia* is disposition (*hexis*), and *energeia* is thus used here to emphasize the *active exercise of virtue*. This interpretation is also supported by Aristotle's discussion on whether or not happiness consists in possessing virtue. He claims that this cannot be the case, 'since it appears possible to possess it [virtue] while you are asleep, or without putting it into practice throughout the whole of your life' (*NE* 1095b33-1096a1). Aristotle explains further:

Now with those who pronounce happiness to be virtue, or some particular virtue, our definition is in agreement; for 'activity in conformity with virtue' involves virtue. But it makes a great difference whether we conceive the good to depend on possessing virtue or on displaying it – on disposition, or on the manifestation of a disposition in action. For a man may possess the disposition without its producing any good result, as for instance when he is asleep, or has ceased to function for some other cause; but virtue in active exercise cannot be inoperative – it will of necessity act and act well. (*NE* 1098b30-1099a4)

It is evident that happiness for Aristotle does not consist in an action or an activity of soul, nor does it consist in possessing virtue. It consists in the active exercise of virtue. This means that happiness cannot merely consist in contemplative activity; for the possibility of happiness, one should contemplate in accordance with theoretical wisdom (*sophia*). What matters is not just what you do but how you do it. Not everybody who acts exhibits a moral virtue. The source of happiness is not the activity of one's soul but the *virtuous activity* of one's soul. In other words, 'virtuous activity of the soul' constitutes happiness. For the possibility of this constitution, some basic external goods might be necessary, but they are not the source of happiness.

This is how we should understand Aristotle's claim that happiness consists in the activity of the soul in accordance with virtue. But what kind of virtue? Aristotle says that if there are several virtues that correspond to the activity of soul, then this activity should be in accordance with the best (*aristin*) and most complete (*teleiostatin*) virtue (*NE* 1098a18-19). Monists take this 'best and most complete virtue' to be theoretical wisdom, while inclusivists claim it to be the composite of all virtues. Neither of these answers seems to be satisfactory. Aristotle could have just spelled out what this virtue is or could have said explicitly that it is the composite of all virtues. I suspect that the ambiguity here is a purposeful one, because the best and most complete virtue is contextual and varies according to the particular circumstances. If there are different parts of the soul (indeed, for Aristotle, there are), the virtues relevant for the well-functioning of these parts will be different in kind (indeed, they are so). How are they supposed to be reduced to one virtue?

It is the circumstances that determine which part of the soul needs to be employed and which one of the relevant virtues is the best and most complete for the task. For example, if you encounter an instance of mistreatment of one person by another, the way in which you should react needs to be in accordance with the best and most complete virtue that corresponds well to the situation. In this case, the best and most complete virtue would be justice. Of course, happiness does not merely consist of a single instance of virtuous activity. Happiness, says Aristotle, requires a complete life (*NE* 1098a19; 1100a5). The point is that the source of happiness is the activity of soul in accordance with the best and most complete virtue determined in view of particular circumstances.

This interpretation is neither inclusivist nor monist, but coheres well with the particularism and contextualism of Aristotle's general approach in ethics. Since both the particularist and the contextualist interpretation of Aristotle's approach in ethics is well-established, I will not defend this view here, but will go on with one possible objection.

Aristotle arrives at the aforementioned explanation of happiness with what is known as the function (*ergon*) argument. According to Aristotle, the good of something that has a function is its functioning well (i.e. functioning in accordance with its proper virtue). In order to determine the human good, one first needs to specify the function peculiar to human beings. The function of a human cannot be merely living, because the act of living is shared even by plants. It is the faculty of reason (*logos*) that distinguishes human beings from other life forms. This means that living in accord with reason is the function peculiar to human beings. The human good is then the activity of the rational part of the soul in accordance with virtue. Does this mean that moral virtues such as justice are not relevant for the human good, since moral virtues *seem to* belong to the non-rational part of the soul? If this is true, then our comprehensive interpretation is in danger. If moral virtues belong to the non-rational part of the soul and happiness only involves the activity of the rational part of the soul, then happiness does not involve morally virtuous activities. But according to our interpretation, it does. Are moral virtues indeed non-rational? What is the relationship between moral virtues and reason?

Evidently, Aristotle distinguishes between intellectual (*dianoitikos*) and moral (*ēthikos*) virtues. Prudence (*phronēsis*) is the only practical virtue that is at the same time intellectual. The other practical virtues are moral virtues that regulate the well-functioning of the appetitive part of the soul. Nonetheless, there is a close affinity between the intellectual virtue of prudence and moral virtues. Aristotle explicitly says that without prudence, one cannot be morally virtuous, and without possessing moral virtues, one cannot be prudent (*NE* 1144b31-33). How is this so? Moral virtues determine a good end, and prudence enables one to bring about that end in action. In the earlier example, you may want to protect the mistreated person (the end determined by your virtue of justice), but what needs to be done in order to be just under those circumstances is specified by prudence. Since prudence is an intellectual virtue that belongs to the rational part of the soul, and the exercise of prudence requires the exercise of moral virtues, happiness should involve the activity of soul in accordance with prudence and moral virtues together. We may consider this to be an indirect argument for the view that the activity of the rational part of the soul must also be in accordance with moral virtues. If we could show that moral virtues can in some sense be placed in the rational part of the soul (*pshuche*), then this would be a direct argument. Is there such an argument? I think there is.

In the function argument, Aristotle explains that the kind of life that is peculiar to human beings is the practical life of the rational part of the soul, which has two divisions. Both divisions partake of reason, but in two different manners; one possesses reason, while the other obeys reason. As Aristotle says: 'There remains the practical life of the rational part of man. This part has two divisions, one rational as obedient to reason, the other as possessing reason and exercising intelligence' (*NE* 1098a3-6). Furthermore, Aristotle distinguishes between intellectual and moral virtues based on this distinction in the rational part of the soul:

> If on the other hand it be more correct to speak of the appetitive part of the soul as rational, in that case it is the rational part which, as well as the whole soul, is divided into two, the one division having reason in the proper sense and in itself, the other obedient to reason as a child to its father. Now virtue also is differentiated in correspondence with this division of the soul. Some forms of virtue called intellectual virtues, others moral virtues. (*NE* 1103a1-6)

It is true that moral virtues regulate the well-functioning of the appetitive part of the soul. But the appetitive part of the soul can be considered as rational, for it is capable of obeying reason. Properly speaking, then, moral virtues belong to the second division of the rational part of the soul, for moral virtues are obedient to reason possessed by the first division to which prudence belongs. In other words, while prudence and other intellectual virtues belong to the rational part of the soul understood strictly (i.e. limited to the first division that actually possesses reason), moral virtues belong to the rational part of the soul understood broadly (i.e. involving the second division that is capable of obeying reason). This conclusion might come as a surprise. However, nowhere does Aristotle say that moral virtues themselves are non-rational. On the contrary, as the earlier quotation shows, the introduction of the distinction between intellectual and moral virtues is done right after the qualification of the appetitive part of the soul as rational, that is, as capable of obeying reason.

Since moral virtues also belong to the rational part of the soul, happiness involves the activity of the soul in accordance with moral virtues as well. This conclusion is also supported by another observation. If moral virtues were non-rational, then animals would be capable of acting virtuously. But Aristotle claims that animals cannot be happy, for they are not capable of noble acts: 'We have good reasons therefore for not speaking of an ox or horse or any other animal as being happy, because none of these is able to participate in noble activities' (*NE* 1099b32-35). From this quotation, it is also evident that happiness, for Aristotle, consists in not only theoretically virtuous activity but also morally virtuous activities. In general terms, the source of happiness is the activity of the rational part of the soul in accordance with the best and most complete virtue, where the best and most complete virtue is determined in view of the particular circumstances. Since moral virtues also belong to the rational part of the soul understood broadly, the best and most complete virtue under certain circumstances may be a moral virtue.

Our interpretation so far is compatible with inclusivism, but for different reasons. The main shortcoming of inclusivism is that it cannot give us a comprehensive view of *NE*, for it cannot provide us with an inclusivist interpretation of Book X, Chapters 6–8, where Aristotle discusses the relation of happiness to philosophical activity. Before we look into this, we shall first encounter an insightful version of monism, for our view is clearly in opposition to the basic tenet of monism.

II Encountering a monist account

Monist accounts take happiness to be philosophical activity. Since happiness, for Aristotle, is the end of all human activities (i.e. the end for the sake of which all other activities are pursued), monists are committed to the view that morally virtuous activities are valuable for the sake of philosophical activity. The mainstream monist account gives an instrumentalist explanation of the 'for the sake of' relationship between morally virtuous activities and philosophical activity.[3] There are two interrelated problems with this interpretation: (a) Not all of morally virtuous activities are instrumentally valuable for the possibility of contemplation. Hence, the moral virtues that are not instrumentally connected to contemplation seem to lack intrinsic value. (b) Some immoral activities might turn out to be instrumentally valuable for maximizing contemplation. Instrumentalist interpretation opens the gate to the undesired conclusion that one should be moral to the extent that one can maximize contemplation and it is legitimate to pursue the immoral activities that maximize contemplation.

Gabriel Richardson Lear has recently provided us with an elegant defence of monism that aims to avoid this undesired conclusion. After summarizing this novel account presented in her book *Happy Lives and the Highest Good* (2004), I will point out some of its shortcomings. According to Richardson Lear, morally virtuous activities are middle-level ends. Recall that for Aristotle, middle-level ends are pursued both for their own sakes and for the sake of happiness. Since Richardson Lear agrees with monism, that happiness does not involve morally virtuous activities, and argues that morally virtuous activities are middle-level ends, she needs to explain how morally virtuous activities are choiceworthy for the sake of happiness that is considered to be exclusively philosophical activity. She argues that the 'for the sake of' relation between middle-level ends and happiness as philosophical activity can best be understood as a form of approximation. On this view, middle-level ends such as morally virtuous activities are choiceworthy for the sake of philosophical activity because they approximate philosophical activity.

There are three problems with Richardson Lear's account: (a) Her account of approximation cannot explain the relationship between philosophical activity and some of the middle-level ends such as pleasure, honour and intelligence (*nous*). (b) Practical knowledge may indeed approximate theoretical knowledge. But morally virtuous activities not only require practical knowledge but also involve action. How is virtuous action supposed to approximate theoretical activity which is devoid of action? (c) According to Aristotle, morally virtuous activities are not middle-level ends; it is not the activity of virtue but the possession of virtue that counts as a middle-level end.

Richardson Lear may avoid the first problem by claiming that her account does not aim to explain the relationship between philosophical activity and other middle-level ends. This seems to be the case, as she explains:

> I suspect there will be a variety of ways in which middle-level ends are choiceworthy for the sake of happiness. The account of how the happy person seeks honor for the sake of happiness may not be the same as the account of how he chooses his friends for the sake of happiness. But, since there is a special problem about the status of moral virtue, I will devote the rest of this discussion to understanding how it is that the activity of moral virtue can be choice worthy for the sake of an independent good, such as theoretical contemplation, without undermining its own intrinsic desirability. (Richardson Lear 2004: 46)

Richardson Lear's account of approximation is then limited to the relationship between philosophical activity and morally virtuous activities. But this means that her monist account is incomplete, for it does not explain the relationship between philosophical activity and middle-level ends in general. We may leave aside this as a minor problem and turn to the second problem; this is more crucial because it rests at the heart of the thesis of approximation.

According to Richardson Lear's thesis of approximation, morally virtuous activities are choiceworthy for the sake of philosophical activity because they approximate it. Our question is this: How do morally virtuous activities which involve action approximate philosophical activity that is devoid of action? What kind of analogy is there between the two? First, nowhere does Aristotle mention any relation of approximation between morally virtuous activities and philosophical activity. Richardson Lear seems to agree on this: 'Admittedly, Aristotle never explicitly says that excellent practical reasoning is good because its essence is defined with reference to wise contemplation' (Richardson Lear 2004: 90). In order to provide us with an analogy between practical reasoning and theoretical contemplation, Richardson Lear introduces a novel notion of 'grasping truth' in the following manner:

> Reason, like our capacity for nutrition, is a part of the soul; it is, in other words, a life capacity, according to Aristotle. Thus its activation is a way of living. Since the function of the whole rational soul is truth, we can call this way of living 'grasping the truth' or as I will tend to say, 'living truthfully'. (Richardson Lear 2004: 99)

Notice, however, that 'grasping truth' or 'living truthfully' is not Aristotle's terminology. But it is on the basis of the notion of truthfulness that Richardson Lear makes an analogy between practical reasoning and theoretical reasoning. As she claims:

> Theoretical and practical reasoning are analogous, then, because, when done well, both are ways of being truthful. They are genuinely distinct, however, because the

objects of the two kinds of reason demand different activities if they are to be grasped successfully. (Richardson Lear 2004: 103)

We first need to understand the scope of Richardson Lear's analogy. What does 'grasping practical truth' (i.e. 'grasping truth' in the practical case) consist of? On our common understanding, 'grasping practical truth' means understanding practical truth or having the knowledge of practical truth. If 'grasping practical truth' consists of having the knowledge of practical truth, then the analogy between grasping practical truth and grasping theoretical truth is based on the apparent analogy between the knowledge of practical truth and the knowledge of theoretical truth. This limited scope sustains a legitimate analogy. But it does not help us with our original problem. We need an analogy between morally virtuous activities and theoretical activity. Based on the analogy between the knowledge of practical truth and the knowledge of theoretical truth, we cannot claim that morally virtuous activities (which involve not only the knowledge of practical truth but also the action accompanied by correct desire) resemble theoretical activity (which does not involve action, but is limited to the knowledge of theoretical truth). Contrary to our common understanding, Richardson Lear conflates grasping practical truth with morally virtuous activities. Hence according to her terminology, grasping practical truth involves the knowledge of practical truth *and* action accompanied by correct desire. In other words, grasping practical truth is a matter of making good choices. We might want to follow Richardson Lear on this and agree that one can define 'grasping practical truth' as she does. But when we change the meaning of grasping truth in the practical case in this manner, we lose the apparent analogy we could make between grasping practical truth taken as understanding practical truth and grasping theoretical truth as understanding theoretical truth. Richardson Lear is aware of the problem:

> But if grasping truth in the practical case is a matter of making good choices while grasping truth in the scientific case is a matter of contemplating demonstrations of truths from known principles, we may begin to doubt how similar these two modes of truthful living really are. Why should we think we have not stretched the meaning of truth beyond recognition when we apply it to choices and actions as well as to propositions? (Richardson Lear 2004: 103)

Richardson Lear does not answer these crucial questions and seems to be aware that they are crucial when she claims:

> We will, of course, want to know why choice is the appropriate way to grasp practical truth, while all other truth can be grasped by reason alone. I leave that question, however, for a fuller study of Aristotle's moral epistemology. (Richardson Lear 2004: 106)

This is not a legitimate suggestion, for it presupposes that 'grasping truth' or 'living truthfully' is Aristotle's own terminology, and that choice is the appropriate way to grasp practical truth for Aristotle. Evidently, Aristotle lacks the notion of truthfulness as Richardson Lear defines it. Aristotle indeed claims that the end of practical reasoning is action and that choice is the principle of action. Nonetheless, we cannot claim that for Aristotle 'choice is the appropriate way to grasp practical truth, while all other truth can be grasped by reason alone', simply because Aristotle has a notion of practical truth that is distinguishable from choice. According to Aristotle, virtuous action is based on good choice, and good choice involves practical truth and correct desire. In the following passage of *NE* VI, Aristotle explicitly claims that while theoretical good consists in truth alone, practical good consists in truth in agreement with correct desire:

> In the case of thought concerned with contemplation, however, which is neither practical nor productive, what constitute its being good or bad are truth and falsity, because truth is the characteristic activity of everything concerned with thought. But in the case of what is practical and concerned with thought, its being good consists in truth in agreement with correct desire. (*NE* 1139a 27-31)

One might have an understanding of the practical truth but lack the correct desire. Such is the situation of an incontinent person. If choice were the appropriate way to grasp practical truth for Aristotle, then he would not be able to distinguish between an incontinent person and a self-indulgent person as he did in *NE* VII. According to Aristotle, both choose to follow their base desires, but an incontinent person understands the relevant practical truth (i.e. he understands that what he does is not good, and what is good is such and such), while a self-indulgent person lacks an understanding of the relevant practical truth (i.e. he believes that what he does is good). If choice were the appropriate way to grasp practical truth, then there would not be any difference between an incontinent and a self-indulgent person, for their choices are the same.

Furthermore, it is possible to achieve an understanding of practical truths about other people's actions. If practical truth were not distinguishable from virtuous action (that arises from a good choice based on practical truth and correct desire), we would not be able to understand and judge other people's actions. In *NE* VI 10, Aristotle, however, clearly distinguishes practical understanding (*sunesis*) from prudence in the following way:

> Understanding or good understanding, the quality in virtue of which we call men 'persons of good understanding' or 'of good understanding', is not the same as scientific knowledge in general. ... For understanding does not deal with the things that exist forever and are immutable, nor yet with all of the things that come into existence, but with those about which one may be in doubt and may deliberate. Hence it is concerned with the same objects as prudence. Understanding is not however the same thing as prudence; for prudence issues commands, since its end is a statement of what we ought to do or not to do, whereas understanding merely makes judgments. ... Thus understanding does not mean either the possession or acquisition of prudence; but when we employ the faculty of opinion to judge what another person says about matters that are in the sphere of prudence, we

are said to understand (that is, to judge rightly, for right judgment is the same as good understanding), in the same way as learning a thing is termed understanding it when it means employing the faculty of scientific knowledge. (*NE* 1142b35-1143a16)

Aristotle explains that understanding in practical matters is judgement about what concerns prudence. For instance, we make judgements about whether someone's action is good or not. In other words, we arrive at an understanding of practical truth through right judgement, and when our judgement is about our own situation and accompanied by correct desire, we choose to act in accordance with prudence.

From these considerations about the situation of an incontinent person and a person of good understanding, it follows that Aristotle has a notion of 'understanding practical truth' distinct from choice and action. If our interpretation of Aristotle is correct, then Richardson Lear's notion of 'grasping practical truth', on which it necessarily involves choice and action, is not Aristotelian. Unless Richardson Lear gives an explanation of how an activity that involves action can approximate an activity that does not involve action, her thesis of approximation cannot solve the problem of monism. Unfortunately, Richardson Lear does not give us such an explanation, but leaves it for 'a fuller study of Aristotle's moral epistemology'. It is doubtful that Richardson Lear's thesis of approximation can be substantiated by a fuller study of Aristotle's moral epistemology, simply because 'grasping truth' is not Aristotle's own conception.

There is another reason to be sceptical about Richardson Lear's thesis. As it turns out, her initial assumption that morally virtuous activities are middle-level ends is not Aristotle's own view. But without this assumption, the project of substantiating her thesis of approximation falls apart. Recall that middle-level ends are pursued for their own sakes and for the sake of happiness. Since Richardson Lear considers morally virtuous activities to be middle-level ends, she takes on the project of explaining how morally virtuous activities are choiceworthy for the sake of happiness that she considers to be philosophical activity.

According to Aristotle, however, it is not the activity of virtue but the possession of virtue that is a middle-level end. The only passage where Aristotle suggests that virtue is a middle-level end is the following:

> Happiness in particular is believed to be complete without qualification, since we always choose it for itself and never for the sake of anything else. Honour, pleasure, intellect, and every virtue we do indeed choose for themselves (since we would choose each of them even if they had no good effects), but we choose them also for the sake of happiness, on the assumption that through them we shall live a life of happiness; whereas happiness no one chooses for the sake of any of these nor indeed for the sake of anything else. (*NE* 1097a34-b6)

Here Aristotle takes the possession of every virtue to be worth choosing for its own sake and for the sake of its actualization, which constitutes happiness. Richardson Lear also casts doubt on her own assumption that, for Aristotle, morally virtuous actions are middle-level ends when she says:

> Let me be clear. Nothing that Aristotle says in the opening book of the *Nicomachean Ethics* suggests that morally virtuous action is a middle level end. (He says that moral virtue is a middle level end, and that is presumably in part because it is worth choosing for the sake of its actualization). And yet it is important for us to see that there are suggestions in *NE* I that some virtuous activity or other may turn out to be teleologically subordinated to the highest good. (Richardson Lear 2004: 43)

Richardson Lear then appeals to the function argument in *NE* I 7 and argues that if one form of virtuous activity turns out to be happiness, then other forms of virtuous activity will be teleologically subordinated to it. This possibility suggests that some morally virtuous activities may turn out to be middle-level ends. Here is how Richardson Lear explains this:

> Thus, if one form of virtuous human functioning is most final, that ought to mean that the other forms of virtuous activity are teleologically subordinated to it. Aristotle does not emphasize the subordination of the other forms of virtuous activity, but it is entirely appropriate to infer that this is what he has in mind. Excellent functioning is an ultimate or final end; thus if one such kind of activity turns out to be more final than another, that means that the latter is worth choosing for the sake of the former. That is just what it means for one end to be more final than another. Thus we see Aristotle leave room in *NE* I.7 for the possibility that some virtuous activities are middle level ends. (Richardson Lear 2004: 45)

Nowhere does Aristotle claim that morally virtuous activities are middle-level ends. Neither does he mention any possibility of subordination among different forms of virtuous activities. Aristotle does not even argue that happiness consists of one form of virtuous activity. The more we make one assumption after another, the more we seem to move away from Aristotle's view. Richardson Lear, however, claims that in the light of *NE* X, we can retrospectively interpret *NE* I 7–8 in the way she does:

> I do not mean to suggest that in *NE* I 7–8 Aristotle is already saying that there is certainly a teleological hierarchy of rational virtuous activities, much less that the exercise of some other virtue is more final than the exercise of those moral virtues with which Aristotle's well-bred audience is familiar. That argument does not come until *NE* X. But in retrospect we can see that he is laying the groundwork for his argument that this one highest virtuous activity is contemplative. And that means that morally virtuous action is choiceworthy for its own sake and for the sake of something higher. (Richardson Lear 2004: 45)

This means that there is no independent argument for the assumption that for Aristotle morally virtuous activities are middle-level ends. It is on the assumption that happiness consists of one form of virtuous activity, that is, philosophical activity, that morally virtuous activities might be interpreted as middle-level ends. We should then turn to *NE* X, where Aristotle discusses the relationship between happiness and philosophical activity.

III What kind of life is the happiest life?

In *NE* X 6–8, Aristotle addresses the question: What kind of life is the happiest life? Already in Book I Aristotle claimed that there are three candidates for a life of happiness: the life of enjoyment, the life of politics and the life of contemplation. The life of enjoyment associates happiness with bodily pleasures. This is a vulgar conception of happiness because animals also pursue bodily pleasures. Hence, this life does not even count as a happy life. Aristotle's main concern in *NE* X 7–8 is the comparison between the life of politics and the philosophical life. This discussion also has significance for the debate between monists and inclusivists. Monists, appealing to Aristotle's conclusion that the philosophical life is the happiest life, claim that happiness consists solely in philosophical activity. On this view, morally virtuous activities are valuable instrumentally (as means to maximize contemplation) or through approximation to contemplation. Inclusivists mostly are puzzled about how to interpret this section.

The main problem has to do with the formulation of the debate. Both monist and inclusivist accounts presuppose that the life of politics is the same as the life of morally virtuous activities. Aristotle's comparison between the philosophical life and the life of politics is then interpreted to be a comparison between the philosophical activity and morally virtuous activities. Since Aristotle privileges the philosophical life over the life of politics, from the aforementioned reasoning, it follows that it is better to be a philosopher rather than a virtuous person. But this is not a sensible conclusion, especially from the comprehensive perspective of Aristotle's ethics.

For a healthy debate, we need to distinguish between the two senses of *politikos*. In one sense, *politikos* means 'political', and in another sense, it means 'social'. Political activities consist of practices that pertain to the administration of a state (subject of politics), while social activities regulate one's relationship with others (subject of ethics). It is the failure to keep this distinction in view that prevents us from resolving the current debate. Aristotle himself appeals to such a distinction in several places. For instance, in *NE* VI.8, he clearly distinguishes between political prudence and ethical prudence in the following manner:

> And in fact, the political and prudence have the same characteristic, though their being is not the same. Of the prudence that is concerned with a city, one part is architectonic, namely, the legislative; the other, concerned with particulars, bears the name that is common to them 'the political'. … Prudence also is commonly understood to mean especially that kind of wisdom which is concerned with oneself, the individual; and it is this that bears the common name 'prudence'. (*NE* 1141b25-30)

There is then a distinction between political prudence concerned with a city and ethical prudence concerned with oneself. This means that one might be prudent in one's own life without being a politician. Indeed, this is the primary (or essential) sense of being prudent. Since ethical prudence requires the exercise of moral virtues, one can perform morally virtuous actions without being a politician. One might not have any interest in the art of ruling others, but this will not prevent one from performing noble actions in one's social life. In other words, the life of politics is not equivalent to the life of morally virtuous activities as it is supposed in our contemporary debate. On the contrary, for Aristotle, it is even doubtful whether politicians are genuinely virtuous. He explicitly distinguishes between 'political character' and 'noble character' in the *Eudemian Ethics* (hereafter *EE*):

> But there is also a state of character that is political character, and this character is of the following sort. There are those who think that one ought, it is true, to possess virtue but for the sake of the things that are naturally good; hence though they are good men (for things naturally good are good for them) yet they have not nobility, for it is not the case with them that they possess fine things for their own sake. ... But he who thinks that one ought to possess the virtues for the sake of external goods does fine things only by accident. (*EE* 1248b18)

This is also supported by Aristotle's initial claim in *NE* I that the life of politics aims at an external good, namely, honour: 'Cultivated men, on the other hand, and men of action think that the good is honour – for this may be said to be the end of the life of politics' (*NE* 1095b 22-24).

From these quotations, it follows that the life of politics aims at external goods, primarily honour, hence political men exercise virtues for the sake of external goods. Noble men, however, act virtuously for the sake of acting virtuously. This qualification also supports the view that it is a mistake to consider the life of politics as the life of morally virtuous activities. To summarize, in *NE* X 7-8, Aristotle compares the philosophical life and the life of politics. Since the life of politics is not the same as the life of morally virtuous activities, this comparison cannot be reduced to a comparison between the philosophical activity and morally virtuous activities. This is also evident from what Aristotle says already in *NE* X 8:

> But the philosopher being a man will also need external well-being, since man's nature is not self-sufficient for the activity of contemplation, but he must also have bodily health and a supply of food and other requirements. Yet if supreme blessedness is not possible without external goods, it must not be supposed that happiness will demand many or great possessions; for self-sufficiency does not depend on excessive abundance, nor does moral conduct, and it is possible to perform noble deeds even without being ruler of land and sea: one can do virtuous acts with quite moderate resources. This may be clearly observed in experience: private citizens do not seem to be less but more given to doing virtuous actions than princes and potentates. It is sufficient then if moderate resources are forthcoming; for a life of virtuous activity will be essentially a happy life. (*NE* 1178b33-1179a9)

According to this passage in its context, someone who has chosen the life of philosophy over the life of politics can be a morally virtuous person with moderate resources. Notice, however, Aristotle not only says that it is possible to perform noble deeds even without being ruler of land and sea but also emphasizes that a life of morally virtuous activity is essentially a happy life. Regardless of one's occupation in life, happiness essentially consists in a life of morally virtuous activities. Of course, philosophical activity is distinct from morally virtuous activities. But a philosophical life should involve morally virtuous activities if it is to satisfy the essential condition of happiness. Aristotle already presupposes this in his discussion when he says that the philosopher 'being a man and living in the society of others, he chooses to engage in virtuous action' (*NE* 1178b5-7). If Aristotle's comparison were to be between the philosophical activity and the morally virtuous activities, this sentence and the previous paragraph would not make sense at all.

When we take the life of politics to be the life of morally virtuous activities, Aristotle's comparison between the philosophical life and the life of politics is reduced to a comparison between the philosophical activity and the morally virtuous activities. But Aristotle does not make such a comparison. What then is the subject of comparison? There are two possibilities depending on what we understand by the end of political life. As we have explained earlier, according to the common interpretation, the life of politics takes the end to be honour and associates happiness with honour. This kind of political life is indeed the subject of Aristotle's comparison with the philosophical life in *NE* X 7-8. It is true that the politician who targets external goods acts virtuously. However, he does so not for the sake of acting virtuously but for the sake of external goods, primarily for the sake of honour. As Aristotle explains in *NE* X 7, the politician conceives happiness as something distinct from his virtuous activities:

> But the activity of the politician also is unleisured, and aims at securing something beyond the mere participation in politics – positions of authority and honour, or, if the happiness of the politician himself and of his fellow citizens, this happiness conceived as something distinct from political activity (indeed we are clearly investigating it as so distinct). If then among practical pursuits displaying the virtues, politics and war stand out pre-eminent in nobility and grandeur, and yet they are unleisured, and directed to some further end, not chosen for their own sakes: whereas the activity of the intellect is felt to excel in serious worth, consisting as it does in contemplation, and to aim at no end beyond itself, and also to contain pleasure peculiar to itself, and therefore augmenting its activity: and if accordingly the attributes of this activity are found to be self-sufficiency, leisuredness, such freedom from fatigue as is possible for man, and all the other attributes of blessedness: it follows that it is the activity of the intellect that constitutes complete human happiness. (*NE* 1177b12-25)

Here Aristotle also recapitulates his argument for the view that the life of contemplation constitutes complete happiness in comparison to the life of politics, which aims at some external good distinct from its own activity. Recall that happiness also involves morally virtuous activities. The life of morally virtuous activities constitutes the essential happiness for man, whereas the life of philosophy accompanied by morally virtuous activities constitutes complete happiness. Can we then not call the life of politics essentially happy since it involves morally virtuous activities? The politician mistakenly associates happiness with honour; nonetheless, he performs morally virtuous actions. In general terms we can put the question in this manner: Can we call someone happy who acts as a happy man would but not for the sake of happiness? Interestingly, this question also applies to the case of someone who pursues the life of philosophy not for the sake of contemplation but for the sake of reputation he will receive for his publicized thoughts. Could we call such a life (completely) happy? Aristotle does not explicitly address this question. Nonetheless, an Aristotelian answer would clearly be negative because, according to Aristotle, one can be considered to be virtuous on the condition that one acts with knowledge, deliberately chooses the action, and chooses it for its own sake (*NE* II.4 1105a31-32). The same negative answer applies to the case of the politician who seeks an end external to the virtuous activities that he displays; we cannot call the life of such a politician happy.

But can there not be another kind of political life, a life of politics that does not aim at any external good? Can we not imagine a politician who acts for the sake of virtuous activity? Indeed, according to Aristotle, the *true* politician's aim is to make citizens virtuous and capable of performing noble actions, and that is why he should also study human soul and virtue (*NE* 1102a 8-10, *NE* 1102a 19). This appears to be a noble aim. Why is then one supposed to pursue theoretical wisdom rather than political prudence? Aristotle does not make this comparison in *NE* X. As I have just explained, the subject matter of Aristotle's discussion is the life of politics that aims at an external good. Nonetheless, early on what Aristotle says in *NE* VI, might provide us with an answer:

> It is clear that theoretical wisdom must be the most perfect of the modes of knowledge. ... It must be a combination of intelligence and scientific knowledge: it must be a consummated knowledge of the most exalted objects. For it is absurd to think that the political science or prudence is the loftiest kind of knowledge, inasmuch as man is not the highest thing in the world ... there exist other things far more divine in nature than man, for instance, to mention the most visible, the things of which the celestial system is composed. (*NE* 1141a16-b2)

Since there are more divine beings than human, the study of human is secondary to the study of these other beings, which constitute the proper subject of contemplative activity. From this perspective, the life of a true politician, which requires the study of human soul and virtue so as to make citizens virtuous, is the second-best life. Recall further that according to the commonly understood sense of politics, political life aims at an external good, primarily honour. Aristotle does not seem to give much credit to such a life.

Early on, we argued that we should not conflate morally virtuous activities with the activities of a politician. According to Aristotle, as a social being, each person is supposed to regulate his life in accordance with moral virtues so as to achieve the essential form of happiness. This essential form of happiness is what distinguishes human beings from animals. As we quoted early on, Aristotle claims: 'We have good reasons therefore for not speaking of an ox or horse or any other animal as being happy, because none of these is able to participate in noble activities' (*NE* 1099b32-35). Nonetheless, a life of morally virtuous activities is not the happiest (*eudaimonestatos*) life human beings are capable of achieving. Through contemplation, human beings can become divine. Aristotle explains the following concerning the life of contemplation:

> Such a life as this however will be higher than the human level: not in virtue of his humanity will a man achieve it, but in virtue of something within him that is divine. ... If then the intellect is something divine in comparison with man, so is the life of the intellect divine in comparison with human life. (*NE* 1177b26-32)

If we follow Aristotle's distinction between practical reason and theoretical reason, we realize that practical reason, the realm of the ethical, is what distinguishes humans from animals and theoretical reason, the realm of philosophical contemplation, is what makes humans divine. For 'the activity of God, which is transcendent in blessedness, is the activity of contemplation' (*NE* 1178b23). That is why the life of philosophy for Aristotle is not only the happiest (*eudaimonestatos*) but also the most blessed (*makarios*) one. As he says: 'The whole of the life of the gods is blessed, and that of man is so in so far as it contains some likeness to the divine activity' (*NE* 1178b27-28).

As we have quoted before, Aristotle claims that the philosopher pursues a morally virtuous life. From Aristotle's perspective, the life of philosophy presupposes the life of morally virtuous activities. There is then a hierarchical relationship between the life of philosophy (which presupposes the life of morally virtuous activities) and the life of morally virtuous activities (devoid of contemplation). Naturally, the former is higher in rank than the latter; while the former is the happiest life understood as blessedness, which makes humans divine, the latter is the essential form of happiness that distinguishes humans from animals. As Aristotle explains further in NE X 7-8, the life of philosophy is the happiest life while the life of morally virtuous activities is happy in a secondary way.

> And what we said above will apply here as well: what is proper to each thing is by nature best and pleasantest for it; for a human being, therefore, the life in accordance with intellect is best and pleasantest, since this, more than anything else, constitutes humanity. So this life will also be the happiest. The life in accordance with the other kind of virtue is happy in a secondary way, since the activities in accordance with it are human. For we do just actions, courageous and the other actions in accordance with the virtues, in relation to each other, observing what is proper to each in contracts, services and actions of all kinds, and in feelings as well; and all of these are manifestly human. (*NE* 1178a5-14)

According to our comprehensive interpretation, Aristotle's portrait of the relationship between happiness and virtuous activities is more subtle than it appears. Morally virtuous activities done for their own sake with moderate resources constitute the essential happiness for human. The life of philosophy accompanied by morally virtuous activities constitutes complete happiness (*teleia eudaimonia*), or what we may call blessedness (*makarios*). The life of politics which aims at honour is not a happy life. The true politician whose aim is to make citizens virtuous, however, pursues the second best life possible for human. There is a noteworthy option that is left for consideration, that is, the life of contemplation not accompanied by morally virtuous activities. Aristotle, however, is silent about the merit of this life and its relation to happiness. But the answer seems to be evident. Since morally virtuous activities constitute the essential condition for the possibility of happiness, a life devoid of morally virtuous activities cannot be a candidate for happiness. In other words, human beings cannot become divine before exceeding the mere form of being animal.

IV Conclusion

The current debate between the monists and inclusivists, however, is blind to this hierarchical relationship between various forms of life with respect to happiness. This has two main reasons. Primarily, as we have claimed in the introduction, there are two distinct questions that Aristotle addresses with regard to happiness: (a) What does happiness consist in? and (b) What is the happiest life? Monist and inclusivist accounts, however, disregard the distinctness of these questions and subsume them under the single question: (c) What is happiness? When the question is formulated in this manner, Aristotle's answer to question (a) is taken to be a definition of happiness, and his answer to (b) is taken to be the form of life that fits this definition. But Aristotle's answers do not allow for a coherent interpretation within this framework. Aristotle does not give us a simple definition of happiness. The whole book is devoted to the exploration of happiness from various aspects. What is taken to be a definition in our current debate, namely, the answer to question (a), is just one aspect of this exploration where Aristotle explains the source of happiness. For Aristotle, happiness consists in activity of the soul in accordance with virtue. Although the source of happiness is activity in accordance with virtue, this constitutive principle is not sufficient for bringing about a lifetime of happiness; as he explains in other parts of the book, happiness also requires some basic external goods. But these external goods do not constitute the source of happiness.

Once Aristotle is thought to have given us a definition of happiness in the form 'happiness is activity of soul in accordance with virtue', it is then legitimate to search for the activity that satisfies this definition. It is most natural to take this activity to be philosophical activity, for in his answer to question (b), Aristotle claims that the life of philosophy is the happiest life. That is roughly how we arrive at the monist conclusion that happiness is philosophical activity. We have already explained the shortcomings of monism. Inclusivist accounts are not in a better position since they follow the same reasoning. Rather, they are perplexed about how to interpret Aristotle's claim that the life of philosophy is the happiest life.

This brings us to the second reason why monists and inclusivists are blind to the hierarchical relation among various forms of life with respect to happiness. Both monists and inclusivists presuppose that the life of politics is the life of morally virtuous activities. Since the debate is formulated based on this presupposition, we are forced to make a choice between being a philosopher and being a morally virtuous person. This choice, however, is clearly wrongheaded. We have explained why this presupposition is not part of Aristotle's view. Aristotle distinguishes not only between the life of politics and the life of morally virtuous activities but also between the life of a politician who aims at an external good such as honour and the life of a true politician who aims to make citizens virtuous. All these different forms of life have their distinct relation to happiness and a hierarchical relationship among themselves. In order to understand this, we need to distinguish between the essential form of happiness achieved through morally virtuous activities from the higher form of happiness (understood as blessedness) achieved through philosophical contemplation. The former form of happiness is what distinguishes human beings from animals, while the latter is what makes them divine. Naturally the latter cannot be achieved without the former, that is to say, one cannot be divine and blessed without first going beyond the mere form of being animal. Only a comprehensive reading of *NE* and alertness to Aristotle's various questions enable us to reach this conclusion.

Notes

1 Examples of inclusivist accounts include Ackrill (1974) 1980; Crisp 1994; Cooper (1987) 1999; Irwin 1985; Irwin 1991; Keyt 1983; Roche 1988; White 1990. Examples of monist accounts include Cooper 1975; Hardie 1965; Heinaman 1988; Kenny 1992; Kraut 1989; Richardson Lear 2004.
2 Translations of Aristotle are my interpretations based on the original Greek text in view of Crisp (2004), Rackham (1934) and Rowe (2002).
3 For instrumentalist interpretations, see Cooper 1975; Kraut 1989.

Bibliography

Ackrill, J. ([1974] 1980), 'Aristotle on Eudaimonia', in A. O. Rorty (ed.), *Essays on Aristotle's Ethics*, 15–33, Berkeley: University of California Press.
Broadie, S. and C. Rowe (2002), *Aristotle: Nicomachean Ethics*, Oxford: Oxford University Press.
Cooper, J. ([1975] 1986), *Reason and Human Good in Aristotle*, Indianapolis: Hackett.
Cooper, J. ([1987] 1999), 'Contemplation and Happiness: A Reconsideration', in *Reason and Emotion*, 118–37, Princeton: Princeton University Press.
Crisp, R. (1994), 'Aristotle's Inclusivism', *Oxford Studies in Ancient Philosophy*, 12: 111–36.
Crisp, R. (2004), *Aristotle: Nicomachean Ethics*, Cambridge: Cambridge University Press.
Hardie, W. (1965), 'The Final Good in Aristotle's Ethics', *Philosophy*, 40: 277–95.
Heinaman, R. (1988), 'Eudaimonia and Self-Sufficiency in the *Nicomachean Ethics*', *Phronesis*, 33: 31–53.
Irwin, T. (1985), 'Permanent Happiness: Aristotle and Solon', *Oxford Studies in Ancient Philosophy*, 3: 89–124.
Irwin, T. (1991), 'The Structure of Aristotelian Happiness', *Ethics*, 101: 382–91.
Kenny, A. (1992), *Aristotle on the Perfect Life*, Oxford: Oxford University Press.

Keyt, D. (1983), 'Intellectualism in Aristotle', in P. Anton and A. Preus, *Essays in Ancient Greek Philosophy*, vol. 2, 364–87, Albany: State University of New York Press.

Kraut, R. (1989), *Aristotle on the Human Good*, Princeton: Princeton University Press.

Rackham, H. (1934), *Aristotle: Nicomachean Ethics*, Cambridge: Harvard University Press.

Rackham, H. (1952), *Aristotle: The Eudemian Ethics*, Cambridge: Harvard University Press.

Richardson Lear, G. (2004), *Happy Lives and the Highest Good*, Princeton: Princeton University Press.

Roche, T. (1988), 'The Perfect Happiness', *Southern Journal of Philosophy*, 27 (supp.), *Aristotle's Ethics*: 103–25.

White, S. (1990), 'Is Aristotelian Happiness a Good Life or the Best Life?' *Oxford Studies in Ancient Philosophy*, 8: 103–43.

5

'Going through time together'

Aristotelian friendship and the criterion of time

Eleni Leontsini

I *Philia* and *suzēn*: The criterion of time and the test of friendship

My aim in this chapter is to examine whether Aristotle, in his discussion of friendship, strongly advocates that the most important element is that of 'living together', or 'spending time together', or 'sharing lives' (τὸ συζῆν/*to suzēn*). Thus, the key question I would be dealing with in this chapter is 'How important is living together in Aristotle's account of friendship?', exploring at the same time the different ways in which living together (τὸ συζῆν/*to suzēn*) could be important. The 'living together' criterion is pinpointed in almost all contemporary discussions on Aristotle's notions and kinds of *philia*, but it is mentioned, nevertheless, only *in passim* by Aristotle in some passages in both the *Nicomachean* and the *Eudemian Ethics*, and it is never extensively elaborated in his works.[1]

A clarification regarding the Aristotelian notion of *suzēn* is needed here. *Suzēn* is crucial for both our personal life and for political life in general (*bios idiōtikos* and *bios politikos*). Aristotle clearly relates political life with *suzēn*, and thus with *philia*. But I should make clear, at this point, that in this chapter of course I am merely referring to the notion of *suzēn* in relation to it being a necessary condition of *philia* and mainly of being a *philos* to one another, and not to *suzēn* overall. *Suzēn* is an important Aristotelian political notion in general, which is prominent in both his moral and political theory, since, as Aristotle points out, '*suzēn* is the result, the *ergon* (ἔργον/*ergon*) of *philia*, since *philia* is the pursuit of a common social life' (*Pol.* III.9.1280b38-40). In fact, one could argue that 'living together' (*suzēn*) is in the core of Aristotelian political theory, especially in *Politics*, Book I, but also throughout the *Politics*, as well as in the *Nicomachean* and *Eudemian Ethics*, and in the *Magna Moralia*, where the importance of *suzēn* for political life is clearly demonstrated, that is, the importance of living in the company of others.

As we know, one of the basic ideas of *Politics* I.1–2 is that the *polis* (πόλις) is a natural entity like an animal or a human being. Two additional ideas are that a human being (*anthrōpos*/ἄνθρωπος) is by nature a political animal, and that the *polis* is prior to the individual. In fact, *Politics* I.1-2 is mainly dedicated to arguing for the naturalness of the *polis*, in the sense that the *polis* is natural because human beings have a natural tendency to live in city-states (*poleis*) and can only achieve their good within the *polis*. The *polis* is an association for the sake of the most sovereign good, and it comes into being for the sake of life (ζῆν/*zēn*) but exists for the sake of the good life (εὖ ζῆν/*eū zēn*). These passages imply that the citizens must share a common conception of the good. The *polis* is natural in the sense that only by living together within the *polis* can human beings achieve their true good (*agathon*), since the point which is made here is that only those fortunate enough to live together (*suzēn*) in a *polis* have a chance of a truly good life.

For Aristotle, there are different ways in which living together could be important, and there are numerous passages that demonstrate this. *Suzēn* is not only implied in Aristotle's famous pronouncement in *Pol* I.1.1253a2-3 that 'a human being is by nature a political animal' but also most clearly stated in *NE* IX.9.18-19, where Aristotle argues that 'a human being is political and to live with others is according to nature' (πολιτικὸν γὰρ ὁ ἄνθρωπος καὶ συζῆν πεφυκός/*politikon gar ho anthrōpos kai suzēn pephukos*).[2] 'Living together' is vital for human life, either personal or political, since 'an association depends on friendship – after all, people will not even take a journey in common with their enemies' (*Pol* IV.11.1295b23-25), since 'it is thought to be the special business of the political art to produce friendship, and people say that excellence is useful because of this, for those who are unjustly treated by one another cannot be friends to one another' (*EE*.VIII.1.1234b22-25).

In addition, it is important to point out that 'living together' is also associated with the common or public interest (τὸ κοινῇ συμφέρον/*to koinē sumpheron*) of all the citizens, towards which all non-deviant constitutions should aim at:

> Since people formulate partnerships (συμπορεύονται/*sumboreuontai*) with a view to some particular interest (*sumpheron*), and to provide anything that they need for the purposes of life; and it is for the sake of the public interest (τοῦ κοινῇ συμφέροντος) that the political community too seems both to have come together originally and to endure, for this is what legislators aim at, and they call just that which is to the public interest. (*NE*.VIII.9.1160a11-14)

Justice is indeed closely connected to *suzēn*, since:

> the laws in their enactments on all subjects aim at the public interest (τοῦ κοινῇ συμφέροντος) either of all or of the best or of those who hold power, or something of the sort; so that on one sense we can call those acts just that tend to produce and preserve *eudaimonia* and its components for the political society. (*NE*.V.I.9.1129b15-19)

It should be pointed out that in everyday political life 'the models of friendship in Classical Greece were based at least in part upon patterns of exchange which were themselves governed by the status of individuals as "insiders" or "outsiders", friends or enemies, creating expectations of the way relationships should work' (Mitchell 2002: 178). This meant that, in everyday political life at least, friendship was related to ideology (i.e. *polis* ideology), since 'Greek political world was, at least in part, built upon friendship networks and ideas of repaying favours, and because the alliances and relationships between states were constantly shifting and changing, friends could be forced to become enemies' (Mitchell 2002: 191). Hence, *philia* and *suzēn* were often used interchangeably as an example regarding political relations.

But the notion of *suzēn* that I am concerned with in this chapter is that which has to do with *suzēn* in relation to personal *philia*, that is, whether *suzēn* (spending time together) is a necessary condition for friendship. So to return to *philia* and to the 'criterion of time', if the criterion of 'living together' (τὸ συζῆν/*to suzēn*) is indeed an important condition (as it has been argued by most commentators), then this criterion may also have a bearing on Aristotle's threefold conception of friendship. For example, according to Sarah Broadie and Christopher Rowe, 'the all-important element of living together' is a necessary condition for the friendship relation and should be included in Aristotle's general definition of *philia* (Aristotle 2002: 408). Michael Pakaluk makes an even stronger claim than Sarah Broadie and Christopher Rowe when he argues that, according to Aristotle, 'the highest expression of friendship is simply "spending time" or "sharing in thinking with one's friend"', connecting this with leisure, since 'only in spending time with a friend do we enter into a relationship with another person that closely resembles this relationship that, at the same time, one has to oneself' (Pakaluk 2005: 260–1). Also, Nancy Sherman (1991: 118–56) makes a similar strong point arguing that, in Aristotle's view, the good life is a life lived among friends, and, in particular, among friends of virtue or good character, contrasting this emphasis on attachment and intimacy with the themes of a more impartialist ethics, such as the one Kant presents (Stern-Gillet 1995: 47; Schollmeier 1994: 54–6; Price: 159–60; Urmson 1988: 112–17; Hughes 2001: 168–79).

It is unclear though what 'all-important' really means in this context, and it is unclear whether 'all-important' and 'most important' mean quite the same thing; something that is not clarified by Sarah Broadie and Christopher Rowe in the aforementioned definition they provide. It is interesting as well that, besides the previously mentioned Aristotelian scholars, Alexander Nehamas in his recent book on friendship, although he only discusses the Aristotelian foundations of friendship in one chapter, also thinks the 'criterion of time' to be important (2016: 11–36). Most notably, Martha Nussbaum has argued that there are in Aristotle eight 'requirements for friendship': (a) mutuality in affection, (b) independence (the object of *philia* must be seen as a being with a separate good, not as simply a possession or extension of a *philos*; and the real *philos* will wish the other well for the sake of that separate good), (c) mutual benefiting in action, insofar as this is possible, (d) living together, (e) trust, (f) mutuality in pleasure, (g) mutual helping, and (h) mutual attraction. Hence, Martha Nussbaum considers 'living together' to be 'a requirement for friendship'. Furthermore, for Nussbaum, there are three additional mechanisms of friendship: (a) mutual influence, (b) shared activity, and (c) emulation and imitation (mirror friendship). Hence, Nussbaum renders 'shared activity'[3] as one of the three important mechanisms of Aristotelian *philia* (1986: 357–9).

But, it is interesting that W. K. C. Guthrie, being very careful with the ancient text as he always was, succinctly pointed out that, in a later chapter (*NE*.IX.9.1170b11), living together (τὸ συζῆν) is said to involve sharing thoughts, not simply 'feeding in the same place like cattle' (Guthrie 1981: 386, f. 3). Therefore, contrary to the earlier interpretation that takes the 'criterion of time' to be a necessary condition for friendship, I will argue that 'going through time together' is not a necessary condition nor an essential element of Aristotle's general definition of friendship[4] and that, despite the importance that the 'criterion of time' ('spending time together') does indeed have for the sustainability of a *philia* (of whichever kind), it should not be taken literally as 'living together' in a continuous and uninterrupted way, but that it should be understood in a much broader sense if Aristotle's account of *philia* is to have any standing. But also, as I will establish, Aristotle himself intended it this way, as it is apparent in various other passages of the Aristotelian text.

Therefore, the key issues to be asked are: (a) Is it correct to say that living together is 'all-important'? and (b) What does this really mean? It is plausible to argue that one cannot truthfully claim to be friends with someone unless s/he has spent some time with them. In other words, having spent time with X is a necessary condition of being friends with X. But it is not at all clear how much time one needs to have spent together in order to count as friends, and whether one can still be friends with someone if s/he has not had any contact with them for a long time. Hence, the key question is whether living together is important simply for deciding whether a relationship counts as friendship or whether it is also important for determining what kinds of friendship are best.[5]

This is of course a very complex issue in relation to the friendship relation and the conception of friendship in general, whether ancient, modern or contemporary. Undoubtedly, one should spend enough time with someone so as to become good friends with her or him, since it is only *via* 'spending time together' that it is possible for both to know each other's character and their life story, appreciate one another and to love each other truly. Even if recriminations in friendship will occur, these are most likely to happen when friends spend time together rather than when being apart where distance usually idealizes the object of love and does not allow each other to realize their faults of character. Friendship is really put at test when the friends spend time together. Spending time together and, hence having recriminations with one's friend, is maybe the most important 'test of friendship', since it is only *via* disputes, fights and conflict that one will consciously decide that the other person is hers or his friend, despite the recriminations (*NE*.IX.3-5). It is only then that the friends realize that they truly love each other, when they are offered a chance to forgive one another and to give a second chance, or even a numerous set of second chances, to their friend.

Having said that, one should also be careful to point out that distance can indeed put the friendship also at test, in the sense that distance makes the friends to loose contact with one another and could also cause recriminations merely because of the 'absence' of the other, which might not only 'alienate' the *philia* but also weaken the love that the friends have for each other.

As stated earlier, Aristotle argues that one should give his/her friend a numerous opportunities of 'second chances', and that s/he should always be willing to forgive, understand and sustain the friendship at any cost, despite the recriminations or the changes in the character of the friend (*NE*.IX.3-5). In fact, Aristotle insists that, even if a friend acted badly and even became bad, one should try to persevere in the friendship that once existed (*NE*.IX.3-4), unless s/he realizes that her/his friend is 'incurable in malice / wickedness' (τοῖς ἀνιάτοις κατὰ τὴν μοχθηρίαν/*tois aniatois kata tēn mochērian*), since it both difficult and unbefitting to become lovers of evil (πονηρὸν/*ponēron*) or to love an evil person (φιλοπόνηρος/*philoponēros*) (*NE*.IX.3.1165b18; also *NE*.I.3.1165a36ff and mainly *NE*.I.3.1165b17-22). Hence, as pointed earlier, an important 'test of friendship' is indeed the 'test of time' because it is only then that one understands the true character of one's *philos*.

II The object of love and the forms of Aristotelian friendship

It is useful to clarify the Greek notion of *philia*, which, at first sight, seems to be very different from the concept of 'friendship', at least in its contemporary ordinary use in any modern language. As it has been pointed out by most standard treatments of Aristotle's notion of friendship, the meaning and the definition of the Greek concept of *philia* is much wider than that of 'friendship', including all kinds of intimate love relations between both sexes (Annas 1977: 532–54, Schofield 1999: 82–99, Price 1989; Schollmeier 1994). As John Cooper points out,

> The field of *philia* covers not just the (more or less) intimate relationships between persons not bound together by near family ties, to which the words used in the modern languages to translate it are ordinarily restricted, but all sorts of family relationships (especially those of parents to children, children to parents, siblings to one another, and the marriage relationship itself); the word also has a natural and ordinary use to characterise what goes in English under the somewhat quaint-sounding name of civic friendship. (Cooper 1999: 312–13)

Most important though is that the meaning of Greek *philia* in general, and Aristotle's in particular, is 'lost in translation', since, as David Konstan rightly points out, 'Aristotle is not, in the first instance, interested so much in friendship itself as in the nature of affectionate ties or relations in general' and 'the inveterate custom of translating *philia* as 'friendship' rather than 'love' or 'loving relationship' has produced some awkwardness in English versions of the ethical treatises and, on occasion, error as well' (Konstan 1997: 67–8). Of course, one should not forget that Aristotle even includes *erōs* as a form of friendship in various passages in the *Nicomachean Ethics*, let alone that he defines *erōs* as an 'excess of *philia*' (ὑπερβολὴ φιλίας/*huperbolē philias*): 'For it would be impossible to love too many people. This is also why one cannot be in love with too many people. Because *erōs* (being in love) is an excess of *philia*, and that can only be felt towards one person; therefore, a strong *philia* too can only be felt towards a few people' (οὐδὲ γὰρ ἐνδέχεσθαι δόξειεν ἂν πολλοῖς εἶναι φίλον σφόδρα. Διόπερ οὐδ' ἐρᾶν πλειόνων· ὑπερβολὴ γάρ τις εἶναι βούλεται φιλίας, τοῦτο δὲ πρὸς ἕνα· καὶ τὸ σφόδρα δὴ πρὸς ὀλίγους) (NE.IX.10.1171a10-13).

Aristotle illustrates extensively the different varieties of love, intimate relations and friendship that he mentions in his discussion in the relevant books of the *Nicomachean Ethics* and the *Eudemian Ethics*, but also in various passages in the *Rhetoric* and the *Politics*. Examples of *philia* describing relationships such as those of all sorts of family relationships, like those of parents to children, children to parents, siblings to one another, the marriage relationship itself, erotic love, friendships of fellow citizens, fellow tribesmen, shipmates, slaves and even thieves, can be found in *NE*.VIII.11.161b12 and *EE*.VIII.10.1242a1, but also in the *Generation of Animals*, III.2.753a13. For example, Mary Blundell discusses the many levels and varieties of *philia* under three main headings: family, fellow citizens and personal friends (Blundell 1989: 39–49). Nevertheless, it is not clear whether the Greek term *philos*, when it is used as a noun, applies to all these varieties of Aristotelian *philiai*, like, for example, the family relationships, since as it is a term used mainly to describe personal friendships in the ordinary use of the term, as David Konstan has successfully argued (Konstan 1996: 71–94), but also political friendships (Leontsini 2013a: 129–41). The adjective is, of course, used in a much wider sense, in the sense that the question is really about the meaning of *philos* and *philia* when it is used as a noun.

Philein mostly denotes 'loving feeling', so in that sense *philia*, in some contexts at least (if not all), is much closer to 'love' in the modern sense than any other ancient Greek word, and indeed it does mean love in most contexts. This is a line of argument that is also followed by Suzanne Stern-Gillet (1995), and I need to admit here that personally I have not been adopting this line of interpretation of '*philia* as love' consistently nor literally in most of my previous work (Leontsini 2013b: 21–35 and Leontsini 2007: 159–209), although I have now come to agree with both David Konstan and Suzanne Stern-Gillet, since this is the only way for the Aristotelian notion of *philia* to make any sense given Aristotle's notion of it in all his works. But it should be noted though that the Greeks used *erōs* to denote 'erotic love', the kind that involves sexual desire (*epithumia*), that is, *sunousia* (intercourse), while the word *agapē* (love) does not occur in Aristotle and was only put into usage much later by the Christian authors in the notion of Christian love (*agapē*). The word '*agapan*' (to love) does occur in Aristotle, but only as a synonym of *timan* (to honour), *boulesthai* (to want), *aireisthai* (to prefer) and *diōkein* (to pursue). The connection between love and friendship was also made in Latin, as Cicero points out in *De Amicitia* (VIII. 26): 'For the first thing to bring people together in a relationship is love (*amor*), from which friendship (*amicitia*) derives its name' (Leontsini 2007: 171, f.17).

In the *Nicomachean Ethics*, Aristotle starts his discussion concerning love stressing that *philia* 'is a virtue or implies virtue' and 'is most necessary with a view to living':

> For without friends no one would choose to live, though s/he had all other goods; even rich people and those in possession of office and of dominating power are thought to need friends most of all; for what is the use of such prosperity without the opportunity of beneficence, which is exercised chiefly and in its most laudable form towards friends? Or how can prosperity be guarded and preserved without

friends? ... And in poverty and other misfortunes people think friends are the only refuge. (*NE*.VIII.1.1155a313)

Philia, according to Aristotle, undoubtedly entails at least two important constitutive features, affection and an altruistic concern for the friend's good,[6] since, as it is clearly stated by Aristotle in many passages, in all cases it is much more important to love than to be loved: 'In being loved, on the other hand, people delight for its own sake; hence it would seem to be better than being honoured, and friendship to be desirable in itself. But it seems to consist in loving rather than in being loved' (δοκεῖ δ'ἐν τῷ φιλεῖν μᾶλλον ἢ ἐν τῷ φιλεῖσθαι εἶναι/*dokei de en tō philein mallon ē en tō fileisthai einai*) (*NE* VIII.8.1159a25-28).[7]

Now, an objection that could be raised is that the use of word 'altruistic' may be anachronistic here, but not only is this the standard exegesis of Aristotle's element of *philia* as 'loving being more important than to be loved', but most importantly, it is indeed in the core of Aristotle's notion of friendship to mainly presuppose a one-sided relationship (giving without hoping to get in return). Contrary to friendly alliances in political action, as was mentioned in the first section of this chapter, Aristotelian personal friendship is not reciprocal, as the *Rhetoric* passage stated next clearly indicates. It is only in the kind of civic friendship as a form of public interest[8] that Aristotle advocates where political friends retain the aspects of mutual awareness and liking, the reciprocal wishing the other well for that other's sake, and the concern to do things for their friend.[9]

But a much more important objection that could be raised to the aforementioned is whether all friendships involve affection and altruistic concern, since one could rightly argue that these would not apply to utility friendships, the third and 'lowest' kind of *philia*, the one that is referred to by Aristotle as the useful (χρήσιμον/*chrēsimon*). It is true that this is problematic and that there is a tendency to be denied that this kind of *philia* is a real one. But, as Suzanne Stern-Gillet (1995: 38) has pointed out: 'It is a fact that less than fully virtuous people do not generally lack friends and companions; to deny the name of friendship to such associations would clearly not only do violence to the observed facts (τὰ φαινόμενα/*ta phainomena*) but also reduce the status of primary friendship to that of a generally unattainable ideal.'[10]

This is quite important for the understanding of Aristotle's normative notion of friendship at least in the *Nicomachean Ethics*. When examining Aristotle's distinction between the three kinds of friendship and the notion of political friendship, one should bear in mind this core common to all friendly associations. This is clearly demonstrated in the *Rhetoric* where Aristotle argues that love (*filein*) and concern for others (Annas 1993: 249) is part of the normal meaning of 'friendship':

> We will begin by defining friendship (*philia*) and friendly feeling (*to filein*). Let friendly feeling, or loving (*to filein*) be defined as wishing for someone what one thinks to be good for their own sake and not for one's own, and being inclined, so far as you can, to bring these things about. A *philos* is one who feels thus and excites these feelings in return. Those who think they feel thus towards each other think themselves friends (*philoi*). This being assumed, it follows that your *philos* is

the sort of person who shares your pleasure in what is good and your pain in what is unpleasant, for your sake and for no other reason. (*Rhet* II.3.1380b36-1381a5)

This passage from the *Rhetoric*, as it has been argued, is essential for the understanding of Aristotle's notion of *philia* in the corresponding books of both the *Nicomachean* and the *Eudemian Ethics*, since it is in this passage that Aristotle indicates the core common to all friendly associations. It is suggested that the central idea contained in friendship is that of doing well by someone for his or her own sake, out of concern for him or her and not, or merely, out of concern for oneself. This theme is of course essential to Aristotle and we find it all throughout his moral and political works (e.g. good constitutions versus deviant ones), as I have elaborated in the first section of this chapter. But this is not to say that the difference between good constitutions and bad ones does not fall into the three classifications of friendship, as Aristotle at length compares the constitutions with *philia* and justice (*dikaiosunē*) in *NE* VIII.9, arguing that the first is altruistic, while the others are egoistic in the sense that the deviant ones do not aim at the common or public or general interest (*koinē sumphēron*), as of course he does in *Politics* Books III and IV in many passages, but also in the *Nicomachean Ethics* in two additional important passages (*NE*.V.I.1129b15 and *NE*. VIII.9.1160a14).

John Cooper argues that this definition from the *Rhetoric* states the core of Aristotle's own analysis of *philia*, since 'the parties love one another for their characters and not merely because they enjoy or profit from one another's company' (Cooper 1999: ibid). John Cooper maintains that this kind of *philia* (which he labels as 'character-friendship') is distinguished from the other two forms of friendship in that the description under which one loves the other is a description of that other's whole. Nevertheless, Cooper argues that this 'core' element of *philia* is also present in all three kinds of *philiai* that Aristotle analyses, at least in a loose sense.[11] I should point out here though that, although I do endorse Cooper's interpretation (in a loose sense at least, as far as other-concern is involved), I do not think that the term 'character-friendship' successfully describes Aristotle's notion of this kind of friendship, but that this is best described by Sarah Broadie as 'excellence-based friendship' (Broadie and Rowe 2002: ibid), a term that I will also be adopting henceforth. In addition, not all friendships involve genuine affection and altruistic concern, since this would not clearly apply to utility friendships.

Aristotle sustained that friendship is one of the most important forces that motivates *koinōnia* into action and holds it together, since '*philia* is the pursuit of a common social life' (*Pol* III.9.1280b38-39), and argued that friendship is even more important than justice since it generates concord (*homonoia*) in the city (*NE* VIII.1.1155b21-27): 'In all communities of exchange, this sort of justice holds people together' (*NE*.V.3.1132b31) and 'reciprocity preserves cities' (*Pol*.II.1.1261a32). Other people are vital to us because we need others in order to communicate and interact with them, 'for a human being is a social being and his nature is to live in the company of others' (*NE*.IX.9.1169b18-19). Aristotle attributed a special kind of meaning to the idea of *philia* by sustaining that 'society depends on friendship – after all, people will not even take a journey in common with their enemies' (*Pol* IV.10.1295b23-25). According to Aristotle, 'it is thought to be the special business of the political art to produce *philia*, and people say that excellence is useful because of this, for those who are unjustly treated by one another cannot be friends to one another' (*EE*.VIII.1.1234b22-25).

There are also several other passages where Aristotle stresses the aforementioned point. For example, in *NE*.IX.9.1166a1-10, where he discusses the origins of *philia* relations towards our neighbours and where he specifies the ways that we distinguish the various kinds of *philia* in relation to ourselves, Aristotle points out that

> some people define a friend as someone who wishes and does what is good, or what appears to be good, for the sake of his/her friend; or someone who wishes his/her friend to be and to live for his/her own sake – this is the attitude of mothers toward their children, or friends who have come into conflict. Others define a friend as someone who spends time with another and chooses the same things as s/he does; or someone who shares in the sorrows and joys of his/her friend – and this quality too is found in mothers in particular.

But, as Aristotle points out in *NE*.IX.4.1166b 30-1167a 3, goodwill (εὔνοια / *eunoia*), although it seems to be a characteristic of *philia*, it still is not friendship, since goodwill can arise even towards people we do not know and without them being aware of it, but friendship cannot. In this sense, goodwill is not even affection (φίλησις/*philēsis*), since *philēsis* involves intimacy, while *eunoia* can spring up suddenly.

Aristotle's distinction between the three kinds of friendship is well known: *philia* that arises from (a) excellence or goodness (*aretē* or *agathon*), (b) pleasantness (*ēdu*) and (c) usefulness (*chrēsimon*) (*NE*.VIII.2.1156b27 and *EE*.VIII.9.1236a32), which are better understood when we, first, come to know the object of love (*philēton*); 'for not everything seems to be loved but only the lovable, and this is good, pleasant, or useful', and for people 'to be friends, then, they must be mutually recognised as bearing goodwill and wishing well to each other for one of the aforesaid reasons' (*NE*. VIII.1.1155b17-1156a5). Corresponding to the object of love, there are three kinds of friendship equal in number to the things that are lovable (*NE*.VIII.6.1158a6-10). The different reasons for loving someone depend on whether one loves them for their utility, their pleasantness, or their goodness or their excellence (*NE*.VIII.2.1156a10-24). 'Excellence-based friendship' is the friendship of people who are good, and alike in goodness; such friends wish well alike to each other *qua* good, and they are good in themselves (*NE*.VIII.2.1156b6-8). It is obvious from Aristotle's analysis that, of all three kinds of friendship, excellence-based friendship is the one to be preferred, since this kind of friendship 'is the complete (τέλεια/*teleia*) kind, as it also implies the advantages of the other two kinds (1156b7ff)' (Broadie and Rowe 2002: 409).

Various passages in the *NE* (VIII.1.1155b21-27; VIII.6.1158a9; VIII.3.1166b30-1167a3; VIII.4.1166a1-10; IX.10.1171a5), and the passage in the *Rhetoric* (II.3.1380b36-1381a5), seem to suggest that all three kinds of friendship, including the variety of political friendship that derives from utility or 'common advantage'[12] and aims at the common interest (*to koinē symferon*),[13] entail at least two important constitutive features: affection and an altruistic concern for a friend's good. According to Aristotle, x and y are friends if and only if (1) x and y know each other, (2) x and y have mutual goodwill (*eunoia*) for the other's sake, (3) x and y feel affection (*philia*) for each other, and (4) x and y recognize (2) and (3) (Leontsini 2007: 175).

III 'Living together' as an essential requirement for friendship: *Chronos, kairos* and *philia*

As stated in the beginning of this chapter, my aim is to argue that the 'criterion of time' is not an essential part of the general definition of friendship offered earlier. As mentioned previously, it has often been argued that the criterion of time should also be introduced in reference to the so-called requirements of friendship. Some think that 'living together' is – either for Aristotle or in general – an essential requirement for friendship. But how is 'shared activity' to be understood? And, what exactly does it mean? And, most importantly, how does Aristotle understand it in his analysis of *philia*?

It is true that Aristotle does mention *in passim* that to achieve 'excellence-based friendship' or any other kind of *philia* for that matter, living together and sharing common activities daily is an important requirement. In fact, Aristotle mentions in the *Nicomachean Ethics* that ideally friends should 'spend their days together' or 'go through time together' (*NE*.VIII.3.1157a24, VIII.6.1158a9, IX.10.1171a5), since it is important to achieve a thorough experience of the other's character and habits to have this sort of day-to-day association, if people are to eventually become friends with one another.

It should be noted though that in the two of the three passages just mentioned (*NE*.VIII.6.1158a9 & IX.10.1171a5) Aristotle chooses both times to use the verb συνημερεύειν (*sunemereuein*) ('to spend the day together'), and he chooses to do so when describing cases that the friendship has not yet being fully realized, that is, it has not yet become a 'real' friendship, since in these cases the desire to become friends (to befriend one another) is present (*eunoia*), but this is not enough unless one gets to know the character of the other well and *sunemereuein* is important for a friendship to spring into action and eventually to hopefully flourish. As he says in *NE*.VIII.6.1158a9: 'But such people may bear goodwill (*eunoia*) to each other; for they wish one another well and aid one another in need; but they are hardly friends, because they do not spend their days together (*sunemereuein*) or delight in each other (*chairein allēlois*), and these are thought the greatest marks of friendship.' So, the mention of the 'criterion of time' in this context refers to friendships that have not yet become actual ones; that is, these are not *already* established friendships.

Also, in *NE*.VIII.3.1157a20-30, his reference is to 'excellence-based friendship', the kind of *philia* that he anyway thinks it is very rare to achieve, and that a person should consider himself or herself lucky if s/he manages to acquire even one or the most, if s/he is so lucky, two such friends in her/his lifetime, and the point Aristotle is making there is explicitly about this 'first' kind of friendship:

> But it is natural that such friendships requires time (*chronos*) and familiarity; as the proverb says, people cannot know each other well till they have 'eaten salt

together'; nor can they admit each other to friendship or be friends till each has been found lovable and been trusted by each. Those who quickly show the marks of friendship to each other wish to be friends but are not friends unless they both are lovable and know the fact; for a wish for friendship may arise quickly, but friendship does not.

It is obvious though from the passage just quoted that again in this case Aristotle's point is that for one to be able to acquire 'excellence-based friendship', one needs first to get to know the other well, and that his main point is that this kind of *philia* should be tested over a long period of time: *en pollō chrono dedokimasmenon* (*NE*.VIII.3.115724). Aristotle again is not advocating that friends should spend all their time in constant company. His point is that 'excellence-based friendship' requires the 'test of time' in order to be classified as such.

Nevertheless, it should be pointed out that in Aristotle's account of excellence-based friendship, living together and shared activity are complex. He argues that, although there are three different kinds of friendship, it is still meaningful to ask which of them is best. It can be assumed that one kind of friendship is better than another if it contributes more to a life of virtuous activity. Utility and pleasure-based friendships might indirectly contribute to such a life, but Aristotle would argue that excellence-based friendships are essential to it. It would be difficult, if not impossible, to live a life of virtuous activity if one did not share this with other people of excellent character. So living together is not just a necessary condition of calling someone a friend. Rather, it is an essential part of the good life and Aristotle in effect argues this point in *EN*.IX.9.

One should of course explore what Aristotle means by 'living together' more extensively in excellence-based friendships. It clearly means more than 'living in the same house', and it must include shared activity, but I wonder whether Aristotle's account of excellence-based friendship means more than that, as in *NE*.IX.9 quoted earlier, for example, he seems to envisage a more intense relationship. No doubt, all kinds of friendship require some kind of continuity over time, but this does not mean that friends must always be in one another's company. However, the situation may be different in the case of excellence-based friendships. In *NE*.VIII.3, Aristotle seems to say that these require time, and the distinctive features of this kind of friendship, as described in *NE*.IX.9, require time in a way in which the others don't. Nevertheless, I do not think that this means that even the best kind of friendship requires us to be continuously in one another's company. We could also notice that Aristotle thinks that, when considering whether someone is truly *eudaimōn*, we should look at their life as whole. A truly happy life would include friendships, and these must extend over time, but Aristotle is not committed to saying we must necessarily have lifelong friendships, or that someone who outlives his friends has not had a good life.

But at the same time, in other passages, Aristotle also seems to think that it is not always important for friends (once they have truly become friends of whichever kind) to spend their days together in constant company, since he is suggesting that it is not always necessary that the people that we love will be always with us. It is true that some people find their enjoyment in living in each other's company, and bestow good things on each other, but 'others are asleep or separated by distance, and so do not engage in these activities of friendship, but nevertheless have a disposition to do so; for distance, does not dissolve friendship without qualification, but it does dissolve its activity' (*NE*. VIII.9.1157b5-13). Aristotle also seems to think that it is a rational and appropriate reaction that correctly corresponds to the value of personal affection in a good human life to value people who are dead as well as people who are alive. As he points out in the *Rhetoric*, 'We consider it a virtue in people, if they love their friends equally both present and absent, both living and dead' (*Rhet*.II.4.1381b24-26). But also from the beginning of the *NE* I.8.1099b2-4, Aristotle argues that 'nobody will entirely live well, if he is both solitary and childless; still less, perhaps, if he has terribly bad children or friends, or has good ones who die'.

The 'shared activity' condition for friendship might be a sufficient (and of course a desirable one), but is not a necessary one, in the sense that the 'living together' condition is not necessary for one to be able to be friends with someone. Reciprocal services, mutual contact and joint projects can be pursued, and indeed they often are in most friendships, and especially in the kind of the 'excellence-based friendship' without fully satisfying the 'living together' criterion. Ideally, these shared activities would had been intensified and maybe better performed if it were possible for friends to always live together at each other's company.

Hence, Aristotle's classification of the three types of friendship and the definition of *philia* derived from it is not undermined by the 'living together' criterion. In fact, the way Aristotle describes on various passages the criterion of time is indicative of this. He merely mentions once that 'living together' is important, while he uses phrases such as 'spending time together', of 'sharing lives' and 'of going through time together'. There are occasions (for some many, for others fewer) that arise for friends to 'spend time together' and various ways of 'sharing one's life'.

The mention of *chronos* (time) reveals some further points I would like to raise in this chapter related to *philia* and the 'criterion of time'. As Lambros Couloubaritsis has successfully argued (Couloubaritsis 2016: 167-200; Couloubaritsis 2018: 21-38), it is in fact *kairos* (moment)[14] and not *chronos* that is the 'dominant' notion of 'time' that Aristotle advances in his ethical works.[15] *Chronos* refers to *bios*, while *kairos* refers to *praxis*, and Aristotle's ethics are of course concerned with *praxis*. In addition, wherever Aristotle uses the verb *dein* (δεῖν) in the *Nicomachean Ethics*, it is *kairos* that he is referring to. Especially, in the case that a moral agent is obliged to make moral choices, it is again *kairos* that determines her/his moral choice, since moral choices and especially overriding moral dilemmas cannot be taken at leisure, at the length of time, but one needs to make them instantly at the moment they arise. It is a fact that in the discussion of *philia* in both the *NE* and *EE* Aristotle uses *chronos* (time) and never *kairos*.[16] But, this does not undermine my point about the importance of *kairos*, since *chronos* is the commonly used word for 'passing time together', and Aristotle here follows the common usage of the word *chronos*, being consisted with his endoxic method.

This is so because it is the notion of *kairos* that is implied here, since *kairos* is needed for *eunoia* (good will) as the most important condition for creating a friendship to grow into a true *philia*. That is, friendship can materialize only because of *kairos*, because of our ability to seize on the moment of mutual friendly feeling. Unless one 'seizes the moment' when mutual good will (*eunoia*) arises, then s/he will never develop *eunoia* into *philia*. This is in a way similar to what Michel de Montaigne will later describe in his discussion of friendship in his famous quote: 'If I am pressed to say why I loved him, I feel it can only be explained by replying: "Because it was he; because it was me"' (Montaigne 2004).

It should be noted that this notion of *eunoia* that Aristotle stresses in relation to the very first motivation that might lead us eventually to establish a friendship is important for not only Aristotelian philosophy but also as far as our general understanding of human relations in general as it is at play in our everyday activities. Aristotle is quite right to relate *eunoia* to *kairos*, and this is apparent in numerous everyday examples. I will merely mention a few here, so as to illustrate my point further. For example, why is it that, when one watches a political debate or a talk show on television consisting of a panel of speakers, s/he does not really know personally or might even never have come across them before, one suddenly starts supporting the x or y speaker and not someone else? It is because one takes a liking, a goodwill, towards this person, maybe because one likes her/his mannerism, her/his face, the way the speaker is dressed, or her/his political ideas of course and the arguments s/he presents.[17] This is precisely the function of *eunoia*. This is mere *eunoia* that it is unlikely to lead to friendship. But in other cases it does. If I attend or present a paper at a conference, there are many colleagues I will meet for the first time, without ever meeting them before in my life, but I will not of course develop *eunoia* towards all of them. Even with the ones that I will feel immediate good will towards them and enjoy their company throughout the conference, for us to continue our communication and to eventually develop a friendship, it would require for both of us to acquire mutual goodwill and friendly feeling and affection in order for our relation to turn into friendship, and especially an 'excellence-based friendship'. But the fact that I met this person at a conference was of course merely accidental since for whatever reasons one of us might not had been able to attend it. Hence the notion of *kairos* is vital in these cases. It was merely *kairos* and *eunoia* that eventually turned us into friends.

Having produced this argumentation, one should not take lightly though the excellence-based friendship, the 'primary' or 'virtue' friendship that is based on *aretē* (Price 1989: 103–30). One should also take into account seriously that the 'criterion of time' might be a necessary condition for excellence-based friendships, since Aristotle is not simply concerned with the necessary or sufficient conditions for calling someone a friend. At *NE*.VIII.1.1115b13-15, he argues that, although there are three different kinds of friendship, it is still meaningful to ask which of them is the best. It is obvious that for Aristotle, a kind of *philia* is better if it contributes more to a life of virtuous activity. Utility and pleasure-based friendships might indirectly contribute to such a life, but Aristotle would argue that excellence-based friendships are essential to it. It would be difficult, if not impossible, to live a life of virtuous activity if one did not share this with other people of excellent character. Therefore, sharing activities together is not just a necessary condition of calling someone a friend. It is an essential part of the good life. These points are relevant to the questions about 'going through time together'. No doubt, all kinds of friendship require some kind of continuity over time, but this does not mean that friends must always be in one another's company. However, the situation may be different in the case of excellence-based friendships, since in *NE*.

VIII.3, Aristotle seems to say that these require time. One could argue, however, that the distinctive features of this kind of friendship, as described in *NE*.IX.9, require time in a way in which the others do not. However, it does not mean that even the best kind of friendship requires us to be continuously in one another's company. We could also notice that Aristotle thinks that, in considering whether someone is truly *eudaimōn*, we must look at their life as whole. A truly happy life would include friendships, and these must extend over time, but Aristotle is not committed to saying we must have lifelong friendships, or that someone who outlives his friends has not had a good life,[18] like in the passages I presented previously.[19]

IV Conclusion

The many examples referring to erotic love (*erōs*)[20] in the *Nicomachean Ethics* that Aristotle puts forward in his discussion of *philia* support even more the aforementioned point on *eunoia*, *kairos* and *philia*, as well as my overall argument that the 'criterion of time' should not be considered as an essential requirement of friendship. There are two important passages that are crucial to the understanding of *philia* in relation to time (*kairos*). The first is found in the *Nicomachean Ethics*, where Aristotle, while comparing *erōs* with *philia*, describes the pleasure that we experience from the view of the object of our love but also the crystallization of our love for that person when we desire her or her/his presence independently on whether this person is absent:

> Goodwill seems, then, to be a beginning of friendship, as the pleasure of the eye is the beginning of love. For no one loves if he has not first been delighted by the form of the beloved, but he who delights in the form of another does not love her/him, but only does so when he/she also longs for her/him when absent and craves for her/his presence. (*NE* IX.5.1167a3-8)

A second similar passage is found in the *Rhetoric*: 'Indeed, it is always the first sign of love, that besides enjoying some one's presence, we remember her/him when she/he is gone; and we love when we actually feel pain because she/he is not there no longer' (*Rhet* I.11.1370b16-22).

Both passages clearly indicate that distance, that is, absence from one other's company, is a vital element for the creation of both *philia* and *erōs*. Hence, distance is an important aspect of love and friendship, not only for its establishment but also vis-à-vis its sustainability. Once people are friends, 'spending time together' is of course a most desirable condition as well, but not a necessary one. Friendship can certainly survive the 'test of time', and, especially if it does, it is then proven to be a genuine kind of *philia*, and sometimes even one of the supreme kinds, that of 'excellence-based' one. To repeat it once again, 'going through time together' therefore is not an essential element of Aristotle's general definition of friendship and the 'criterion of time' should not be taken literally as 'living together' in a continuous and uninterrupted way, but should be understood in a much broader sense if Aristotle's account of *philia* is to have any standing at all.

Notes

I am greatly indebted to Richard Stalley for providing me with extensive comments, textual evidence and valuable insights on the final draft of this chapter, and of course for his excellence-based *philia*, which he has so generously and ἀφειδῶς provided me for so many years. I am also grateful to Lambros Couloubaritsis for offering me useful points and bibliography on the notion of *kairos* in Aristotle. For insightful discussions and helpful comments on the first and final version of this chapter, I am also greatly indebted to Andrius Bielskis.

1. Abbreviations: *NE* (*Nicomachean Ethics*), *EE* (*Eudemian Ethics*), *Pol* (*Politics*), *Rhet* (*Rhetoric*). Translations from Aristotle's *Nicomachean Ethics* and *Politics* are from Ross (1980) and Stalley (1995) respectively, and the translations of Aristotle's other works are from Barnes (1984), with many alterations of my own. I will be indicating when the translation is solely my own.
2. The translation is mine.
3. In a similar way, Elizabeth Telfer, in her influential paper on friendship, which had re-opened the discussion on friendship in analytic philosophy, refers to the 'shared activity' condition for friendship, arguing that there are three types of activity which are all necessary conditions of friendship (the 'shared activity' condition for friendship): (a) reciprocal services, (b) mutual contact and (c) joint pursuits (Telfer 1971: 223–4).
4. According to the definition of Aristotelian *philia* that I have formulated, for Aristotle x and y are friends iff: (1) x and y know each other, (2) x and y have mutual goodwill for the other's sake , (3) x and y feel affection for each other, and (4) x and y recognize (2) and (3). (Leontsini 2007: 175).
5. This is a point I owe to Richard Stalley.
6. In the same way, as Annas has pointed out, 'Aristotle's account of personal friendship can be seen as trying to answer the questions raised in Plato's *Lysis* concerning the altruistic nature of friendship and the relation between liking and thinking good' (Annas 1977: 532–54).
7. In fact, all of *NE*.VIII.8 is dedicated to the importance of loving than being loved.
8. Yack (1993: 110) labels Aristotelian political or civic friendship as 'shared advantage friendship' and Leontsini (2013) as 'common advantage friendship', but in all the Aristotelian texts, the word used is 'interest' (*supheron*), which is the word I believe to be the correct one, translation wise, but also philosophically wise.
9. For clarifying this potential criticism with which I disagree with, I am indebted to Andrius Bielskis who raised it to me in our discussions.
10. For having the opportunity to address this serious criticism, I am grateful to Richard Stalley who raised it in his comments to the first draft of my chapter.
11. I have argued elsewhere that this also applies to Aristotle's notion of *politikē philia* as well (Leontsini 2013b: 21–35).
12. For an analysis of political friendship as 'common advantage friendship' (Leontsini 2013b: 25–9). Although almost all English translators of Aristotle's works translate Aristotle's notion of '*to koinē symferon*' as 'common advantage', and in the aforementioned chapter, I have also adopted this translation and, hence, interpretation, I now believe that this translation is misleading and unfair towards the Aristotelian text, since 'advantage' does not accurately attribute neither the ancient meaning of the Greek word nor Aristotle's intentions. It is apparent

throughout the *Politics* (esp. Bks I-IV) and in both the *Nicomachean Ethics* the *Eudemian Ethics* that Aristotle uses the term '*to koinē symferon*' consistently to denote that in a political community, no matter what its constitution is (provided it is not a deviant one), the people who rule should always do so having in mind the 'interest of the others' ('*to eteron symferon*', *HN*.V.I.1130a1), that is, 'concern for others', the very same idea which is dominant in his discussion of *philia* in the *Nicomachean Ethics*. See also note 13.

13 'Common' or 'public' or 'general' interest or 'interest' in general is neither quoted nor discussed at length very often in the *NE* : 'Interest' is referred in some places in the *NE* such as *kalon* and *ūdū* (*NE* 1104b31), *kalon* (*NE*1168a12), *kalon* (*NE* 1140α29 & 1127a5), *agathon* (*NE* 1140α27), *to allō* (*NE* 1130a5), to *eautō* (*NE* 1141b5 & 1160b2), *to paron* (*NE* 1134b35, *to kata symferon* (*NE*1134b35), *to syferon diōkein* (*NE*1156a27), *ta symferonta agnoein* (*NE* 1110b27), *to antixoun symferon* (*NE*.1155b5) *to dokoun symferon kai to kalon* (*NE* 1169a6). It should be noted that in all the aforementioned cases, the term 'interest' is always quoted in relation to that of the 'common or public interest', either in a positive way (as in the case of good, *agathon*) or in contrast of that of the public interest (as in all other cases when Aristotle is usually referring to the notion of personal interest which aims at personal non-altruistic gain and not self-preservation).
14 It should be noted here that the importance of the notion of *kairos* in Ancient Greek philosophy in general has been made prominent in contemporary philosophy and ancient scholarship by the extensive research conducted by Evanghélos Moutsopoulos in numerous papers and books he has published over the years (Moutsopoulos 2007; Moutsopoulos 2010).
15 It should be noted that the notion of time in Aristotle's *Physics* is only that of *chronos* and not of *kairos*, unlike for example in the Sophists or in Plato (Couloubaritsis 2016: 168–73).
16 *Kairos*, that is, seizing the moment, implies of course that there is a right time for something and that one seizes it (in the way we seize the opportunity when the right moment for doing something is there) rather than remain passive and do nothing (i.e. not acting on the opportunity). This is a point for which I am grateful to Andrius Bielskis for drawing my attention to it.
17 This is an example that was provided to me by Lambros Couloubaritsis.
18 As I pointed out previously, Aristotle argues that 'nobody will entirely live well, if he is both solitary and childless; still less, perhaps, if he has terribly bad children or friends, or has good ones who die' (*NE*.I.8. 1099b2-4).
19 For this paragraph, which raises the point regarding excellence-based friendships, I am greatly indebted to the extensive comments that Richard Stalley kindly provided me.
20 For the connection between *erōs* and *kairos*, see Moutsopoulos (1989: 15–19).

Bibiography

Annas, J. (1977), 'Plato and Aristotle on Friendship and Altruism', *Mind*, 86: 532–54.
Annas, J. (1993), *The Morality of Happiness*, Oxford: Oxford University Press.
Aristotle (1980), *Nicomachean Ethics*, trans. D. Ross, Oxford: Oxford University Press.
Aristotle (1995), *The Politics*, trans. Ernest Barker, revised by R. F. Stalley, Oxford: Oxford University Press.

Aristotle (2002), *Nicomachean Ethics*, trans. intro & commentary by S. Broadie and C. Rowe, Oxford: Oxford University Press, 2002.
Barnes J., ed. (1984), *The Complete Works of Aristotle*, 2 vols., Princeton: Princeton University Press.
Blundell, M. (1989), *Helping Friends and Harming Enemies: A Study in Sophocles and Greek Ethics*, Cambridge: Cambridge University Press.
Cooper, J. (1999), *Reason and Emotion*, Princeton, NJ: Princeton University Press.
Couloubaritsis, L. (2016), 'La question du temps dans l'*Éthique à Nicomaque*', in D. Sfendoni-Mentzou (ed.), *Le temps chez Aristote*, 167–200, Paris: Vrin-Ousia.
Couloubaritsis, L. (2018), 'L'organisation complexe du temps chez Aristote', in E. Moutsopoulos and M. Protopapas-Marneli (eds), *Aristotle: Timeless and Scientific Timely*, 21–38, Athens: Academy of Athens.
Guthrie, W. K. C. (1981), *A History of Greek Philosophy VI. Aristotle: An Encounter*, Cambridge: Cambridge University Press.
Hughes, G. J. (2001), *Aristotle on Ethics*, London: Routledge.
Konstan, D. (1996), 'Greek Friendship', *The American Journal of Philology*, 117 (1): 71–94.
Konstan, D. (1997), *Friendship in the Classical World*, Cambridge: Cambridge University Press.
Leontsini, E. (2007), *The Appropriation of Aristotle in the Liberal-Communitarian Debate*, with a foreword by R. F. Stalley, Athens: National and Kapodistrian University of Athens, Saripolos Library.
Leontsini, E. (2013a), 'Sex and the City: Plato, Aristotle, and Zeno of Kition on *Erôs* and *Philia*', in E. Sanders, C. Thumiger, C. Carey and N. J. Lowe (eds), *Erôs in Ancient Greece*, 129–41, Oxford: Oxford University Press.
Leontsini, E. (2013b), 'The Motive of Society: Aristotle on Civic Friendship, Justice, and Concord', *Res Publica*, 19 (1): 21–35.
Leontsini, E. (2015), 'Justice and Moderation in the State: Aristotle and Beyond', in Guttorm Fløistad (ed.), *Philosophy of Justice*, 27–42, Heidelberg: Springer.
Mitchell L. G. (2002), *Greeks Bearing Gifts: The Public Use of Private Relationships in the Greek World, 435-323BC*, Cambridge: Cambridge University Press.
Montaigne, Michel de ([1580] 2004), *On Friendship*, trans. M. A. Screech, London: Penguin.
Moutsopoulos, E. (1989), 'Éros kairos', *Revue Philosophique de la France et de l'Étranger*, 179 (1): 15–19.
Moutsopoulos, E. (2007), *Kairicité et liberté*, Athens: Academy of Athens.
Moutsopoulos, E. (2010), *Reflets et résonances du kairos*, Athens: Academy of Athens.
Nehamas, A. (2016), *On Friendship*, New York: Basic Books.
Nussbaum, M. (1986), *The Fragility of Goodness: Luck and Ethics in Greek Tragedy and Philosophy*, Cambridge, MA: Harvard University Press.
Pakaluk, M. (2005), *Aristotle's Nicomachean Ethics: An Introduction*, Cambridge: Cambridge University Press.
Price, A. (1989), *Love and Friendship in Plato and Aristotle*, Oxford: Clarendon Press.
Schofield, M. (1999), 'Political Friendship and the Ideology of Reciprocity', in M. Schofield, *Saving the City*, London: Routledge: 82–99.
Schollmeier, P. (1994), *Other Selves: Aristotle on Personal and Political Friendship*, Albany: State University of New York Press.
Sherman, N. (1991), *The Fabric of Character: Aristotle's Theory of Virtue*, Oxford: Oxford University Press.

Stern-Gillet, S. (1995), *Aristotle's Philosophy of Friendship*, Albany: State University of New York Press.
Telfer, E. (1971), 'Friendship', *Proceedings of the Aristotelian Society*, 71: 223–4.
Urmson, J. O. (1988), *Aristotle's Ethics*, Oxford: Blackwell.
Yack, B. (1993), *The Problems of a Political Animal*, Berkeley and Los Angeles: University of California Press.

6

Byzantine Thomism

Aristotelianism and Thomas Aquinas' reception in Byzantium

Athanasia Glycofrydi-Leontsini

Introduction

In this chapter, I will discuss the importance of the translation of Latin works (Glycofrydi-Leontsini 2003: 175–85) for the formation of late Byzantine philosophical and theological debates, and especially the substantial interest in Thomas Aquinas among the Byzantines that led to the formation of Byzantine Thomism, a historical movement connected with the intellectual and diplomatic contacts between Byzantines and Latins in the fourteenth century, the century before the Union of Florence (1439) and the Fall of the Byzantine Empire to the Ottoman Turks (1453). I shall focus on the reception of Thomas Aquinas in Byzantium and the contribution of Demetrius Cydones to the formation of the first Byzantine School of Thomism in the East. Especially, I shall discuss Demetrius Cydones' translation into Greek of three of the four sections of Thomas Aquinas' *Summa Theologica*, and I will present the *editio princeps* of the *Secunda Secundae*, which I have undertaken some years ago under the auspices of the research project directed by academician professor emeritus Evanghélos Moutsopoulos to edit from the manuscripts and to publish the most philosophical part of Aquinas work in which there is a synthesis of Aristotelian 'virtue ethics' with Christian 'law ethics'.

I Philosophical and theological controversies in late Byzantium

In the two final centuries of the Byzantine Empire, the so-called Palaiologan period (1261–1453), a troubled but culturally brilliant period characterized as the Byzantine Renaissance, a group of outstanding scholars such as Theodore Metochites, Nikephoros Gregoras, Nikephoros Choumnos, Georgios Pachymeres, Maximus Planudes, Cardinal Vasilius Bessarion, Georgios Gemistos Plethon and Georgios Gennadios

Scholarios, among others, produced original works in philosophy and science; all these thinkers believed in the value and utility of ancient civilization and its achievements, and led to the development of Byzantine humanism, a movement that spread from Constantinople, the capital, to other centres such as Thessaloniki and Mystras, which had many features in common with the Italian humanism of the Renaissance (Graig 2000: 160-5).

At the final phase of Byzantine philosophy, which coincided with the end of the empire, a philosophical controversy took place over the primacy of Plato and Aristotle, the two main ancient philosophers, which marked a revival of Byzantine philosophical thought (Karamanolis 2003: 253-80). The debate started in 1439 when Georgios Gemistos, the so-called Plethon (1355/60–c.1452),[1] a scholar, who had the benefit of an excellent education, and have established in Mystras a kind of a Platonic Academy, travelled to Florence as a participant in the Council of Union (Dendrinos 2007: 135-52).[2] In Florence, he delivered a series of lectures on Plato which had a great impact on the Latin intellectuals, and reinvigorated Greek studies in Renaissance Italy. During his stay in Florence, he published his short work Περὶ ὧν Ἀριστοτέλης πρὸς Πλάτωνα διαφέρεται (De differentiis) (Lagarde 1973: 312-43)[3] in which he criticized Aristotle's philosophy comparing it with Plato's philosophy, focusing on Aristotle's differences from Plato in different topics concerning logic, the soul and the intellect, ethics, the fifth element, Aristotle's conception of teleology, causality and determinism and motion. At the beginning of his treatise he draws a contrast between the ancient philosophical tradition which preferred Plato, and the Western philosophical tradition, especially the Scholastics, who, following Averroes, defended the great merit of Aristotle's philosophy (Karamanolis 2003: 261). Plethon was a student of Demetrius Cydones, and it is not inappropriate to say that he knew Cydones' translations of *Summa contra Gentiles* and *the Summa Theologica* (Demetracopoulos 2001). Shortly after the publication of *De differentiis*, in the last half of 1443 or the first half of 1444, Georgios Scholarios, a layman who ran a school of philosophy in Constantinople in the 1420s and 1430s, devoted to Aristotle and an admirer of Aquinas,[4] defended Aristotle against Plato in his work Κατὰ τῶν Πλήθωνος ἀποριῶν ἐπ' Ἀριστοτέλει, a treatise usually mentioned as *Contra Plethonem* (Petit, Jugie & Siderides 1928-36: 1-118); he argues that 'the Platonic commentators in late antiquity maintained that Platonic and Aristotelian philosophy are quite compatible and rather complementary' (Karamanolis 2003: 262), and thinks that Plethon misrepresents the Ancients and ancient Platonism. On the other hand, Scholarios claims that 'Plethon represents a special kind of Platonism, namely that of Proclus' (Karamanolis 2003: 268). He also thinks that Plethon had a limited understanding of Plato, and that his aim was to present Platonic philosophy as being closer to Christian views. Plethon replied, criticizing further Aristotle's philosophy in his work Πρὸς τὰς Σχολαρίου περὶ Ἀριστοτέλους ἀντιλήψεις, that can be mentioned as *Contra Scholarii* (Maltese 1988), as well as Scholarios, whom he accused for lack of understanding of the Aristotelian views.

Other intellectuals offered their contribution in this philosophical debate. I should mention here the fact that Aristotle's philosophy enjoyed in Byzantium a remarkable revival in the eighth, ninth and tenth centuries, and again from the eleventh century onwards. In the eleventh century, Michael Psellos inaugurated a period of long discussions among the followers of Plato and Aristotle, which were passed from Byzantium to the West (Tatakis 1977: 139). Actually, in the tenth century, the Byzantines started the discussion on the primacy of Plato and Aristotle and contributed to the renaissance of the classical studies regarding philosophy (Tatakis 1977: 116–119 and 133–5). In fact, the debate on the merits of Platonic or Aristotelian philosophy in the two last centuries of Byzantine history (fourteenth and fifteenth centuries) contributed to the widening of the philosophical communication between the Byzantines and the Westerners. In the fifteenth century, Scholarios, who became the first patriarch under Ottoman Rule, defended Aristotle and established him as the standard philosophical authority of the Orthodox Church. In his study of Aristotle's works, he shows Aquinas' influence (Livanos 2006; Plested 2012; Podskalsky 1974: 305–23) as he adopts the Scholastic method of a philosophical commentary. He spent many years translating, summarizing, and commenting on Aquinas' works, and often preferred to translate Aquinas' commentaries on the Aristotelian works rather than write new ones (Karamanolis 2003: 268–9). In addition, it should be mentioned that the Scholastics had adopted Aristotle's philosophy, while for centuries Aristotelianism was part of the official ideology of the Orthodox Church (Karamanolis 2003: 280).

There were other scholars involved in the philosophical debate on whether Plato or Aristotle was more important (Karamanolis 2003: 280). These were Matthew Kamariotes, Theodore Gazes, Michael Apostoles and Andronikos Kallistos to name but a few. The most bitter in the whole controversy was George Trapezountios, conventionally termed 'George of Trebizond' (1395–1472/3), who wrote a treatise in Latin called *Comparationes philosophorum Aristotelis et Platonis,* published in 1458, in which he praised Aristotle and criticized Plato. Cardinal Bessarion, an ardent Platonist, responded in 1469 with his polemical work *In calumniatorem Platonis,* in which he took an intermediary position between Platonists and Aristotelians (Tatakis 1977: 261–84). The Byzantine scholars were engaged in discussions concerning their philosophical tradition and in re-reading the ancient texts and their commentators. From the middle of the fourteenth century onwards, the discussions focused mostly on which philosophy was closer to the Christian doctrine – Plato's or Aristotle's – but the debate progressed in favour of Aristotle, who was eventually established as the philosophical authority of the Orthodox Church (Mohler 1942).

At that time, the Latin influences on Greek intellectuals were strong as the Cydones brothers continued to translate Latin texts of Augustine, Aquinas, Hervaeus Natalis and others into Greek (Ebbesen 2003: 15–30 and 27). In theology, the Latin influences are apparent in the Hesychast debate of the 1330s between Barlaam of Calabria and his opponent Gregory Palamas, and later in the Palamite and anti-Palamite debate. In the fourteenth century, the Hesychast debate between Nikephoros Gregoras (1290/3–1358/61), Barlaam of Calabria (*c.*1290–1348) and Gregorios Palamas (*c.* 1296–1359) and his followers led to a great theological controversy (Tatakis 1977: 243–61).

Hesychasm, related to a specific type of monastic praying, led the physical experience of the divine energy through the so-called silent prayer (Ebbesen 2003: 26). Hesychasm is characterized as the anti-logical movement in the fourteenth century (Ierodiakonou 2003: 219–36), and was a movement associated with Thessaloniki that had a considerable impact on Byzantine philosophy and mainly on the survival of Orthodoxy. The controversy over Hesychasm derives from the Greek word ἡσυχία (*hesuchia*), whose meaning is tranquillity or inner stillness, and it culminated in Gregory Palamas being in opposition to the Scholastic Barlaam the Calabrian (1337–1341) concerning the method of prayer and contemplation of the Byzantine monks who claimed to be able to achieve communion with God through inner quietude and silence.

This debate was mainly about theological issues concerning the existence of God and his divine attributes, about philosophical issues concerning discussions on logic, and the differences between Platonism and Aristotelianism; it was also connected with politics, especially as far as the relations between the Byzantine State and the Latin West, as this debate had also a certain impact on the attempts to bring about the Union of the Churches. Gregoras had a strong opposition to Aristotelian syllogistic. He tried to persuade the Byzantines not to take part in discussions with the Latin theologians, criticizing them because they were using Aristotle's syllogisms. He believed that a purified intellect in the state of grace had no need of Aristotle's syllogisms.

In addition, Barlaam and Palamas also discussed about the use of Aristotelian logic to prove the Christian dogma and whether it was appropriate to use Aristotelian logic in theology. They also discussed about God's substance and his divine energies. Barlaam claimed that we were able to know God's divine attributes by using dialectical syllogisms based on the doctrines of the Bible scriptures and divinely inspired theories of ancient philosophy about the created world, while Palamas claimed that logical demonstrations, based on the revealed wisdom of the Christian Fathers, should be used to prove the Christian dogmas about God's attributes. According to him, it is faith and grace, and not the rationality of pagan philosophy, that plays a significant role in our attempts to understand God himself. The Palamas–Barlaam dispute, although grown out of an important theological issue, soon became a question concerning the use of Aristotelian logic in theology (Ierodiakonou 2003: 228).[5] In the end, Barlaam's works and his treatment of logic were appreciated by the Cydones brothers, Demetrius and Prochorus, who translated Aquinas' *Summa contra Gentiles* and *Summa Theologica* (Prochorus translated the *Tertia Pars*), all of which were re-examined by Byzantine scholars like Cardinal Bessarion and Scholarios. It is not wrong to claim that Hesychasm actually grew out of two basic metaphysical controversies: (a) Can there be a distinction between God's essence and His attributes that are 'real'?, and (b) Is the light that is perceived in contemplation the same as that on Mount Tabor, and is that light created and temporal or increate and eternal?

The Thomists and anti-Thomists debate in the middle of the fourteenth century should be characterized as a reaction towards the Latin influences on Greek intellectuals; Demetrius Cydones, chief minister of the Emperor John Cantacuzene (1347–1354), although deeply interested in theological issues from a philosophical standpoint, did not enter in a debate with the Hesychasts. His hostility to Palamism on philosophical matters was strengthened by his discovery of Thomas Aquinas who, according to him, knew Plato and Aristotle better than the Greeks themselves. His younger brother Prochorus, a monk on Mount Athos and the leader of the anti-Hesychast faction in the 1360s, challenged Palamism from a Thomist viewpoint and developed the patristic argumentation using a Thomist method of argumentation (Russell 2003:

153). Prochorus' anti-Palamite activities led to his trial and condemnation in 1368, and after that event, Demetrius Cydones was involved in the anti-Palamite debate and seemed to be the leader of the opponents of Palamism. Demetrius Cydones and his followers turned to study Aquinas' works in order to discuss the place of philosophical knowledge and ethics in Christian thought and life. Between 1354 and 1368, Demetrius Cydones wrote the treatise *De personarum proprietatibus in Trinitate ad Constantinum Asanem* in which he discusses the simplicity of God, an anti-Palamite theme, and argues, following Saint Thomas' rational arguments, that the distinctions between the substance and the attributes of God are not real but merely conceptual. While the Hesychasts gave an independent existence to the attributes, Cydones argued that God's attributes such as wisdom are not separate entities from God himself. He also states that 'the properties of fatherhood and sonship, aspiration and procession are of a different kind from the other attributes and have a real existence, not as properties qualifying a subject but as relations within the Godhead: these real relations are the subsistent divine Persons' (Russell 2002: 153–174 and 157, f. 21, 22, 23, 24). The anti-Palamite debate on theological matters has its merits, and Byzantine Thomism, exercised for years by Demetrius Cydones' pupils, made important contributions to metaphysics, especially in questions concerning the divine constitution, and God's attributes in relation to his essence.

II *Contacts between Byzantines and Latins in the fourteenth century*

One of the most noteworthy examples of these contacts is the diplomatic and scholarly career of Demetrius Cydones (Kianka 1981; Ryder 2010), who flourished in the latter half of a turbulent century marked by destructive civil wars, social unrest, urban violence and defeats at the hands of the Ottoman Turks. It was also a period of intellectual ferment from within, such as the Hesychast controversy and new currents of thought from without, such as Thomism and Scholasticism. Of these, the best known was the theological method and synthesis of Thomas Aquinas, introduced to Byzantium in the 1350s and 1360s by the translations of Demetrius Cydones and his brother Prochorus. The influence of Thomas Aquinas on the Cydones brothers and their followers was strong, and it spread through the intellectual milieu of Constantinople. The pro-Thomists' and anti-Thomists' debate is an intellectual and theological controversy of the age, which had a certain impact on the internal Byzantine controversy over the theology of Gregory Palamas, the defender of the Hesychasts monks, and was related to the far-reaching problem of the relations with the Latin church. Demetrius Cydones' high esteem for Aquinas' scholastic doctrines and his use of dialectical argumentation in theology is explicitly expressed in his *Correspondence*, his *Apology* and in his *Defense of Thomas Aquinas*. Aquinas' understanding of Aristotelian philosophy, and his synthesis of Aristotelian philosophy and Christian doctrine was brought to Byzantium mainly by Demetrius Cydones' translations of his major and best-known works, the *Summa contra Gentiles* and the *Summa Theologica*. Thomas' philosophical influence was prolonged in the East until the eighteenth century. Generally speaking, the Latin influence on Greek intellectuals from the eleventh century onwards was apparent, especially through the Greek translations of Latin texts (Ebessen 2003: 25–8; Benakis 1996: 35–47).

Demetrius Cydones (c.1324–c.1397/8) held the position of Mesazōn from 1347 to 1354 and served successfully the Palaiologan emperors John V and Manuel II; his younger brother Prochorus (1333/4–1369/70), a monk at Mount Athos and the leader of the anti-Hesychast faction in the 1360s (his activities brought him a notoriety that led to his trial and condemnation in 1368); and Demetrius' 'Latinophron' companions, Manuel Kalekas, Andreas and Maximus Chrysoberges, who went to Italy and were among the early bearers of Greek culture to the Italian Renaissance, as well as later figures such as Cardinal Bessarion, who considered Saint Thomas 'an effective successor of the Aristotelian school' (Papadopoulos 1974: 113), and Gennadius Scholarios, an ardent Aristotelian, were all attracted by Thomistic thought, which spread in Byzantium through Demetrius Cydones' translations and defences of Aquinas (Glycofrydi-Leontsini 1975: 429–32).

Actually, this small but vigorous minority made efforts to persuade their countrymen of the merits of Thomism and of the importance of the political and religious rapprochement with the Latin world (Jugie 1928: 385–402; Papadopoulos 1974: 274–304; Tym 1974: 837–912; Kianka 1981: 264–86).[6] Demetrius Cydones in particular was able to inspire a first period of Scholasticism in the East that endured, until it was forcibly crushed by Orthodox religious and secular authorities towards the end of the fourteenth century. Demetrius Cydones' opposition to Palamism on account of its incompatibility with the scholastic philosophical tradition was strengthened by his discovery of Thomas Aquinas, who seemed to him to have a better grasp of Plato and Aristotle than did the Greeks themselves (Glycofrydi-Leontsini 1975: 429–32). Cydones showed little personal interest in Aquinas' most purely philosophical works, the commentaries on Aristotle, none of which he translated. Instead, it was Aquinas' use of philosophy in works of theology that won his approval and admiration. Cydones recognized the superiority of Aquinas over the 'Greek wisdom' because he was arguing philosophically for the truth of the Christian faith, while Plato and Aristotle argued for the truth of pre-Christian concepts which were now superseded by divine revelation. Demetrius' great attraction to the works of Aquinas was based on Aquinas' affirmation of the basic validity of Greek philosophy in a Christian context that helped him towards solving for himself the controversy over the theology of G. Palamas. In opposition to Palamas' reluctance to admit any positive value to pagan Greek thought in Christian theology, Cydones and other anti-Palamites approved the validity of using a philosophical or speculative method in theology (Kianka 1981: 264–86; Plested 2012).

The translations of Latin texts were of great value to the Greeks in preparing them for the encounter with the Latins at the Council of Florence (1439). Significant theologians, such as Nilus Cabasilas, Joseph Bryennius and, later, Georgios Scholarios, the first Ecumenical Patriarch under Ottoman Rule, learned from the translations of the Cydones brothers the methods of Thomism without compromising their orthodoxy. The benefit derived by the West was much greater, for it was the members of Cydones' circle who led the way in satisfying the new passion in Italy for Greek learning. Manuel

Chrysoloras became the first official teacher of Greek in the West, when in 1397 he accepted a five-year contract from the Florentine Studio to teach Greek grammar and literature. In addition, he and the younger of the Chrysoberges brothers were active in the negotiations for the church union that culminated in 1438-9 in the Council of Florence. The movement that began as a protest against Palamism from within Orthodoxy thus had influential consequences for subsequent relations between the Latin and Greek churches. This sudden expansion of horizons contributed to the turbulence of Byzantine intellectual life in its final days, known as the debate between Thomists and anti-Thomists (Papadopoulos 1976). It led to the compromise attempted later by Georgios Scholarios (c.1400-post 1472), mentioned earlier, who tried to justify Palamas' doctrine of the impossibility of 'seeing' God's 'essence' by appealing to Thomas Aquinas' interpretation of God's vision in the *Quaestiones quodlibetales* (Jean Chortasménos 2000: 397-442). Scholarios, a strong Christian Aristotelian, was the principal defender of the Thomistic fusion of Christian theology with Aristotle in the Byzantine philosophical and theological debates.[7]

III *Demetrius Cydones' encounter with Thomas Aquinas*

Demetrius Cydones was born about 1324 in the city of Thessaloniki and received his education there. Among his teachers was Nilus Cabasilas, who became bishop of Thessaloniki before his death about the year 1363. His family was one of the wealthiest in Thessaloniki, with connections with the imperial court in which Demetrius held an important position for years. His government career spanned nearly for forty years (1347-86), involving three emperors, during which time Demetrius was in and out of key positions in the government, but usually in office. As a government official in Constantinople, he was concerned not merely with day-to-day administrative business of the empire but also with policy-making on the highest level during a time of serious emergency (Kianka 1980: 57-71). During the years of service for John VI (1347-54), his duties at the palace brought him into contact with many Westerners, whose requests to the emperor were channelled through his office. He soon discovered that the official interpreters were not adequate for the task. He decided to learn Latin himself, and with the emperor's approval, he found an excellent teacher in a Dominican friar in Pera, the Genoese colony across the Golden Horn from Constantinople, who came to live with him at the palace. After learning the fundamentals of the language, he started reading from Aquinas' *Summa contra Gentiles*. Charmed by the language, method and mastery of Aristotelian philosophy, he began to translate it into Greek to prove to his friends that the Latins were worth reading. He translated some passages from Thomas Aquinas' *Summa contra Gentiles*, which he read to the emperor, who was so impressed that he urged Demetrius to undertake a translation of this work into Greek, a translation completed on the afternoon of 24 December 1354, which he entitled Τὸ τοῦ Θωμᾶ καθ' Ἑλλήνων βιβλίον. The emperor who had encouraged him to translate this work, saying 'that it would be of great advantage to the cause of the Greeks in the future', had his own copy, and his example was followed by other Byzantine notables. The success of this translation encouraged Demetrius to continue his translating work, and he produced during the next decade a partial translation of Aquinas' *Summa Theologica*, with the help of his brother Prochorus, who completed the translation by translating the *Tertia Pars* of the *Summa Theologica*, and also some smaller treatises (*De aeterminate mundi contra murmurantes*, *De ente et essentia* and the preface of Aquinas' commentary in Aristotle's *Metaphysics*), an Augustinian *florilegium*, Anselm of Canterbury's *De processione Spiritus Sancti*, and various other Latin patristic and scholastic texts. Demetrius Cydones had a political and an intellectual programme that led him to convert to Roman Catholicism around the year 1360 and to pursue of the policy of rapprochement with Western Europe, that, he believed, was the natural and the only possible ally of the faltering empire. The mission to Rome in 1369 with John V in the presence of the Pope was concerned with theological matters, but also with diplomatic negotiations since Demetrius was convinced that Byzantium's only hope for survival was an alliance with the Pope and Western Europe.

Demetrius' translations are all of Latin theological works. Besides Aquinas' *Summa contra Gentiles* and *Summa Theologica*, he translated other minor works by Aquinas (Papadopoulos 1976: 56–64),[8] as well as Augustine's *Soliloquia* and *Sententiae*, and works by Fulgence, Anselm, Pierre de Poitiers and Nicoldi de Monte Croce (Glycofrydi-Leontsini 2003: 184–5). That was due to his interest in the intellectual controversies of his age: on the one hand, the internal Byzantine controversy over the theology of Gregory Palamas, the defender of the Hesychasm monks, and on the other hand the far-reaching problem of relations with the Latin church. Cydones was not a theologian but an educated layman who opposed to Palamism. He had a profound knowledge of the Latin language and of the Greek classical heritage, and through his translating activity, made possible a dynamic dialogue between the Byzantines and the Latins. He was deeply interested in theological issues from a philosophical standpoint and was the first to translate Thomas Aquinas' major works *Summa contra Gentiles* and *Summa Theologica*. After Cydones' discovery of Thomas Aquinas, who seemed to him to have a better grasp of Plato and Aristotle, a group of pro-Thomist scholars was composed who were well informed about Western culture through their reading of Latin literature and their travelling to Western Europe mostly for diplomatic and intellectual reasons.

IV The edition princeps of the Secunda Secundae

My interest in Cydones translations started before the year 1976 when I edited in a critical edition the first book of the *editio princeps* of the *Secunda Secundae* of his *Summa Theologica*, which was based on five principal manuscripts, among the thirty extant codices containing the complete translation (Vaticani Graeci 612 and 611, Parisini Graeci 1235 and 1237, and Oxoniensis Bodleianus Roe Graecus 21). The translation was compared with the Latin text in the following editions: (a) *Thomas Aquinas, Summa Theologica* (edited P. H. M. Christmann et al. (Albertus-Magnus Acedemie: Walberberg bei Koln, 1959, 1960, 1966) and (b) *Saint Thomas Aquinas, Summa Theologiae* (Latin text and English translation, Introductions, Notes, Appendices and Glossaries, edited by T. C. O' Brien, vols. 31 ff. (Blackfriars, London–New York, 1966-75)). It was included in the series *Corpus Philosophorum*

Graecorum Recentiorum under the direction of E. Moutsopoulos (Chortasménos 2000: 397–442; Leontsinis and Glycofrydi-Leontsini 1976). In the course of time, four other volumes appeared (Demetracopoulos and Bretanou 1980; Sideri and Photopoulou 1979; Kalokairinou 2002); more recently vol. 19, edited by A. Glycofrydi-Leontsini and I. D. Spyralatos, was published (Glycofrydi-Leontsini and Spyralatos 2011), while vol. 20, which includes questions 101–122 (Glycofrydi-Leontsini and Spyralatos 2019,) has recently been published in the publication series of the work.

In the introduction of vol. 19, as editors placing the text in the general frame of the *Summa Theologica*, we presented the subject matter of religion and virtue that is treated in the chapters of that volume, and we discussed the manuscripts of the work and Cydones' characteristics as a translator. The text is followed by an apparatus criticus and an apparatus fontium page by page, and the volumes concludes with two indices, the *Index locorum sacrae scripturae* and the *Index nominum and locorum*. In his review of the aforementioned volume, associate professor George Arabatzis considers 'Cydones' translation as belonging to a series of similar works undertaken after the Byzantines' reconquest of Constantinople from the occupying crusaders in 1261, most probably with the desire to understand better the Latin mentality' (Arabatzis 2016: 501–3). G. Arabatzis observes in his review that in the preface of the volume (pp. 7–12)

> E. Moutsopoulos sums up his long-held relevant positions: (I) Kydones's rendition initiates Modern Greek philosophy since it is then and through this translating work that began the introduction of foreign philosophical masterworks into Greek philosophical discourse; (II) the translation is rightly situated as a proper philosophical work since Kydones pursued a middle path between the Latin original and the Aristotelian Greek text that he knew so well, trying to be loyal to both Aquinas and Aristotle. (Arabatzis 2016: 502)

The language of the translation is in scholarly attic Greek that was used at the time by intellectuals in Constantinople. I have argued that Cydones translated Aquinas *ad verbum* with the original text of Aristotle at his side, though occasionally changes in tenses and mood as well as periphrastic language were introduced; many times, he corrected the Aristotelian text, which has been changed in the Latin translation used by Aquinas, as it is apparent in numerous examples that can be found in his translation. In this way, Demetrius provided us with an accurate and readable Greek text (Glycofrydi-Leontsini 2003: 311–19) that clarifies Thomas Aquinas' major contribution towards a better understanding of Aristotle's *Ethics* that is well established in his *Summa Theologica*, especially in his *Secunda Secundae*, in which Aquinas discusses the three theological virtues – faith, hope and charity – and the four cardinal moral virtues – prudence, justice, fortitude and temperance – with their ramifications, and makes a synthesis of Aristotelian 'virtue ethics' with the Christian 'law ethics'. It has been suggested that Aquinas' Aristotelianism, especially insofar as his attempt to transform desire for moral ends is concerned, differs from Aristotle's thought in three ways: *theoria* (θεωρία) becomes that vision of God, which is the goal and satisfaction of human desire; the list of the virtues is modified and extended; and the concepts of the telos and that of the virtues are interpreted in a framework of law which has both

Stoic and Hebrew origins (MacIntyre 1967: 15-16). It is well known that the *Secunda Secundae* contains detailed teaching on individual moral topics and that it was modelled on the *Nicomachean Ethics* on which Thomas worked. Cydones says in his *Apology* that he had not enough time for his translation, and in many cases, he is closer to the original text than to the Latin text as quoted in the *Summa Theologica*. As it is noted, the Latin text 'Nihil enim est ita proprium amicitiae sicut convivere amico' ('Nothing so marks friendship as duelling together') (2a2ae 23, 1) was translated by Cydones as 'οὐδὲν γὰρ οὕτως ἴδιόν ἐστι τῆς ἀγάπης (agape) ὥσπερ τὸ τῷ φίλῳ συζῆν (suzēn)' ('Nothing is more particular to love than living with one's friend') (Cydones 1982: 25), while in the Aristotelian passage we read 'οὐδὲν γὰρ οὕτως ἐστὶ φίλων ὡς τὸ συζῆν' ('Nothing is similar to friends living together') (suzēn), *NE*. IX 6, 1157b19 (Glycofrydi-Leontsini 2003: 181). I should also add that although Aquinas had divided his text into *quaestiones, articuli and objectiones* at the beginning of each chapter, Cydones simply used the word ζήτημα (zētēma) without making further division (Glycofrydi-Leontsini 2003: 179, f.25). He has also translated the medieval and scholastic term *Summa* in the manuscripts of the *prima pars* as σύνοψις (sunopsis) or σύνταξις (suntaxis), while in the *Secunda Secundae* in the titles of the manuscripts added as title Τὰ Ἠθικά/*Ta Ēthika* (Arabatzis 2016: 501-3). As far as Cydones' method of translating *ad verbum* is concerned, it should be pointed out that this was a typical method used by translators of Greek texts that changed during the Renaissance when the Byzantine scholar Manuel Chrysoloras, according to a Florentine student, taught that 'conversion into Latin *ad verbum* was worthless ... a complete perversion of the meaning of the Greek. He [scil. Chrysoloras] said it was necessary to translate *ad sententiam* without changing the character of the Greek in any way' (Glycofrydi-Leontsini 2003, 182, f. 31). Cydones wanted to render an accurate and readable text, and his competence and skill as a translator were highly appreciated by the intellectuals as well as by the Orthodox theologians in Constantinople. I must mention the *didaskalos* Joseph Bryennius, who was acquainted with both Latin language and scholastic thought, who in his works quoted and refuted passages of the *Summa Theologica*. In a letter to Cydones written in 1395 he remarks praising his scholarly qualities: 'The accuracy of his translation (ἑρμηνεία/hermēneia) of the language of the Romans [i.e. Latin] to that of the Greeks, his sense of temperance, humility, modesty, eloquence and elegant voice' (Glycofrydi-Leontsini 2003: 184, f.35).

Overall, Cydones' translations of Thomas Aquinas' texts is important for us to understand the cultural exchange between Byzantium and the Latin West, but at the same time, it helps us better to understand St Thomas position on different topics, and especially his encounter with Aristotelian philosophy. There are many similarities and differences between Aristotle and Aquinas, who, as it is well known, admired Aristotle, referring to him as *illus philosophus* (Owens 1999: 38-59). It is interesting to add the views expressed by the scriber of the MS. Paris. Gr. 1237, f. 1, in the margin: (a) 'εἴθε Θωμᾶ μὴ ἦσθα γεγονὼς ἐν τῇ δύσει ἀλλὰ ἐν τῇ ἀνατολῇ, ἵνα ἦσθα ὀρθόδοξος, καὶ ἵνα ἐφρόνεις καὶ περὶ τῆς ἐκπορεύσεως τοῦ ἁγίου πνεύματος ὀρθῶς, ὡς καὶ περὶ τῶν ἄλλων καλῶς λέγεις' ('I wish Thomas that you were not born in the West but in the East, so as to be a Greek Orthodox Christian, and also so as to believe in the emanation of the Holy Spirit in the right way, in the same way that you speak so rightly about everything else'),[9] and (b) 'οὗτος σοφὸς πλὴν τοῦ εἶναι Λατῖνος καὶ Βαρλααμίτης, μᾶλλον δὲ Βαρλαὰμ Θωμαίτης ἦν καὶ Λατῖνος, τὰ ἄλλα θαυμάσιος' ('This was a wise man, apart from been a Latin and a follower of Barlaam, but probably it was Barlaam that was Thomist and a Latin, but he was in any other respect excellent') (Leontsinis & Glycofrydi-Leontsini 1976: 16, 7–12). Cydones made possible 'L'hellenisation du Thomisme au XIVe siècle' (Moutsopoulos 1975: 131–6) with his translations, and he contributed to the history of Aristotelianism. Yet since he had not written commentaries on the Aristotelian works, there is no evidence to establish whether he was an Aristotelian or a Platonist. I have to add here that the ongoing Plato–Aristotle debate, especially in the fifteenth century, made clear that a variety of interpretations of Platonism and Aristotelianism were at play among Greek scholars such as Bessarion (Karamanolis 2001). Nevertheless, Aristotle was an authority in the East till the seventeenth century as Aristotelianism was introduced in the Greek thought by Theophilos Corydalleus (1572–1646), a Greek scholar who was trained in Rome and Padua, and who participated in the 'back to Aristotle' movement that swept the Latin schools after scholars had seen the disastrous results of the sixteenth-century attempts to get rid of 'the Philosopher' (Ebessen 2003: 27–8).

Notes

1. Gemistos Plethon was born in Constantinople and studied there under Demetrius Cydones, who inspired him with his love of philosophy. He spent the most of his life in Mystras (Peloponnese), one region under Byzantine sovereignty at that time, and served as adviser to the Despots of Morea until the end of his life. In Mystras, he founded a school for advanced philosophical studies and had a selected circle of students; among them were Georgios Scholarios, Ioannis Argyropoulos, Demetrius Chalcocondyles, Basilius Bessarion and Isidore of Kiev. In the Council of Union, he joined a large delegation of clergymen and laymen and participated at the request of Emperor John VIII Palaiologos.
2. After his participation in the Council of Ferrara-Florence (1438–1839), Plethon, who was before in favour of the church union, changed his position.
3. An English translation of this treatise can be found in Woodhouse 1986: 192–214.
4. Scholarios argued strongly for union with the Latin West at the Council of Florence, but returning to Constantinople, he changed his mind and became an anti-unionist; out of favour with the pro-union imperial court, he retired to a monastery, from 1445 to 1453, and wrote pamphlets against the union.
5. The Barlaam–Palamas controversy is well known, and it is important to mention that Barlaam was condemned by the Ecumenical Synod of 1341 and returned to Italy while Palamas became archbishop of Thessaloniki and after his death was declared a saint.
6. Demetrius rejected the traditional Byzantine view that the world was divided into two groups, the Byzantines themselves, who were the heirs of Plato and Aristotle, and everyone else, including the Latins, who were 'barbarians', incapable of any intellectual achievements. For him, the strength of the Byzantine Empire had been broken by the Latin conquest of 1204, and its attempted recovery in the reign of Michael VIII had been undermined by the civil wars and the fourteenth-century Turkish conquests.

7 The history of Christian thought in the East is often presented as a series of controversies: the Christological controversies, the iconoclast controversy, the filioque controversy and the Hesychasm controversy. As far as the philosophical presuppositions that shaped the Eastern Christian world view and the question of where philosophy ends and theology begins within the Eastern context, it is sufficient to note that the authors of this period discuss philosophical issues such as the status and meaning of nature, the relationship between body and soul, the sensible and the intelligible, the interconnection of theory and practice, and above all, the nature of God and the possibility of human communion with the divine. The discussion on *energeia* crystallized a long tradition of Christian thought until the end of the thirteenth century, just before the Hesychast controversy.

8 Demetrius Cydones is reported to also have translated *De rationibus fidei contra Saracenos, Graecos et Armenos ad cantorem Antiochenum, De articulis Fidei et Ecclesiae sacramentis ad archiepiscopum Panormitanum, Devotissima exposition super symbolum apostolorum* (Papadopoulos 1967: 56–64).

9 A similar view is expressed by Scholarios in the margin of cod. Vatic. Gr 433, f. 81 containing the synopsis (ἐπιτομή/epitomē) of the *Prima Secundae* of *Summa Theologiae*: 'Εἴθε, ὦ βέλτιστε Θωμᾶ, μὴ ἐγένου ἐν Ἑσπέρᾳ, ἵνα καὶ εἶχες ἀνάγκην τῶν ἐκτροπῶν τῆς Ἐκκλησίας ἐκείνης ὑπερδικεῖν τῶν τε ἄλλων καὶ ἥν ἐπὶ τῇ τοῦ Πνεύματος ἐκπορεύσει εἶναι τῇ διαφορᾷ τῆς θείας οὐσίας καὶ ἐνεργείας ἐπεπόνθει· ἦ γὰρ ἄν καὶ ἐν τοῖς θεολογικοῖς σου ἀδιάπτωτος ἦσθα ὡς καὶ ἐν τοῖς ἠθικοῖς τούτοις εἶ' (Papadopoulos 1967: 154). Scholarios appreciated Aquinas for his Aristotelianism, whom he associated with Christianity against paganism (Jugie 1935: 517–30).

Bibliography

Arabatzis, G. (2016), *Demetrios Kydones, Thomas Aquinas's Summa Theologica in Greek Language* (Review of vol. XIX. Ed. A. Glycofrydi-Leontsini and I. D. Spyralatos) (Corpus Philosophorum Graecorum Recentiorum, II 19, Athens: Foundation for the Research and the Edition of Modern Greek Philosophy, 2011, 356pp.), *Mediaevistik*, 29: 501–3.

Benakis, L. G. (1996), 'Lateinische Literatur in Byzanz, Ubersetzungen philosophischer Texte', in G. N. Constantinides, N. M. Panagiotales, E. Jeffreys and A. D. Angelou (eds), *Φιλέλλην: Studies in Honour of Robert Browning*, 35–42, Venice: Istituto Ellenico di Studi Bizantinie Postbizantini di Venezia.

Chortasménos, J. (2000), 'L'enseignement de la logique, le tomisme à Byzance', in Willehad Paul Eckert (ed.), *The Greek Manuscripts in the 15th and 16th Centuries*, 397–442, Athens: National Hellenic Research Foundation.

Craig, E. (2000), 'Byzantine Philosophy', *Routledge Encyclopedia of Philosophy*, vol. 2, 160–5, London: Routledge.

Demetracopoulos, J. (2001), *Πλήθων και Θωμάς Ακυινάτης. Από την ιστορία του Βυζαντινού Θωμισμού*, Athens: Parousia.

Dendrinos, C. (2007), 'Reflections on the Failure of the Union of Florence', *Annuarium Historiae Conciliorum*, 39: 135–52.

Ebbesen, S. (2003), 'Greek-Latin Philosophical Interaction', in K. Ierodiakonou (ed.), *Byzantine Philosophy and its Ancient Sources*, 15–30, Oxford: Clarendon Press.

Glycofrydi-Leontsini, A. (1975), 'La traduzione in Greco delle opera di Tommaso d'Aquino', *Nicolaus*, 3: 423–8.

Glycofrydi-Leontsini, A. (2003), 'Demetrius Kydones as a Translator of Latin Texts', in C. Dendrinos, J. Harris, E. Harvalia-Crook and J. Herrin (eds), *Porfyrogenita, Essays on Byzantine History in Honour of Julian Chrysostomides*, 175–85, London: Aldershot.

Ierodiakonou, K. (2003), 'The Anti-Logical Movement in the Fourteenth Century', in K. Ierodiakonou (ed.), *Byzantine Philosophy and Its Ancient Sources*, 219–36, Oxford: Clarendon Press.

Jugie, M. (1928), 'Demetrius Cydonès et la théologie latine à Byzance', *Echos d'Orient*, 27: 385–402.

Jugie, M. (1926–1935), *Theologia* dogmatica christianorum orientalium ab ecclesia catholica dissidentium, 5 vols., Paris: Letouzey et Ané.

Karamanolis, G. (2001), *Plato and Aristotle in Agreement? Platonists on Aristotle from Antiochus to Porphyry*, Oxford: Oxford University Press.

Karamanolis, G. (2003), 'Plethon and Scholarios on Aristotle', in K. Ierodiakonou (ed.), *Byzantine Philosophy and Its Ancient Sources*, 253–80, Oxford: Clarendon Press.

Kazhdan, Alexander P. (1991), *The Oxford Dictionary of Byzantium*, Oxford: Oxford University Press.

Kianka, F. (1980), 'The Apology of Demetrius Kydones. A Fourteenth-Century Autobiographical Source', *Byzantine Studies*, 7: 57–71.

Kianka, F. (1981), 'Demetrius Kydones (c.1324-c.1397): Intellectual and Diplomatic Relations between Byzantium and the West in the Fourteenth Century', PhD thesis, Fordham University, New York.

Kretzmann, N. et alia (1990), *The Cambridge History of Later Medieval Philosophy. From the Rediscovery of Aristotle to the Disintegration of Scholasticism 1100–1600*, Cambridge: Cambridge University Press.

Κυδώνη, Δημητρίου (1976), Θωμά Ακυινάτου Σούμμα Θεολογική εξελληνισθείσα, CPhGR, vol. II. 15, 2a2ae, 1–16, eds. G. Leontsinis and A. Glycofrydi-Leontsini, Athens.

Κυδώνη, Δημητρίου (1979), Θωμά Ακυινάτου Σούμμα Θεολογική εξελληνισθείσα, ed. Ph. Demetracopoulos, vol. II. 16, 2a2ae, 17–22, Athens.

Κυδώνη, Δημητρίου (1980), Θωμά Ακυινάτου Σούμμα Θεολογική εξελληνισθείσα, eds. Ph. Demetracopoulos and M. Bretanou, vol. II. 17A, 2a2ae, 23–33, Athens.

Κυδώνη, Δημητρίου (1982), Θωμά Ακυινάτου Σούμμα Θεολογική εξελληνισθείσα, eds. S. Sideri and Ph. Photopoulou, II.17B, 2a2ae, 34–56, Athens.

Κυδώνη, Δημητρίου (2002), Θωμά Ακυινάτου Σούμμα Θεολογική εξελληνισθείσα, ed. E. Kalokairinou, vol. II. 18, 2a2ae, 57–79, Athens.

Κυδώνη, Δημητρίου (2011), Θωμά Ακυινάτου Σούμμα Θεολογική εξελληνισθείσα, eds. A. Glycofrydi-Leontsini and I. D. Spyralatos, II. 19, 2a2ae, 80–100, Foundation of Research and Editions of Neohellenic Philosophy.

Κυδώνη, Δημητρίου (2019), Θωμά Ακυινάτου Σούμμα Θεολογική εξελληνισθείσα, eds. A. Glycofrydi-Leontsini and I. D. Spyralatos, II. 20, 2a2ae, 101–22, Athens.

Lagarde, B. (1973), 'Le De Differentiis de Plethon d'après l'autographe de la Marcienne', *Byzantion*, 43: 312–43.

Livanos, C. (2006), *Greek Tradition and Latin Influence in the Work of George Scholarios: Alone Against All Europe*, Piscataway, NJ: Gorgias.

MacIntyre, A. (1967), *A Short History of Ethics*, London: Routledge & Kegan Paul.

Maltese, E. V. (ed.) (1988), *Georgius Gemistus Plethon Contra Scholarii pro Aristotele objectiones*, Leipzig: Teubner.

Mohler, L. (1942), *Kardinal Bessarion als Theologe, Humanist und Staatsmann*, 3 vols, Aalen: Scientia Verlag.

Moutsopoulos, E. (1975), 'L'Hellénisation du Thomisme au XIVe siècle', *Annuaire scientifique de la faculté de philosophie de l'Université d'Athènes*, 24: 131–6.

Owens, J. (1999), 'Aristotle and Aquinas', in N. Kretzmann and E. Stump (eds), *The Cambridge Companion to Aquinas*, 38–59, Cambridge: Cambridge University Press.

Papadopoulos, S. (1974), 'Thomas in Byzantium', *Theologie und Philosophie*, 49: 274–304.

Papadopoulos, S. (1976), Ἑλληνικαὶ μεταφράσεις Θωμιστικῶν ἔργων. Θωμισταὶ καί Ἀντι-Θωμισταὶ ἐν Βυζαντίῳ, Αθήναι.

Petit, L., M. Jugie and X. A. Siderides (1928–36), *Oeuvres complètes de Gennade Scholarios*, 8 vols. Paris.

Plested, M. (2012), *Orthodox Readings of Aquinas*, Oxford: Oxford University Press.

Podskalsky, G. (1974), 'Die Rezeption der thomistischen Theologie bei Gennadios II Scholarios (ca. 1403-1472)', *Theologie und Philosophie*, 49: 305–23.

Russell, N. (2002), 'Palamism and the Circle of Demetrius Kydones', in C. Dendrinos, J. Harris, E.Harvalia-Crook and J. Herrin (eds), *Porphyrogenita, Essays on Byzantine History in Honour of Julian Chrysostomides*, 153–74, London: Aldershot.

Ryder, J. (2010), *The Career and Writings of Demetrius Kydones: A Study of Fourteenth-Century Byzantine Politics*, Leiden: Brill.

Tatakis, B. N. (1977), *The Byzantine Philosophy*, trans. from French into Greek by E. Kalpourtzi, Athens: Society for the Studies of Neohellenic Civilization and General Education.

Tym, T. (1974), 'Prochoros und Demetrios Kydones', in W. P. Mainz (ed.), *Thomas von Aquino: Interpratation und Rezeption*, 837–912, Mainz: Matthias Grünewald Verlag.

Woodhouse, C. M. (1986), *Gemistos Plethon: The Last of Hellenes*, Oxford: Oxford University Press.

Part 2

Modernity, conflict and MacIntyrean Aristotelianism

7

Aristotelianism, Austinianism and the problem of the good

Kelvin Knight

Alasdair MacIntyre has urged philosophers to 'begin with Aristotle and J. L. Austin by recognizing the multiplicity and heterogeneity of uses of "good", "bad", "better", and "worse"' (MacIntyre 2014; 47; cf. MacIntyre 2013: 23, 2016: 13). To do this is to give 'the *first* word' to 'ordinary language', as Austin proposed in his influential 1956 Presidential Address to the Aristotelian Society (Austin 1957: 11; Austin's emphasis). The speech 'made Aristotle's treatment of voluntariness popular' (Sorabji 1980: 249) in 'dispos[ing] of the problem of Freedom' (Austin 1957: 6) when judging actors' responsibility for their actions, and for their actions' consequences. If Aristotle did not precisely begin his works of practical philosophy by attending to ordinary language, we know from his naming of the aims of action 'goods', his sensitivity to ordinary language (including to homonyms and synonyms, and to its use in rhetoric and poetic drama), shared meanings and the logic of predication (especially but not only in his *Organon*) the great attention he paid to ordinary language. More straightforwardly, it is how MacIntyre began his 1967 *A Short History of Ethics* in analysing Homer's 'prephilosophical history of "good"' (MacIntyre 1967: 5–13), and in going on to analyse its usage by Plato, Aristotle and others. It is also how he eventually decided to begin what, in 2016, became *Ethics in the Conflicts of Modernity*.

In the case of each philosopher, making such a beginning involved stepping back from what had become philosophical convention and presupposition. Aristotle stepped back from Plato's idealism, Austin stepped back from the battle between Oxford's so-called realists and its Greenian, Bradleian and Kantian-cum-Aristotelian idealists (Austin 1968), and MacIntyre stepped back from Austin and analytic philosophy in returning to Aristotle and Homer. Even so, each only stepped back so far. Aristotle progressed from Plato, in analysing the logic of propositional language and in bringing ideals down to earth as aims of action and nature. MacIntyre progressed from Austin as well as from Aristotle, because Austin dug deeper into grammar and more widely across its uses than Aristotle's 'scrappily and inexactly' conducted analyses (Austin 1961: 38) could ever have done. Austin – like MacIntyre, a classics graduate – was able to explore to such depth and breadth because of the ways in which others had broken the ground of philosophical tradition to readdress language's logic. Two philosophers had recently dug deep, all the way down through logic's proposed laws, to discover language's bedrock of practice. One was Martin Heidegger, who followed what he understood to have been Aristotle's route through logic, and then carried on through Homeric prehistory in an attempt to escape philosophical tradition altogether. This was an approach taken by Hans-Georg Gadamer (Gadamer 1986) but was rejected by MacIntyre. The other excavator was Ludwig Wittgenstein, whom both Austin and MacIntyre followed.

Upon hitting bedrock, Wittgenstein had taken issue with Augustine. Against Augustine's analysis of words' use to refer to and name real (and, by humans but not by God, fictitious) things, the late Wittgenstein had ranged his own analysis of the full multiplicity and heterogeneity of linguistic usage (Wittgenstein 2009: 5^{e}ff.). In this, his digging may be compared to that of Heidegger in undermining any traditional idea of truth as propositions' correspondence to reality. Neither Austin (Strawson 1971: 149–249) nor MacIntyre followed far in that direction. Austin took a route left aside in Wittgenstein's observation that 'words are also deeds' (Wittgenstein 2009: 155^e §546), first categorizing statements and exclamations into kinds of act, and then categorizing the logical parts of intentional utterance as conventional, purposive and consequential action. MacIntyre's more particular concern has always been with intentionality in the use of moral language.

That MacIntyre was a Wittgensteinian and Austinian long before he was a convinced Aristotelian is evident from his 1951 master's thesis, in which he followed them by taking 'the most important step in ... understanding ... the significance of moral judgements' (MacIntyre 1951a: 74): that of abandoning any theoretical search for their *referents* and, instead, analysing their *use*. In this, he followed Austin's critique of emotivists' 'descriptive fallacy' (Austin 1946: 174; emphasis omitted),[1] discerning in their propositions 'a disguised form of the referential view of moral language' (MacIntyre 1951a: 5). Taking modern natural science as their paradigm of rationality, emotivists maintained that *the* function of language is to *describe* (and thereby explain) reality. Finding nothing objectively real to which moral terms correspond, they concluded that it is only the speakers' subjective emotions that moral language refers to. Against this, Austin argued that language is used to perform many kinds of action (Austin 1962), of which description is only one.[2] MacIntyre knew this to be true. Having become a Marxist and joined the communist party, he knew that moral terminology was available for ideological, propagandistic and manipulative purposes. As he affirmed, 'moral judgements are performatory' (MacIntyre 1951a: 2). As he would write after Austin's premature death, in 1960:

> A name [Austin's] no longer has a bearer,
> A sentence that was true [he lives] is false,
> Yet something lives.
> Distinctions which he drew are his survivors,
> We utter his and our performatives. (MacIntyre 1960: 369)

MacIntyre followed Austin in taking promising to be an especially significant kind of social action, primarily because 'one binds oneself by saying "I promise"' (MacIntyre

1951a: 54); one does not merely describe reality, but *changes* it, by putting oneself under an obligation and committing oneself to a future course of action. Such a commitment may be made by speaking in a wedding; when one says 'I do' a bride and groom are 'not *describing* the action [they are] doing, but *doing* it' (Austin 1946: 174; Austin's emphases). Intentionally, the two thereby become one. Two physical beings create a marriage. By using language in a law-governed way, they change their relation to one another and, also, to the wider society of individuals, of couples and of families. As MacIntyre adds to what was said by Austin, the significance of this change is fully ethical. If the marriage is to the right person, at the right time and for the right reasons, then the action may be called good in a way that is paradigmatic of the term's moral usage. The point of promising and of marrying is not to describe the world but to change it, and the point of marrying is to change both one's own world and that of one's significant other for the better. MacIntyre's hope was to discriminate between sustainable kinds and false theories of moral judgement and action.

Hope was fulfilled in MacIntyre's 1981 *After Virtue*. His *Short History* had remained Austinian in exploring the heterogeneous uses of moral concepts. He got beyond heterogeneity in *After Virtue*. Emotivism, he argued, was both true and false: it was false as a theory of a universal logic of moral propositions, but true as a description of how such propositions were used in modernity's particular, post-Enlightenment culture. The problem of moral and political practice was that ordinary ethics, and ordinary ethical language, was subject to a scepticism warranted by the failure of Locke, Kant, Bentham and heterogeneous others to sustain any non-teleological moral theory against the valid criticisms that each made of the others. The consequence was that belief in ordinary moral precepts collapsed, having been undermined by extraordinary, unsustainable theories that purported, but failed, to justify such precepts. Radical scepticism was exemplified by Nietzsche, who initiated the deconstruction of all moral theory including that classical tradition of the virtues of which it had been the Enlightenment's project to supplant. Against that project, and against Nietzsche, MacIntyre now argued for re-adoption of an intentionally referential use of moral language and for resumption of the traditional search for an agreeable concept of the human good, completion and 'end', or *telos*. The logic of such a theoretical and practical 'quest' was that such a goal could provide a sustainable justification of moral precepts, as the means by which imperfect, 'untutored' human beings may move towards its, and their own, realization. This logical, theoretical relation between the concepts of the human good and of that good's constitutive excellences, or virtues, was still best exemplified by Aristotle's original account, not least because his account exemplified how philosophical theory could express ordinary ethical practice by using the ordinary, Greek vocabulary of goods and the various virtues in expressing the best of ordinary, Greek practice. Such practice, MacIntyre proposed, exemplified how a culture could be entirely unemotivist in its use of moral language and its enforcement of moral norms. Therefore, soon after *After Virtue*, he stopped naming its historical referent a capacious 'tradition of the virtues' and started using the fully philosophical moniker 'Aristotelianism'.

Aristotelianism might be thought to have supplanted Austinianism in *After Virtue*. Certainly, this is how the book was widely perceived by most philosophers, whether analytic or continental. Certainly, Austin himself had bequeathed ample grounds for objection to the book's departure from careful analysis of ordinary, contemporary language. Most notable, again, was his 1956 address. He employed the old Stagirite to undermine the modern presupposition of individuals' unconditional freedom and consequent culpability for the foreseeable consequences of their own actions; he would not use him to defend other presuppositions from analytic interrogation. Having used Aristotle to dispose of Kantianism's 'traditional' conception of human freedom (Austin 1957: 6), he now attempted to undermine Aristotelianism's traditional conception of the human good. Concurring with emotivists, he therefore issued

> a general warning in philosophy. It seems to be too readily assumed that if we can only discover the true meanings of each of a cluster of key terms, usually historic terms, that we use in some particular field (as, for example, 'right', 'good' and the rest in morals), then it must without question transpire that each will fit into place in some single, interlocking, consistent, conceptual scheme. Not only is there no reason to assume this, but all historical probability is against it, especially in the case of a language derived from such various civilisations as ours is. We may cheerfully use, and with weight, terms which are not so much head-on incompatible as simply disparate, which just don't fit in or even on. Just as we cheerfully subscribe to, or have the grace to be torn between, simply disparate ideals – why *must* there be a conceivable amalgam, the Good Life for Man? (Austin 1957: 29; Austin's emphasis)

Breaking from Austin was no easy thing for MacIntyre to do. He marked the break by denouncing as 'barren' the 'notion that the moral philosopher can study *the* concepts of morality merely by reflecting, Oxford armchair style, on what he or she and those around him or her say and do' (MacIntyre 2007: xvii; MacIntyre's emphasis). This was the notion informing those conversational 'Saturday Morning Meetings' famously hosted by Austin (Warnock 1973). What he objected to most was the elitist and exclusionary ex-'public school' style in which such philosophizing was conducted. Without denying the virtuous 'clarity', 'wit' and 'patience' with which Austin did philosophy (MacIntyre 1962), MacIntyre saw greater good in the work of those without whose readiness to sacrifice the rewards of talking with the rich there could have been little progress in philosophy and no record of it. Scrappiness and inexactness need not be an intellectual vice. As even Austin liked to insist, under some circumstances, it is entirely reasonable to maintain that 'France is hexagonal' (Austin 1962a: 142–3). It all depends on what one is doing.

Denunciation of style and method could not be enough; MacIntyre had to do more. He argued, at length, that his conception of the good life for humankind was no unquestioned presupposition. He did so in another, classicist style, still familiar to Oxonian philosophers, by reflecting, analytically, on ethics in the conflicts of antiquity. Then, there was conflict between rival and incompatible goods, virtues and courses of action, between which persons were apt to be torn. He therefore refused 'the presupposition' of Plato, Aristotle and, he added, Aquinas that the virtues are united by 'a cosmic order which dictates the place of each virtue in a total harmonious scheme of human life' (MacIntyre 2007: 142). Against that presupposition he deployed Sophocles' enactments of tragically ineradicable conflict. This juxtaposition of the tragedians against the philosophers represented a false opposition that had been presented by Austin. For Austin, he proposed, '*Either* we can admit the existence of rival and contingently incompatible goods which make incompatible claims to our practical allegiance *or* we can believe in some determinate conception of *the* good life for man.' Austin's failure to acknowledge the possibility that we might be able to do both, and 'that there may be better or worse ways for individuals to live through the tragic confrontation of good with good' was, he countered, likely due to an unquestioned presupposition of Austin's own (MacIntyre 2007: 223–4; MacIntyre's emphases). The point of ethics he argued, against Austin, even if not yet entirely with Aristotle, is precisely to educate human desire and action towards some determinable conception of the good life under imperfect, conflictual conditions.

Despite refusing to heed Austin's warning, and despite disparaging his style of philosophizing, MacIntyre continued to give ordinary language the first word in his own most titanic effort to rethink moral theory. It was attention to a multiplicitous cluster of ordinary uses of 'good' that led him to his middle way through Austin's false dichotomy. Out of that multiplicity, he began to elaborate a social theory of ethical judgement, action and goods. 'A moral philosophy', he proposed, 'characteristically presupposes a sociology' (MacIntyre 2007: 23).

After Virtue's sociology of practices and institutions exceeded both ordinary language and Austin's 'way of doing philosophy', his 'linguistic phenomenology' of speech acts (Austin 1957: 8). The book did so still more, and more famously, in another, related way. It argued that in social contexts, other than those it specified as practices, the use of moral terms had become detached from their literal meaning, and that, to this extent, linguistic usage had come to be how it is described by emotivists. While Austin had pointed out what emotivism missed, MacIntyre pointed also to what it illuminated about our post-Enlightenment, emotivist culture. In the context of state and corporate institutions, and most especially of their 'manipulative' management, ordinary moral language had indeed become as manipulative and meaningless as both Nietzsche and emotivists alleged (MacIntyre 2007: 194). The narrative recounted in MacIntyre's second, longer history of ethics was intended to give a causal explanation of this contemporary moral culture, as a consequence of the failure of the Enlightenment's non-teleological moral theories. The book's sociology was intended 'to lay bare the empirical, causal connection between virtues, practices and institutions', to have 'strong empirical implications' and to provide 'an explanatory scheme which can be tested in particular cases' (MacIntyre 2007: 196; cf. Beadle 2017).

MacIntyre's moral philosophy, his adoption of a sociological kind of teleology, provided *After Virtue*'s grounds for fully contravening Austin's general, philosophical warning. This contravention was not in using such functional concepts as farmer; it was in allowing that there might be something in Aristotle's analogical extension of such conception to humanity as a natural kind. MacIntyre's claim about usage in the history of Western philosophy was that 'it is only when man is thought of as an individual prior to and apart from all roles that "man" ceases to be a functional concept' (MacIntyre 2007: 59). In this sense, his sociology and moral philosophy entailed that the human good and end is much more than an amalgam; it is 'a conception of *the* good' which 'transcend[s] that limited conception of the virtues which is available in and through practices', and is therefore able to guide the ordering of those other goods that are each internal and limited to a particular practice (MacIntyre 2007: 219; MacIntyre's emphasis). As yet, in *After Virtue*, he insisted that the quest for such a human good, both by ordinary persons in understanding their own lives and by philosophers working within a tradition, 'presupposes' a 'background account' of shared social practices directed to their particular, internal goods (MacIntyre 2007: 187). By understanding such goods within both the living of lives and the pursuit of truth, it remained possible to conceive of the human good as something to be practised, virtuously.

> The virtues therefore are to be understood as those dispositions which will not only sustain practices and enable us to achieve the goods internal to practices, but which will also sustain us in the relevant kind of quest for the good, by enabling us to overcome the harms, dangers, temptations and distractions which we encounter, and which will furnish us with increasing self-knowledge and increasing knowledge of the good. The catalogue of the virtues will therefore include the virtues required to sustain the kind of households and the kind of political communities in which men and women can seek for the good together and the virtues necessary for philosophical enquiry about the character of the good. We have then arrived at a provisional conclusion about the good life for man: the good life for man is the life spent in seeking for the good life for man, and the virtues necessary for the seeking are those which will enable us to understand what more and what else the good life for man is. (MacIntyre 2007: 219)

Politically, the good may be understood as something of an amalgam. The idea that particular goods and activities might be amalgamated in political communities in which people can seek for the good together, as a fully comprehensive and architectonically ordered common good, was what had been hoped by those Oxonian Aristotelians whom the likes of Austin had replaced. Their ranks and hopes had been reduced by the disillusionment of the First World War, and then still more by the Second World War. When, before that second war, Austin defended Aristotle's enquiry into the human good from an anti-idealist critique issued by the holder of the White's Chair – which had previously been occupied, until his death, by the leader of those Aristotelians, T. H. Green, and more recently by the dean of Aristotle scholarship, W. D. Ross – he already felt no need to refer back to their idealized Aristotle (Austin 1968). Shortly after the war began, he commended Aristotle's enquiry into why people 'call different things by the same name' in '*actual* ... not *ideal*' language, before warning against misuse of the 'word ... "fascist"' (Austin 1961: 38, 40; Austin's emphases).

By the time Austin issued his presidential warning to the Aristotelian Society – long after returning from war as a multinationally decorated hero of Britain's sedentary and analytic military intelligence (Warnock 1969: 9–10) – he had himself become the White's professor. While Oxford philosophy reclined in his armchair, the world beyond remained altogether less relaxed. The year before, he had travelled to Harvard, to deliver what became his definitive account of speech acts; he focused upon their authors' intentions in issuing them, from which he differentiated their intended and unintended consequences. He ended by claiming that attention to what 'the word "good"' was used to do would have shown 'why what I have said is interesting', and that clarity about its use would not be reached before the ideal of 'a complete list' of usages and their 'inter-connections' (Austin 1962: 162). This was an ideal to which he never came close. Instead, he issued his warning.

What, then, did Austin intend by his act of warning? Certainly, a great deal. At Harvard, the year before, he had presented 'warning' (primarily, of a bull being about to charge) as a paradigm case of a speech act. Given this, we can be certain that he considered himself '*right* to … warn … in the sense of … whether, on the facts and [his] knowledge of the facts and the purposes for which [he was] speaking, and so on, this was the proper thing to say' and do (Austin 1962; Austin's emphasis). Clearly, his intent was partly to continue clearing away 'the jargon of extinct theories, and our own prejudices too, as the[ir] upholders or imbibers' (Austin 1956: 8). What is less evident is his political intent. Although he was no political philosopher, he was certainly a political animal. It may therefore be germane to recall his pre-war warning of the danger of fascism and his calling for the anti-fascist war in which he served with such distinction. Unfortunately, his post-war philosophy bore little sign of his experience beyond such observations as the military utility of regarding France as hexagonal. What we do know is the warning's more immediate political context.

In October 1956, Britain was at the height of another 'cold' war, this time against the Soviet Union. This raised none of the difficulties that Oxford philosophers had experienced from wars against modern idealism's German homeland, since they all regarded Soviet terminology as ideological and manipulative. The morning before Austin delivered his lecture, on 29 October, Israel had invaded Egypt. The day before, the Soviet Red Army had been told by Hungary's communist government to leave the country. Poland had been undergoing its own anti-Leninist October Revolution for weeks. For this reason, and because of his influence on the 'contextualizing' of canonical texts in the history of political thought (Skinner 2002), his warning should be understood within the context of an ideological conflict. In that conflict, Western intellectuals made a virtue of pluralism in opposition to the vice of communist totalitarianism. Even if Aristotle was not often accused of totalitarianism, Plato was (Popper 1945), and Hegel's culpability for both fascism and Marxism was so standardized that even Oxford's few remaining idealists had given up defending him, for fear of being regarded as complicit. The political danger allegedly lurking in the jargon of past theories and present prejudices was therefore well known.

When Austin attacked the idea of a 'single, interlocking, consistent, conceptual scheme', he was, we may infer, warning against ideological as much as philosophical misuse of the idea of *the* human good. His warning would be elaborated upon to great effect by two of his old friends from the Senior Common Room of pre-war All Souls College: Stuart Hampshire, who shared many of Austin's moderately leftist sympathies, and Isaiah Berlin, who shared less (MacIntyre 2013: 26). We may further infer, therefore, that besides its 'perlocutionary' (to use one of Austin's technical departures from ordinary English) consequence of reducing judicial appeal to free will and increasing judicial use of excuses, his Presidential Address had the further effect of encouraging philosophers to supplement political scientists' advocacy of institutional pluralism with a pluralism and heterogeneity of values. Whatever his intentions, the political consequence of his warning was to strengthen the Cold War's liberalism of fear.

In October 1956, Austin's warning was accepted by MacIntyre, who, that month, attacked Marxism's 'jargon', its self-image as a 'conceptual scheme' and its claim that certain concepts are falsely ideological, arguing, in alliance with Austin, 'that any concept can be used ... to mystify' (MacIntyre 1956: 369). The target of his critique was John Lewis, who had already been the leading philosopher of the Communist Party of Great Britain when he was a member, in the late 1940s. The passage to which MacIntyre took especial exception was Lewis's accusation that Aristotle's 'rigidly formal [syllogistic] logic reflect[ed] and justif[ied] a static order of society', to which a part of his lengthy response was to ask what was reflected by Aristotle's natural and teleological 'doctrine of change'. To ask this was to challenge Marxists' simplistic contrast of their own materialism to others' 'idealism', by which they denoted 'a failure to take causal explanation seriously', to which MacIntyre responded by defending 'those of a positivist or analytical stand-point' even more than Aristotle (MacIntyre 1956: 366–8). In fact, Lewis himself resisted the contrast (Roberts 1997: 117–19), being 'a moralist ... deeply imbued with philosophic traditions of English Christian nonconformism and ... British idealism' (Roberts 1997: 104). These influences had been evident in, for example, the third longest contribution published in UNESCO's famous human rights symposium a few years earlier. Here, Lewis had followed Green more closely than Marx. Amidst others' scepticism about such rhetoric, he affirmed 'rights as based upon human needs and possibilities and the recognition by members of a society of the conditions necessary in order that they may fulfill their common ends' (Lewis 1949: 54). No matter; in 1956, MacIntyre – still far more leftist in his sympathies than Austin, although no more sympathetic to that actually existing state socialism, which he still characterized as Stalinist – was even less willing than Austin 'to let sleeping dogmatists lie' (Austin 1961: 43).

After Virtue reversed MacIntyre's 1956 judgement that no concepts are particularly ideological. He here turned Bentham's critique of rights as 'fictions' upon its author's own utilitarianism. To human rights and utility, he added a third 'moral fiction': the idea of 'bureaucratic managerial expertise' (MacIntyre 2007: 62–78). Institutionalized in both state and corporations, managerial manipulation was 'perhaps the most culturally powerful' manifestation of emotivist belief and behaviour (MacIntyre 2007: 76, 25–32, 85–9, 106–8). Stalinism no longer seemed the threat it had been twenty-five years earlier. The manipulativeness of its language appeared transparent in Britain, and even in Eastern Europe its cultural power seemed to have almost ended. What seemed undiminished were the Western rhetoric of managerial efficiency and individual rights.

It was against liberalism that that MacIntyre developed his Aristotelianism. The good life for human beings was exactly that which he now posited as the core concept into which philosophy should enquire. In *After Virtue*, he had been equivocal as to whether the term's true meaning was susceptible of discovery. All that he claimed was that there remain good reasons, both practical and theoretical, to suppose that it is in one's own good to quest for the good life. The reasons he elaborated in his 1988 *Whose*

Justice? Which Rationality? and his subsequent *Three Rival Versions of Moral Enquiry* were partly theoretical and partly practical. Whatever Austin had intended in weighing 'historical probability' against conceiving the human good, MacIntyre intended more in arguing that philosophy is inseparable from its history. In *After Virtue*, he suggested something like an Enlightenment, stadial conception of history, on which view the emergence of philosophy out of Homeric society might be paradigmatic for all 'heroic', prephilosophical societies, including that Germanic one to which classical civilization succumbed. From *Whose Justice?* onward, he entertained an altogether more pluralistic conception of both cultural and philosophical tradition, in which Aristotelianism is one tradition among others, both Western and non-Western, for which no more final claim can be made than that it is the best theory so far. When theorizing from within his tradition, however, his conception of the human good lost its earlier equivocation and became increasingly determinate.

The human good became, for MacIntyre, something additional to an aspirational object for which people quest. As humans' *telos* or 'final end', it became the premise or 'first principle' for all enquiry within the Aristotelian tradition (MacIntyre 1998a). That it is a first principle that can withstand sceptical, critical scrutiny, MacIntyre inferred from the scrutiny to which he had subjected it, from a plurality of perspectives, for over thirty years. As a premise, it informs an entire conceptual scheme. This scheme is not, on his account, neatly interlocking and unchangingly consistent. Indeed (as he indicates in his contribution to this volume), it is not even neatly one single scheme. As a tradition, it is always changing. What makes it the best theory so far is, he claims, threefold: first, theoretically, its proponents' self-consciousness as practicing members of a tradition helps make it the best theory of what a philosophical theory really is; second, its continuing use of real ethical concepts and terms, such as 'goods' and the names of the virtues, helps make it the best theory of real ethical language and practice, thought and action; finally, the theory continues to provide sustainable justification of such practice, and of uninstitutional, shared practices. He has long invoked the logic of Aristotle's practical syllogism in saying that the conclusion of practical reasoning is not simply judgement but action. Theoretically, all apparent conflicts between different goods and the exercise of different virtues should be resolvable, by reference to a comprehensive teleology of the good life. Sophocles' tragic conflicts are resolvable through the exercise of practical rationality (MacIntyre 1988: 124–45; Sorabji 1980: 295–8). In this, it might be thought that MacIntyre accepted Austin's dichotomy, differing from Berlin and Hampshire in settling on its other side.

While remaining sensitive to the multiplicity and heterogeneity of linguistic usage, MacIntyre has acknowledged the case for Augustinian realism. In indicting moral fictions, he is now closer to both Augustine and Marx than to Bentham. He credits Thomas Aquinas as the greatest theorist of the human good, specifying that his own Aristotelianism is Thomistic. In *Whose Justice? Which Rationality?*, he described how Aquinas had synthesized the previously rival Augustinian and Aristotelian traditions into a single, coherent conceptual scheme. *After Virtue* now carries a prologue in which he admits that 'it is only because human beings have an end towards which they are directed by reason of their specific nature, that practices, traditions, and the like are able to function as they do' (MacIntyre 2007: xi). Acknowledging the reality of coherent philosophical rivals, his proposition that Aristotelianism is rationally superior in its theoretical correspondence to empirical reality rests upon a sub-sociological conception of a common, human good. Having dug down through social practice, he has hit Thomistic Aristotelianism's philosophical bedrock of theology. The singularity of the human good is underwritten by the singularity of the God of the philosophers, and of Augustine. Whereof one cannot speak philosophically, thereof one may, *qua* philosopher, be silent. Although MacIntyre continues to think that Aristotelian and Thomistic practical philosophy should be open to amalgamating with enquiries that resume from where Marx's philosophizing left off, after theorizing with Feuerbach's assault on Christianity's alleged alienation of the human good (MacIntyre 1998b), he has happily allowed 'theistic elements in [his] account' to alienate faithful followers of Berlin, Hampshire or Bernard Williams (MacIntyre 2016: 231).

The MacIntyre of 1956 *might* have been shocked. Then, he had ridiculed the alleged dogmatism of Lewis's works by comparing them with 'those manuals *ad mentem Divi Thomae* which vex the lives of Catholic theological students' (MacIntyre 1956: 366). That the MacIntyre of 1981 would *not* have been shocked is clear from his acknowledgement of two Catholic, Thomistic Aristotelians – the continental Jacques Maritain, as well as the analytic Peter Geach – as the philosophers from whom he had 'learnt most' (MacIntyre 2007: 260), although the fact that Maritain, arguably modernity's greatest Thomist philosopher, also disdained such manuals might indicate that even the MacIntyre of 1956 need not have been surprised. The MacIntyre of 1950 should have been pleased. Before completing his MA thesis, his first publication had followed an unnamed Maritain in differing from a named Sartre and a praised Austin. Against Austin's dismissal of Thomism's traditional appeal to analogy (Austin 1961: 39–40, 42), he defended 'a proper understanding' of such 'analogical predicat[es]' as 'goodness' and, especially, 'existence' (MacIntyre 1951b: 58). When, much later, he expressly defended Thomism against modern and postmodern opponents, he admitted that, beneath its textbooks' appearance of dogmatic homogeneity, the reality was almost of 'too many Thomisms' (MacIntyre 1990: 58–81). Within that variety, MacIntyre distances himself from Maritain. If he shares something with the 'critical realism' with which Maritain (Maritain 1995: 75–144) opposed Aristotle to Kant, he nonetheless denies the 'personalism' with which Maritain followed Kant's theorization of humans' separation from social roles. Most notoriously, he repudiates the way in which Maritain, joining Lewis in the UNESCO symposium (Maritain 1949), allowed human rights to eclipse the human good.

After Virtue's cautiously provisional conclusion about the human good has been replaced by a determinate conception of the good life, which both recognized goods' attributive heterogeneity and argued for the possibility of their rational, hierarchical ordering. Ethically and psychologically, one's objects of desire should be ordered within a conception of one's own good, in society with others; sociologically and politically, heterogeneous goods and practices should be ordered for the common good. Since Austin's binary choice was now accepted by MacIntyre, so too was the coexistence of rival traditions. In *Whose Justice?*, he presented a binary opposition of kinds of good more general and basic than that of morally educative goods internal to practices and potentially corruptive goods external to them. 'Goods of excellence' or virtue internal to persons he opposed to 'goods of effectiveness', such as skills, which might be used for good or ill. Aristotelianism stood for the subordination of effectiveness to excellence; its rivals elided the distinction (MacIntyre 1988: 30–74). Beneath the dichotomy resided the first principle of the human good, as goal.

In *Dependent Rational Animals: Why Human Beings Need the Virtues*, he advanced a robustly factual, causal and naturalistic account of that good. As he now confessed, he judged himself to have been 'in error in supposing an ethics independent of biology to be possible' (MacIntyre 1999: x). He had moved a long way from Austin, putting language in its place within a teleology of humans as animals and of animal practices as pre-linguistic. Ethics emerges out of human evolution, along with human language. More recently, he has described how our power of speech enables us to enquire, narrate, share and criticize reasons, 'formulate complex and detailed intentions', 'identify … common goods' and pursue temporally distant goals, as goods.

> The key moment in distinctively human development occurs when someone first makes use of their linguistic powers to pose the question 'What is the good of doing this or that, of making this or that happen or allowing this or that to happen?', and is understood as inviting from others or from himself some statement of reasons for and against any particular answer, reasons which can then be evaluated. From then on human projects, human responses to good and bad fortune, and human relationships were taken to be intelligible in terms of the good and the bad, the rationally justifiable and the rationally unjustifiable. So that there came a time when our predecessors were able to ask 'Is it a good thing or a bad thing to fall helplessly in love?' and to consider such responses as 'That depends on whom or what you fall in love with' and 'A bad thing if it happens too often'. (2016: 225–6)

Such a contemporary Aristotelianism may be contrasted with what might be constructed from Austin's premise. Austin's disposal of 'the problem of Freedom' may be understood, historically, as a disposal of Kant's moral rigorism and as a return to an empiricist conventionalism exemplified by David Hume. On this view, the proposition that norms cannot be inferred from facts was only incorrectly attributable to Hume (MacIntyre 1971; MacIntyre 1988: 310–11), even if Hume could be understood as a progenitor of emotivism or expressivism (MacIntyre 2007: 47–56, 229–32; MacIntyre 2016: 45–6, 79–85) in regarding only means and not ends to be susceptible to reason. Hume grounded this moral anthropology in a naturalistic 'science of man' (MacIntyre 1965: 16), in which humans were accustomed by the artificial virtues, underlain by their natural passions and prudence, to act in conformity with social convention and law. Such conventionalism was shared by Wittgenstein (Bloor 1997). The sociology that he and Austin presupposed was one of heteronomous rule-following. In this way, one may move from one's sense of the way the world is, as rule-governed, to an understanding of how one ought to act, in accordance with the rules. This was seen by one of Austin's keenest followers, John Searle, who first made the move in the Austinian terms of speech acts (Searle 1964; Searle 1969): 'It is internal to the concept of promising that in promising one undertakes an obligation to do something' and 'necessarily commits oneself' to 'the internal constitutive rules of the institution' (Searle 1969: 189, 195). 'Ought' denotes such commitment. Thereafter, he moved from ordinary language to an extraordinary description of 'the structure of human civilization' (Searle 2010), using as his vehicle performative declarations. Austin had listed among speech acts such 'declarations' as 'I declare war' (Austin 1962: 7, 40, 155), counting as ordinary language users such officials as cricket umpires, marriage-officiating priests and war-declaring politicians. Whereas he and Wittgenstein concerned themselves with the rules of grammar, Searle was concerned with how linguistically created rules and institutions confer 'status functions' and powers (Searle 1995: 41–3, 94–112). It was, of course, a declaration that initiated the US independence, which was institutionalized by a constitutional convention. What most impresses him is the way that state laws allow the creation of corporations, which can then create their own official rules and roles. He claims this as a 'social ontology' and 'metaphysics' of collectively intended institutions (Searle 1995: 5, 3), including a 'deontology' of institutionalized 'desire-independent reasons for action' (Searle 2010: 80–9, 127–32). Ethics is reduced to rule-following. Having exceeded whatever Austin might have intended by the expression linguistic phenomenology, Searle now exceeded the bounds of language in tracing the 'evolutionary' (Searle 2010: 4, 94) steps 'from electrons to elections and from protons to presidents' (Searle 2010: 3); from mind-independent 'brute facts' to the emergent 'institutional facts' (Searle 2010: 10–11, 21–4, 90–124) 'of money, government, marriage, private property, and so on' (Searle 2010: 88), including defence against 'the Bentham-MacIntyre style of skepticism' (Searle 2010: 176) of human rights' Universal Declaration.

Although MacIntyre need have no time for Searle's manoeuvres (Knight 2013), we might think that he has made some similar moves. In narrating the philosophical formation of that native of Wrocław, Edith Stein, he studied the work of her mentor, Adolf Reinach (MacIntyre 2006), which has often been compared with that of Searle (Mulligan 1987; Smith and Zelaniec 2012; Salice and Schmid 2016) and, more recently, of Austin (Salice and Uemura 2018: 28–31). As he later noted, at the core of Reinach's work 'was his theory of the social act and of promising as a type of social act' (MacIntyre 2012: v). Social acts, Reinach specified, are those freely intentional and causally 'spontaneous acts which are in need of being heard' and understood by others (Reinach 2012: 19). As MacIntyre acknowledges, 'every system of civil law' presupposes an understanding of promising (MacIntyre 2006: 55), and of 'the meaning and force' of promising in generating 'an obligation to and a legitimate claim on the part of the person to whom it is addressed' (MacIntyre 2006: 59). Nonetheless, Reinach's phenomenology was more than linguistic, allowing that the good might be more than a linguistic construct. Whereas 'language ... is irremediably general and universal', any adequate ethics must be able to address the practical 'particularities and singularities that we encounter' (MacIntyre 2010: 2).

It was only after having begun thinking of what eventually became *Ethics in the Conflicts of Modernity* that MacIntyre perceived the need to get back to philosophical basics: to our conflicting desires, to practical reasoning about their achievement and ordering, and to our understanding of what has been achieved and what remains to be done. Having wanted to move Aristotelian discussion of practical reasoning about common goods on to reasoning about politics, he realized that this would only have point once the possibility of shared reasoning about rationally desired goods and their pursuit had been more firmly established. He therefore returned to where he had begun, restating what he had learnt from Austin about shared uses of 'good', from Geach about its attributive use, and from Aristotle about how attributive uses may be teleologically amalgamated and ordered into a defensible conception of the human good, and isolating his general argument from his narrative of the history of ethics, with all its particularities.

Central to that theoretical argument is a robust, if incomplete, conception of the human good as an object of desire greater that any mere amalgam. This is not to deny the heterogeneity of goods; it is to claim that such heterogeneity points beyond all of its constituents to a desire for something that exceeds them all. The quest for such a good may be conceived by Marxists as communism, by Christians as God (MacIntyre 2016: 243–315) and, as MacIntyre long ago suggested (MacIntyre 1953), by the likes of Lewis as both. For Austin, as for Berlin, Hampshire and Williams, and for contemporary expressivists, this is a mistake. MacIntyre has never made it his task to convince them that they are wrong. His task is to get straight about Aristotelianism's disagreement with them, and about how best to respond to their theoretical challenge. Once that philosophical defence had been mounted and clarified, it should be possible to progress in reasoning about how best to act in conflicts characteristic of modernity, not least in defending common goods against corruption by institutionalized pursuit of money, power and status. Such practical defence should always be expressed in ordinary language about goods and virtues. MacIntyre's own general warning to philosophers is that they must never pretend to have the last word. Even if they take the final good as their first principle, they must understand themselves as participants in a tradition of ongoing enquiry into how the idea of the good should inform pursuit of common, human good.

Notes

I thank Alasdair MacIntyre and participants in the 2016 International Society for MacIntyrean Enquiry conference, held at the University of Wrocław, for comments upon a short, early draft of this chapter.

1 Despite expressly referring to Austin, MacIntyre does not list any source in his bibliography. This is a simple oversight; he *does* list John Wisdom's paper, upon which Austin's was a commentary. That the relation of Austin to MacIntyre is nonetheless one of similitude as well as influence is apparent from the MA's anticipation of what Austin was to say in 1956 of excuses, of the Aristotelian resonance of thinking about freedom and responsibility (e.g. MacIntyre 1951a: 3–4), and from the fact that most of Austin's writings were not published until after his death.
2 He also objected that, if 'good' can be said to be unempirical, then the same may be said of 'reality' (Austin 1962b: 62–70, 71–3).

Bibliography

Austin, J. L. (1946), 'Other Minds', *Proceedings of the Aristotelian Society supplementary*, 20: 148–87.
Austin, J. L. (1956), 'A Plea for Excuses: The Presidential Address', *Proceedings of the Aristotelian Society, New Series*, 57: 1–30.

Austin, J. L. (1961), 'The Meaning of a Word', in J. L. Austin (ed.), *Philosophical Papers*, 23–43, Oxford: Oxford University Press.

Austin, J. L. (1962), *How to Do Things with Words: The William James Lectures Delivered at Harvard University in 1955*, ed. J. O. Urmson, Oxford: Oxford University Press.

Austin, J. L. (1968), '*Agathon* and *Eudaimonia* in the *Ethics* of Aristotle', in J. M. E. Moravcsik (ed.), *Aristotle: A Collection of Critical Essays*, 261–96, London: Macmillan.

Beadle, R. (2017), 'MacIntyre's Influence on Business Ethics', in A. J. G. Sison, G. R. Beabout and I. Ferrero (eds), *Handbook of Virtue Ethics in Business and Management*, 59–67, Dordrecht: Springer.

Bloor, D. (1997), *Wittgenstein, Rules and Institutions*, London: Routledge.

Gadamer, H. G. (1986), *The Idea of the Good in Platonic-Aristotelian Philosophy*, trans. P. Christopher Smith, New Haven: Yale University Press.

Geach, P. (1956), 'Good and Evil', *Analysis*, 17 (2): 33–42.

Hare, R. M. (1952), *The Language of Morals*, Oxford: Oxford University Press.

Knight, K. (2013), 'Rules, Goods, and Powers', in Ruth Groff and John Greco (eds), *Powers and Capacities in Philosophy: The New Aristotelianism*: 319–34, London: Routledge.

Lewis, J. (1949), 'On Human Rights', in UNESCO (ed.), *Human Rights: Comments and Interpretations*, 54–71, London: Allan Wingate.

MacIntyre, A. C. (1951a), 'The Significance of Moral Judgements', MA diss., University of Manchester.

MacIntyre, A. (1951b), 'Analogy in Metaphysics', *Downside Review*, 69: 45–61.

MacIntyre, A. C. (1953), *Marxism: An Interpretation*, London: SCM Press.

MacIntyre, A. (1956), 'Marxist Tracts', *Philosophical Quarterly*, 6 (25), October: 366–70.

MacIntyre, A. (1960), 'On the Death of an Oxford Philosopher', *New Statesman*, 59 (1513), 12 March: 369.

MacIntyre, A. (1962), 'A Philosophical Classic', *The Guardian*, 2 February: 8.

MacIntyre, A. (1965), 'Introduction', in A. MacIntyre (ed.), *Hume's Ethical Writings: Selections from David Hume*, 9–17, London: Macmillan.

MacIntyre, A. (1967), *A Short History of Ethics: A History of Moral Philosophy from the Homeric Age to the Twentieth Century*, London: Routledge and Kegan Paul.

MacIntyre, A. (1971), 'Hume on "Is" and "Ought"', in A. MacIntyre (ed.), *Against the Self-Images of the Age: Essays on Ideology and Philosophy*, 109–24, London: Duckworth.

MacIntyre, A. (1988), *Whose Justice? Which Rationality?* London: Duckworth.

MacIntyre, A. (1990), *Three Rival Versions of Moral Enquiry: Encyclopaedia, Genealogy, and Tradition*, London: Duckworth.

MacIntyre, A. (1998a), 'First Principles, Final Ends and Contemporary Philosophical Issues', in K. Knight (ed.), *The MacIntyre Reader*, 171–201, Cambridge: Polity Press.

MacIntyre, A. (1998b), 'The *Theses on Feuerbach*: A Road Not Taken', in K. Knight (ed.), *The MacIntyre Reader*, 223–34, Cambridge: Polity Press.

MacIntyre, A. (1999), *Dependent Rational Animals: Why Human Beings Need the Virtues*, London: Duckworth.

MacIntyre, A. (2006), *Edith Stein: A Philosophical Prologue*, London: Continuum.

MacIntyre, A. (2007), *After Virtue: A Study in Moral Theory*, 3rd edn, London: Duckworth.

MacIntyre, A. (2010), 'Danish Ethical Demands and French Common Goods: Two Moral Philosophies', *European Journal of Philosophy*, 18 (1): 1–16.

MacIntyre, A. (2012), 'Foreword', in Adolf Reinach (ed.) and J. F. Crosby, *The Apriori Foundations of the Civil Law, Along with the Lecture 'Concerning Phenomenology'*, v–vii, Frankfurt: Walter de Gruyter.

MacIntyre, A. (2013), 'On Having Survived the Academic Moral Philosophy of the Twentieth Century', in F. O'Rourke (ed.), *What Happened in and to Moral Philosophy in the Twentieth Century? Philosophical Essays in Honor of Alasdair MacIntyre*, 17–34, Notre Dame: University of Notre Dame Press.

MacIntyre, A. (2014), 'Philosophical Education against Contemporary Culture', in *Proceedings of the American Catholic Philosophical Association*, 87: 43–56.

MacIntyre, A. (2016), *Ethics in the Conflicts of Modernity: An Essay on Desire, Practical Reasoning, and Narrative*, Cambridge: Cambridge University Press.

Maritain, J. (1949), '" Introduction" and "On the Philosophy of Human Rights"', in UNESCO (ed.), *Human Rights: Comments and Interpretations*, 9–17 and 72–7, London: Allan Wingate.

Maritain, J. (1995), *Distinguish to Unite or the Degrees of Knowledge*, trans. Gerald B. Phelan et al., Notre Dame: University of Notre Dame Press.

Mulligan, K. ed. (1987), *Speech Act and Sachverhalt: Reinach and the Foundations of Realist Phenomenology*, Berlin: Springer.

Popper, K. R. (1945), *The Open Society and Its Enemies Vol. 1: The Spell of Plato*, London: Routledge and Kegan Paul.

Reinach, A. (2012), 'The Apriori Foundations of the Civil Law', in A. Reinach (ed.) and J. F. Crosby, *The Apriori Foundations of the Civil Law, Along with the Lecture 'Concerning Phenomenology'*, 1–142, Frankfurt: Walter de Gruyter.

Roberts, E. A. (1997), *The Anglo-Marxists: A Study in Ideology and Culture*, Lanham: Rowman & Littlefield.

Salice, A. and G. Uemura (2018), 'Social Acts and Communities: Walther Between Husserl and Reinach', in A. Calcagno (ed.), *Gerda Walther's Phenomenology of Sociality, Psychology, and Religion*, 27–46, Cham: Springer.

Salice, A. and H. B. Schmid eds (2016), *The Phenomenological Approach to Social Reality: History, Concepts, Problems*, Cham: Springer.

Searle, J. R. (1964), 'How to Derive "Ought" from "Is"', *The Philosophical Review*, 73 (1): 43–58.

Searle, J. R. (1969), *Speech Acts: An Essay in the Philosophy of Language*, Cambridge: Cambridge University Press.

Searle, J. R. (1995), *The Construction of Social Reality*, New York: Free Press.

Searle, J. R. (2010), *Making the Social World: The Structure of Human Civilization*, Oxford: Oxford University Press.

Skinner, Q. (2002), 'Interpretation and the Understanding of Speech Acts', in Q. Skinner (ed.), *Visions of Politics vol. 1: Regarding Method*, 103–27, Cambridge: Cambridge University Press.

Smith, B. and W. Żełaniec (2012), 'Laws of Essence or Constitutive Rules? Reinach vs. Searle on the Ontology of Social Entities', in Francesca De Vecchi (ed.), *Eidetica del Diritto e Ontologia Sociale: Il Realismo di Adolf Reinach*, 83–108, Milan: Mimesis.

Sorabji, R. (1980), *Necessity, Cause, and Blame: Perspectives on Aristotle's Theory*, London: Duckworth.

Strawson, P. F. (1971), *Logico-Linguistic Papers*, London: Methuen.

Warnock, G. J. (1969), 'John Langshaw Austin: A Biographical Sketch', in K. T. Fann (ed.), *Symposium on J. L. Austin*, 3–21, London: Routledge and Kegan Paul.

Warnock, G. J. (1973), 'Saturday Mornings', in I. Berlin (ed.), *Essays on J. L. Austin*, 31–45, Oxford: Oxford University Press.

Wittgenstein, L. (2009), *Philosophical Investigations*, trans. G. E. M. Anscombe, P. M. S. Hacker and J. Schulte, 4th edn, Oxford: Wiley-Blackwell.

Virtues and the common good

Alasdair MacIntyre reads Aristotle

Christof Rapp

Aristotle is famous for stressing the impact of the legislation in the city-state on the moral development of its citizens. Also, it is crucial for Aristotle's political theory that a city-state is the kind of community that strives for a common good or purpose and that citizens are assessed according to their contribution to the realization of this common purpose. At first glance this looks pretty similar to Alasdair MacIntyre's approach to virtue ethics, especially with respect to the role of communities and questions of justice. These similarities notwithstanding, this chapter attempts to pinpoint some crucial differences. Above all, it turns out to be difficult for any community-relative conception of the virtues to integrate Aristotle's appeal to human nature. Moreover, one might question whether Aristotle would be willing to join MacIntyre in rejecting community-independent standards of justice. MacIntyre's interpretations of Aristotle are too complex to do justice to them in their entirety here. However, the general contours of his reading seem to be clear.

1 Background: The revival of Aristotelian ethics

One of the most influential debates in contemporary political theory was, and to some extent still is, the dispute between liberalism and communitarianism. It is well known that modern communitarianism essentially stems from a critique of liberal conceptions of the state and – connected with this – a critique of modern moral philosophy in general. To some extent, the critique was a reaction to John Rawls's thought experiment of the so-called veil of ignorance, which, according to the critique, presupposes the conception of a socially and historically unconditioned self. This conception in turn is seen as inspired by early modern philosophy, among others the philosophy of Immanuel Kant. Thus, if the theoretical sources of liberalism are to be found in certain intellectual developments of modernity, it makes sense to outline an alternative that draws on pre-modern thinking or is at least intellectually kindred to pre-modern ideas. In this regard, communitarianism situated itself very similarly to the simultaneously emerging virtue ethics, which was originally motivated by the critique of the theories of deontology and consequentialism prevailing in modern moral philosophy and was then further developed through an appeal to premodern theories of virtue (see most notably Anscombe 1958; Williams 1985). Now so-called pre-modern ethics is itself an extremely complex and multifaceted endeavour; Aristotle or the 'Aristotelian tradition' are regularly involved in these appeals to pre-modernity, since Aristotelian ethics, which was taken up in the Middle Ages by Thomas Aquinas and adapted to a Christian framework, is considered at a very general level the major alternative to modern moral philosophy insofar as Aristotle was concerned – very roughly speaking – primarily with happiness and the virtues rather than duties and rights, and insofar as the morality of the individual seems, in his thought, to be intimately connected with the morality of the political community.

The object of Aristotle's political philosophy is the Greek city-state, the *polis*. The city-state represents the kind of political community that Aristotle was closest to and most familiar with due to his own life experience. Although it was during Aristotle's lifetime that Alexander the Great, who Aristotle had taught for several years, founded a world empire, which de facto lessened the significance of the city-state as the paradigmatic political form of community, nonetheless, this important historical change is, for whatever reasons, not really reflected in Aristotle's writings; his political thinking remains entirely oriented around the traditional city-state – and in this it differs in important ways from a modern liberal constitutional state. The city-state described by Aristotle comes closer in several regards to the communitarian ideal than to the modern liberal conception. For Aristotle, the city-state should only include a few thousand citizens, so that it is possible for people to know one another. Moreover, it was a common practice that the city-state took on responsibility for certain religious–cultural tasks. Finally, Aristotle sees it as one of the central tasks of the legislator to take care of the citizens' upbringing, that is, above all, the formation of their character. Thus in this understanding of the city-state there is no fundamental separation of the political and public sphere from a private sphere responsible for moral content and questions of belief, which means that the city-state and its parts do not strive for any kind of neutrality in such questions; to the contrary, the city-state seems to offer the most suitable form to achieve an agreement about the content of moral education and character formation. For these reasons it seems quite natural to turn to Aristotle when we seek alternatives to the modern liberal understanding of the state.

The debate between communitarianism and liberalism is sometimes put rather pointedly as the question of whether to give precedence to the good or to the right and rights. Whereas liberalism gives priority to the rights of liberty that are meant to enable the individual to develop their own conception of the good, it is essential to communitarian theses that substantial notions of right, justice and rights can only result from a substantial conception of the good. In this sense, proponents of communitarianism argue for the priority of the good, whereas proponents of liberalism consider the individual rights of liberty to be foundational. If we reduce the controversy to this simple set of alternatives, then Aristotle seems to belong among the friends of the good more than the friends of rights. For, first, Aristotle's *Nicomachean Ethics* begins with a theory of the good, or more precisely the highest good; from this Aristotle develops the conception of human happiness; from this in turn the Aristotelian theory of virtue emerges; and justice finally makes an appearance among the individual virtues, in the vicinity of which it might be possible (if at all) to situate rights. Second, Aristotle stresses repeatedly that the state community, that is, the city-state, exists for the sake of a good. This all sounds at first glance very much like a prioritization of the good, suggesting that in this regard as well Aristotle is intellectual kin to communitarians.

2 Alasdair MacIntyre's 'Aristotelian' theory of virtues

One important source of the revival of Aristotelian virtue theory is Alasdair MacIntyre's *After Virtues* (1981). In this book, he famously invokes Aristotelian ethics as an alternative to Friedrich Nietzsche, and more generally to developments deriving from the philosophy of enlightenment. Since he undertakes to ground virtues in practices that are inextricably connected with small communities, his ideas have been associated with the movement of communitarianism as sketched earlier. At any rate, MacIntyre's reading of Aristotelian virtues (especially in *After Virtue*) represents the most straightforward attempt to understand virtues as deriving from the ethical life of particular communities. This attempt has inspired political philosophers and Aristotle scholars alike. This in itself is a reason to look a little more closely into his claims. For MacIntyre the concept of practice is pivotal. He conceives 'practices' as cooperative, socially founded activities that possess their own particular standards of excellence (MacIntyre 1981: 187). There are inherent goods of a practice that can only be achieved through the acknowledgement of those particular standards of excellence. Every practice has a history (MacIntyre 1981: 190); the standards of excellence peculiar to the practice are moulded by all those persons who have previously participated in the practice. In entering a practice, a person places herself in a relation to all previous participants of the practice, such that the participation in such a practice always goes hand-in-hand with the acknowledgement of a certain tradition and certain standards of this tradition (MacIntyre 1981: 190). Virtues then get defined in reference to such a practice. MacIntyre conceives virtue as 'an acquired human quality, the possession and exercise of which tends to enable us to achieve those goods which are internal to practices and the lack of which effectively prevents us from achieving any such goods' (MacIntyre 1981: 191). Moreover, this practice-relative concept of virtue gets connected with MacIntyre's ideas on the narrative conception of the self and the role of tradition (MacIntyre 1981: ch. 15). No one is in a position to seek the good or exercise the virtues as an individual (MacIntyre 1981: 220). The virtues uphold the relation to those traditions that provide historical context to the life of the individual (MacIntyre 1981: 223). 'Hence the individual's search for his or her good is generally and characteristically conducted within a context defined by those traditions of which the individual's life is a part' (MacIntyre 1981: 222). Here the narrative phenomenon of being-embedded is decisive. The history of a practice is embedded within a larger tradition and only becomes comprehensible within this larger tradition, just as the life of an individual is embedded within the history of a series of traditions. The good life for the Athenian commander from the fifth century BCE is thus different from the good life of a nun in the Middle Ages or a peasant in the seventeenth century. The point is not just that these persons lived under different social circumstances;

> it is also that we all approach our own circumstances as bearers of a particular social identity. I am someone's son or daughter, someone else's cousin or uncle; I am a citizen of this or that city, a member of this or that guild or profession; I belong to this clan, that tribe, this nation. Hence what is good for me has to be the good for one who inhabits these roles. (MacIntyre 1981: 220)

Practice, goods, inherent ends, community, friendship, activities, virtues – this all sounds like genuinely Aristotelian terminology; and in fact MacIntyre develops his virtue theory from his own special interpretation of the Aristotelian theory of virtue (MacIntyre 1981: ch. 12) and calls his theory 'clearly Aristotelian' (MacIntyre 1981: 197). At the same time, he explicitly distinguishes himself from Aristotle, rejecting in particular Aristotle's appeal to a fixed human nature – MacIntyre speaks of Aristotle's 'metaphysical biology' (MacIntyre 1981: 148, 162, 196). If we follow MacIntyre's strategy of throwing together the Aristotelian concepts of the good, practice and virtue, the result for the political community is that it follows a project recognized as good by the community (MacIntyre 1981: 151, 156) and that it is only from this project and the associated practices that we can ascertain the virtues that are necessary to achieve the inherent goods of this practice. Moreover, every reflection on the good and the virtues can only be meaningful from within a certain tradition and in consideration of the particular social role of the person in question. Taken together, this yields a picture that, despite the inspiration MacIntyre takes from Aristotle, and despite the Aristotelian-seeming terminology, ultimately contradicts several core statements of the historical paradigm.

3 Aristotle's general account of the good

Aristotle's ethics concerns itself in a central passage with the good and goods; in the *Nicomachean Ethics*, the systematic basis of the entire treatise seems to consist in his theory of the highest good. In terms of the alternatives discussed earlier as to whether priority should be given to the good or the right, Aristotle again winds up with the communitarians in the camp of friends of the good. Since Aristotle does not shy away from naming concrete goods – for example, health, beauty, strength, virtues, good repute, many and good friends, and many and good descendants[1] – his ethics seems more 'material', that is, filled with concrete content, than 'formal' or 'procedural' (which is generally associated with the liberal position). Now it should be noted that Aristotle's characterization of such things as goods does not say much more than that people commonly view these things as worth choosing and worth striving for in themselves. Such a list of goods is compatible with quite diverse moral standpoints, since everything depends on the weighting of the various goods. Thus, Aristotle argues for the priority of the inner goods of the soul, namely, the virtues, over the bodily goods (e.g. health, strength) and external goods (e.g. good repute and good luck);

he supports this with, among other things, arguments that an ambivalent use could be made of all goods with the exception of the virtues (*Rhetoric* I 1, 1355b4-5), and that there could be an excess of all other goods but not of virtue (*Politics* VII 1). This represents in a sense the first step in a philosophical structuring and hierarchization of the goods acknowledged at the level of common sense. This hierarchization goes further in the first book of the *Nicomachean Ethics* when Aristotle determines the highest good. It is determined through the formal criterion that it is always sought for its own sake and never for the sake of something else (*NE* I.7). Aristotle tries to show that only *eudaimonia*, happiness or the happy life, is of this type. All agree on this point, according to Aristotle, that *eudaimonia* is the highest good, the only controversy is what this highest good consists in (*NE* I.7.1097b22-24). Thus, it is clear that the identification of happiness and the highest good or end is not yet meant as any substantial position. It is decisive for the Aristotelian conception of the good that he wishes to determine the good generally as the goal of human action, which could manifest itself quite differently in different domains and actions. The discussion of the good and the highest good is thus a methodologically crucial step within Aristotle's moral philosophy, since it establishes *eudaimonia* as the reference point of all human action; *eudaimonia* is understood as specifically human well-being and requires in turn the exercise of certain excellences/virtues, such that Aristotelian ethics can essentially be structured through the exploration of these excellences/virtues.

Thus, the prominence of the concept of the good in Aristotle's ethics should be confused neither with the communitarian thesis of the priority of the good over the just nor with MacIntyre's idea of a particular community. For Aristotle's general theory of the good as he presents it at the beginning of his ethics does not concern a particular substantial conception of the good as a precondition for a substantial understanding of the just, but rather accounts for the general structures of intentional striving and action that then help to justify the particular position of *eudaimonia* as the end point of human actions. At this point, we might think that the discussion of the highest good only gives us the general teleological structure of the ethics, and the content of happiness and thus the ultimate goal of striving would then be whatever various groupings or various individuals recognize as good and worth striving for.[2] In fact Aristotle proposes a somewhat different strategy that aims at outlining, at least in broad strokes, what can be considered the good life of a human. The decisive step occurs in the so-called *ergon* argument.

4 The role of the *ergon* argument in Aristotle's moral philosophy

Everyone agrees, says Aristotle, that *eudaimonia*, the happy life for humans, is the highest good – that which we all strive for and which all planned and intentional action ultimately aims at. How can this goal be more closely delimited? Aristotle first uses the formal properties of the highest good to show that certain forms of life are not suited to exhibit happiness for structural reasons (*NE* I.5). For example, if the highest good, and thus happiness, represents something that is a final goal that no one ever pursues for the sake of something else, then the life dedicated to acquiring money cannot have a structure suited to exhibit happiness, since money is something that essentially serves the acquisition of other things and thus cannot be meaningfully pursued for its own sake.

Above all, Aristotle seeks, in the famous *ergon* argument in *NE* I.7, to give at least a general outline of what the good life consists in for humans. The *ergon* is the purpose, end or specific function of each thing. Plato had already argued using the notion of *ergon* and showed that there is a specific *ergon* of the eye or the shears (Plato, *Republic* I 352e f.). The *ergon* argument in Aristotelian ethics is meant to show, from the specific nature of the human soul, what the good or end for the human as human is. In this argument, Aristotle reasons that since only the human possesses a soul with the capacity to reason, this is the *ergon* of the human that distinguishes us from other creatures and from lifeless things. The reason can be employed or activated well or poorly. If it is used well, then we say that it behaves in accordance with excellence/virtue (*aretē*). Moreover, it is decisive for *eudaimonia* that individual humans do not just possess reason as a disposition, but rather actually develop and exercise or deploy their reason. Accordingly, human happiness or the good life for the human as human is determined among other things by the exercise of the soul in accordance with its specific excellence/virtue. As mentioned, this is only meant to be an approximate outline of happiness (*NE* I.7.1098a20-22), but it essentially holds for all humans and is based on that which characterizes all humans: their rational soul.

As a vague outline of a determination, this definition provides no details, no detailed life-plans and no concrete decisions; Aristotle himself seems to allow for a certain plurality of life forms conducive to happiness when in his sophisticated weighing of the theoretical and the practical form of life in Book X, Chapters 6–9 of the *Nicomachean Ethics*, he places the theoretical life above the practical life, but nonetheless concedes that there is also a form of happiness that corresponds to the practical life. But this plurality remains quite limited. The good specific to the human must be related to the exercise of reason. Since reason occurs in two different ways in the rational part of the soul and in the part of the soul that is itself non-rational but capable of listening to reason, there are two kinds of virtue or excellence: the excellence of the rational part of the soul with its various intellectual capacities (intellectual or dianoetic virtues) and the excellence of the non-rational part of the soul, also called 'character'; when the latter is in accord with reason or responds as the rational part of the soul would command, then it achieves an excellence peculiar to what we could also call 'character virtues' or 'ethical virtues'. Thus, achieving a happy life means, for every person, leading a life in accordance with the character virtues and the intellectual virtues. The practical or political life, in which the character virtues are predominant, has to make use of at least *one* intellectual virtue, namely *phronēsis*, without which there can be no true character virtues. The theoretical life on the other hand, which is dedicated to the preferential exercise of the intellectual capacities and in particular the theoretical capacities, cannot do without certain positive and praiseworthy character traits, since every human as a bodily and social creature has to come to terms with certain needs and social challenges.

This rough outline of happiness, which Aristotle develops from the nature or essence of the human, contains unequivocal normative guidelines as to which forms of life are suitable to happiness and which are not. Both the life that consists in the exercise of character virtues and the life that consists in the exercise of intellectual virtues are good or happy because in each of these, one of the parts of the soul peculiar to humans is in a good state or is exercised in a good manner. Thus, Aristotle's *eudaimonia* does not consist primarily in a subjectively felt state of happiness, but rather in the objectively assessable activity in accordance with excellence (*aretē*) of the part(s) of the soul peculiar to the human. From our modern perspective, we might find this plausible or not – but it is clear that Aristotle's philosophical concept of virtue/excellence would be completely meaningless and objectless without this reference to the nature and peculiar function of the human soul. The virtue/excellence that serves as part of the *definiens* of human happiness in Aristotle's outline of the happy life is not just any ability or disposition that appears useful or advantageous to us in order to achieve something good, but rather it is the good, excellent state of the human soul. Thus, when MacIntyre's reading of Aristotelian virtues tries to jettison precisely this central theoretical piece of the Aristotelian ethics that he finds undesirable, it robs Aristotle's conception of virtue of no less than its philosophical core. Of course, Neo-Aristotelians are free to combine various pieces of Aristotle's moral philosophy into a novel construction, but it would be problematic to claim that such a philosophically gutted theory of virtue is still 'Aristotelian'.

The proponents of MacIntyre's 'Aristotelianism' seek to conceal this problem by distinguishing Aristotle's good practical philosophy, as it were, from what they consider his obsolete and outdated theoretical philosophy.[3] The *ergon* argument, its preconditions and its direct implications are ascribed to the obsolete theoretical part,[4] and it is thought that one can easily leave it aside along with other historical peculiarities of Aristotelian ethics (such as the distinction between Greeks and barbarians). MacIntyre coined the term 'metaphysical biology' for this purpose in order to characterize the thematic complex connected with the *ergon* argument as an isolatable and dispensable aberration in Aristotelian thought.

5 Does Aristotle's ethical thinking rely on 'metaphysical biology'?

With the claim that Aristotle's teleology rests on a 'metaphysical biology' (MacIntyre 1981: 148, 162, 196), MacIntyre clearly wishes to mark off what he considers a particularly untenable Aristotelian theorem. Since MacIntyre very much wants to draw on Aristotle's teleological structure of actions, hence his practical teleology, this term implies a thesis about the purportedly problematic conflation of practical and theoretical philosophy on Aristotle's part. The formulation clearly refers to the idea of a predetermined goal or end in the nature of a species. The reference to biology is meant to suggest that Aristotelian ethics rests on biological judgements about the essence of the species, whereas the reference to metaphysics implies that the corresponding biological judgements of Aristotle are not really supported empirically and scientifically, but rather biased by a particular metaphysics – one that for example dictates assumptions about the place of humanity in the cosmos. If such a conglomerate of assumptions were in fact the foundation for Aristotle's ethics and political philosophy, then without question, one would be well advised to dispense with these assumptions relentlessly.

The question of whether Aristotle's *ergon* argument (see section 4) was meant to found practical-moral thought on factual judgements borrowed from the science of his time was the subject of controversial dispute in the literature of the past decades. This kind of discussion was not uncommon at the time *After Virtue* appeared; Bernard Williams, for example, in a publication in the 1980s, likewise accused Aristotle of seeking an Archimedean point in an absolute understanding of nature (Williams 1985: 52). Since then at least a majority of authors have rejected this criticism as unjustified, partly on philosophical grounds and partly on exegetical grounds. On the one hand, there are philosophical tendencies that assess the appeal ancient philosophy makes to nature more positively, elaborating the advantages of a 'rich', simultaneously descriptive and normative concept of nature, which moreover is not taken from natural philosophy but rather conceived from the perspective of the acting and morally reflective person (see, for example, Annas 1993; Nussbaum 1988; McDowell 1998). On the other hand, it is worth asking whether Aristotle's statements on the specific abilities of the human soul do in fact rely on questionable theses of Aristotelian biology or Aristotelian metaphysics. It is true that Aristotle's natural philosophy defends a picture of the soul that is compatible with his practical philosophy (for example in his *De Anima*), yet his conception of virtues does not directly use any of the specifications of his natural philosophy. At least the essential statements Aristotle makes about the human soul in connection with his conception of virtue – namely, that it possesses reason and that within the soul we can distinguish a rational and a non-rational part – can be made plausible without the metaphysically more ambitious and controversial theorems about the soul as form and about the status of forms in relation to matter. It is telling that in this context, for the division of the soul into a rational and a non-rational part, Aristotle himself refers the reader to his exoteric writings meant for a broader audience (see, for example, *NE* I.13, 1102a26-27), and does not refer to his natural-philosophical investigations. Thus, it seems that the Aristotelian ethics can make autonomous use of its distinction between a rational and a non-rational part of the soul without needing any recourse to the results of biology. Observations like these might suggest a general picture of Aristotle's ethics according to which appeals to human nature are not seen as the biological-metaphysical and, as it were, external fundament for normative claims, but rather as the result of an agent's reflection on the potential and the limits of human agency. For example, one could refer to *NE* I. 2, where Aristotle points out that if there is a supreme good for the sake of which people ultimately do what they do, and which is chosen only for its own sake and not for the sake of anything else, it would be of great importance for the conduct of life to know more about this supreme good – just as it is important for the archer to have a well-defined target (1094a22-26). If indeed the appeals to human nature are derived from efforts like these, that is, from efforts aiming at the clarification of the conditions of a good and happy life, nature is deployed not as a set of objectively given ahistorical facts, but is just one factor within an inquiry that is conducted from the agent's internal perspective; this kind of inquiry can lead for example to the result that certain ways of living are more, while others are less, suitable for attaining the good and happy life. Also, Aristotle never tires of emphasizing in this context that this kind of inquiry can only provide a rough outline of what the good life consists in – and such a rough outline (*tupos*) can be interpreted and filled in different ways, which might be sensitive to different social-historical backgrounds and to individual capabilities and preferences.

We could summarize this discussion by saying that Aristotle's appeal to nature does not necessarily presuppose any substantial recourse to controversial and purportedly obsolete theorems of biology or metaphysics. Far from rejecting the appeal to a human nature and dismissing it as a historical curiosity, there are contemporary philosophers who defend Aristotelian naturalism as the key to upholding an objective concept of the good. In any case however – whether or not one wishes to go as far as the proponents of a Neo-Aristotelian naturalism – the project of defending a genuinely Aristotelian ethics without *any* reference to human nature seems very unpromising.

6 Universalist or community-relative grounding of Aristotelian virtues?

Aristotle's concept of the excellence/virtue of the soul is one thing, collecting and describing individual virtues recognized at his time is quite another; it is here if anywhere that a historical-societal dimension foreign to the *ergon* argument in itself seems to come into play. If we look at Aristotle's catalogue of concrete virtues, above all the so-called character virtues, then we recognize a few of the virtues still appreciated today (justice, temperance, generosity and perhaps also courage), but we also find several other virtues that seem quite inseparable from the cultural and political circumstances in the Athens of Aristotle's day. With virtues such as *megaloprepeia*, for example, the impossibility of any halfway-usable translation already confronts us with the historical contingency of this virtue; in English we use something like 'magnificence', but the expression does not capture what Aristotle really meant, namely, a virtue that relates to the appropriate financial support of elaborate public events. Other virtues seem familiar and trans-historical by name, such as courage, but reveal themselves to be false friends upon closer examination, for while we would happily elucidate the value of courage using examples of civil courage, Aristotle insists that courage is a virtue of warriors that can only be manifested in life-threatening situations of a battle.

In view of examples like these, we will not be very tempted to claim that these virtues are derived from human nature in a universalist manner. Authors who actually uphold such a universalist conception (see, for example, Nussbaum 1993) are assuming a quite idealized picture of Aristotelian virtues – a picture in which exactly one virtue is correlated with each of the areas of human life (see, for example, Höffe 1998). This way of picturing the grounding of Aristotelian virtues is not implausible, but it is idealized to some extent, since in fact such a derivation of virtues from the elementary domains of human life (unlike the way it is done by Nussbaum 1993) is not found anywhere in Aristotle; he does not even attempt a complete listing of the various domains of life. Moreover, this picture abstracts from the often clearly historically bound[5] and sometimes very narrowly conceived[6] concrete descriptions of individual virtues. Finally, this way of presenting Aristotelian virtues regularly pushes aside the question of gaps in the Aristotelian catalogue of virtues: wouldn't a universalistic virtue ethics (derived from the essential domains of human life) also provide a virtue for coping with suffering, illness, loss and death – and not just for death in battle? This would at least be something that would concern all human beings alike. Aristotle himself mentions emotions that relate to the achievements and possessions of others, and that could cause a significant amount of 'emotional disorder', but why does he not include in his ethics a virtue that could help us to deal with these emotions? In short, if the universalist reading is not entirely persuasive in view of the concrete examples and the gaps he leaves, wouldn't a community-based reading be preferable here – for example, with the argument that despite the ambitious statements from Book I of the *Nicomachean Ethics* about the philosophical foundation of the virtues (see section 3) Books II through V bring out the entire breadth and complexity of lived morality in the particular historical context of Athens in the fourth century BCE? We could then, like MacIntyre, say that Aristotle lacks any sense for the specifically historical (MacIntyre 1981: 147) and for this reason said nothing about the historical contingency of the Athenian virtues he described, but that with his descriptions of virtues in Books II to V of the *Nicomachean Ethics* offers a paradigmatic analysis of the grounding of virtues in the traditional practices of Athenian aristocrats in the fourth century BCE.

Clearly neither the community-based nor the universalist reading offers a sufficient characterization of the role of the characterization of particular virtues in the Aristotelian ethics. We should concede then to the universalist interpretation that virtues for Aristotle are founded in human nature, and we should concede to the community-based reading that there is no purely deductive way to get from the abstract philosophical idea of an excellence of the human soul to the full breadth of descriptions of individual virtues and that the concrete, historically embedded morality of the Athenian aristocracy in Aristotle's time probably supplied additional constraints. To see what connects both conceptions, we need to briefly delve into Aristotle's famous doctrine of *mesotēs*, his idea that character virtues always aim at a mean.

This *mesotēs* doctrine is the decisive link between the conception of virtue as excellence of the specifically human soul on the one hand and the multiplicity of character virtues on the other. This is so in the following sense: virtue/excellence conceived as the excellence of the non-rational part of the soul is a character disposition on the basis of which one carries out right actions and has the appropriate emotions; for if a character disposition were the origin of wrong actions and inappropriate emotions, it could not possibly be manifesting the excellent or best possible state of this part of the soul. Now what does it mean to carry out the right action and to have the appropriate emotion? Generally speaking, for Aristotle, this means avoiding wrong actions and inappropriate emotions; and since actions and emotions can be wrong or inappropriate in two different directions, namely, in the direction of too much and the direction of too little, a virtue aims at a mean – insofar as the mean is that area between too much and too little. For this reason, character virtues for Aristotle are always a mean (between two bad character traits) and make it possible for us to hit a middle in the area of emotions and actions, namely, the right actions and emotions. This, I take it, is Aristotle's philosophical account of what it means to be a virtue or excellence. How does he get from this most general and formal account to the concrete multitude of individual types of virtues? Does he do so by deducing the right character disposition for each of the different areas of human life from this general account? This would more or less correspond to the universalist reading sketched earlier, with all of its weaknesses. Thus it seems more adequate to say that Aristotle puts this philosophical account to the test using the acknowledged virtues of his day, and that he browses the vocabulary of popular morality for character dispositions that are virtuous in the sense that they hit a mean (and thus avoid the fallacious tendencies of too much and too little). The outcome of this encounter, as we may put it, between a philosophical account of virtue and the popular morality of his time is that several of the virtues acknowledged by his fellow citizens, if they are only analysed correctly according to the *mesotēs* doctrine, can in fact be understood as correct character dispositions and thus as manifestation of the excellent state of the corresponding part of the soul. Other dispositions, by contrast, which are also to be classified as correct and virtuous according to the *mesotēs* doctrine, are simply lacking any denomination in everyday language. And in still other cases, popular morality offers characterizations of behaviours that are generally esteemed as virtuous, but cannot, according to Aristotle's philosophical analysis, qualify as real excellences of the soul.

If this is a suitable description of Aristotle's way of proceeding, then it is true that Aristotle's catalogue of virtues reflects the concrete virtues of his historical context; but it is not true that they are recognized as virtues because they are the virtues of this particular community; rather, Aristotle only recognizes those virtues given in his historical community as real virtues or excellences because they correspond to his philosophical account of virtue (and thus aim at a mean, avoid the fallacious excesses). This philosophical account in turn cannot be separated from the idea that virtues have to qualify as the manifestation of the excellence of the human soul (or a part of it), and this latter idea is not dependent on the concrete morality of a particular political community.

7 MacIntyre and Aristotle on the common good of the community

Since Aristotelian ethics in the narrow sense can only be separated with great difficulty from the notion of a constant human nature, we might think that it is not Aristotle's ethics oriented around the happiness of the individual, as he develops it in the *Nicomachean Ethics* and *Eudemian Ethics*, but rather his theory of the political community, the object of the *Politics*, that serves as the real model for communitarians. And in fact, in his book *Whose Justice? Which Rationality?* Alasdair MacIntyre gives considerable weight to the *Politics* and emphasizes that the *Nicomachean Ethics* also cannot be understood without the *Politics* (MacIntyre 1988: 102).[7] While in his discussion of Aristotle in *After Virtue* MacIntyre relies primarily on the *Nicomachean Ethics*, his picture of Aristotle in *Whose Justice?* rests above all on *Politics* I and VII as well as excerpts from *Nicomachean Ethics* V and VI. Most notably, he appeals to the beginning of *Politics* I (MacIntyre 1988: 96–8), where Aristotle argues in the famous *zôon-politikon*-passage that it is part of human nature to live in a political community, and that anyone who is not capable of belonging to a state community or who does not need to due to her own autarchy must be either an animal or a god (Aristotle, *Politics* I 2, 1253a26-29). MacIntyre concludes that whoever is isolated from the justice of the *polis* does not have any standards of justice at their disposal (MacIntyre 1988: 98). For MacIntyre, Aristotle is here expressing the idea 'that it is within one specific kind of social context that the intellectual and moral virtues of human beings characteristically have to be exercised and that apart from certain features of that kind of social context the concept of those virtues must for the most part lack application' (MacIntyre 1988: 99). Accordingly, there are no external standards[8] by which the *polis* can be assessed: 'Justice, both as a virtue of the individual and as an ordering of the social life, is only to be achieved within the concrete institutionalized forms of some particular *polis*. The norms of justice have no existence apart from the actualities of each particular *polis*' (MacIntyre 1988: 122).

Aristotle's *Politics* in fact contains a number of thoughts that can be further developed in the terms of communitarian theory or along the lines of *Whose Justice? Whose Rationality?* The most noteworthy is the intimate connection between ethics and political theory correctly emphasized by MacIntyre; Aristotle emphasizes the continuity between ethics and political theory, for example, by referring in the final chapter of the *Nicomachean Ethics* to the necessity of implementing the virtues and by describing this as the task of the legislator, which is meant to motivate the subsequent discussion of legislation – one of the central themes of the *Politics*. In terms of the communitarian potential of Aristotle's *Politics*, so to speak, it is no less important that Aristotle explicitly defines the city-state as being founded for the sake of a particular good, namely, the highest good (*Politics* I.1,1252a1-3). The city-state arises, according to Aristotle, for the sake of the self-sufficient life (in terms of the provision of that which is necessary for life) and persists for the sake of the good life (*Politics* I. 2,1252b27-30). The good life as a communal good or end of a city-state is clearly not conceivable for Aristotle without the exercise of particular virtues, such that there is a direct connection between the end of a state and moral norms; in this sense, Aristotle also argues in *Politics* VII 1- 2 that the happiness of the state and the happiness of the individual are of the same type. He explicitly distinguishes the state from communities that only exist for pragmatic purposes, such as a trading cooperation or a military alliance (see *Politics* III 9). Here we could see a proximity to MacIntyre's idea that a community is founded 'to achieve a common project, to bring about some good recognized as their shared good by all those engaging in the project' (MacIntyre 1981: 151).[9] Moreover in various contexts of his *Politics*, Aristotle points out that different city-states could have different conceptions concerning the content of this communal good and the standards of justice. If the conception of the communal good has direct implications for the abilities and virtues recognized as praiseworthy, then this seems to come close to the communitarian ideal. It is not least of all one of the primary motifs of the *Politics* that the functioning of a city-state presupposes the exercise of certain virtues by its citizens. A city-state or *polis* worthy of the name, Aristotle even says, would have to ensure that the citizens acquire certain virtues (*Politics* III 9, 1280b5-8).

In all these regards Aristotle's political theory seems closer to the communitarian picture and closer to the picture suggested by MacIntyre than to its rival liberal conception. However, upon closer examination we also find significant differences.

8 Whose justice?

City-states differ in their constitutions, and accordingly in their standards of justice as well. Of course, Aristotle was familiar with many historically grown constitutions; he himself arranged a collection of 158 constitutions. However, he does not go so far as to say that each of these constitutions is bound to its own conception of the just. What interested him about the plurality of standards of justice was that the significant forms of constitution differ in the prevailing conceptions of the type of merit to be considered in distributing public offices and goods (this is a discussion that stretches above all across the chapters 8–11 of *Politics* III). In an oligarchy, the rule by the few wealthy ones, the oligarchs themselves at least tend to make the wealth they bring in the single standard for the distribution of goods and public offices. They argue that their disproportionately large financial support must be honoured by a correspondingly disproportionate share of rights to rule and of the communally acquired profits. This does not rule out the possibility that there could be other conceptions of just distribution in the same city-state held, for example, by the less wealthy citizens. In a democracy, the rule by the relatively impecunious many, in contrast, the democrats at least argue that all citizens should be equal in status as free citizens, and thus must all be considered equally in the distribution of goods and access to public offices. This is the conception that corresponds to the ruling group in a democracy, but this does not mean that this conception will be shared without exception by all citizens of the democratically ruled city-state. Finally there is the aristocracy, the rule by the educated and virtuous ones, in which at least those educated and virtuous persons argue that the virtue they bring to bear including their competence in good guidance of the city-state counts more than money and freedom, and thus they should be given correspondingly privileged access to governmental offices.

This discussion reveals a factual plurality of conceptions of justice. The question is what type of merit is to be valued more highly in questions of distributive justice. This plurality is however starkly limited; it essentially relates to the primary forms of state constitutions. Thus, it does not relate to the concrete difference between, let us say, Sparta and Thebes, but rather to the typological difference between various forms of constitution. Moreover, Aristotle does not simply juxtapose these various conceptions, but expresses a certain preference for the argument that neither money nor freedom, but rather virtue and knowledge (or competence), make a decisive contribution to the true highest end, the good and happy life. Hence the various claims raised by oligarchs, democrats and aristocrats can all be reassessed. Moreover, it is by no means the case that one has to be socialized within an oligarchy, a democracy or an aristocracy to claim wealth, freedom or virtue as the decisive contribution. This is shown by political conflicts, which often precisely involve the clash between the claims of oligarchically minded citizens and democrats within one and the same city-state, such that, as Aristotle describes again and again in *Politics* IV to VI, a reasonable balance needs to be found between these opposing, but not entirely unjustified claims.

This seems to be a completely different sort of consideration than the one MacIntyre develops from the problem of distributive justice. He takes this dispute between oligarchs, democrats and aristocrats as paradigmatic for different situations of any type that bring with them varying principles for just distribution.[10] And he takes distributive justice in turn as paradigmatic for any kind of exercise of virtue.[11] To assess what a just distribution would be, we need a common project and a common conception of the goals, which would make one contribution appear more meritorious than the other[12] – and this is itself a question of the appropriate experience and upbringing. It then follows directly from this, for MacIntyre, that there can be no polis-independent criteria for the assessment of justice.

9 No external standard?

A strict community-relative interpretation of the plurality of conceptions of justice in the various city-states (see section 8) would have to postulate that there can be no external standards of justice. Aristotle, however, seems to be far from drawing this conclusion. He keeps comparing various types of constitution and explicitly uses standards of justice in doing so. The most significant example of this is his juxtaposition of good and so-called 'degenerate' or 'unnatural' constitutions (*Politics* III 7). Essentially, those constitutions are considered good in which the ruling person or group rules for the benefit of all participating citizens, whereas Aristotle criticizes the constitutions in which the ruling person or group rules to their own benefit at the cost of the other citizens. Aristotle sees this latter tendency in tyranny (the sole ruler exploits the citizens for his own profit) and in oligarchy (the rich rule only for the benefit of the rich) as well as in those forms of democracy[13] in which the numerous poor seek to enrich themselves at the cost of the affluent. If in any form of constitution, the legitimate claims of certain groupings (e.g. the poor, the uneducated or the affluent) are systematically infringed upon or ignored, then the affected citizens are being ruled unjustly. This is the sharpest criticism that Aristotle levels at any individual type of constitution. While he can tolerate the fact that many states live under difficult conditions and thus cannot strive for a good life for all citizens in accord with the exercise of the virtues, and in fact have to be content with mere survival (*Politics* III 6, 1278b24-30), the aforementioned constitutions violate, on his view, the very nature or essence of a city-state, since by their nature city-states are founded for the good and self-sufficient life of their participating citizens (and their 'nature', that is essence, consists in being a community serving the good and self-sufficient life of its citizens). In this sense, constitutions that only serve the benefit of the rulers are 'unnatural'. And this, if anything, is what I call an 'external standard'.[14]

10 Political virtues

Using the notion of a common goal for a community that decisively determines what the citizens of a particular community consider good, MacIntyre suggests a quite plausible understanding of the virtues: the virtues or excellences in a community are those capacities that are considered praiseworthy in this particular community because they contribute to the realization of its common goal. Since achieving such a good in any community with a division of labour requires various capacities (as Aristotle also admits), MacIntyre can also establish a connection between Aristotle's political theory and the theorem that the good for the individual person is always measured by their particular social role as well.

We can also find in Aristotle a description that seems to come very close to this picture in reference to what Aristotle calls the 'civic' or 'political' virtues (see *Politics* III 4). The *polis*-relative virtues have to orient themselves around the constitution of that city-state, such that these virtues can also differ depending on the constitution (*Politics* III 4, 1276b30-34). Moreover, it would be fatal for a city-state if all of its citizens had the same abilities and virtues; hence at the level of the political or civic virtues role-specific abilities are needed, just as a ship needs good rowers but also good pilots. So far, so good. However, this description raises the question of how these political virtues relate to the virtues that were discussed in the ethical writings, namely, the ethical virtues (in *Politics* III 4 Aristotle calls them 'the virtues of the good or excellent human'). This question leads, as is so often the case with Aristotle, to a complex discussion with a differentiated conclusion – namely, to simplify it somewhat: on the one hand, it turns out that the virtue that those governing a city-state should have above all else, namely, practical reason (*phronēsis*), is identical with the eponymous virtue that distinguishes a good, excellent person. On the other hand, it turns out that all other political virtues are of a different type than the virtues discussed in the ethics, for they are role-specific and *polis*-relative, whereas the virtues of ethics, as Aristotle says, are always one and uniform (*Politics* III 4, 1276b32). This means, first, that the *polis*-relative and role-specific model of virtues corresponds to the political virtues in Aristotle but does not correspond to the true virtues. And it means, secondly, that Aristotle does not hesitate to contrast the political virtues dependent on the common goal of a city-state with the standard of a *polis*-independent human virtue.

Aristotle emphasizes in various contexts how important a well-ordered city-state is for the acquisition of the virtues. He also believes that laws have an educational mandate that essentially extends and supplements the upbringing in the family. For just as parents use praise and reproach, reward and punishment to bring their children to associate good actions with agreeable experiences and bad actions with disagreeable or painful experiences, well-made laws should not only prevent illegal actions but also educate the citizens to wholeheartedly reject wrong actions and to enjoy doing good and noble actions. This training is meant, in both the private and the legal domain, to operate on the non-rational part of the soul through sensations of pleasure and displeasure, and to so shape the character of the citizens that they act virtuously and in accordance with the laws without reluctance. Thus, Aristotle establishes an exceptionally close connection between the acquisition of virtues and legislation. However, he is fully aware that this represents an ideal, since the legislation of most actually existing city-states is by no means oriented around the virtues. In the time of Plato and Aristotle, the Spartan constitution was thought to place particular value on educating citizens in the virtues; yet Aristotle criticizes this constitution quite sharply, as it only concerns itself with a certain part of human virtues, namely, the martial virtues (see *Politics* II 9). It follows that legislation in the majority of states contributes rather little to the acquisition and reinforcement of the virtues. Hence for Aristotle the pluralism in the conception of the good and the just stems from the fact that most actually existing states are lagging behind the ideal of state education in the virtues. If Athens and Sparta remain behind the ideal envisioned by Plato and Aristotle of virtue-oriented legislation, there must be a concept or content to these virtues that can be determined independently of the particularities of Athens and Sparta. The good for the human as a human in Sparta is no different from the good for the human as a human in Athens.

11 The virtues of dependent beings

MacIntyre's understanding of Aristotelian ethics significantly evolved through the years. As already indicated, we cannot do justice to all the subtle moves and nuances within his interpretations of Aristotle. However, MacIntyre's work *Dependent Rational Animals* (1999) marks an important realignment in his use of Aristotle and thus deserves to be briefly considered.

The main innovation in this book, deriving from the Paul Carus Lectures delivered in 1997, consists in the discovery of what MacIntyre calls the 'human animality'. For this insight, he draws again on Aristotle, for Aristotle was a philosopher who took the commonality between human and non-human beings quite seriously. This is true in many respects; most notably, Aristotle's account of the soul acknowledges that human and non-human animals have the nourishing and perceptive soul (as well as the kinds of desires connected with these) in common. Also, human and non-human animals are both self-movers, that is, they can set themselves into motion, whenever they desire a perceived or imagined object. More than that, Book IX of the *Historia Animalium* engages in detail with the character traits of different species of animals and adopts for this purpose a vocabulary by which we usually describe the behaviour and habits of human beings. Using Aristotle's *Historia Animalium* for the human animality thesis, MacIntyre is particularly impressed by Aristotle's depiction of the intelligent behaviour of dolphins (MacIntyre 1999: 22). Nonetheless, there is of course a different strand in Aristotelian philosophy, namely, when it comes to human reason and rationality, which in some important sense is peculiar to human beings.[15] Indeed, Aristotle sometimes speaks of the complex nature of human beings (see, for example, *Nicomachean Ethics* VII.14, 1154b20-26) – 'complex' because they are mortal like all other animals on the one hand, but through their intellect also possess a spark, as it were, of divinity. This is by no means an argument against the project of exploring the animality of human beings with the help of Aristotle; it is rather a cautionary note, to which we will get back in a minute.

MacIntyre's new project in *Dependent Rational Animals* comes with an important retraction concerning the use of Aristotelian philosophy; with regard to the metaphysical biology-thesis from *After Virtue* he says: 'Although there is indeed good reason to repudiate important elements in Aristotle's biology, I now judge that I was in error in supposing an ethics independent of biology to be possible' (MacIntyre 1999: x). He justifies this turn by the thought that an account of the good, of rules and of the virtues must be able to explain how the corresponding form of life is possible for beings that are biologically constituted as we are; also, our initial animal condition must be regarded as the origin of a development into a certain way of life. Clearly, this is a major departure from the point of view we discussed above, and this new orientation is more likely to do justice to the Aristotelian approach (see the discussion in section 5). Taking these biological conditions into consideration, MacIntyre comes to focus firstly on the development of human beings and secondly on their dependency and vulnerability. It becomes obvious that, especially in the early stages of human development, human beings are not born as independent rational reasoners, but as animals and dependent beings. In order to acquire practical reason and virtues each individual is dependent on suitable parents, teachers and their virtues. The description of this peculiar development that MacIntyre offers (MacIntyre 1999: 81–98) is in many respects reminiscent of, and in conformity with, Aristotle's discussion of character development in *Nicomachean Ethics* Book II, even though Aristotle is of course not his only and not even his main source for this part of the discussion. It is important for MacIntyre's new account that not only the child and the adolescent but also grown up, adult agents remain dependent in many respects. In order to uphold their social relationships, agents need what MacIntyre now calls 'virtues of acknowledged dependence' (ibid: 119-28); as for example virtues of giving and receiving, the virtue of exhibiting gratitude and so forth. Friends, colleagues, family members are the most important protection against moral errors, he says; for example, they help and correct us when we are about to go astray in our practical reasoning (ibid: 96). For ideas like these, MacIntyre can again draw on Aristotle, in particular on his treatment of virtuous friends (ibid: 160-1), who mutually support each other in their attempt to attain the virtues. There is, however, one tenet in Aristotelian ethics that MacIntyre takes to be incompatible with his picture of dependent animals, which is Aristotle's ideal of the *megalopsychos* (ibid: 127), the high-minded person, for Aristotle describes this person approvingly as being ashamed of receiving benefits, thinking that it is a mark of superiority to convey rather than to accept benefits. MacIntyre diagnoses here the illusion of self-sufficiency, an illusion typical of rich and powerful people who think that they can do without society.

One brief remark on the *megalopsychos*. True, the characteristic of the high-minded person that MacIntyre quotes may echo an aristocratic ideal of independence and, perhaps, masculinity, of Aristotle's days. Still, the quoted characteristic does not concern the definition and essence of the *megalopsychos*. The corresponding virtue is essentially responsible for dealing with honours. The high-minded person is one who is never mistaken about whether she does or does not deserve a particular honour in relation to her real merits and accomplishments, whereas people who lack this particular virtue tend to expect and to demand honours and signs of recognition that they do not actually deserve. In order not to fail in dealings with honour, it is thus vital to come to an unbiased assessment of one's own merits and achievements. This again is not possible without paying attention to what friends and fellow citizens think about one's merits. In fact, Aristotle seems to think that honour is ultimately about the attempt to gain approval of one's qualities through other people's opinions (see NE VIII.8,1159a23-24). From this perspective, the *megalopsychos* displays a kind of dependence with regard to self-knowledge or self-assessment that MacIntyre could easily implement into his framework.

More importantly, MacIntyre's new openness regarding the constraints of human nature may lead to the questions of (i.) why, out of all marks of human beings, it is only their supposed 'animality' that matters, and (ii.) why animality has just these implications of dependence and vulnerability. Generally speaking, one could read the project of *Dependent Rational Animals* as paradigmatically showing that any account of virtues should, to some extent, take the conditions of human beings as human beings into account. MacIntyre demonstrates that such a perspective is not bound to lead to the kind of ahistorical and inflexible essentialism that he has always rejected. Why then should this project be confined to saying that human beings are animals and thus inherit animal-like dependence and vulnerability? Regarding (i.), one might say that evoking Aristotle for the animality of human beings is only half the story – given that Aristotle would insist that human beings have a complex nature (see earlier), namely, the biological, animal-like nature plus the distinguishing characteristic of rationality. With regard to (ii.), finally, it could be worthwhile recalling that it is not only dependence and vulnerability that animals and human beings have in common but also a wide range of perceptions, pleasures, pains, needs, drives and so forth. Admittedly, many of these aspects are touched upon under the heading of human beings' 'corporeality', which they share with other animals; still, one could wonder why the social dependence and vulnerability alone get all the attention. Again, if, as MacIntyre now acknowledges, it is impossible to account for the good and the virtues independently of 'biology' or, as Aristotle would prefer to say, independent of the specific human nature, there is no longer any strong reason for restricting this project to particular strands within this human nature.

12 Concluding remarks

MacIntyre's philosophy is obviously inspired by many different traditions; still it aims at sketching a philosophy of the good, the virtues and the community, and not at the exegesis of particular historical figures. Hence the question of whether this philosophy rests on an exegetically tenable reading of any historical role model is only of secondary importance. When MacIntyre refers to philosophers of the past such as Aristotle, this often comes without any claim to give a historically accurate interpretation of the pertinent texts. So the preceding discussion was not meant to be evaluating him on the basis of the details of his interpretation of Aristotle. Nor was it meant to show that the Aristotelian position is superior in any way to MacIntyre's. This chapter was concerned primarily with the philosophical question of whether Aristotle – apart from all exegetical controversies and subtleties – by and large upholds a theory that is related in spirit to the several positions defended by MacIntyre. Yet the answer to the question of whether Aristotle is intellectually related to the suggested account(s) of the good, the virtues and the community does have a certain systematic relevance. Insofar as MacIntyre's philosophy of virtue presupposes a sharp criticism of certain modern developments, the appeal to Aristotle – the paradigm of premodern ethics – takes on an indirectly legitimating function. When he is playing off a putatively premodern way of thinking against a modern one, it is of some interest whether the ancient role model is suitable for the job it is supposed to do.

Notes

1. At least he lists these goods in chapter I 5 of the *Rhetoric*; however, the dialectical context of this chapter should serve as a warning not to ascribe too much significance to this list.
2. This is how the MacIntyre commentator Lutz characterizes the intention of *After Virtue*: 'Where Aristotle seeks an explanation of teleology in the metaphysics of substances composed of matter and form …, MacIntyre's *AV* [= After Virtue] simply rescinds from the metaphysical question altogether. *AV* studies the phenomena of teleology in intentional actions and social practices, whole human lives, traditions, and institutions. … the teleology of MacIntyre's *AV* is socially discovered, but remains metaphysically unexplained' (Lutz 2012: 173f.).
3. See, for example, Knight 2007: 1, who distinguishes between the 'ethical image' and 'its theoretical projector'.
4. The MacIntyre commentator Lutz sees the core of the obsolete theoretical preconditions on Aristotle's part in a theory of 'teleologically ordered substances' (2012: 173). This theoretical background has been disproven, he says, by modern science, in particular through the discovery of chromosomes; thus it only makes sense for modern thinkers such as MacIntyre to dispense with such a falsified natural philosophy (Lutz 2012: 174f.). Lutz seems to assume that the modern biological theory of inheritance discredits the metaphysical concept of form – however, to my mind, the discovery of chromosomes seems to be the most minor problem with Aristotle's ethics. One can defend versions of essentialism without defending Aristotle's metaphysical account of form, and whether or not we adopt a metaphysics of forms seems to be quite independent of the discovery of chromosomes.
5. See the abovementioned example of courage.
6. The Aristotelian virtue of truthfulness, for example, is no broad trans-situational character trait like our honesty, but rather concerns only the appropriateness of the representation of one's own merits and assets.
7. This book also includes an in-depth discussion of Aristotelian epistemology. I regret that I am not able to comment on it in this chapter.
8. See MacIntyre 1988: 122: 'So there is no standard external to the *polis* by which a *polis* can be rationally evaluated in respect of justice or any other good.'
9. MacIntyre goes on here to write: 'As modern examples of such a project we might consider the founding and carrying forward of a school, a hospital or an art gallery' (p. 151).

10 See MacIntyre 1988: 106: 'But in all of them he will especially need to learn both to understand the principle of just distribution and to be moved by a disposition to abide by it. To do so he will have to come to recognize who owes which good to what persons in a variety of situations, something which in Aristotle's view requires experience and habituation, as well as right reason.'
11 See MacIntyre 1988: 106: 'Justice thus occupies a key position among the virtues.'
12 See MacIntyre 1988: 106f.: 'But concepts of desert have application only in contexts in which two conditions are satisfied. There must be some common enterprise to the achievement of whose goals those who are taken to be more deserving have contributed more than those who are taken to be less deserving; and there must be a shared view both of how such contributions are to be measured and of how rewards are to be ranked.'
13 Precisely speaking, in *Politics* III Aristotle lists democracy under the bad 'degenerate' forms of constitution; this could give the modern reader the impression that Aristotle was hostile to democracy. The truth is that he recognizes a positive form of rule by the people – this obtains when the poor majority rules for the benefit of all. He calls this constitution 'polity' after the Greek term for all constitutions, '*politeia*'.
14 The recognition of 'external' standards is also expressed in Aristotle's influential remark that political justice is on the one hand lawful, on the other hand natural (*Nicomachean Ethics* V 9, 1134b18ff.) The meaning of this concept of the naturally just is controversial and often gets overestimated in the Aristotelian tradition. It seems clear however that Aristotle wishes to appeal to notions of justice that are not dependent on one *polis* or another. For MacIntyre's attempt to trace natural justice (as he calls it) to the justice of the best *polis*, see MacIntyre (1988: 120f).
15 MacIntyre (1999: 5) says: 'And Aristotle's account of human beings as distinctively rational has sometimes been interpreted as though he meant that rationality was not itself an animal property, but rather a property that separates humans from their animality. Aristotle did not of course make this mistake.' It would be nice, if MacIntyre were right on that, but there are reasons for being more cautious. While MacIntyre bases this claim on Aristotle's ascription of *phronēsis* and foresight to certain animals, it is not clear that terms like *phronēsis*, courage or cowardice retain their original meaning when applied to non-human animals.

Bibliography

Annas, Julia (1993) *The Morality of Happiness*, Oxford: Oxford University Press.
Anscombe, G. E. M. (1958), 'Modern Moral Philosophy', *Philosophy*, 33: 1–19.
Höffe, Otfried (1998), 'Aristoteles' universalistische Tugendethik', in Klaus-Peter Rippe and Peter Schaber (eds), *Tugendethik*, 42–68. Stuttgart: Reclam.
Knight, Kevin (2007), *Aristotelian Philosophy: Ethics and Politics from Aristotle to MacIntyre*. Cambridge: Polity Press.
Lutz, Christopher Stephen (2012), *Reading Alasdair MacIntyre's after Virtue*, New York: Continuum.
MacIntyre, Alasdair (1981), *After Virtue: A Study in Moral Theory*. London: Duckworth.
MacIntyre, Alasdair (1988), *Whose Justice? Which Rationality?* Notre Dame/Indiana: Notre Dame University Press.

MacIntyre, Alasdair (1999), *Dependent Rational Animals: Why Human Beings Need the Virtues*. London: Duckworth.

McDowell, John (1998), *Mind, Value, and Reality*, Cambridge, MA: Harvard University Press.

Nussbaum, Martha C. (1988), 'Aristotle, Nature, and Ethics', in J. E. J. Altham and Ross Harrison (Hrsg.), *World, Mind and Ethics: Essays on the Ethical Philosophy of Bernard Williams*, 86–131, Cambridge: Cambridge University Press.

Nussbaum, Martha C. (1993), 'Non-Relative Virtues: An Aristotelian Approach', in Martha Nussbaum and Amartya Sen (eds), *The Quality of Life*, 242–69, Oxford: Oxford University Press.

Rapp, Christof (1994), 'Was Aristotle a Communitarian?' *Graduate Faculty Philosophy Journal*, 17, 333–49.

Williams, Bernard (1985), *Ethics and the Limits of Philosophy*, Cambridge, MA: Harvard University Press.

Williams and MacIntyre on the human good and ethical objectivity

Apostolos Malakos

Introduction

One possible reading of MacIntyre's project is to situate his work within a spectrum of diverse, diverging, but gaining momentum and strength after the 1970s, theoretical attempts to rediscover rational foundations for ethics and morality. MacIntyre's work could be placed within a current of moral quasi realism, moral objectivism, or at least anti-scepticism and rationalism that took many forms and included Neo-Aristotelianism, Thomas Nagel's moral realism, pragmatism, Christine Korsgaard's neo-Kantianism, Levinasianism, contractarianism and many more. Such attempts have been responding to a variety of challenges to the claims for objectivity in social sciences in general and in philosophy and ethics in particular, and included, not only philosophical and theoretical but also pervasive cultural critiques in favour of radical contingency, expressivism, the non-discursive, the non-conceptual and the absurd in theory, art and everyday decision-making.

Starting with the devastating neo-romantic Nietzschean critique of morality, but also including various intuitionist and emotivist critiques, literary prioritizations of the irrational, post-Heideggerian anti-humanist challenges to subject-centred ontological and epistemological claims, poststructuralist and deconstructionist critiques of reason as 'totalizing', postmodernist identifications of modernist discourses as strategies for domination and many other forms, these challenges were probably predominating the intellectual landscape of Western academia not so long ago. While all these challenges to some of the illegitimate ambitions of modernism were valuable in many respects, they tended to be totalizing themselves, legitimizing perspectivism, asserting the radical incompatibility of alternative views and leaving no room for any processes or standards for reflective resolution. A measure of the success of the rationalist responses of which, according to this reading, MacIntyre's work can be thought of as an important part, may be that the anti-rationalist backlash is not predominant anymore.

With regard to ethics and philosophical attempts to ground and justify moral claims in some form of practical rationality, MacIntyre, despite espousing Nietzsche's condemnation of the Enlightenment project, does not agree with Nietzsche's central thesis against morality, namely,

> that all rational vindications of morality manifestly fail and that therefore belief in the tenets of morality needs to be explained in terms of a set of rationalizations which conceal the fundamentally non-rational phenomena of the will. (MacIntyre 2007: 117)

Such a reading of MacIntyre's work within a whole spectrum of rationalist attempts to ground the objectivity of ethics is overshadowed by at least two central tenets of his thought: namely, his perceived criticism of every kind of universalism[1] and his insistence on the incompatibility or incommensurability of traditions of theoretical and practical enquiry. A Neo-Aristotelian position does not necessarily entail those two viewpoints, and this chapter aims to challenge the validity of the claims inherent in both these positions.

In what follows, I will examine and evaluate Bernard Williams' influential critique of Aristotle's project, which includes both criticisms of Aristotle's conception of the 'good', and Aristotle's views about 'what is the best life to live' for a human being *qua* member of the species. Dealing with the former, first, I will identify three particular conceptual considerations about 'goodness' as such, and state Williams' conclusion, and then, second, dealing with the latter, I will identify again three kinds of argument that for Williams disqualify any kind of 'direct route from considerations of human nature to a unique morality and a unique moral ideal' (Williams 1993: 62). Third, I will present a critical exposition of MacIntyre's account of human flourishing based on a close reading of his text. *Ethics in the Conflicts of Modernity* (hereafter *ECM*) is in my view breaking new ground in pooling together Aristotelian and Thomistic resources, and MacIntyre's remarkable ability of synthesis to address the issues involved in Aristotle's teleology and his conception of the human good. While MacIntyre gives very substantive and nuanced answers as to what he considers as necessary components of an adequate conception of the human good, he postpones his full, direct answer regarding the final good's specific content and gives it after his reply to Williams. Fourth, I will examine MacIntyre's reply, trying to establish to what extent it is compelling or not and what are the problems remaining for the Neo-Aristotelian model after Williams' critique and MacIntyre's reply and positive account of the human good. My contention will be that significant problems remain which cannot be solved within the limits of Neo-Aristotelian resources. I will then suggest that the inadequacies of such a conception of the good such as MacIntyre's, as well as any such Aristotelian conception, expose a central contradiction and a lacuna in the Aristotelian project, which Williams has helped us understand. In particular, the tension between Aristotelian species formalism – which in effect is some form of universalism – and political particularism, which could be seen as a particular ancient version of the modern tension between subjective freedom and intersubjective morality.

1 Williams' conceptual critique of the 'good'

Williams advances at least three major series of arguments about the conceptual uses of the adjective good. First, he points out that 'good' in some of its uses should be thought of as an attributive rather than a predicative adjective, with the consequence 'that it is logically glued to the substantive it qualifies' (Williams 1993: 39–40)[2], meaning that an assertion that something is good can be adequately understood only if we can answer the question 'a good what?'. He also suggests that 'a good F' does not mean something like 'better than most F's'; in other words, that even if we assume good to be a comparative, the uses of good do not get 'unstuck from its substantive' (Williams 1993: 42).

Second, Williams proceeds to claim that since good is always so intimately related to the substantive it qualifies, the sense of any kind of statement including the phrase 'a good F' can be adequately understood only if this phrase is taken as a whole. This implies that the phrase 'a good F', for some Fs, partly takes its meaning by what fills the place of F, and this would further imply that the notorious distinction between fact and value will be disproved for cases such as this, since it is evident that factual knowledge, an understanding of what F is and does, will determine the truth or falsity of the judgement 'this is a good F'.

Third, however, Williams goes on to question whether this is the case for any filling of F, and makes the case that

> the fact/value distinction may not hold as a general distinction but is useful for a more restricted use concerning the goodness of some things, and more particularly, persons qua human beings and qua some of the more particular social roles a person may have. (Williams 1993: 46–7)

Williams shows that although in the cases of functional descriptions of artefacts or descriptions of human beings that refer to their job skills or roles, the meaning of the whole phrase 'a good F' is partly, at least, determined by what fills F, in the cases of less functional or non-functional descriptions of activities of human beings, the knowledge about F does not provide criteria for determining a good F, and some form of evaluation is implied when goodness is added. The point is that for some roles or activities, as for parenting, one can have a clear understanding of what it means to be a parent, without the criteria that are implied by the term good parent being implicit in the concept of a parent as such. In other words, whereas for some terms like a footballer, the term itself may be largely sufficient to imply what a good footballer is, for some other terms, of which a human being *qua* human being is the most important, the term itself is not sufficient to imply what makes somebody a good human being. In this way, the fact/value distinction here might hold, not in the absolutistic sense of the factual knowledge being irrelevant to the evaluation, but in the sense that this knowledge, while it might be necessary, it is not sufficient for the evaluation. This suggestion seems to me crucial for understanding the logic, the attraction as well as the limitations of the Aristotelian ethical edifice. Let us follow closely here the *Nicomachean Ethics*:

> Every craft and every line of enquiry, and likewise every action and decision, seems to seek some good; that is why some people were right to describe the good

as what everything seeks. But the ends [that are sought] appear to differ; some are activities, and others are products apart from the activities.³

It is indeed significant to focus on how Aristotle moves from using twice the term 'good' (αγαθόν) in the singular, to using the term end (τέλος) in the plural. Keeping in mind the far-from-clear-cut distinction between good and end (in Greek τέλειον meant something reaching its goals, completed and therefore, at least potentially, perfect), Aristotle seems to keep the term good in the singular because he has in mind to argue for the existence of one, highest good for the sake of which all the other ends are aimed at. A bit further he argues:

> Suppose, then, that the things achievable by action have some end that we wish for because of itself, and because of which we wish for the other things, and that we do not choose everything because of something else-for if we do, it will go on without limit, so that desire would prove to be empty and futile. Clearly, this end will be the good, that is to say, the best good.⁴

Here Aristotle defines the good as that which is, first, an end in itself, and, second, this end for the sake of which we choose other ends. So 'the good' is a kind of end, the highest end that human activity can aim at, and only this end that fulfils these two criteria. But in which sense do those two further criteria transform an end into a 'good'? Somebody who aims at gaining power at the expense of others and has no ethical qualms, taking care to appear just, might be able, in furthering these aims, to act in such ways for the sake of 'gaining lasting power', which to him or her might be the final good, adjusting his other activities to further this final good. This seems to me to show that the aforementioned two criteria do not necessarily transform ends into goods, a 'τέλος' into an 'αγαθόν'. If by good one means something more than an end, if a final good is not only something that is an end in itself for the sake of which other things are pursued, but more importantly that end in itself *for the sake of which it is good to aim at particular ends*, that end brings in a claim, both for itself and its 'lower' ends, for a particular kind of goodness, an 'ethical' or evaluative sort of goodness to go together with the functional one. A third criterion needs to be assumed here; the characteristic that transforms a final end into a final good, a quality of goodness for the sake of which presumably it is good to aim at all particular ends that further the final good. It is not the content of the final end that necessarily make it 'good', but an evaluative judgement that adds the quality 'goodness'. This means, however, that the definition of 'the good' as 'the end for the sake of which it is good to ...' involves some measure of circularity. Williams' argument's force shows its pertinence here, because the point is precisely that functional considerations, which have to do with the nature of an activity, may be sufficient in some cases to lead from an 'end y' to a 'good y', but cannot operate in identifying the highest good of an activity when the nature of the activity is not exhausted by one, particular function. Indeed, as Williams suggests:

> In any ordinary understanding of good, surely, an extra step is taken if you go from saying that you want something or have decided to pursue it to saying that it

is good. ... The idea of something's being good imports an idea, however minimal or hazy of a perspective in which it can be acknowledged by more than one agent as good. (Williams 2006: 58)

Of course, one cannot rule out the possibility that, despite (practical) reason's requirement for systematicity and some measure of closure, there might not be a good, one good, that serves as the end 'for the sake of which' other ends are perceived. There might be a plurality of goods which may be pursued for their own sakes and, even if not contradicting or being in tension with each other *a priori*, they certainly prove so a posteriori, that is, in practice. Such practice requires standards or norms to guide it. Goods are not ordered by themselves, nor are they ordered by human nature as such.

Concluding the conceptual analysis, I think that Williams builds a strong case that is corroborated by Aristotle's text in the *NE*, asserting that for some things, especially for human beings *qua* some of their functions and *qua* members of the species, even if we had a perfectly clear idea of their nature, we could not gain an understanding of what it means for them to be 'good' as such. The concept of 'good' presupposes in its use some kind of evaluative standard that tends to remain concealed but involves even implicitly an expectation for some form of agreement with others.

2 Williams' substantive critique of the final good according to human nature

On the basis of this analysis of the uses of the term 'good', Williams moves to identify three substantive objections to the attempt to elicit unquestionable ethical goods from specific characteristics of human nature. First, some preconceptions and presuppositions have already been used; in other words, some evaluative principles have already been assumed and have been made use of, in selecting one particular characteristic of human nature as the fundamental, defining one, for example, rationality. If one used other evaluative principles, s/he might be led to identify different distinguishing characteristics of human nature, for example, as Williams says, killing others for fun. To the objection that such a distinguishing characteristic takes human beings as they are or as they tend to be when the virtues are no more present, and not as they could or should be according to the potentiality of their nature, let me point out here, and I will elaborate further later, that Aristotle himself claims that for human beings, 'true goodness is rare', although presumably 'goodness' is almost always present for roses or animals which tend to reach their final end of flourishing and for whom 'goodness is presumably common'.

Second, this leads to the suggestion that there is an inherent ethical ambiguity in whatever distinguishing characteristics one might choose for human nature. If one takes sociality as the distinguishing mark of man, it turns out that this is a precondition both for the ethical demands of the Others in the Levinasian sense and for the complete disregard of any such demands and acts of unimaginable cruelty to Others. Both attitudes entail sociality. Third, if one were to take rationality as the distinctively human characteristic, s/he would still be dependent on an inbuilt evaluation of rationality as more fully human and 'good' than say emotionality, and would therefore tend to underestimate the importance of emotions and passions in human lives. Emotions and non-rational beliefs tend to be very complex and resistant to transformation via rational argument or training and habituation, and, although there may always be various forms of communication and osmosis between our rational and emotional selves, these forms involve complicated two-way processes of influence. This, moreover, does not necessarily mean that there are some fundamental non-rational choices of the mysterious 'will' that form the ground for practical rationality. It might be the case that the complex whole of a self, a 'desiring *nous*', in Aristotle's words, is motivated towards practical reasoning and acting not only by direct or indirect desires but also by emotional factors which are never fully formed before and without some determination by processes of reasoning, but operate in continuous interaction with desires and practical reasoning in ways that no factor can be thought of as necessarily determining the outcome.

Williams concludes by stating that insights on the distinguishing characteristics of human nature, of what human beings are and do, contribute of course to an understanding of what morality is. He does claim, however, that different views of what human nature consists in, and divergent evaluative principles of judging which 'parts' or 'potentialities' of this nature are 'good', will lead to differing views of the content of ethical virtues and moral norms. Let me conclude here my summary of Williams' critique of the Aristotelian model of the good life by pointing out to a further substantive point. Williams suggests that the duality inherent in the Aristotelian conception of the good life between the final good of civic life made possible by practical rationality and the good of contemplation sustained by theoretical reason not only is not accidental but also leaves one with no conceptual resources to either choose the one over the other or bridge the gap between them. Despite the centrality of his account of practical life in the *polis* as the highest form of human good, Aristotle is disposed to regard a life of *theoria* as a yet higher form of good. Yet, Williams argues, he and his system is unable 'to provide any account of how the intellectual activities are to be brought into relation to the citizenry activities' (Williams 1993: 58).

Aristotle is committed to such a duality not only because of his dual conception of reason, as practical and therefore as leading to acts, and theoretical concluding in propositions, nor just because of his distinction between the unchangeability of parts at least of the cosmos as opposed to the changeability of the sub-lunar universe and human affairs, but also because his conception of human nature includes both a finite and an infinite part that are served by different kinds of reason. But how are these two parts to be mediated, since on the whole they are served not only by two different parts of reasoning but seem also to contradict the demands of each other in many actual everyday life choices? Why should one bother about others, or the polis, after s/he has used them for a good education, and now reaches for the firmament above; and if one does care, how is s/he to decide what takes priority, when and to what extent, in shaping her life and in making concrete, particular choices? Again, here, some evaluative principle would be required for these choices.

3 MacIntyre's account of the human good

Let me move now to MacIntyre's complex reply to Williams' critique by first pointing out that MacIntyre acknowledges the force of this critique and the depth of Williams' thought not only explicitly (MacIntyre 2016: 150) but also in the way he puts at the centre of *ECM* an attempt to give a positive account of the human good in a Neo-Aristotelian way that would, among other things, put to rest Williams' criticisms.[5] In what follows, I will try to present the main points of this account, before going on to MacIntyre's direct reply to Williams' critique.

MacIntyre starts by describing some formal characteristics of diverse human goods, suggesting that disagreements about goods exemplify, in most cases, different understandings of the priorities that we tend to assign to various goods and the rank ordering of those goods that each of us holds (MacIntyre 2016: 15–16). He goes on to contrast the ways other animal species are dependent for their goods on their biological nature, which limits their interaction with their environment, with the ways human beings are enabled by their biological nature for a widespread and in-depth interaction with their environment. This complex interaction enables human beings to redirect the use of natural resources in developing their own specific purposes, and gradually transform not only their environment but also more importantly themselves (MacIntyre 2016: 24–6). They become able for such transformative action by developing two interrelated capacities, linguistic (MacIntyre 2016: 26–7) and rational, which together have the cumulative effect that human beings develop the capacities to communicate complex sets of intentions to each other, to co-operate and develop new forms of associative activities, to ask questions and look for and find answers about the truth or falsity of their assertions and inferences, and finally to tell stories to themselves and others about 'their heroic enterprises and tragic failures', and thus to develop a distinguishing type of agency as they become reflective learners:

> So for now let me remark only that, on the view that I have begun to outline, rational enquiry into and consequent disagreement about what human flourishing consists in in this or that set of circumstances is itself one of the marks of human flourishing. (MacIntyre 2016: 25–6)

MacIntyre goes on to suggest that whereas human beings do tend to agree about what it is for other animal species to flourish, they tend to disagree about what it is to flourish for themselves, because this latter depends on the specific and very diverse cultures they inhabit, which provide specific 'sets of evaluative standards' (MacIntyre 2016: 27–8). He, therefore, points out that the original problem of deciding what is the particular type of human flourishing, has now been transformed into a problem about how to stand back from, and move beyond, the standards and evaluative principles of our own culture and judge other culturally conditioned accounts in view 'of the realities of human flourishing' (MacIntyre 2016: 28) per se. Here MacIntyre introduces Aristotle because he suggests that Aristotle achieved exactly that, that is, he used resources of his own culture to move beyond it and make claims that hold for any culture, proposing 'standards that he was able to present as deserving the allegiance of any adequately rational enquirer' (MacIntyre 2016: 28). As he moves on to explain how it was that Aristotle achieved that, MacIntyre presents Aristotle's 'core conception' of human flourishing in four headings, by reiterating the main distinguishing characteristics he has given earlier, that is, linguistic, rational, social and cultural capacities, adding however a crucial dimension of our cultural conditioning:

> Our nature is such that we find ourselves directed by our upbringing, if we have been adequately educated, toward ends *that we take to be goods* and we have some conception, even if initially inchoate, of what it would be for someone to achieve those ends in such a way that their life would be a perfected human life. (MacIntyre 2016: 29; emphasis mine)

MacIntyre seems to suggest here that we always already operate within broadly defined, but nevertheless particular conceptions, of the human good that are culture specific, and therefore would be fundamentally different from other such conceptions. He fails to show, however, how it is possible on this model in which 'we take ends to be goods', to step beyond one's cultural conditioning and produce an account of human flourishing as such. Moreover, MacIntyre's strategy up to now is to establish, through the identification of what he takes to be some structural characteristics of human nature, the features of language, rationality and sociability as its distinguishing marks. In doing so, MacIntyre aims to give at the same time, and almost imperceptibly and gradually, a substantive description of that nature, making therefore his account of human development and flourishing a matter of description of facts. As he implicitly recognizes, though, the development of practical rationality through the use of our linguistic capacities results also in the development of multiple and recurrent cases of failure of reason, which sometimes might not be particularized failures but complete breakdowns, presumably due to the parallel emergence of very influential non-rational forces and because of recurrent bouts of irrationality. In a similar vein, his belief in the capacity of humans to learn from mistakes may be challenged. His portraying of a largely rationalistic story of our evolution might then be challenged in favour of a much more complex story that gives more emphasis on our emotional development, as Williams would claim. In other words, at the point of his argument, when the distinguishing characteristics of human nature he identifies stop being just structural characteristics and take some substantive content, some evaluation has already taken place for this particular kind of content rather than that. Let me also note in passing here that, according to Aristotle, deliberation cannot furnish the ultimate end of human life, but can only take place within the horizon of one ultimate end which cannot be deliberated upon but is somehow given. This ultimate decision does not need to be an expression of a non-rational choice, but, according to Aristotle, can be accomplished by our reason through a direct act of apprehension or intuition of something that is not demonstrable as such and therefore not a conclusion of theoretical reason, nor deliberated upon and therefore not a conclusion of practical reason either. On Aristotle's account it is nonetheless something we *know* – by intuiting its truth, something we arrive at by exercising an intellectual capacity. But as we choose all other ends for the sake of the final good, there is no other good for the sake of which our ultimate good will be chosen and, therefore, according to Aristotle, there can be no inferred reasons for which we choose this final end. We simply intuit it, and my point here is that this intuition is somehow evaluative; it is not a presuppositionless apprehension of the obviousness of a truth, but always asserts some assumed value, some ascription of goodness.

Coming back to the main line of argument, I think the point can be made that MacIntyre's case up to now is very interesting in what he describes but, in fact, condenses a very complex, long-term evolution into a rationally biased, short version that omits very significant areas of human development, regarding the emergence of complex emotional set ups and non-rational structures of belief. In other words, one could legitimately claim that this account takes as its point of departure a specific view about what it is to flourish as a human being, and projects this view backwards. The point, here, is not whether MacIntyre's account is partly correct, which it probably is, or valuable, which it definitely is, but rather whether, as I think he makes it to be, is free of evaluative presuppositions.

After some interesting digressions, which contrast the account given so far with expressivist and Nietzschean accounts of the human good, MacIntyre takes up the same line of argument in chapter 1.8, admitting that the story he has given so far falls short of providing an account of what the particular form and content of human flourishing is, and what is required is 'an account of the structures of human activity and of how our uses of 'good' and its cognates find application within and to those structures' (MacIntyre 2016: 49). He goes on to suggest that the most important of our ends that identify the lives we are going to lead are formed incrementally and transformed gradually as we grow older and, therefore, we should not think about them as formed from an early stage in our development (MacIntyre 2016: 50). It is also the case that not only our ends but we as agents are also transformed, and that, therefore, the content of the various virtues required for us to flourish cannot be given in advance and that 'in the life of practice there are no fully adequate generalizations to guide us' (MacIntyre 2016: 51). He then reiterates and expands on the points he has already made about sociability and rationality to the effect that we depend on others in order to learn, and that our final end will have to be the end of 'rational activity as such, an end to be contrasted with those various and particular ends' (MacIntyre 2016: 53). Again, however, he seems not to have come closer to answering the question about what the specifically human final end is, and he reiterates the question:

> Such a final good is by contrast unqualifiedly good and stands to those other goods as a measure stands to what is measured. So what does or could be such a final good? (MacIntyre 2016: 54).

He proceeds, perhaps surprisingly, to say that it is too soon to ask this question. MacIntyre makes some more very useful suggestions about the characteristics that such a good must have, namely, that it is only after we have recognized the fragility of our goodness and our tendency to fail that we might be able to recognize the goodness that our lives might possess and to be contented with their outcomes (MacIntyre 2016: 54), and, more significantly, that if one accepts the view that there is nothing beyond our finite nature, one might conclude that *'there is no final end, no ultimate human good to be achieved'* (MacIntyre 2016: 55–6; emphasis mine). So the question remains, and the answer is postponed and produced after the reply to Williams, although here we have some clear intimation of what it might be and that perhaps the final good of human activity is 'inescapably theological', in MacIntyre's own words. The issue arises, of course, of whether this begs the question about how all those humans, who are not inspired by such a vision, structure their lives around an ultimate good. Presumably they fail to do so.

4 MacIntyre's reply to Williams

Let us move forward now to MaIntyre's reply to Williams' critique, which proceeds in four stages. First, MacIntyre responds to Williams' claim that Aristotle's model of the human good cannot account for error and failure. MacIntyre is correct in pointing out that Aristotle does provide a nuanced account of cases of failure like the failure of the intemperate, the akratic, the imprudent, the one who ascribes more importance than is due to goods like pleasure and money, and the failing practical reasoner and suggests that for Aristotle,

> to err is to act from a desire for some object that the agent has no good reason to desire. So to act, whether intemperately or acratically, is to have insufficiently disciplined passions. (MacIntyre 2016: 221)

But why do desires seem so recalcitrant? Why does education by parents, friends and others fail so often so as to make failing not an exception but a widespread fact of the human condition? What is it in the search of the particularly human good that makes it so easy to miss the mark? I think the example of the akratic, who has the practical wisdom to realize that one should at least postpone satisfying some of their desires, but fails to do so, shows here the limitations of the Aristotelian account. If desires and passions and emotions make more often than not their own claims and resist habituation and transformation, isn't Williams correct in highlighting the probability that a rationally biased conception of human nature pays insufficient attention to the emotional set up?

Aristotle, in particular, claims in the *NE* that 'goodness is rare'. How are we to understand this assertion, however, within his model, given his teleology? For goodness to be rare, the human case, alone among all species, must surely be contradicting the teleological assertion. Aristotle in *Metaphysics* θ makes the crucial point that 'rational powers' (μετά λόγου) as opposed to 'irrational ones' (άλλογες) are characterized by their ability and tendency to choose between good and bad. Humans choose their ends, whereas other animals or plants are directed determinedly towards their good. But why do humans display the tendency to choose so often, perhaps more often than not, the bad rather than the good? As MacIntyre himself admits, Williams' contention that Aristotle's teleology works better with plants and other animals than it does for human beings is essentially correct, and this is because a human being, unlike other animals, needs a principle to make a choice between good and bad ends. It is not true that we are simply socialized through practices and adopt just various culturally conditioned goods that are more or less given. We also freely adopt some principles of choosing the good together with some conceptions and principles of what counts as a good. And these principles that we adopt are very often bad principles because they exemplify regimes of injustice, power, money and status and individual as well as collective strategies of deception and self-deception. The substantive issue in a kernel is that even if we take up some given conception of what a good is and a standard for choosing that good, we cannot but have justified, explicitly or implicitly, this adoption by some kind of explicit or implicit normative statement, which even if, to an extent, culturally conditioned, we legislate ourselves. The searching for such a principle is a problem of normativity, and I think Kant is right in insisting that our reason operates and should operate normatively, that is, it does not look only for goods but as it does so, legislates for principles, which to some extent take some universalizing form and allow us to distance ourselves from particular social practices we are socialized in.

Second, MacIntyre goes on to respond to Williams' claim that Aristotle is mistaken in assuming that there is a distinguishingly human form of the good life. To do so, he provides a series of arguments that an Aristotelian account should employ in responding to this claim. He first suggests that any Aristotelian account of the human good should point out that it is a matter of fact that there is a set of goods that, whatever one's cultural milieu, it would be difficult to deny:

> They are at least eightfold, beginning with good health and a standard of living – food, clothing shelter – that frees one from destitution. Add to these good family relationships, sufficient education to make good use of opportunities to develop one's powers, work that is productive and rewarding and good friends. Add further time beyond one's work for activities good in themselves, athletic, aesthetic, intellectual and the ability of a rational agent to order one's life and to identify and learn from one's mistakes. (MacIntyre 2016: 222)

It might seem here that finally some indisputable substantive account of what the human good should include has been reached. But this is not the case, because all these goods are indisputable to the extent that they are part of *sustaining* life, maintaining and nourishing and helping one to grow; in other words, insofar as they refer to the sustenance and flourishing of the human species *biologically*. To the extent that by flourishing we do not mean biological flourishing any more, and by human nature we refer to a point beyond biological nature to some kind of flourishing *qua* human as a cultural species, all these eight characteristics, even health itself, are defined differently in diverse cultures and contrasting principles of evaluation enter in their definition. A Nazi tradition of (distorted) practical rationality and ethical enquiry, as I am sure existed in Germany in the late 1930s, understood even 'good health', never mind 'good mental health', 'good family' and 'good education', very differently from the way a citizen of classical Athens would understand them. Does this mean that all traditions are indeed incompatible? Now it seems to me that *some* traditions are indeed incommensurable, but the claim that all are, seems counterintuitive. And not merely because there would not be the extent of exchange and commonality among traditions that there is, but for a more substantive reason: traditions that accord a central role to practical rationality tend to share some characteristics that have to do with the nature of reason itself or the human nature understood as rational. Moreover, as Christine Korsgaard has suggested, cultural particularism can go only so far without contradicting itself, because if it claims that human beings fully conceive themselves as members of particular cultures and form their practical identities accordingly, then the *universal* fact is established that for all human beings, practical identities are formed, at least in part, by particular social bonds (Korsgaard 1996: 118–19). The claim that human beings live and need to live in communities is a universal claim.

Third, MacIntyre attempts to respond to Williams' suggestion that to take humans as first and foremost rational animals is unfounded and arbitrary, and at any rate is not a matter of fact but involves some presupposed evaluative standard. MacIntyre reiterates his point about the distinctiveness of linguistic capacities, which enable humans alone to be self-reflective and critical of their own reasoning, and suggests that this distinguishing characteristic leads human beings to a key moment in their development when, for the first time, they make use of their linguistic capacities to ask questions of the type 'what is the good of doing this or that …' (MacIntyre 2016: 225). From these two interrelated points he then goes on to claim that

> human beings have distinguished themselves from other animal species … by realizing a determinate form of life participation which requires a grasp of and an ability to find application for the concept of a good, the concept of a reason, and a number of related concepts. (MacIntyre 2016: 226)

But, of course, Williams, or Kant for that matter, would have no problem with that, and I see nothing specifically Aristotelian about this claim. MacIntyre seems to finally concede that until now his reply to Williams has not been sufficiently substantive or at least that Williams would not be satisfied by it, and he suggests that after all Williams is right about the limitations of teleological accounts of the human good, because, although in each social role we are initiated into the ends of this role, the question remains about how are we to integrate those diverse activities and put their various ends in a hierarchy of goods that will be defined by a substantive, final, ultimate end, 'the good' according to which it is best to act *qua* humans (MacIntyre 2016: 226–7). As must have become evident by now, Williams' critique proves to be difficult to counter because any Aristotelian account of the good is committed to two related but, at least to an extent, contradictory claims, namely, that the good of humans *qua* humans is defined teleologically in a naturalistic way as it is for any species, and that especially for humans it is culturally conditioned as well. As the standard Aristotelian is committed to both claims, s/he is then looking for the universal solely in human nature and understands cultural factors in solely particular forms but in each of those claims she is in error. The human good is not provided in naturalistic terms, because the functional 'good' of 'human nature' does not operate by itself in human lives. It is mediated by culturally defined goods, which always involve the claims to goods and demands on each of us made by specific others, and therefore rival claims and demands enter a contestable public space. To the extent that they involve the development of forms of rationality, they are based on generalizing judgements not only about the good of this or that particular human group or society but also about the human good in general (in the Kantian sense). Particular cultures are not just loci of particular and 'local' claims, but at the same time and always are loci of universalizing and purportedly universalizable claims, even in cases where these claims are unethical.

As Ernst Cassirer was arguing correctly, but largely in vain, to a hostile audience, including the then-young Levinas, against Heidegger in the 'magic mountain' of Davos in 1929, human activity is always form producing, there is no pure existence or 'thrownness' (*Geworfenheit*) as such.[6] Human activity presupposes taking a stand about the goodness of that or the other, always from a particular standpoint, but in a way that transcends that standpoint in the sense of making a more general claim. Despite their failures, human beings go on failing, sometimes gravely worse, sometimes better, but they keep striving for some kind of transcendence. And this is a condition for the possibility of their existence as ethical beings. This striving for transcendence of any kind of naturalism and particularism is perhaps the defining characteristic of the ethical as such, and it includes the exercising of not only empirical freedom as freedom of choice but also transcendental freedom as autonomy to legislate for myself and others. This moral legislation has ontological repercussions, because good and evil exist as potentialities, but, through our choices, become actualities. Nobody can live without raising her sights beyond the limiting horizon if she is to remain within the human species *qua* ethical species, and indeed this is the way philosophy's and art's certain venerable tradition was and is visualizing being in the world. In Seneca's words 'the soul traverses the whole world', in Chrysippus' 'the immersion in the whole' (ο ποντισμος στο Ολον) and in the same vein Aristotle's suggestion in the last book of the *Nicomachean Ethics* to strive for immortality, Aquinas' *beatitudo*, Kant's transcendental freedom and Levinas' claim about the infinite demand of the Other's face.

It is for this reason, of course, that I find MacIntyre's final reply to Williams and positive account of the human good so interesting as he adopts Aquinas' central insight about the ultimate human good:

> It may seem paradoxical, but is not, to express that insight by saying that on his view we complete and perfect our lives by allowing them to remain incomplete. A good life is one in which an agent, although continuing to rank order particular and finite goods, treats none of these goods as necessary for the completion of her or his life, so leaving her or himself open to a final good beyond all such goods. ... Does one have to be a theist to understand one's life in these terms? Of course not. Whether Aquinas is right about the presuppositions of such a life is one thing. What the character of such a life is quite another. (MacIntyre 2016: 231)

It seems to me that MacIntyre, in providing us here with his definition of the final human good, allows for multiple definitions of the ways finite human beings strive for infinitude. In doing so, he moves beyond Aquinas' particular definition, even if he himself accepts Aquinas theological vision. Moreover, MacIntyre seems implicitly committed here to the claim that to the extent that a human being or a particular community strive for infinitude, they quest for some kind of movement beyond their finite boundaries and assert universalist aspirations

Conclusion

The issue that I think remains, regarding Williams' critique of Aristotelian and MacIntyrean combination of naturalism and particularism, is related to Williams' claim that the distinctive human good is not given by our biological *telos*, nor by our finite human nature, and whatever it may be, it is, at least to an extent, not a matter of fact but a matter of using one evaluative standard over another. MacIntyre, however, as also Aristotle, Aquinas, Kant and Levinas, may be correct that, if the human good is not given by our finite nature, it must at least include a horizon of infinity that transcends it. But which are the sources of this transcendence? Does this infinite horizon have a topos? Or is it an ethical utopia, a land of fiction and myths? Are we duped by morality, as Levinas asks? Does this mean that we are back to Nietzsche in the sense that, even if this topos existed, it would be grounded on some non-rational act of the will? Not necessarily, but a condition for the possibility of grounding moral transcendence beyond subjectivism and particularism is to philosophically bridge the gap between individual autonomy and ethical intersubjectivity. As I tried to show in this chapter, however valuable in many respects, the Aristotelian account of the human good cannot solve this particular impasse. And this is perhaps because any such pre-modern account cannot bridge the divide between what Hegel called established and reflective morality, and between objective morality and subjective freedom, because 'this principle of subjective freedom is a later growth, it is the principle of our modern days of culture' (Hegel 1995: 98–9). But even modern accounts have to face the main thrust of Williams' critique of morality and show how subjectivity, this strange unity of self-consciousness and agency, is not limited to finite, psychological subjectivity and, therefore, able to provide disputable, but in principle intersubjective, ethical standards. 'In principle' is crucial here, because it means that what is important is not whether an evaluative standard is universally accepted as true but, even if it fails or conflicts with other such claims, whether it can ground subjective maxims of action that make a valid (not necessarily true) claim for being categorically imperative, in the discursive space opened up by a free legislative activity that is not only empirical but also transcendental. The sense of transcendental here being that, as an agent, one is not just free, but also able and bound, even unwittingly, to legislate not only for oneself but also for others – in plain English, to give and justify reasons for their choices according to some kind of intersubjective criterion. What *only* remains then is to ground the intersubjectively contested ethical claims of human beings, who are emotionally complex, dependent and autonomously legislating rational animals, capable although failing, to recognize the unique ethical demands of every single Other which is at the same time a not-other. But, of course, in MacIntyre's words, 'the joke is in the word only'.

Notes

1 I write 'perceived' here because MacIntyre is not against any possible kind of universalist argument. He accepts that unconditional rules and principles are needed if shared deliberation is to exist and, more to the point, that these rules are given in virtue of our nature as rational agents. I take this to mean that these principles, 'what Aquinas called the precepts of natural law'(MacIntyre 2016: 57) are the same for any culture. Despite that, however, MacIntyre unfortunately affords very little space in his work on the nature and role of these precepts in the functioning of reason.
2 The point here is that the sentence 'that is a yellow bird' is analysable into the sentence 'that is a bird and it is yellow', unlike the sentence 'he is a good cricketer' which is not analysable into the sentence 'he is a cricketer and he is good'.
3 Aristotle, *Nicomachean Ethics*, 1094a1-6, translated by Terence Irwin (second edition), (Indianapolis: Hackett Publishing Co., 1999) from now on *NE*.
4 *NE*,1094a18-23.
5 See especially chapter 1, 'Desires, goods and "good": Some philosophical issues'.
6 See here Peter E. Gordon, 2010, *The Continental Divide: Heidegger, Cassirer, Davos*, Cambridge, MA: Harvard University Press.

Bibliography

Aristotle (1999), *Nicomachean Ethics*, trans. Terrence Irwin, Indianapolis: Hackett Publishing Co.

Cooper, John M. (1975), *Reason and Human Good in Aristotle*, Cambridge, MA: Harvard University Press.

Gordon Peter, E. (2010), *The Continental Divide: Heidegger, Cassirer, Davos*, Cambridge MA: Harvard University Press.

Hegel, Georg Wilhelm Friedrich (1995), *Lectures on the History of Philosophy II: Plato and the Platonists*, Lincoln: University of Nebraska Press.

Korsgaard, M. Christine, (1996), *The Sources of Normativity*, Cambridge: Cambridge University Press.

MacIntyre, Alasdair (2007), *After Virtue: A Study in Moral Theory*, London: Duckworth.

MacIntyre, Alasdair, (2016), *Ethics in the Conflicts of Modernity*, Cambridge: Cambridge University Press.

Williams, Bernard, (1993), *Morality, An Introduction to Ethics*, Cambridge: Cambridge University Press.

Williams, Bernard (2006), *Ethics and the Limits of Philosophy*, London: Routledge.

10

Alasdair MacIntyre's Nietzschean anti-modernism

Golfo Maggini

I

In the first chapter of *Ethics in the Conflicts of Modernity*, Alasdair MacIntyre goes back to a discussion on expressivism in ethics that he started a long time ago. Examples of the 'imagined expressivist' he targets are, among others, Harry Frankfurt, Simon Blackburn and Alan Gibbard. The issue here is no less than what 'is at odds between expressivists and NeoAristotelians' (MacIntyre 2016: 31 cf.). There is no doubt that expressivists insist on the significance of the psychology of morality, but MacIntyre seems to find not a mistake or a fallacy, but a serious lacuna in what they claim about morality. Talking in the name of moral psychology, though, expressivists evoke Nietzsche – and Freud – as their idols. But is Nietzsche the prototype of the 'imagined expressivist' (Blackburn 2007: 281–96) MacIntyre refers to? Is his Overman a prototype of the 'expressivist agent', someone who 'exemplifies an expressivist stance' in opposition to the stance of a 'Neo-Aristotelian agent'? (MacIntyre 2016: 59) The answer to this question is not an easy one, as it is quite obvious that Nietzsche's moral stance cannot be reduced to that of a classical expressivist of the twentieth-century moral philosophy, except, perhaps, from Bernard Williams: 'Williams' rejection both of modern conceptions of morality and of the Christianity which he saw as the precursor of those conceptions led him to follow Nietzsche in an attempt to recover from the ancient Greek world – from its tragedians and historians rather than from its philosophers – alternative ways of understanding human relationships and transactions' (MacIntyre 2016: 68 cf.).[1] It is, therefore, not fortuitous that MacIntyre's attack on Bernard Williams' anti-theoretical stance in ethics is recurrent in the 2016 book to the point of making of him his main rival moral philosopher.[2]

Nevertheless, the question remains as to the critique of Nietzsche himself: Does MacIntyre somehow assimilate Nietzsche, for instance his genealogical method, to Williams in the same way as he makes the latter comply with writers such as D. H. Lawrence and Oscar Wilde? My answer to this question is negative. In my view, Nietzsche, in terms analogous to Charles Taylor or Martha Nussbaum, is not easy to assimilate to an expressivist or post-expressivist stance, and this is in part true of MacIntyre's entire interpretative thread, which never assimilates Nietzsche to his postmodernist adepts and never sees him as a Foucauldian stereotype. MacIntyre's interpretation of Nietzsche, even when he comes to criticize Williams' appropriation of Nietzschean genealogy, shows a deep sensitivity and openness to the German philosopher's genuine insights, and even to his transformative critique of modernity's moral mirror images, which largely resemble his own. These background resemblances seem to have more of a performative than an assertoric character, as they set forth their common rejection of modern principle-based morality, either deontological or utilitarian, as well as their insistence on the internal link between morality and human flourishing.[3] (MacIntyre 2016: 47–8) This is even more so as Nietzsche is one of the very few moral thinkers, along with Augustine and Marx, who brought forth the tensional, intrinsically conflictual and dynamic, never to be conceived as pure and monolithic, nature of ethics:

> to be a moral agent is to have the potentiality for living and acting in a state of tension or, if need be, conflict between two moral points of view. And this is never simply or mainly a tension or a conflict between points of view at the level of abstract and general theory. It is always primarily a tension or a conflict between socially embodied points of view, between modes of practice. (MacIntyre 2006: 193)

But let us move back from the 2016 book to the previous stages of MacIntyre's self-reflecting interpretation of Nietzsche.

II

In his 1994 interview to Giovanna Borradori, while commenting on his earlier treatments of modern ethics, Alasdair MacIntyre remarks that the 'notion of choosing one's own morality makes no sense; what makes sense is the much more radical notion of choosing to displace and overcome morality. So *A Short History of Ethics* should perhaps have ended by giving Nietzsche the final word, instead of leaving him behind two chapter earlier' (Borradori and MacIntyre 1994: 146). He goes on to qualify Nietzsche's philosophy as the ultimate answer to the systematic inconclusiveness that was the outcome of Enlightenment and post-Enlightenment moral philosophy, concluding with a self-critical remark on his 1967 book: 'From a methodological viewpoint, it is today clear to me that while I was writing *A Short History*, I should have taken as a central standpoint what I learned from R.G. Collingwood: that morality is an essentially historical subject matter and that philosophical inquiry, in ethics as elsewhere, is defective insofar as it is not historical' (Borradori and MacIntyre 1994: 146). Though the main references here seem to be Renaissance thinker Gianbattista Vico, R. G. Collingwood and even hermeneutic philosophers such as Hans-Georg Gadamer, MacIntyre's self-critique has a much broader scope as it thematizes a shift in his understanding of morality in general and modern morality in particular leading to the recognition of its constitutive historicity. So, the question to ask has to do with the core of the critique addressed to Nietzsche in *A Short History of Ethics*, as there is clearly a divergence between this initial, critical standpoint and his later position on Nietzsche's morality. Here I take the 1999 *Dependent Rational Animals* as a later, critically important instance.

In *A Short History of Ethics*, MacIntyre introduces Nietzsche as the end point of nineteenth-century philosophy, expressing about him the same reservations regarding the vagueness and empty formalism of his Overman or the Will to Power as those against Kant's categorical imperative:

> What worries us in Nietzsche is perhaps like what worries us in Kant ... the conscientious moral agent dominated by the form of the categorical imperative is in fact licensed to do anything at all – provided he does it conscientiously. What looked like a restrictive guide to conduct is in fact empty of restriction. So likewise, and more crudely, with the notion of the Superman. In the name of the Will to Power what might one not do? (MacIntyre 1998: 218)

At the opposite edge of this timeline, in *Dependent Rational Animals*, the treatment of Nietzschean morality gravitates around the virtues of dependence. In playing Nietzsche's account of friendship in *Thus Spoke Zarathustra* against Aristotelian φιλία, MacIntyre points out that:

> to a remarkable extent Nietzsche offers us an inverted mirror-image of the friendship required by the virtues of acknowledged dependence. ... Nietzsche thus confronts us with a radical alternative way of thinking about dependence and independence in human relationships. ... Yet, although we can learn from Nietzsche we cannot learn from him as one who is able to participate with us in rational conversation, criticism, and enquiry. (MacIntyre 2001: 164–5)

What lies between *A Short History of Ethics* and *Dependent Rational Animals* is by no means without significance: the much-commented dilemma 'Nietzsche or Aristotle' from *After Virtue*, the short but important remarks on Nietzsche in *Whose Justice? Which Rationality?* (1988) and, last but not least, the systematic account of Nietzschean genealogy in *Three Rival Versions of Moral Inquiry* (1990). It is my view that what MacIntyre designated in his 1994 interview as morality being a historical subject matter bears structural resemblances to Nietzsche's genealogical critique of Enlightenment morality, especially his criticism of the latter's claim to absoluteness, objectivity and superiority to other moral traditions. In fact, the historical perspective on morality can also be ascribed to Nietzsche without necessarily linking it to a moral subjectivism and, even more, to moral relativism. The latter's critique has, nevertheless, been in many instances MacIntyre's main argument against Nietzschean genealogy. What I will argue, then, is that MacIntyre's reduction of the latter to the relativistic threat to rationality has to do with the hasty identification of Nietzsche himself with Nietzsche-inspired thinkers, such as Michel Foucault.

III

In chapter 9 of *After Virtue*, right in the middle of the book, MacIntyre introduces a dilemma put in the form of a disjunction: Nietzsche *or* Aristotle? Strangely enough, the question does not seem to follow naturally from the previous chapters, which, roughly speaking, are engaged in a negative task, that is, in the polemic against the Enlightenment project and its alleged failure. Chapter 9 is, then, to be perceived as a strategic move within the whole plan of the book, as it is later on, in chapter 18, that MacIntyre's polemic finds its constructive counterpart, that is, the account of virtues starting from virtue in archaic societies and concluding with what might come *after* virtue. It is at this point, that is in the book's concluding chapter, that MacIntyre returns to the question posed in chapter 9 with the obvious claim to answer it: instead of 'Nietzsche or Aristotle?' it is, then, 'After Virtue: Nietzsche *or* Aristotle, Trotsky *and* St. Benedict', a combination which sounds strange to the naïve reader or commentator due to the use of these four names in a conjunctive or disjunctive manner (Solomon 2003: 136–7). Naturally, the two philosophers are evoked here not as separate instances in the history of moral philosophy, but as *types* – Aristotle exemplifying the classical view of man and Nietzsche the late modern cultural of subjectivism and emotivism. It is doubtless that MacIntyre's treatment of Nietzsche's counter-Enlightenment project is by no means circumstantial or fortuitous, but of critical importance for his *plan d'attaque* on the Enlightenment project. In a remarkable "tour de force", MacIntyre constructs Nietzsche as his other self.

In what follows, I will try to account briefly for MacIntyre's theses using several of the arguments advanced by Richard J. Bernstein.[4] Bernstein argues that MacIntyre's 'story line', which resembles by all means the kind of genealogical 'unmasking' of which Nietzsche has been the initiator, focuses on a harsh critique of emotivism in its many facets within mature modern societies, not as a theory, but foremost as what 'has been embodied in our culture' (MacIntyre 2007: 21). This critique culminates in his appeal to Nietzsche in chapter 9, where, on the one hand, Nietzsche is identified as the initiator of suspicion and distrust vis-à-vis modernity as such, whereas, on the other hand, an either-or problematic is put forth: either one is a Nietzschean, meaning that s/he diagnoses the state of the Enlightenment project as a failure *après coup*, or one takes the stance against this retrospective evaluation of modernity and stands for a more radical position, that is, the rejection altogether of modernity as what should have never occurred in the first place (MacIntyre 2007: 111). This either-or structure is, for Bernstein, the climax of the whole questioning: 'For the alternative posed by MacIntyre is not just one view of morality versus another – it is, rather, morality versus no morality' (Bernstein 1984: 8). Strangely enough, this is the point where Bernstein's treatment reveals a real paradox: from chapter 9 on, MacIntyre is supposed to part from Nietzsche by presenting an account of the virtues that could effectively build on one of the two sides of the either-or structure. Is this really the case? For Bernstein, it is not: 'One might even claim that what MacIntyre has shown us *thus far* really supports Nietzsche's case; that what MacIntyre decoded is the champion of Nietzsche. Why? Because he not only shows that there are incompatible and incommensurable lists and theories of virtue, but has failed *thus far* to show how we can "rationally" adjudicate among rival claimants'

(Bernstein 1984: 9). But if Enlightenment morality led us to a situation of moral disagreement and perpetual conflict over competing truth claims, neither is the story line of the virtues a continuous one nor does it succumb to a single criterion of rational justification and truth. Now, if this is the case, what would be the difference between MacIntyre's and Nietzsche's deconstructive move? The latter has already drawn attention to the incommensurable and incompatible claims of Enlightenment morality. So, it may be asked whether MacIntyre poses any good alternative to that critique of Enlightenment which he accuses of being conducive to the eclipse of values and nihilism. Bernstein does not opt for the easy way. He, thus, builds his critique upon MacIntyre's three structural bases for the virtues, that is, practices, the narrative unity of a single human life and the idea of a moral tradition, noting that, with regard to all three bases, there is no dramatic difference between Nietzsche and MacIntyre himself (Bernstein 1984: 16).

IV

If the critique of late modern emotivist culture lies at the heart of MacIntyre's attack on Nietzsche in *After Virtue*, there is an important hermeneutic change in subsequent analyses, in his 1988 *Whose Justice? Which Rationality?* as well as in its aftermath, *Three Rival Versions of Moral Inquiry*. But this brings us back to our initial questioning about MacIntyre's self-critique of his late recognition of the radical historicity of moral traditions, in the light of an enlarged understanding of what rationality is. In *Whose Justice? Which Rationality?* the focus of criticism is not just Nietzsche himself – if Nietzsche was ever to be the topic on its own – but post-Enlightenment theorists, who define themselves mainly as post-Nietzscheans, accused of moral perspectivism conducive to relativism: 'Post-Enlightenment relativism and perspectivism are thus the negative counterpart of the Enlightenment, its inverted mirror image. Where the Enlightenment invoked the arguments of Kant or Bentham, such post-Enlightenment theorists invoke Nietzsche's attacks upon Kant and Bentham' (MacIntyre 1989: 353). While MacIntyre's main subject matter here is the rational inquiry into the historical unfolding of traditions, the postmodern Nietzschean theorist seems to be MacIntyre's steady companion, and not without good reason. In similar terms to him being the inverted mirror of the Enlightenment thinker, MacIntyre conceives his own rational inquiry as the inverted mirror of the post-Nietzschean thinker:

> Perspectivism, in this once more like relativism, is a doctrine only possible for those who regard themselves as outsiders, as uncommitted or rather committed only to acting a succession of temporary parts. ... From the standpoint afforded by the rationality of tradition-constituted enquiry it is clear that such persons are by their stance excluded from the possession of any concept of truth adequate for systematic rational inquiry. (MacIntyre 1989: 368)

In similar terms, in *Three Rival Versions of Moral Inquiry*, Nietzsche's genealogical project comes as a reply to the encyclopaedic project of setting universal standards, compelling to all rational agents, within which the often-rival claims of different communities and cultural frameworks can be evaluated. Nevertheless, the claim to objectivity and universality is, so to speak, a self-defeating one, and a genealogist such as Nietzsche is the first to acknowledge this fact:

> Psychologically what is taken to be fixed and binding about truth – Nietzsche would of course have said the same about knowledge and duty and right – is an unrecognized motivation serving an unacknowledged purpose. To think and speak of truth, knowledge, duty, and right in the late nineteenth-century mode, the mode in fact of the Ninth Edition, is to give evidence of membership in a culture in which lack of self-knowledge has been systematically institutionalized. (MacIntyre 1994: 35)

Hence, the hermeneutic preconception of the complex relationship between the encyclopaedist and the genealogist is nothing more than the necessary misrepresentation of the one by the other: from the perspectivism of the encyclopaedist, the genealogist is a proponent of relativism and an enemy of rationalism, whereas from the standpoint of the genealogist, the encyclopaedist adopts a naïve stance towards moral knowledge and truth being entangled in conceptual schemes and metaphors unrecognized by him as such (MacIntyre 1994: 43). Nevertheless, and in contrast to the complete failure of the encyclopaedist tradition to perceive itself a tradition, for MacIntyre, the genealogist has made a decisive step further, that is, 'the transformation of the moral inquirer from the participant in an encyclopaedic enterprise shared by all adequately reflective and informed human beings into an engaged partisan of one such warring standpoint against its rivals is an accomplished fact' (MacIntyre 1994: 56). Consequently, the discontinuity or even the crisis within the modern moral establishment produced by such a genealogist as Nietzsche is irreversible, because it revealed a fundamental truth, which is nowadays prevailing:

> So far as large-scale theoretical and conceptual structures are concerned, each rival theoretical standpoint provides from within itself and in its own terms the standards by which, this is at least what its adherents claim, it should be evaluated, rivalry between such contending standpoints includes rivalry over standards. There is no theoretically neutral or even a pre-theoretical ground from which the adjudication of competing claims can proceed.' (MacIntyre 1994: 173)

Hence, the historical and cultural embeddedness of moral inquiry is to be accepted by the genealogist and MacIntyre alike, the main difference between them being that the latter acknowledges the necessity to take the quest for rational justification a step further.

V

What would be the outcome of the twists and turns of MacIntyre's critique of Nietzsche, which we have followed very briefly here? First, it is quite clear that what he has in mind while criticizing Nietzsche is not always or foremost Nietzsche himself, but a certain reception of Nietzsche by postmodern thinkers who elaborated on his genealogy, such as Michel Foucault.[5] As far as the critique of Nietzsche's genealogical project is concerned, Nietzsche's identification with his postmodern adepts is of critical importance as it definitely narrows down the scope of MacIntyre's critique: 'It is all too easy to conclude further that therefore, when one large-scale theoretical and conceptual standpoint is systematically at odds with another, there can be no rational way of settling the differences between them. And Nietzsche's genealogical heirs do so conclude, for this as well as for other reasons' (MacIntyre 1994: 173). A second point to consider in MacIntyre's critique is his 1999 account of Nietzsche as an 'inverted mirror' of his own stance towards modernity and late modernity, a statement that merits much greater attention. Last but not least, it is important to distinguish between at least two phases in his treatment of Nietzschean morality. In the first phase Nietzsche is designated as an ultra-modern, that is, as the ultimate moment in the evolution of modern individualistic Enlightenment thought – mainly in *After Virtue*: 'But it now turns out to be the case that in the end the Nietzschean stance is only one more facet of the very moral culture of which Nietzsche took himself to be an implacable critic' (MacIntyre 2007: 259). In the second phase – from *Whose Justice? Which Rationality?* on – Nietzsche is perceived as an anti-modernist and, even more, as an anti-theorist:

> Nietzsche's final standpoint, that towards rather than from which he speaks, cannot be expressed as a set of statements. Statements made only to be discarded – and sometimes taken up again – in that movement from utterance to utterance in which what is communicated is the movement. Nietzsche did not advance a new theory against older theories, he proposed an abandonment of theory.[6] (MacIntyre 1994: 49)

But even in these terms, MacIntyre's account of Nietzsche does not seem to fully appreciate the hermeneutic complexity and fecundity of some keys ideas in the latter's treatment of morality, such as the use of perspectivism in his value theory[7] or even his harsh critique of Enlightenment individualism and liberalism: 'The Nietzschean stance turns out not to be a mode of escape from or an alternative to the conceptual scheme of liberal individualist modernity, but rather one more representative moment in its internal unfolding. And we may therefore expect liberal individualist societies to breed "great men" from time to time. Alas!'[8] (MacIntyre 2007: 259). MacIntyre gives us a short but eloquent account of perspectivism in *Three Rival Versions of Moral Inquiry*: '[Nietzsche] takes there to be a multiplicity of perspectives within each of which truth-from-a-point-of-view may be asserted, but no truth-as-such, an empty notion, about *the* world, an equally empty notion. There are [for Nietzsche] no rules of rationality as such to be appealed to, there are rather strategies of insight and strategies of subversion' (MacIntyre 1994: 42). Nevertheless, it is important to ask: is perspectivism in Nietzsche equivalent to what here MacIntyre takes it to be? One thing that is decisive for MacIntyre's whole interpretation is that he relates closely Nietzsche's moral perspectivism with contemporary emotivist theories in ethics, as for him to translate these post-Nietzschean claims into this idiom is at once to recognize both the resemblances and the differences between such claims and a type of theory in academic moral philosophy advanced in different versions by Charles L. Stevenson and Simon Blackburn (Stevenson 1944; Blackburn 2014).

But is Nietzsche's perspectivism synonymous to relativism? MacIntyre argues that 'from the standpoint of the genealogist no tradition can be rational, but in this case for reasons which equally undermine any claim that particular methods or principles are ever as such rational'[9] (MacIntyre 1994: 117). And, even more importantly, does the claim to rationality give us the right to endorse one of the moral traditions as superior to the others in order to allegedly avoid genealogical relativism? This is at least what Richard Bernstein argues in criticizing MacIntyre's hermeneutics of tradition: 'Despite MacIntyre's apparently tolerant claims in acknowledging the "legitimacy" of radically incommensurable traditions of justice and practical rationality, there is an *implicit* cultural imperialism in his view. For it is a necessary consequence of his claims that a given tradition *may* contingently turn out to be rationally superior to all its rivals' (Bernstein 1991: 64).

These subtle conceptual distinctions are in large part forgotten by MacIntyre when he criticizes Nietzsche's relativism, or even his irrationalism, though they are known to him as conceptual clarifications (MacIntyre 1989: 352–3, 367–9). This is also the case when he treats Nietzsche as a moral or cultural relativist or as an ultra-individualist succumbing to a Weberian reading of Nietzsche – and I am here alluding to the account by Thomas D'Andrea of the way in which the early MacIntyre plays Nietzsche against Marx leading to the idea that Marxism ended up in succumbing to modern liberal individualism by espousing a Weberian, Nietzsche-inspired moral and political ideal. Many stimulating alternatives could be given against this reductionist move, such as the prevailing of a perfectionist rather than an individualistic ideal of the self in Nietzsche, beautifully analysed by Stephen Mulhall in a recent paper where he plays an Emerson-inspired Nietzsche against the postmodern one.[10] (Mulhall 2013: 215–8)

To summarize my argument, there is a Janus-head structure in what MacIntyre does as far as Nietzsche is concerned. On the one hand, there is clearly a strategic way of interpreting him via the attack on his postmodern, historicist and potentially relativistic, reading. Thus, Nietzsche becomes, hermeneutically speaking, MacIntyre's 'inverted mirror', as he is the enemy he constructs in order to make his way across the impasses of late modernity. On the other hand, there are two positive moments in this hermeneutic encounter. First, what MacIntyre claims in many instances as the idea of 'my own tradition' is not far away from Nietzsche's perspectivism, in the sense that they both are not forms of subjectivism or relativism. It is in this sense that in a recent challenging paper Stephen Mulhall describes Nietzsche's distance from his postmodern legacy as due to his hidden alliance with American perfectionism and Emerson in particular, for whom he had openly expressed a lifelong admiration: 'For Nietzsche's Emersonian reformulation asks whether your apparently flourishing life is truly yours or whether it has in truth gone dead for you – whether its vitality is mere appearance, so that you find yourself haunting your own existence' (Mulhall 2013: 213). Second, MacIntyre's historical account of ethics resembles Nietzsche's genealogical method in morality in that they both have to be parts of a more comprehensive *Kulturkritik*, that is, a critique of cultural forms that transcends the level of normative or even meta-ethical positions. This is especially evident, for example, in MacIntyre's discussion of the emotivist self. Emotivism's meta-ethical critique stands at a distance from Nietzsche's existential commitment to ethics, and MacIntyre emphasizes on many occasions that this is not accidental:

> There is thus a double case to be made against any Neo-Aristotelian point of view. Expressivists charge that it fails to recognize the truth in expressivism concerning the meaning and use of normative and evaluative sentences and the nature of moral judgment … Nietzscheans charges that it presents what is not just a false account of human flourishing. … For the expressivist Neo-Aristotelianism is false. For the Nietzschean it is corrupting. (MacIntyre 2016: 48)

Thus, MacIntyre could well be considered as a post-Hegelian and a post-Wittgensteinian, but primarily as a post-Nietzschean in the strongest possible sense of the term, for the harsh critique of metaphysical foundationalism, individualism, abstract rationalism, moral formalism and proceduralism, and of modern man's loss of projection upon the future because of no authentic historical awareness. What seems indeed to remain intact in this complex hermeneutic encounter is what MacIntyre wrote in his 1990 *First Principles, Final Ends*: 'A theory about the predicaments of contemporary philosophy … requires the construction of something akin to what Nietzsche called genealogy', adding later on that this construction would be necessary even without being a Thomist (MacIntyre 1990: 57–8). This statement condenses the argument for a historically aware moral inquiry which characterizes MacIntyre's critique of modernity as a tradition, while witnessing at the same time a deep kinship to Nietzsche, even if it takes the form of an 'inverted mirror' hermeneutic relation.

Notes

1. See Bernard Williams (1993: 4-14) and also, more importantly, his *Truth and Truthfulness* where he sets forth the critical for the whole history of ethics opposition between theory, and its standard of truth, and anti-theory in ethics, with its standard of truthfulness: 'His [Nietzsche's] aim was to see how far the values of truth could be revalued, how they might be understood in a perspective quite different from the Platonic and Christian metaphysics which had provided their principal source in the West up to now' (2002: 18). Williams' stance, therefore, is close to that of Nietzsche and his critique of Platonism and idealism in ethics; this proximity grows even bigger, when Williams openly characterizes his moral standpoint as a form of 'skepticism without reductionism' (Andrew Pyle, ed. (1999), 143).
2. See mainly pp. 150–65 of Alasdair MacIntyre (2016), which are part of the core chapter of the book that deals with the relationship between morality and modernity.
3. Though the MacIntyre of *Ethics in the Conflicts of Modernity* has Marx and Aristotle in mind, when discussing human flourishing, it is no accident that he prefers Nietzsche to Harry Frankfurt when it comes to 'the importance of the first person pronoun' (MacIntyre 2016: 47). What the modern expressivist will recognize is that 'she will, insofar as she follows Nietzsche, interpret anti-expressivist views as expressions of an inability or a lack of will on the part of those who hold them to admit to the

underlying motivation of their judgments and actions, an inability to recognize who and what they are'. (ibid. 48). But, for MacIntyre, the Neo-Aristotelian stance is not an impersonal one, thus, he does not agree with the 'reflective expressivist' agent, who would argue that the Neo-Aristotelian agent engages in a 'corrupting' moral stance (ibid.).

4   See Richard J. Bernstein (1984), and MacIntyre's reply (1984), 30–41. On another occasion, Bernstein points out the quasi-Hegelian manner of MacIntyre's historical approach to modern moral philosophy which moves around the notion of emotivism (Richard J. Bernstein (1991), 21–2).

5   See MacIntyre's comment on Foucault's famous essay on the uses of history in Nietzsche 'Nietzsche, la genealogie, l'histoire' (1971): *Three Rival Versions of Moral Inquiry*, 49–51. Another important post-Nietzschean to be equally criticized is Gilles Deleuze: *Whose Justice? Which Rationality?*, 368.

6   On the differentiation between the 'theory critics' and the 'morality critics', see Nietzschean literature in Brian Leiter (1997), 250–85.

7   As Buket Korkut suggests: 'Contrary to what MacIntyre suggests, Nietzsche's *perspectivism* is *not* a version of emotivism; it does not involve subjectivity of individual moral judgments. ... In other words, Nietzsche's perspectivism does not arise from his observations of individuals' moral judgments as expressions of subjective will nor does it claim that moral judgments are individual preferences, which is the basic tenet of emotivism' (Buket Korkut (2012), 205; Korkut's emphasis). For Korkut, contrary to what MacIntyre implies, Nietzsche engages himself in an intersubjectivist, historically situated interpretation of morality.

8   See in this respect: R. Kevin Hill (1992), 3-12 and Shari N. Starrett's (1992) reply in Shari N. Starrett (1992), 13–20.

9   Gordon Graham contends that 'the genealogist ... subordinates philosophy in history. Because he sees, rightly, that total historical detachment, or radical universalism, is impossible, he swings violently in the opposite direction and concludes that every thought and idea is the creature, and hence the instrument, of its time, to be used or abused in the power struggles of social and political history. Whereas the encyclopaedist is unrealistically ahistorical, the genealogist is an historical relativist' (Gordon Graham (2003), 28).

10 In his paper, Mulhall is largely inspired here by Bernard Williams' critique of MacIntyre on Nietzsche epitomized in his *Truth and Truthfulness* (2002).

Bibliography

Bernstein, R. J. (1984), 'Nietzsche or Aristotle? Reflections on Alasdair MacIntyre's *After Virtue*', *Soundings: An Interdisciplinary Journal*, 67 (1): 6–29.

Bernstein, R. J. (1991), *The New Constellation: The Ethical-Political Horizons of Modernity/Postmodernity*, Cambridge: Polity Press.

Blackburn, S. (2007), 'Perspectives, Fictions, Errors, Play', in Brian Leiter and Neil Sinhababu (eds), *Nietzsche and Morality*, Oxford: Oxford University Press.

Blackburn, S. (2014), *Mirror Mirror: The Uses and Abuses of Self-Love*, Princeton NJ: Princeton University Press.

Borradori, G. and A. MacIntyre (1994), 'Nietzsche or Aristotle? Alasdair MacIntyre', in *The American Philosopher: Interview with Giovanna Borradori*, Chicago IL: University of Chicago Press.

Foucault, M. (1971), 'Nietzsche, la généalogie, l'histoire', in *Hommage à Jean Hyppolite*, Paris: Presses Universitaires de France, coll. Epiméthée, 145–72.

Graham, G. (2003), 'MacIntyre on History and Philosophy', in Mark C. Murphy (ed.), *Alasdair MacIntyre*, Cambridge: Cambridge University Press.

Hill, K. R. (1992), 'MacIntyre's Nietzsche: A Critique', *International Studies in Philosophy*, 24 (2): 3–12.

Korkut, B.-R. (2012), 'MacIntyre's Nietzsche or Nietzschean MacIntyre?' *Philosophy and Social Criticism*, 38 (2): 199–214.

Leiter, B. (1997), 'Nietzsche and the Morality Critics', *Ethics*, 107 (January), 250–85.

Leiter, B. and N. Sinhababu, eds (2007), *Nietzsche and Morality*, Oxford: Oxford University Press.

MacIntyre, A. (1984), 'Bernstein's Distorting Mirrors: A Rejoinder', *Soundings: An Interdisciplinary Journal*, 67 (1): 30–41.

MacIntyre, A. (1989), *Whose Justice? Which Rationality?* Notre Dame: University of Notre Dame Press.

MacIntyre, A. (1990), *First Principles, Final Ends and Contemporary Philosophical Issues*, Milwaukee, WI: Marquette University Press.

MacIntyre, A. (1994), *Three Rival Versions of Moral Inquiry: Encyclopaedia, Genealogy and Tradition*, Notre Dame: University of Notre Dame Press.

MacIntyre, A. ([1967] 1998), *A Short History of Ethics: A History of Moral Philosophy from the Homeric Age to the Twentieth Century*, London: Routledge.

MacIntyre, A. (2001), *Dependent Rational Animals: Why Human Beings Need the Virtues*, Chicago, IL: Open Court.

MacIntyre, A. (2006), *Ethics and Politics: Selected Essays, Vol. 2*, Cambridge: Cambridge University Press.

MacIntyre, A. (2007), *After Virtue: A Study in Moral Theory*, Notre Dame: University of Notre Dame Press.

MacIntyre, A. (2016), *Ethics in the Conflicts of Modernity: An Essay on Desire, Practical Reasoning, and Narrative*, Cambridge: Cambridge University Press.

Mulhall, S. (2013), 'Naturalism, Nihilism, and Perfectionism. Stevenson, Williams, and Nietzsche in Twentieth-Century Moral Philosophy', in F. O'Rourke (ed.), *What Happened in and to Moral Philosophy in the Twentieth Century? Philosophical Essays in Honor of Alasdair MacIntyre*, Notre Dame: Notre Dame University Press.

Pyle, A., ed. (1999), *Key Philosophers in Conversation: The 'Cogito' Interviews*, London: Routledge.

Solomon, D. (2003), 'MacIntyre and Contemporary Moral Philosophy', in Mark C. Murphy (ed.), *Alasdair MacIntyre*, Cambridge: Cambridge University Press.

Starrett, S. N. (1992), 'Nietzsche and MacIntyre: Against Individualism', *International Studies in Philosophy*, 24 (2): 13–20.

Stevenson, Ch. L. (1944), *Ethics and Language*, New Haven: Yale University Press.

Williams, B. (1993), 'Nietzsche's Minimalist Moral Psychology', *The European Journal of Philosophy*, 1 (1): 4–14.

Williams, B. (2002), *Truth and Truthfulness: An Essay in Genealogy*, Princeton, NJ: Princeton University Press.

Part 3

Virtue ethics and modern social and political theory

From field to forest?

Exploring limits of virtue ethics

Joseph Dunne

Introduction

I will introduce what I want to explore in this chapter by reference to three images through which Charles Taylor symbolizes what he sees as Iris Murdoch's distinctive contribution to Anglophone moral philosophy in the second half of the twentieth century. Murdoch, Taylor suggests, helped to release the discipline from the 'corral' – that is to say, from confinement to issues about *what it is right to do*, as determined by principles and rules governing our obligations to others – and to move it out to the 'field', where more expansive questions emerge about *how it is best to live*. Taylor's deeming of this move as an advance for ethical theorizing relates to his strictures on deontological and utilitarian perspectives and his sympathy with a conception of ethical life as defined by aspirations for a full human flourishing, which would be unachievable without the exercise of a range of different virtues. But Taylor sees Murdoch's work as also exemplifying a further desirable move: out of the corral, to be sure, but beyond the field too – and yonder into the 'forest'. This term symbolizes a place in which flourishing, as the overarching good or ultimate end of human living, which frames the horizon of the field, is somehow transcended. Such a shift would occur through an opening in ethical life to the possibility of radical self-transformation through responsiveness to *what can most fully inspire one's love*, when this is a supremely high good that is irreducible to, and might indeed call for a renunciation of, a rich or flourishing life as identified in the field. My purpose in this chapter is to examine the implications of expanding our moral topography so that, beyond constraints of the corral or fulfilments of the field, the forest is acknowledged as defining the ethical horizon of people who find their way into it – if it does not indeed form a more or less unexplored hinterland of all ethical experience. More particularly, I want to consider how a move from field to forest might reframe our understanding of what it is to live a virtuous life.

In elucidation of Taylor's evocative symbols, Aristotle can be assigned a central role: as the thinker who most conspicuously placed flourishing (*eudaimonia*) at the heart of ethics and who has been the most influential figure in the emergence over recent decades of 'virtue ethics', he is, paradigmatically, the philosopher of the 'field'. By contrast, the 'forest' is a more elusive notion. Its congruence with Murdoch's work stems from her resistance to eudaimonist conceptions of 'good' and her emphasis, rather, on ultimate concern with 'the Good' – an emphasis that was shaped by her engagement with Buddhism, Plato and the Jewish-Christian mystic Simone Weil. In my discussion here, I will not focus on Plato and, while 'forest' is a distinctively Buddhist notion, I will attend more closely to a Christian variant of it. No less than Buddhism, Christianity is far from the only tradition to mark out a forest pathway; but it is the one which has been most deeply interfused with Western philosophical reflection, and with which I am most familiar. In considering it here, I will draw on two contemporary Aristotelians: part of the peculiar interest of Charles Taylor's own work and that of Alasdair MacIntyre lies in the fact that both of them champion the virtues of the field, while evincing at the same time, as we shall see, a powerful pull towards the forest.[1]

I Reconnoitring ethical-spiritual terrain

The field is the area in which people seek to live rewarding lives in the light of some more or less explicit conception of what it is for a human life to flourish or go well (which, without annulling their obligations to others, provides the wider context within which these obligations have meaning and force). What Taylor calls the 'life goods' that constitute or conduce to flourishing may be many and varied, including, for example, a happy family life, purposeful and reasonably well remunerated work, solid friendships, a range of interests and pastimes, and devotion to a political or other cause. But key among them too are personal qualities or virtues of character, such as courage, truthfulness, justice, generosity and temperance – qualities that are required by and embodied in the kinds of family life, work, friendship or political commitment that have any likelihood of proving genuinely fulfilling.

What makes these life goods *good* or how are we to understand the flourishing that they comprise? A significant element of any Aristotelian answer to this question will invoke the notion of the function (*ergon*) of a specific kind of being, understanding the flourishing of any being of that kind as occurring to the extent that it fulfils this function well, whether it be a knife, a flute, a cherry tree, a sheep-dog, a flute-player or a human being. We might call this element 'naturalistic' in the sense that it adheres in the latter cases to the biological order of living things and appeals to empirical regularities amenable to any third-person observer (while not discounting of course that human beings are animals to which language and reasoning are natural). This element is plainly formulated in Aristotle's own texts (see especially *Nicomachean Ethics* [hereafter *NE*], I.7) and has featured prominently in recent work in virtue ethics inspired by those texts (e.g. Foot 2003; Hursthouse 2010). Strong arguments can be made for its inclusion in any cogent account of the ethical life of humans. But it does not encourage us to posit anything gestured to by the symbol of the 'forest'.

Now Taylor's own conception of what we meet in the field of ethics gives a crucial role to what he calls 'strong evaluation'. As ethical agents, we cannot avoid making discriminations, with regard to actions, feelings, desires and states, in terms of qualitative distinctions between what is worthy, admirable and deserving of emulation, on the one hand, and what is discreditable, base, or to be shunned, on the other; it is such discriminations that most crucially form our self-understandings and thereby constitute our identities as persons. These strong discriminations have a binding character that is absent from the weaker preferences and aversions of what may be our actually occurrent desires: commanding our admiration and assent, they warrant, if necessary, the redirection and reshaping of these desires. As life goods, the virtues are paradigm examples of what we evaluate strongly in this sense. But it is a key point for Taylor that an adequate understanding of the goodness of life goods – and accordingly of virtues – must also factor in what he calls 'constitutive goods', which are 'features of ourselves, or the world or God, such that their being what they are is essential to the life goods being good' (1996: 12). While lying for the most part in the background of our moral awareness, constitutive goods are those realities that matter greatly to us, most deeply move us or evoke our fullest love – thereby inspiring and empowering us to live out, in our or doing and being, the virtues that they inform and animate. Knowledge and love are reciprocally linked here. Articulation of a constitutive good – in which philosophical discourse can make sense only when inflected by background understandings and acquired habits and cannot displace narrative depiction of paradigm figures or appreciative attention to examples – can serve to strengthen our attachment to it. But, no less, attachment to what is good about any life-good 'can be an essential condition of making finer discriminations about what it means to realize it' (Taylor 1996: 14; this reflects Aristotle's claim that while the deliberative and discriminatory powers of *phronēsis* direct our actions, these powers themselves presuppose a settled commitment to the goods towards which they direct us).

In relation to Aristotle, Taylor's analysis points to our being animals with *logos* as the constitutive good of the *Nicomachean Ethics*. There is something about the status of being a *logos*-bearing animal that deserves to compel our greatest respect, even awe, and to inspire us to realize it most fully in our actions and lives. A concept in the *Ethics* that would then come to the fore – as in some respects even more important than *ergon* – is *to kalon*. This term, whose primary meaning (in Liddel and Scott) is 'beautiful' or 'fair', is usually rendered in translations of the *Ethics* as the 'noble' or 'fine'. A strongly evaluative notion, in Taylor's sense, it is explicitly distinguished by Aristotle from the pleasant and the useful and points to the quality of a virtuous action as being worthy of being done for its own sake – that is to say, as a component of a higher, more noble way of life: to be done 'for its own sake' is to be done 'for the sake of the noble, since this is the end aimed at by virtue' (*NE*. III, 7, 1115b11-14). A purely naturalistic account of Aristotle's ethical thought – in which virtue contributes to human flourishing as the functional realization of inborn capabilities akin to what can be identified in other animals when they are in rude good health – misses something essential in this thought. It misses precisely that element to which the use of *to kalon* should alert us: an element of intrinsic value that is compelling just because failure to respond to it would betray a lack of the most essential ethical sensitivity. If Aristotle's own sense of the exalted dignity of a human being as a *zōon logon echon* can be taken as the constitutive good of his ethical writing, we should perhaps balance this thought with two other complementary considerations. First, relative to the highest beings –

such as God and the heavenly bodies – our status is incomparably lower; or rather, it is as high as it is precisely because we ourselves have a share in the godly through our being endowed with *logos* and *nous*, the 'divine spark' in us.[2] And, second, Aristotle's own sense of nature as applied to living beings which do not possess *logos* or *nous* is imbued with a sense of awe – as is demonstrated in this famous passage from one of his biological works:

> We must not recoil ... from examination of the humbler animals. Every realm of nature is marvellous: and just as Heracleitus is said to have spoken to the visitors, who were wanting to meet him but stopped as they were approaching when they saw him warming himself at the oven – he kept telling them to come in and not worry, 'for there are gods here too' – so we should approach the inquiry about each animal without aversion, knowing that in all of them there is something natural and beautiful (*phusikon kai kalon*). (*Parts of Animals*, 645a, 15–24)

In combating views of ethics that limit it to right action, and to decision procedures that drastically foreshorten the kind of practical reasoning actually operative in our ethical lives, Taylor takes us out of the 'corral'. But his account of the field that I have just briefly reviewed may leave us better placed to see how openings lead from field to forest. This account seeks to bring into relief not only what a person does but also who s/he is and what s/he loves. Aspiration – a certain kind of stretching or being stretched – is essential to ethical awareness and the pattern of living bound up with it.[3] 'Fullness' is a term that Taylor uses to characterize what we are attracted to as ethical agents – a fullness that comes through love of constitutive goods and a greater realization of the life goods that they constitute. The issue that then arises is whether we might be moved by some constitutive goods that could destabilize what we ordinarily think of as life goods – and indeed have the power to draw us beyond life itself. If this were the case, then we would have made a transition, or crossed a kind of boundary, significant enough to make sense of the idea of passing from field to forest.

What is it to be 'beyond' life in the sense intended here? Well, it is not enough that one's sense of what constitutes a worthy life should stretch beyond consideration of one's own good, motivating altruistic action for the good of others – even if these others be remote from one's immediate milieu and (as might be the case for those with deep ecological commitments) even from one's own lifetime. Indeed, it might not be enough if concern for others should lead a person to suffer and die on their behalf; for such heroic privileging of others' lives over one's own could still cleave to the primacy of life, or at least human life, itself. It is the denial of this primacy – and more precisely, when this denial takes the form of an acknowledgement, indeed a full-hearted love, of some supreme good other than life – that one is in the forest. This acknowledgement involves a displacement of the self, the kind of radical reorientation of a person's identity characteristic of a religious 'conversion', as in a Buddhist's shift from self to 'no-self' (*anatta*) or a Christian's submission to God expressed in the words 'Thy will be done'. The self thus constituted – by attachment to a transcendent Good, an attachment that involves a real renunciation – is hardly the same self as the one for whom a flourishing life in the field constitutes the ultimate ethical end. This is not to say that flourishing in the 'field' sense and all the recognizable challenges of ordinary ethical life are suspended. Rather, at least in the cases of the two historical 'religions' just mentioned, they reappear in transfigured form. 'In Christian terms, if renunciation decenters you in relation to God, God's will is that humans flourish, and so you are taken back to an affirmation of this flourishing, which is biblically called *agapē*. In Buddhist terms, Enlightenment does not just turn you from the world; it also opens the flood-gates of *metta* (loving kindness) and *karuna* (compassion)' (Taylor 1996: 21).

In the next section, I will offer a fuller description of the ethical-spiritual landscape of the 'forest', before going on in the third section to consider how this description refocuses our understanding of 'virtue'. Then in a brief concluding section, I will relate this discussion of forest and field to the dominant morality of secular modernity and the challenge it faces from an insurgent Nietzscheanism. While I'm well aware of how strongly contestable the ground to be covered here is, my intention is not apologetic. More than three centuries ago, Pascal wrote: 'People have contempt for religion; they hate it and fear it may be true. To cure this it is necessary to ... show that it is attractive, lovable (*aimable*), so as to make the good wish that it were true; and then to show that it is true' (quoted in Becket 2006: 13). To support 'a wish that it were true', rather than 'to show that it is true', defines the limit of my ambition in the rest of the chapter.

II In the forest

The forest is the place where one is drawn to a highest good beyond life – in the Christian case, a God who loves the world and in whose love we can aspire to share. But the very height of aspiration here unavoidably confronts us with the lowness of our achievement, with the distance separating us from this supreme good. In the light of this good, suffering in the world is made peculiarly manifest. The depredations of war and famine, apparently random natural disasters, human potential wasted or great need unmet, cruelty inflicted on the innocent, oppressions and injustices unrectified, and often even unrecognized: to be drawn to a good God is at the same time to be exposed in one's conscience to all this blighting of human life. But such exposure also confronts one with everything in oneself that obstructs or greatly limits one's capacity to meet the demand that it presents or to discern what, in one's own circumstances, this demand may be.

Adherence to any demanding ethical ideal is likely to be disturbing in this way. Perhaps in moments of special lucidity or experienced wholeness, one is more aligned with the ideal and more freely and fully disposed to respond to it. But such moments may be relatively fleeting and rare. For the rest, one is occupied with daily cares, finding challenge and satisfaction in ordinary responsibilities and tasks, especially in family and work – enough to distract from, though not entirely to extinguish, one's awareness of the more exacting call, which remains as a background source of admonishment and unease. Embarking on a spiritual path brings this background more to the fore and thus entails encounter with the dark or shadow side of oneself; in the Christian tradition, the 'desert' rather than the 'forest' symbolizes the place of such encounter. The shadow is not due to an egregious failure in moral formation or an arrested state of psychological development. It is understood rather as the default or 'normal' condition of human beings, a normality that leaves us hampered in our ability to meet ethical-spiritual demands that we still find inescapably compelling. Only at the summit of spiritual advance, in the lives of those who are truly holy, is this state of disability overcome so that, in the Christian case, they submit unconditionally to the promptings of an *agapē* that has taken possession of their whole being.

It is the distance between such a saintly state and our ordinary condition that one sets out to traverse when one embarks on a spiritual path; and given the scale and nature of this distance, the path is one of transformation. It will consist centrally of practices and disciplines that aim at an unmaking and remaking of one's character. 'Spiritual exercises' is the common expression here, used for centuries in religious communities (associated most easily but by no means exclusively with Ignatius Loyola), but with wider currency in philosophy now partly because of its centrality in Pierre Hadot's *Philosophy as a Way of Life*. This book demonstrates the extent to which ancient philosophy, especially as practised in the Hellenistic schools, did not consist in 'teaching an abstract theory much less in the exegesis of texts, but rather in the art of living' – which, from Plato's *Phaedo* onwards, included most testingly the art of dying. Such practice of philosophy was primarily a therapeutics of the passions, especially of 'unregulated desires and exaggerated fears', which aimed at 'a profound transformation of the individual's mode of seeing and being' (Hadot 1995: 83).[4] Of the two major Hellenistic schools, Stoicism has a spiritual tenor that is characteristically different from that of Epicureanism: whereas the former emphasizes rational sovereignty through the cultivated ability to limit one's care to matters one can affect and to regard those outside one's control from the perspective of an impassive cosmos, the latter encourages a more insouciant and joyful appreciation of the gifts of existence in each moment. But both schools initiated students into practical disciplines designed to increase vigilance and lucid self-presence in the conduct of life.

These disciplines, if only because of their sanction in the Western philosophical tradition, are helpful reference points here. But there are at least three noteworthy differences between them and their Christian counterparts. First, the idea of renunciation has a force in Christianity that it does not have in Stoicism. The Stoic ethical ideal, although in some respects deeply ascetical, does not entail abandonment of anything that can really be regarded as good: what one has to leave behind is properly to be deemed base, trivial, or unworthy of a being endowed with autonomous Reason (*to logistikon* or *to hēgemonikon*).[5] Christian non-attachment, by contrast, requires the surrender of genuine goods – so that there is real conflict between the full-hearted love of God and what we naturally incline to regard as human flourishing; were it otherwise, conversion could not count as *renunciation*, since nothing valuable would have been given up. But precisely because human flourishing is good and willed by God, it is reaffirmed, on the other side of conversion, which is the fundamental act of consent expressed as 'Thy Will be done'. This consent is lived out in a commitment to the flourishing of others, and ultimately, in partnership with God, to 'repairing the world' (or '*tikkun olam*', the Hebrew expression that Taylor invokes in making this same point (2007: 17)). The commitment is variously manifest in the lives of saintly persons throughout the history of all the great world faiths. In the case of Christianity, it is related to the central mystery of the Incarnation – God entering history in fully human form – and to the fact that hope is not for the immortality of the soul so much as for the resurrection of the body. And the contrast here reflects a deep divergence between Christianity and the whole Socratic tradition in Greek philosophy, a divergence dramatically illustrated in the deaths of the two foundational figures: Socrates facing this final ordeal with supreme composure, his rational sovereignty intact – to the point where it was scarcely an ordeal at all – and Jesus enduring and protesting a brutal, agonizing death, for the most part deserted rather than surrounded by his friends.

The second respect in which the practical disciplines of Hellenistic schools differ from those embodied in Christian spirituality relates to their primary role as edification: they involve remaking, but hardly *un*making, the self. Rigorous discipline and ever renewed attention are indeed necessary, and building positive habits involves dealing with recalcitrant passions – but with no great emphasis on a central feature of Christian asceticism: the sense of one's own personal crookedness, that is to say, one's seemingly boundless capacity for evasion, rationalization, and self-deception when faced with the demands of the higher good to which one has, or supposes that one has, committed oneself. A closer parallel here lies in psychoanalysis, which requires the patient not just to confront instinctual material but also to acknowledge and work through his or her own deeply entrenched resistances to doing this truthfully and with integrity (so that it requires, correspondingly, a great deal of strategic intelligence and hermeneutic sensitivity in the analyst's work of 'outwitting'). This is perhaps not very different from the 'purgative' element or the '*via negativa*' – often involving a 'dark night of the soul' – that is inseparable from religious practice, especially the practice of prayer. Alasdair MacIntyre, in whose work St Augustine and Freud have long been significant figures – especially because of their respective concerns with 'the transformation of desire' and 'the complex connections between desire and knowledge' (2004: 7, 3) – offers a striking formulation of analogy here. In a discussion of Augustine, he introduces Freud as a figure 'whose account of sexuality and religion in some respects is an inversion of Augustine's'. But the inversion is so close that it allows this intriguing parallel:

> For both Augustine and Freud there is someone before whom and to whom one talks, so that in the end one's prevarications and concealments and self-justifications are heard as what they are and the truth about oneself, including the truth about one's resistance to acknowledging that truth, is acknowledged. In both cases the talking involves a discipline, in the one case that of prayer, in the other that of psychoanalysis. And both insist that there is no way of evaluating that particular discipline from a purely external point of view, for such evaluation will be frustrated by those same fantasies from which the discipline is designed to free us. (MacIntyre 2009: 29)[6]

MacInytre's point serves also to bring out another, third, aspect of Christian practice, that distinguishes it significantly from a Stoic (and perhaps from a Buddhist) counterpart: its intrinsically relational character, its directedness to an Other in whose presence it is always conducted. If 'talking' is an element here – as it so manifestly is, for example, in the Psalms, central to both Christian and Jewish prayer and liturgy over the centuries – it is not, however, the main element. At least for the contemplative tradition within Christianity, greater emphasis is on listening in silence, and, more generally, on openness and receptivity. To be sure, there must be an active intention to pray; but the most fundamental act in prayer is one of consent to the presence and action of God in one's life, a 'letting go' in which one is radically vulnerable and dependent – and thereby also open to a grace that can never be received on one's own terms. (If there are things to be done in prayer, the greater need is to allow oneself to be undone.) Carried through, such consent has both a purgative and a unitive aspect. Everything that divides one – ambivalent motivation, unresolved conflict or concealed desire – also diminishes one's capacity for presence. And to invite God's presence is to risk having all this – traditionally covered by the term 'sin' – exposed in a process of purification and healing that may be painful, lengthy and hazardous. Still healing is possible because the Other to whom one is exposed offers a love that is tender and merciful. Progress on this path – and 'progress' is hardly the right word, unless in the Beckettian sense of 'fail again, fail better' – is towards unity with this Other, a unity which, through a conversion of one's willing and desiring, allows one to participate in or become a channel of the divine *agapē*.

Two points may be noted here about the complicated nature of the relationship between 'ordinary' flourishing and the 'fullness of life' that opens on the spiritual path. First, it is only with caution that one should refer, as I have just done, to 'healing'. For if healing is identified with a sin-blind psychotherapy aimed at a conflict-free normalcy, then it has no application here. What one needs to be freed from is not a pathology that distinguishes one from healthy people by disabling one as its helpless victim. Rather, it is a form of affliction to which all human beings are prone and in which they are always to some extent complicit. Moreover, healing can be understood only in the context of an acknowledgement that 'God has given a new transformative meaning to suffering' and that 'following him will dislocate and transform beyond recognition the forms which have made life tolerable for us' (Taylor 2007: 655).

Second, while it is important not to collapse 'fullness of life' into ordinary flourishing, and therefore to reject any understanding of religion as a recipe for 'happiness' or 'success', one may still use these positive terms to characterize the post-conversion state if proper acknowledgement is made of just how deeply revised or 'transvalued' their meaning has then become. Indeed it is just such use that one finds in the Beatitudes, the quintessentially Christian teaching of the Sermon on the Mount (Gospel of St. Matthew, 5, 3-10). The venerable formula, 'Blessed are those who …' might equally be rendered as 'Happy are those who …' (in translation of *makarioi* in Greek versions of the gospels). If one has become the kind of person characterized by the qualities recommended in each of the Beatitudes then one truly is happy or flourishing – a fact that may be related to the frequently recurring references to joy, peace and the absence of fear throughout the New Testament. (At the very least, one has unburdened oneself of many of the ways of manufacturing *un*happiness for which we humans have an immense talent.) Here one has to recognize the gulf between renunciation and the *rejection* of happiness, found in extreme form in Schopenhauer, who deeply admired the ascetical element in Christianity as well as Buddhism (see especially Schopenhauer 1966: 573–88, 603–33). It is here too, and precisely in opposition to such misanthropy, that one can make sense of this statement: 'The saints are those who are supremely successful at the exacting task of being human, the George Bests and Jacqueline du Prés of the moral sphere. Morality is not primarily a question of duty and obligation but of happiness or well-being. Why we should want to be happy is ... the very prototype of a silly question' (Eagleton 2013).

This kind of affirmativeness, like much of what I have written earlier, is inseparable from a claim that, for all the awesomeness of divine transcendence and the abyss separating God's being from ours, there is still some basis here for relationship. Moreover, this basis lies not only in God's gratuitous act of entering redemptively into human history but also in the fact that, on their side, human beings are already imbued with a directedness towards God. However protean and vortex-like it may be, human will is not just an engine of futile, self-frustrating desire, as in Schopenhauer's disparagement of it – or indeed a vehicle of untrammelled power, as in Nietzsche's exaltation of it. Christian understanding here is classically expressed by St. Augustine who, as MacIntyre points out, 'like every other ancient author, whether pagan or Christian, takes the intensity of human desire for granted'. 'What we discover in our progress towards self-knowledge', MacIntyre writes, 'is that our desires are inordinate in respect of their finite objects', and

> they are inordinate because they are at once expressions of and disguises for our love of God. We repress in ourselves the knowledge that we are by nature directed towards God and the symptoms of that repression are the excessive and disproportionate regard that we have for objects that substitute themselves for God, objects which, when we achieve them, leave us disappointed and dissatisfied. It is only insofar as we make God the object of our desire, acknowledging that to desire otherwise is to desire against our nature, that our desires in general become rightly ordered and that we are rescued from the self-protection of a will informed by pride. (2009: 28)

III Virtue in the forest

Aristotle's conception of virtue (*aretē*) must seem in some respects congenial to the 'forest' perspective, which, with special attention to a Christian variant, I have just outlined. It is a strength of Aristotle that – concerned with action, emotion and desire, as well as with insight and judgement – he understands virtue as a disposition of one's whole being and, in particular, as expressive of what one loves or delights in. It is a further strength that he acknowledges a certain 'primacy of practice',[7] especially with regard to the process through which virtue is acquired and developed: apart from sustained engagement in conducive *activities* – without which one lacks material for the only kind of reflection that is apposite – one has no chance of becoming virtuous. The corollary of this primacy is that there can be no informed understanding or sensible discussion of virtue by someone who lacks the relevant experience. This does not mean, as MacIntyre tartly observes, that 'in order to become an Aristotelian one first has to become virtuous – even a slender acquaintance with Aristotelians would be enough to dispose of that claim' (2013: 29). But it does mean that some experience of the need for virtue, of its indispensability for the achievement of centrally important individual and common goods, *is* required; no standing start or vantage-point from a neutral ground can compensate for the lack of this 'engaged' or 'insider' perspective. All this, which I take to be standard in any satisfactory account of Aristotelian ethics, is structurally akin to what holds also with regard to the world of spiritually and religiously inflected experience sketched in the previous section.

Still, is there not a great gulf in sensibility, with respect both to what is to be lived and to the kind of reflection that will adequately articulate this living, between this latter world and the world of Aristotelian virtue? This question can be sharpened by briefly tracing a genealogy of the concept of *aretē* before its appearance in Aristotle's texts. As found in Homer, *aretē* refers to any excellence through which a person shows that he is equal to the demands of a well-defined role, paradigmatically that of the warrior on the battlefield. Physical prowess, courage and wily intelligence are the eminent *aretai*. To excel, and thereby to deserve and preserve honour, is to be on one's mettle and, if fortunate, to prevail in face-to-face combat with an opponent; one must contend with unpredictable forces (erupting sometimes within oneself), the imperative not to become a supplicant and the ever present spectre of death. This arduous, unsentimental and deeply agonal ethos, in which mastery mattered above all, is partially sublimated through its deflection into the athletic arena and later the law-court and the assembly. And perhaps we can see it interiorized and further sublimated in the philosophical ethics of Plato and Aristotle, which depict the individual soul as composite, as the scene of conflict – between reason (*logos*) and the unruly elements comprising the other parts of the soul – and as virtuous to the extent that in this conflict it is reason that prevails.

Prima facie, then, to juxtapose our two worlds – of field (in broadly Aristotelian terms) and forest (in broadly Christian terms) – seems to confront us with two very different and apparently opposing rhetorics: one of strength, mastery, prevailing and excelling; and the other of vulnerability, dependence, receptivity, surrender and supplication. A question then arises about the range of qualities that are to count as virtuous – and about which qualities, therefore, are to be added to or subtracted from the proposed catalogue of virtues in the *Nicomachean Ethics*. In *After Virtue*, MacIntyre was already dealing with this question in pointing out that, in the genealogy of Aquinas' list of virtues, historical elements (especially the entrance of Christianity, with its emphasis on its own peculiarly historical character) have intervened to make him consider as virtues qualities such as humility and patience which, if they were to be included at all in Aristotle's tabulation, would more likely appear as *vices* (1984: 177). And in *Dependent Rational Animals*, he goes further by both excising Aristotle's great-souledness (*megalopsychia*) as a virtue – precisely because its comfort in masterful giving is only the obverse of its aversion to vulnerability and receptivity – and adding 'just-generosity', a quality that he associates with 'acknowledged dependence' and finds prefigured in Aquinas' virtue of mercy (*misericordia*) (see 1999: 119–28). This MacIntyrean revision of Aristotle is consonant with what, in terms of the present discussion, might be characterized as movement towards the forest. And there are still other, related qualities that a forest perspective would also include, notably a capacity for forgiveness (already implicit in charity and mercy), purity of heart, poverty of spirit, gentleness, forbearance and a capacity for mourning, as urged in the Beatitudes, as well as reverence and 'fear of the Lord' (this Lord being not only Abba, loving Father, but also creator and sustainer of a universe of incalculable scale and complexity).[8]

If great-souledness, at least, is to be deleted from Aristotle's catalogue, the question arises as to how the remaining virtues, and especially the 'cardinal' ones (justice, courage, temperance and practical wisdom) relate to the forest virtues just mentioned. Issues will arise for instance about whether, when or to what extent in any given case, justice is to be tempered by mercy. Such dilemmas may seem no different from those that can arise anyhow within Aristotle's own plural scheme when the claims of one virtue pull against those of another, and to call therefore for no more than a routine exercise of the master virtue of practical wisdom (*phronēsis*). But things may not be so simple if charity (*caritas*, *agapē*) is now the master virtue, not, to be sure, usurping the role of practical wisdom but informing and animating it and, through it, all the other virtues. And a further question is whether 'forest' virtues, even if they can alter or redirect the exercise of 'field' virtues, may not themselves depend on some of the latter. For example, on the account of prayer given earlier, could a person undergo such chastening encounter with God without mustering courage to face and truthfulness to acknowledge what may emerge in and from this encounter? If the relationship between these two sets of virtues seems reciprocal, since each may influence the other in complicated ways, how can we enquire further about this relationship? Perhaps one fruitful way of doing so is by turning to the process of learning and development, through which virtues are acquired and perfected as a person advances in ethical or spiritual maturity.

Aristotle thinks that childhood is the crucial period for this learning process: as a child, one needs to form good habits of acting, feeling and perceiving. A virtuous person desires and is disposed to do good actions, while recognizing and esteeming them *as* good; his practical intelligence has been refined so that he understands better *why* they are good and is more discriminating and sure-footed in doing them. To have a fair chance of becoming such a person, Aristotle claims, conducive experience and nurture in one's early years are a necessary condition. What happens, however, if this condition is not met – mainly by the adult world of parents, carers and teachers – and this kind of formation does not happen? Let us suppose this to be the case in the following passage:

> It is irrational to suppose that a man who acts unjustly does not wish to be unjust or a man who acts self-indulgently to be self-indulgent [drunkenness is the example]. ... Yet it does not follow that if he wishes he will cease to be unjust and will be just. For neither does the man who is ill become well on those terms. We may suppose a case in which he is ill voluntarily, through living without self-control and disobeying his doctors. In that case it was then open to him not to be ill, but not now, when he has thrown away his chance, just as when you have let a stone go it is too late to recover it; but yet it was in your power to throw it, since the moving principle was in you. So, too, to the unjust and to the self-indulgent man it was open at the beginning not to become men of this kind, and so they are unjust and self-indulgent voluntarily; but now that they have become so it is not possible for them not to be so. (*NE* 3, v, 1104a, 7–22)

One may regard what Aristotle says here as simply true, practically realistic, or deeply pessimistic (even deterministic) – or indeed as all of the above. Two things in any case stand out: first, that a person who routinely acts badly is not to be let off the hook – there is no hint of exculpation or extenuation on grounds of earlier inadequate nurture or instruction: somehow, even 'at the beginning', it 'was in your power'. And, second, once the routine is established, there is no going back – the gravitational pull of established bad habit is irresistible.

Even if one were to accept the first thesis here – which goes against the grain of a great deal of modern psychology and sociology, and may seem at odds even with Aristotle's own insistence on the indispensability of a person's having received a sound early formation – the second, practically more significant, thesis surely deserves challenge. A person of poor character, we are told, is irreformable. But how are we to regard this claim? Can we in good conscience write off perhaps a large proportion of our fellow humans? Indeed, can we be sure that we are not ourselves being written off? For how many of us can claim truly that our own formation was directed towards 'the noble-and-good' (*ta kala kai agatha*), as distinct from many other lesser things, or that our characters are not in serious need of remaking? And even if we were not to be placed among those who are irretrievably beyond the moral pale, should we accept the existence of any such pale? Surely we should reject it, not because of commitment to the risibly foolish claim that everyone actually is good but rather because of repugnance at the thought that many of those who are not good – and in the cited passage Aristotle does not seem to be referring to deep *evil* – are condemned to remain in that state so that they, and we as their friends or fellow citizens, are helpless to do anything about it.

What I am pointing to here may be taken as a lacuna in Aristotle's account of ethical development: actually, despite frequent claims to the contrary, he has little enough to offer about development in childhood, and even less about it in adulthood. To be sure, we might take is as significant that in the *Nicomachean Ethics*, having given his account of flourishing, voluntareity and the virtues (in Books I–VI), and having then analysed moral weakness (in Book VII), he immediately follows this with his account of friendship (Books VIII and IX). A good friend, it is clear, is one's greatest ally in one's attempt to integrate contrary inclinations and to remain on the path of virtue. 'Remain', however, is the important word. For, in Aristotle's view, friendship itself is possible only between those who are *already* committed to virtue, so that mutual help in sustaining this commitment is at the heart of their friendship. This is surely a lofty view of friendship, but one that does nothing to address the issue just raised: the fate of those who are *off* this virtuous pathway.

Here is a big breach between core insights of Aristotelianism and those of Christianity. If Jesus was, as Hannah Arendt suggests, 'the discoverer of the role of forgiveness in the realm of human affairs' (Arendt 1958: 238), this is related to another central concept in the gospel, that of repentance or change of mind/heart (*metanoia*) – which is itself related to the idea of sin. It is perhaps ironic that while Christians differ from Aristotle in seeing human beings both as more deeply embroiled in evil and as called to a more demandingly high level of virtue, they nonetheless see the distance between these two poles as more traversable than Aristotle sees the comparable, and arguably lesser, distance that opens up in his moral ontology. Whereas the very idea of sin is often rejected because it supposedly consigns people to damnation or permanent exclusion (something like what I am finding in Aristotle), it is in fact both bracingly inclusive and, as Taylor points out, dignifying: rather than damning or pathologizing, it accords all of us the dignity of somehow choosing what will not in fact fulfil us but the 'glamour' of which lures us into supposing that it will (Taylor 2007: 619). Instead of a defined line separating two irreducibly different moral types, perhaps we might entertain the more richly complex ethical picture suggested by Charles Péguy: 'What is formidable in the reality of life is not the juxtaposition of good and evil; rather it is their interpenetration, their mutual incorporation, their mutual sustenance, and sometimes their strange and mysterious kinship.' Such a depiction allows Péguy also to write:

> No one is as knowledgable as the sinner in matters of Christianity. No one if not the saint. And in principle, it's the same person. ... The sinner extends his hand to the saint, since the saint reaches out to help him. And all together, the one through the other, the one pulling the other, they form a chain ... of fingers that can't be disconnected. ... The one who is not Christian is the one who does not offer his hand. (quoted in Taylor 2009: 750–1)

One way of expressing the difference between the accounts offered by Aristotelianism and by a spirituality of the forest is that, whereas in the former a failure of formation seems to lead into a moral cul-de-sac, in the latter it can open a path beyond itself towards *transformation*.[9] While this difference lends attractiveness to the forest, we should have no illusions about any easy passage to the envisaged transformation. And here Aristotle's work is in fact helpful. Unlike much of the signature morality of our own age, which is as voluble in canvassing very high standards as it is silent about what might help us to meet them, Aristotle allows little scope for illusion, stressing that virtuous character is formed in and not above the 'middle soul', that is to say, the seat of appetite, emotion, desire and susceptibility to pleasure and pain. And he depicts convincingly the outcome of ethical formation when it *is* successfully carried through: in the virtuous person all this psychic material, 'resisting' and 'opposing' though it may have been in the pre-virtue state, is attuned with a reason capable of truthfully disclosing the noble-and-good (*NE* 1, 13, 1102b13–28).

IV Conclusion: Contemporary bearings

In referring earlier to Aristotle's ethics as a 'sublimation' of the *aretē* of Homeric figures, I intended no disparagement. For while we have come a long way in modern Western culture from that 'pre-Axial' ethos (Jaspers 2011),[10] we may have little reason to suppose that the humans depicted in its heroic literature are essentially different from ourselves. Otherwise we should be more surprised by the vigour with which the ethos of that earlier society has been reimagined and reaffirmed in the philosophy of the past century by Nietzsche and his followers. Nietzscheanism too has its catalogue of favoured virtues, and they are of an aristocratic and assertive bent, aspiring to great achievement, without scruples about risk or cost. There is here an easy contempt for the supposed pusillanimity of standard modern morality – including benevolence, respect for equality, democratic participation and human rights (not to speak of the petty comforts they may assure) – now exposed as little more than a thin disguise for the resentment of the weak against the superiority of the strong. Impatience with restraint (or the 'ascetical ideal' of which Socrates himself is seen as the *ur*-exponent) is linked to a fierce assertion – of life, it may be, but a life willing to expend everything, including itself, in pursuit of 'self-overcoming'. How ever one views this philosophy, its existence and obvious appeal give a keener sense of the tenacity of the most assertive instincts (especially, in Taylor's view, regarding violence and sexuality), the psychic costs incurred in their curbing, and the relative precariousness, therefore, of a moral order such as ours that is based on such curbing. Going further, Taylor suggests that the appeal of Nietzscheanism can be seen as evidence of an 'ineradicable bent' in human beings towards some good 'beyond life' – and of where this bent can take us when it does *not* take us to the forest.[11]

Short of such a provocative claim, bringing the Nietzschean perspective on stage can serve to put pressure on its main contemporary alternative – one or other version of the standard morality mentioned earlier. In this, or any other, morality, 'curbing' can succeed only if it is real sublimation, that is to say, a non-repressive turning around of these instincts so that their energies are deployed to 'higher' ends – without the inevitable 'return' or 'revenge' entailed by their repression. But sublimation is a big ask, and Taylor sees no grounds for complacency about our capacity to pull it off in contemporary liberal-democratic societies (a scepticism surely reinforced by very recent developments in the moral and political climate of these societies). We have indeed learned to internalize many kinds of restraint through disciplinary regimes, the development of which over several centuries has been well exposed in the writings of Norbert Elias and Michel Foucault (Elias 1982; Foucault 1977, 1980). But what moral vision do we have to make such mechanisms of restraint any more than forms of psychic manipulation or coercion (however 'soft' their mode of operation), and how deeply does this vision penetrate to the instinctual level itself? Taylor has no quarrel with the substance of this morality; rather, he laments the widespread failure, as he sees it, to articulate a vision that might support it. We are earnest in the codification and juridification of standards and norms of behaviour – to an extremity of 'corral' consciousness that leads him to speak of 'code fetishism' and 'nomolatry'[12] – but strikingly reticent about what truly ennobles or dignifies, and thus provides *sources* that could inspire or enable us to live up to them. This failure matters especially when these standards are so demandingly, indeed unprecedentedly, *high*. 'High standards', he remarks, 'need strong sources' (1992: 516).[13]

In this chapter, I've tried to articulate a perspective within which a search for strong sources might be less stifled than it often is in contemporary academic philosophy. Do the spiritual, and frankly theological, connotations of this perspective make it suspect or discreditable in the philosophical arena? If such be the case, then this arena is insufficiently responsive to deep 'cross-pressures' in contemporary society and culture – an insufficiency that, as we may hope, will be recognized and addressed by a more expansive discourse emerging in philosophy.[14]

Notes

1 While MacIntyre is a notorious and self-professed 'Aristotelian', the label may seem a looser fit for Taylor, if only because of his less adversarial attitude to modernity. Still, Murdoch twice attaches it to him without comment, and with good reason, in Murdoch (1992: 150–1; 290): his explicit invocations of Aristotle, though rare, are telling (e.g. 1992: 76–7, 86, 125; and 2007: 282, 501, 704) and a recognizably Aristotelian spirit pervades his work, especially on issues of agency and practical reasoning.

2 'Such life [i.e. of contemplation, *theōrētikē*] would be too high for man; for it is not insofar as he is man that he will live so, but in so far as something divine is present in him…But we must not follow those who advise us, being men, to think of human things, and, being mortal, to think of mortal things, but must, so far as we can, make ourselves immortal and strain every nerve to live in accordance with the best thing in us' *NE* X, 7, 1177b26–1178a2.

3 The language here has Nietzschean resonances ('man is a rope stretched between beast and *Übermensch*' – Zarathustra), and Nietzsche has been an important figure, notably for Bernard Williams, in the critique of 'morality' that has accompanied the emergence in recent decades of different versions of virtue ethics. In a book that is markedly different in outlook and tone from Taylor's work, but still interestingly akin to it in the kind of 'vertical tension' that it writes into ethical life, Peter Sloterdijk gives a Nietzschean twist to religious themes in a compendious and often provocative discussion of what drives – and *should* drive – human beings, through ascetical exertions (or 'spiritual acrobatics'), to feats of 'self-surpassing' (Sloterdijk 2014). Nietzsche features as a key protagonist in Taylor's later writings (as he does in MacIntyre's *After Virtue*) because he rejects the primacy of life goods installed in modern secular morality, while *also* repudiating the 'forest' perspective to which Taylor himself is drawn. I return to this point in the final section of the chapter.

4 Hadot points to the affinities, despite marked differences, between his work and Michel Foucault's later writings on ethics. Other comparable work, in Anglophone philosophy, is Nussbaum (1994).

5 These are key terms in, for example, *The Meditations* of Marcus Aurelius.

6 Characteristically, MacIntyre does not regard prayer as only a matter of interior dialogue with God. As he observes elsewhere, 'productive work' can be 'thought of as a kind of prayer and performed as an act of prayer' – though this is a truth all too likely to be obscured in a fragmented culture that consigns prayer to '"religion", religion conceived of as no more than one more compartmentalized area of activity' (2011: 323). My use of 'practice' throughout the chapter is intended to counter subjectivist misconstruals of 'interiority' that occlude the indispensable background of socially shared activity and meaning. MacIntyre's conception of practice emphasizes its close, though complex and strained, relationship with institution and tradition. With respect to spiritual and religious practice, specifically, Taylor's work gives a fuller and more sympathetic picture of the complexities and strains. This comes out in his account of the wider contemporary landscape with its proliferation and 'fragilization' of spiritual approaches (what he calls 'the nova effect'). He is aware that here 'some great realizations of collective life are lost' and that 'massive unlearning is taking place' with respect to 'some of the great languages of transcendence' – but *also* that 'other facets of our predicament in relation to God come to the fore' (so that, for instance, whereas to appreciate in the seventeenth century what Isaiah meant by a 'hidden God' 'you had to be a Pascal … [n]ow we

live it daily'). This kind of historical lens allows Taylor to view the church, at least in its contemporary incarnation, not as 'a grouping of people together on the grounds of their sharing some important property' but rather as 'a skein of relations ... [of] particular, unique, enfleshed people to each other', 'a network of agapē' that 'creates links across boundaries', and the institutionalization of which may easily make us 'living caricatures of the network life' and of the 'communion' proper to it. And this view (much influenced by Ivan Illich) leads him to urge the need for hospitality on the part of contemporary Christians to 'new unprecedented itineraries ... new paths, opened by pioneers who have discovered a way through the particular labyrinthine landscape we live in, its thickets and trackless wastes, to God' (Taylor 2007: 532, 739, 755).

7   'The primacy of practice' does not imply any rejection of theory; rather, the ethical theory of Aristotle, and of contemporary Aristotelians, is one that acknowledges and accounts for this primacy.
8   Virtues mentioned here are linked to 'gifts' and 'fruits' of the Spirit, classically discussed by Augustine and Aquinas in relation to their respective scriptural sources in Isa. 11.1-2 and Gal. 5.22-23.
9   Reference might be made here – partly because it echoe Aristotle's reference to the drinking bouts of the self-indulgent in the cited passage – to the work of Alcoholics Anonymous, work that is transformative on the ethical plane by adhering to a forest spirituality. See, for example, Keating (with Tom S) 2009.
10 A phrase first given currency by Karl Jaspers, the 'axial age' characterizes a period, usually placed between the eighth and third centuries BCE, during which a significant transformation of ethical thinking is claimed to have occurred across several different cultures, associated with pioneering figures such as the Buddha, Confucius, Lao-Tzu, Isaiah and Socrates.
11 The phrase, 'ineradicable bent', occurs in the essay on Murdoch and later in *A Secular Age*.
12 If juridification and fixation with rules and codes is a feature of modern secular morality, it has bulked large also in religious communities. The teaching of Christian morality has been much confined to the corral, fighting shy of forest and field – a fact that may be linked both to the massive return of the repressed in sexual matters now faced by the Catholic Church and to the vehement resistance by some prominent clerics to pastoral initiatives of Pope Francis.
13 In *Sources of the Self*, Taylor elucidates the notion of a 'moral source' and provides his own narrative retrieval of significant sources of modern moral consciousness.
14 A noteworthy text in this regard is Mulhall 2005. By making philosophy porous to theological reflections, Mulhall's interpretation of our ethical predicament diverges sharply from default axioms of Enlightenment thinking, while reading Nietzsche's critique of Christianity as less radical than the auto-critique inscribed in Christianity itself – so that it is, in Stanley Cavell's phrase, Christianity 'in foul disguise'.

References

Arendt, H. (1958), *The Human Condition*, Chicago: University of Chicago Press.
Aristotle (1984), 'Nicomachean Ethics', in J. Barnes (ed.), *The Complete Works of Aristotle*. Revised Oxford translation, Princeton, NJ: Princeton University Press.

Aristotle. *Parts of Animals*, in Barnes 1984.
Barnes, J., ed. (1984), *The Complete Works of Aristotle*. Revised Oxford translation, Princeton, NJ: Princeton University Press.
Beckett, L. (2006), *Reading in the Light of Christ: Writings in the Western Tradition*, San Francisco: Ignatius Press.
Eagleton, Terry (2013), 'Disappearing Acts' [Review of Denys Turner, *Thomas Aquinas: A Portrait*], London Review of Books, 35 (23), (5 December).
Elias, N. (1982), *The Civilizing Process: Vol. 1, The History of Manners, and Vol. 2, Power and Civility*, trans. from French into English by E. Jephcott, New York: Pantheon.
Foot, P. (2003), *Natural Goodness*, Oxford: Clarendon Press.
Foucault, M. (1977), *Discipline and Punish:The Birth of the Prison*, trans. A. Sheridan, New York: Vintage Books.
Foucault, M. (1980), *Power/Knowledge: Selected Interviews and Other Writings, 1972-1977*, ed. Colin Gordon, New York: Pantheon Books.
Hadot, P. (1995), *Philosophy as a Way of Life*, trans. from French into English by A. Davidson, Oxford: Blackwell.
Hursthouse, R. (2010), *On Virtue Ethics*, Oxford: Oxford University Press.
Jaspers, Karl ([1954] 2011), *The Origin and Goal of History*, trans. from German into English by M. Bullock, London: Routledge Revivals.
Keating, T. (with Tom S.) (2009), *The Divine Therapy and Addiction: Centering Prayer and the Twelve Steps*, New York: Lantern Books.
MacIntyre, A. (1984), *After Virtue*, Notre Dame, IN: University of Notre Dame Press.
MacIntyre, A. (1999), *Dependent Rational Animals*, London: Duckworth.
MacIntyre, A. (2004), *Preface to Revised Edition of the Unconscious: A Conceptual Analysis* New York and London: Routledge.
MacIntyre, A. (2009), *God, Philosophy, Universities: A Selective History of the Catholic Philosophical Tradition*, London: Continuum.
MacIntyre, A. (2011), 'Where We Were, Where We Are, Where We Need to Be', in P. Blackledge and K. Knight' (eds.), *Virtue and Politics: Alasdair MacIntyre's Revolutionary Aristotelianism*, Notre Dame: University of Notre Dame Press.
MacIntyre, A. (2013), 'On Having Survived the Academic Moral Philosophy of the Twentieth Century', in Fran O'Rourke (ed.), *What Happened in and to Moral Philosophy in the Twentieth Century?* Notre Dame: University of Notre Dame Press.
Mulhall, S. (2005), *Philosophical Myths of the Fall*, Princeton: Princeton University Press.
Murdoch, I. (1992), *Metaphysics as a Guide to Morals*, London: Chatto and Windus.
Nussbaum, M. (1994), *The Therapy of Desire: Theory and Practice in Hellenistic Ethics*, Princeton: Princeton University Press.
Schopenhauer, A. (1966), *The World as Will and Representation*, trans. E. F. J. Payne, London: Constable.
Sloterdijk, P. (2014), *You Must Change Your Life*, trans. from German into English by W. Hoban, Cambridge: Polity Press.
Taylor, C. (1992), *Sources of the Self: The Making of the Modern Identity*, Cambridge: Cambridge University Press.
Taylor, C. (1996), 'Iris Murdoch and Moral Philosophy', in M. Antonaccio and W. Schweiker (eds), *Iris Murdoch and the Search for Human Goodness*, Chicago: University of Chicago Press [reprinted in Taylor, C. (2011), *Dilemmas and Connections: Selected Essays*, 3-23, Cambridge, MA: Harvard University Press].
Taylor, C. (2007), *A Secular Age*, Cambridge, MA: Harvard University Press.

12

Aristotle and the politics of recognition

Tony Burns

Introduction

In the *Politics* Aristotle claims that a concern for status, honour, esteem, dignity and respect and the like is one of two principal causes of conflict in society, along with the desire for such things as property, money and wealth. For example, in his critique of Plato, he argues that 'civil troubles arise, not only out of the inequality of property, but out of the inequality of honour' (Aristotle 1984b: II, II, 7, 1267a37-38). He maintains that some citizens would be dissatisfied by the introduction of the social system advocated by Plato (i.e. communism) precisely because 'they think themselves worthy of more than an equal share of honours' (Aristotle 1984b: II, II, 7, 1267a38-41, 2011). They would, therefore believe that they had been treated unfairly, in such a society, precisely because they regard themselves as being, not the equals of others, but superior to them. Aristotle goes on to claim that 'this is often found to be a cause of sedition and revolution' (Aristotle 1984b: II, II, 7, 1267a38-41, 2011).

According to Aristotle, it is not just egotism, selfishness or the 'wickedness' of human nature alone that causes conflict (Aristotle 1984b: II, II, 5, 1263b21-22, 2005). Nor is it necessarily always economic deprivation that brings about these things, for 'want is not the sole incentive to crime' (Aristotle 1984b: II, II, 7, 1267a4-5, 2010). Rather, in his opinion, there is another extremely significant cause of conflict, namely, the drive for honour, esteem and to lord it over others, for example, the 'superiority which is claimed by men of rank' (Aristotle 1984b: II, V, 1, 1301b2-3, 2066). Indeed, Aristotle observes that this aspect of human nature is so significant that even in an egalitarian society with a democratic political system, although 'it is assumed that the citizens are equal and do not differ at all', and the citizens 'rule and are ruled by turns', nevertheless it remains the case that 'when one rules and the other is ruled' the former invariably endeavours 'to create a difference' between themselves and the latter in 'outward forms and names and titles of respect' (Aristotle 1984b: II, I, 12, 1259b4-8, 1998). In what follows, I shall connect this aspect of Aristotle's thought to a discussion of his social theory.

I

The politics of recognition and social theory

The association between the politics of recognition, or identity politics, and the history of sociological thought, has been made by Craig Calhoun. Discussing poststructuralist social theory and its approach to identity politics, Calhoun has suggested that 'a sociologist is apt to think that the new, poststructuralist rhetoric of "subject-positions" and "enactments" is an unnecessary reinvention of the familiar vocabulary of status and role'. In Calhoun's view, 'this is one result of the fact that so much of the most prominent recent social theory has been generated outside sociology and too often in ignorance of sociological theory' (Calhoun 2003 [1995]: 197–8; also McBride 2013: 148–51).[1] The work of Emile Durkheim is obviously relevant in this connection. In my view, however, the sociological thought of Durkheim draws upon a long tradition which can be traced back, ultimately, to the writings of the ancient Greeks, especially to Aristotle (Challenger 1994).

Particularly helpful for a discussion of the sociological dimension of the politics of recognition is Cillian McBride's *Recognition*, which was published in 2013. McBride argues that in order to understand the politics of recognition today, 'we must attend to the way the social world is constituted by social norms', that is to say, 'rules which govern social interaction, from the ways we eat, dress, and speak to one another, up to the roles we occupy and the constitution of social, economic, and political institutions' (McBride 2013: 141). He maintains that one's social identity, and hence also one's relationships to others, which are always relationships of both similarity and difference, or of equality and inequality, is associated with or even determined by these roles, norms and institutions. Moreover, according to McBride, one's 'distinction' from others, the manner in which one's identity is different from that of others, 'is inseparable from hierarchy' (McBride 2013: 72). McBride rightly points out that, hitherto, 'standard discussions' of the politics of recognition have not paid sufficient attention to this sociological side of things, or in some cases even addressed it at all. In his opinion, however, given that 'it is such a central feature of social recognition it is very hard to see how it can be avoided' (McBride 2013: 72). I shall argue that the seeds of this sociological dimension to the politics of recognition can be detected in the writings of Aristotle.

McBride claims that in any society, including therefore, presumably, that of ancient Athens, social norms always 'play a key role in regulating action'. They are a guide for the individuals who occupy the roles with which they are associated as to what is 'acceptable' or even required behaviour 'in a given situation'. Those individuals who 'fail to act in the appropriate way' are exposed to a variety of 'social sanctions' or even 'legal penalties'. In this way, McBride points out, 'the desire to be recognized as someone who knows what is expected of them and can be relied on to act appropriately', in any given situation, is a significant 'feature of social control'. In his view, it is a mechanism for the preservation of that system of social order that prevails in all hierarchical societies (McBride 2013: 143). To illustrate this, McBride refers to the social structure of 'premodern societies'. McBride is thinking here, not of the societies of the ancient world, but rather of feudal society in medieval Europe. Nevertheless, his characterization of pre-modern societies does also apply to the society of classical Athens at the time that Aristotle was writing. Pre-modern societies, he says, 'are clearly ordered by rank'. In such societies there is a 'social hierarchy' within which 'each stratum enjoys its own particular set of rights and duties', and in which 'one's social position' and consequent 'social honour or prestige' are distributed 'according to one's station' (McBride 2013: 15). There are occasions when Aristotle says very similar things in his writings.

An important feature of the politics of recognition, according to McBride, is the association that it has with the notion of authority, which, as he correctly observes, is not 'as widely appreciated in the literature on the politics of recognition as it should be' (McBride 2013: 6). McBride insists that 'the struggle for recognition' is always, and indeed 'essentially', a 'struggle for authority' (McBride 2013: 151). This has to do, first, with our 'self-interpretations' and, second, with 'the normative expectations which we have of others and of ourselves, and which others in turn, have of us' (McBride 2013: 136). McBride argues that we sometimes reject the claims that others make upon us that we ought to act in particular ways and 'want them to recognize that we are rejecting their authority to make these demands'. According to McBride, this is a 'central feature' of the 'personal, and social and political conflicts' that are associated with the struggle for recognition (McBride 2013: 5). Again, I shall suggest that this is also true in the case of Aristotle. McBride does not refer to Aristotle. In my view, however, the writings of Aristotle are a significant early source for historians of political thought who, like McBride, think about the politics of recognition in this particular way.

II

Aristotle and social theory

It is not surprising that at least some of those who have written about the history of sociological thought (though not many) have argued that the origins of what today we call sociology can be found in the writings of the ancient Greeks (Abraham 1973: 21–43, esp. 35–9; Barnes 1948: 3–28; Ellwood 1902: 64–74; Gouldner 1965; McCarthy 2003; Zeitlin 1993). For example, Aristotle's discussion of the different types of friendship in the *Ethics* may be regarded as a contribution to social theory, or to the history of sociological thought. There Aristotle offers his readers insights, which are similar to those of the great sociologists of the modern era, such as Emile Durkheim, Max Weber and Ferdinand Tönnies, into the nature of various different types of 'society' (κοινωνία, *koinōnia*).

In the *Nicomachean Ethics* Aristotle asserts that 'there are different types of "society"', and that 'in every society', of whatever particular type, 'there is thought to be some form of justice, and friendship too' (Aristotle 1984a: II, VIII, 9, 1159b25-28, 1833).[2] As examples of small-scale societies within a *polis*, Aristotle refers to dining clubs, 'religious guilds and social clubs' and reading or discussion groups (Aristotle 1984b, II, V, 11, 1313a41-1313b6, 2085; 1984a, II, VIII, 9, 1160a19-21, 1833; 1984b, II, V, 11, 1313a41-1313b6, 2085). He also talks about the sailors who together make up the crew of a ship, and the soldiers who constitute a corps in an army (Aristotle 1984a, II, VIII, 9, 1159b25-31, 1833). In the *Politics*, he refers to the chorus of a theatre company, and to doctors or members of the medical profession (Aristotle 1984b, II, III, 3, 1276b1-6, 2025; II, III, XI, 1282a1-3, 2034).[3] In short, there is a pluralist or, more accurately, a corporatist dimension to the thought of Aristotle, that is often overlooked, or the significance of which has not been sufficiently appreciated by some commentators.

One reason why this is significant is because the societies in question evidently have to do with the private lives of the citizens of a *polis* outside of the family or household. Nor, however, are they overtly or obviously 'political', because they have nothing directly or immediately to do with the life of the citizens of a *polis* in their public capacity as the makers and enforcers of law. Rather, they occupy an intermediate social space between the household and the state, narrowly conceived. In other words, there is evidence to support the view that what Hegel refers to as 'civil society' (Hegel 1979 [1821]: §§182-256, 122-55), and what Hannah Arendt terms the realm of 'the social' (Arendt 1958: 38-49), already existed in Athens at the time when Aristotle was writing. One way of contextualizing the political thought of Aristotle would be to suggest that it can be seen as an attempt on his part to consider the significance of the existence of these societies for Athenian political life.

Although his views on this subject are not entirely consistent, Sir Ernest Barker is one of the few commentators who has accepted that Aristotle does have a social theory and that this social theory is corporatist. Barker insists that Aristotle thought of a *polis* as a 'state and society in one'. For Aristotle it was 'a single system of order, or fused "society-state"' (Barker (1961 [1951]: 5); also Barker 1960: xxii–xxiii, xxv). However, in his view, Aristotle also evidently believed that the society component of this fused society-state had a very specific character. This is so because Aristotle also thought of it as being not smooth and undifferentiated, but rather (more pluralistically) as an internally differentiated or articulated whole. In short, Aristotle thought of it as a larger society (a Society with a capital 'S') that is composed of a number of smaller societies. It is a 'society of societies' (Barker 1961 [1951]: 5; see also Barker 1959: 228, 233-4, 237). Barker translates Aristotle's *koinōnia* as 'association'. Consequently, he states that for Aristotle, the society side of the society-state or city-state nexus that is a *polis* should be thought of as an 'association of associations'. Other commentators capture the same idea by talking about wider society as a 'community of communities' (Figgis 1960 [1907]: 60, 90, 234; Figgis 1997 [914]: 8, 80; Ross 1964: 239), or in the case of Hegel a 'circle of circles' (Hegel 1979 [1821]: Preface, 6; §145, 105; §148, 106; §179, 119; §180, 120).

This is what Aristotle has in mind in Book II of the *Politics* when he criticizes Plato's *Republic*. There he maintains that the state is and ought to be a 'plurality' of different societies. He agrees with Plato that 'unity' is indeed a core value. However, Aristotle argues that it is possible to take a commitment to this value too far, to the complete obliteration of all differences. There should indeed be unity, but not of the kind that Aristotle associates (rightly or wrongly) with Plato and Platonism. For, Aristotle says, 'there is a point at which a state (*polis*) may attain such a degree of unity as to be no longer a state', as when in music 'harmony' is sometimes reduced to 'unison', and a certain 'rhythm' is 'reduced to a single beat' (Aristotle 1984b: II, V, 1263b31-36, 2005).

Barker rightly concludes from this that. for Aristotle, the word 'state' (πολις) has two meanings, associated with a broad and a narrow sense of the term. In the broad sense, it refers to the complex, articulated entity that is a political society, a city-state or a society-state considered as a whole. In the narrow sense, it refers to just one half or one part of that complex entity, namely, its political constitution or system of government, or those of its component parts that have to do with the making and enforcing of laws (Barker 1959: 286fn3). In other words, according to Barker, at least some of the time, when discussing questions of politics Aristotle does occasionally have in mind something like Hegel's 'strictly political state', as something distinct from the non-political sphere of a civil society containing a number of corporate groups (Hegel 1979 [1821]: §267, 163; see also Hegel 1971 [1830]), §523, 256–7; §534, 263; Hegel 1953 [1831]), 51–2). Aristotle does, therefore, envisage the existence of a number of societies at a level intermediate between that of the household and that strictly political state. As in the case of Plato, Aristotle associates these small-scale societies with different occupations or professions. They included such people as doctors, architects, physical trainers, ship-builders and the like.

A similar interpretation of Aristotle has also been made by Nicholas F. Jones who, in *The Associations of Classical Athens*, emphasizes the significance of Aristotle's assertion, made in both the *Nicomachean Ethics* and the *Politics*, that a *polis* might be thought of as a complex articulated whole, or an association of associations, each of which served 'to mediate the relations between the state and the individual' (Jones 1999: 17, 27–8, 45). Drawing on the work of R. G. Mulgan, Jones argues that we need to distinguish between two different senses of the word *polis* or 'state' in Aristotle's writings, a 'wider' or 'inclusive' one and a narrower or 'exclusive' one. According to Jones, the first of these refers to 'the whole of society'. It includes, therefore, 'both the central controlling institutions' that were associated with the 'government' of the Athenian *polis* and also the 'other constituent "communities"' over which they had control. The second sense, on the other hand, refers only to 'the central authority', that is to say, in the case of classical Athens, to 'the democratic government' that prevailed at the time that Aristotle was writing (Jones 1999: 18; Mulgan 2011 [1977]: 16–17).

Much the same distinction was also drawn, in the medieval period, by Marsilius of Padua in his *Defensor Pacis* (1321), who based his account of Aristotle's social theory on what Aristotle says about the various 'parts' of a state in Book IV of the *Politics*. Marsilius argues that 'the parts or offices of the state are of six kinds', namely, 'the agricultural, the artisan, the military, the financial, the priestly and the judicial or deliberative' (Marsilius, 1980 [1956]: I, V, §1, 15). As specific examples of intermediate societies or corporate groups he cites those involved in the activities of spinning, leather-making, shoemaking, all 'species of housebuilding', and in general 'all the other mechanic arts which subserve the other offices of the state directly or indirectly' (I, V, §6, 17). He also refers to the practice of medicine, which, he argues, is 'architectonic to many of the above mentioned arts' (I, V, §6, 17).

Like Barker, Jones and Mulgan, although of course much earlier, Marsilius of Padua also argued that Aristotle distinguishes between two different senses of the notion of the state, a broad sense and a narrow or a strict sense. He says that three of the six groups identified above, namely, 'the priestly, the warrior and the judicial' parts, 'are in the *strict* sense parts of the state', whereas the other three parts, that is to say, the agricultural, the artisan and the financial parts 'are called parts' of the state 'only in the *broad* sense of the term' (I, V, §1, 15). These other three parts are, he says, 'offices necessary to the state according to the doctrine of Aristotle', because without them a state could not exist (I, V, §1, 15). Here Marsilius prefigures in a striking way the distinction that is later drawn explicitly by Hegel between the idea of civil society and that of the strictly political state.

Marsilius's strict sense of the state, associated with a certain narrow set of social functions might, as in the case of Aristotle before him and Hegel after him, be associated with the realm of politics narrowly understood. It is to be contrasted with and opposed to what is evidently and predominantly a private, economic sphere of society. And yet, like both Aristotle and Hegel, Marsilius argues that there is also another, looser sense of the term 'state', according to which each of (or *both* of) these separate spheres, together with the various groups or orders that are associated with them, might plausibly be said to be parts of the state, more broadly understood.

Marsilius refers to the different offices within the state (in the broad sense of the term) that are associated with different administrative or 'superintendent' functions or 'offices'. He quotes Aristotle's remark in the *Politics* that of these 'some are political', whereas others 'are economic' (I, XVII, §12, 96), or, as Aristotle says, 'concerned with household management' (Aristotle 1984b, II, IV, 15, 1299a22-23, 2062). Marsilius attributes to Aristotle, therefore, and also endorses himself, the view that the three parts of the state, understood in the broad sense of the term, which have specifically to do with economic affairs, or the private lives of its citizens, could not strictly speaking be said to be 'political'. Nor strictly speaking should they be regarded as parts of the state at all, narrowly conceived.

On the issue of social administration, or superintendence, Marsilius cites Aristotle's view that 'not all those who are elected or chosen by lot' within a particular *polis* or state 'are to be regarded as rulers', that is to say 'political rulers' (I, XVII, §12, 96; Aristotle 1984b, II, IV, 15, 1299a16-17, 2062). Marsilius argues that at least some of those who have administrative duties because they are in positions of authority can and should be thought of as having an office or function that is *not* strictly speaking 'political' in character. The individuals who occupy these offices are, he maintains, 'different from the political rulers' of a state (I, XVII, §12, 96). As Aristotle says, they must be 'distinguished from political officers' (Aristotle 1984b, II, IV, 15, 1299a17-18, 2062). In the *Politics* Aristotle offers the examples of 'priests' and 'masters of choruses' (Aristotle 1984b, II, IV, 15, 1299a17-18, 2062).

In the *Defensor Pacis*, Marsilius uses Aristotle's example of the 'priesthood' (I, XVII, §12, 96). He attributes to Aristotle the view that in matters of religion there are persons in positions of authority who rule. It is these individuals who are responsible for the administration or superintendence of religious affairs. However, according to Marsilius's account of Aristotle's views, which on this point at least seems to me to be correct, none of this administration is regarded by Aristotle as being strictly speaking a 'political' affair. Aristotle held that in this particular society, and presumably also in other similar societies, as also in the case of the family or household, neither the authority nor the specific form of rule that are present could be said to be 'political', in the strict sense of that term (I, XVII, §12, 96).

In the later history of political thought, Johannes Althusius was to take issue with the views expressed by Aristotle and Marsilius of Padua on this subject. In his *Politica Methodice Digesta* (1603), Althusius insists that 'all symbiotic association and life', including therefore that which exists within a private society or social institution, is 'essentially, authentically, and generically political'. From which it follows, Althusius argues, that even 'the private association is rightly attributed to politics' (Althusius 1964 [1603]: III, 27). From this point of view, the internal affairs of private or non-state societies and social institutions, including what Hegel refers to as 'the struggle for recognition' that arguably takes place within them (Hegel 1977: §§166–230, 104–38), can properly speaking be said to be 'political'. It is, therefore, a legitimate object of concern for students of politics, broadly conceived.

III

Aristotle's classification of the different types of society

It is true that Aristotle does not say very much at all about the intermediate societies identified earlier, or about the different possible forms that they take. He does not have a self-conscious or fully worked out theory that explicitly classifies them into their various types. He does, however, say at least something about this issue. Here we might make two observations. The first has to do with Aristotle's views regarding the question of what it is that binds the individual members of a particular society or group together and motivates them in their interactions with one another. The second has to do with the question of policy-making or decision-making within a particular society or group.

Regarding the first of these issues, Aristotle identifies a number of different reasons why the individual members of a particular society might come together, in addition to the simple pleasure that is provided by friendship or companionship. For example, in the case of religious societies, this is a matter of devotion, or 'for the sake of offering sacrifice' (Aristotle 1984a: II, VIII, 9, 1160a19-21, 1833). In the case of societies whose members meet for educational purposes, to discuss topics of common interest, it is the pleasure that is associated with the pursuit of knowledge (Aristotle 1984b: II, V, 11, 1313a41-1313b6, 2085).

Aristotle also says at one point that, in the case of a number of societies, what binds their members together is the pursuit of 'some particular advantage' that they all have in common. He points out that sailors or crew members might aim 'at what is advantageous on a voyage with a view to making money or something of the kind'. Similarly, he points out that 'fellow-soldiers' might aim 'at what is advantageous in war, whether it is wealth or victory or the taking of a city' (Aristotle 1984a: II, VIII, 9, 1160a10-17, 1833). In the case of at least some of these small-scale societies, then, Aristotle maintains that it is appropriate to talk about 'mere friendships of association', that is to say, temporary friendships that are entered into as a matter of expediency, for reasons of self-interest and in pursuit of a shared or common advantage. Societies of this kind, Aristotle points out, 'seem to rest on a sort of compact' or a contractual agreement between their individual members (Aristotle 1984a: II, VIII, 12, 1161b12-

16, 1835). Affairs of this kind are regulated by the system of rectificatory justice of a *polis,* so far as it has to do with 'voluntary' private transactions (Aristotle 1984a: II, V, 2, 1130b30-1131a9, 1784-85).

These small-scale societies are in effect examples of what Ferdinand Tönnies has in mind when, in his *Community and Association,* he talks about societies that are 'associations' (Tönnies 1955). However, like Tönnies, Aristotle does not assume that all of these intermediate or small-scale societies are integrated in the same way. In particular, he does not think that all societies are associations (*Gesellschaft*). He suggests that in at least some societies, not least in the family or household, the principle that ties the individual members together is not egotism or self-interest. As in the case of Tönnies's communities (*Gemeinschaft*), then, Aristotle suggests that in the case of other types of societies, the interactions that take place between their members are more obviously ethical in character. In societies of this kind, he thinks that what binds the members to one another are the ties of duty.

So far as the issue of decision-making within these various different types of society is concerned, Aristotle suggests that some societies are based on the principle of order, hierarchy and authority, whereas others are not. He implicitly makes the distinction, which Hugo Grotius, writing much later, in his *The Laws of War and Peace* (1625), makes explicitly between 'equal societies' and unequal ones (Grotius 2005 [1625]), I, I, §3, 2, 136-37). Drawing directly on the writings of Aristotle as his source, Grotius maintains there that of 'societies, some are equal', such as those that are composed of 'brothers, citizens, friends, allies' and so on, whereas 'others [are] unequal', and exist by 'pre-eminence, as Aristotle terms it', such as those that are constituted by 'parents and children, masters and servants, king and subject, God and man', in all of which 'some are governors and others governed'. Grotius associates the latter with what 'may be called a right of superiority' and the former with 'the right of equality' (Grotius 2005 [1625]), I, I, §3, 2, 136-37).

The distinction that Aristotle draws implicitly between equal and unequal societies can be mapped on to his distinction between those societies that are associations and those that are communities. If we do this then, four theoretical possibilities are generated. In principle, we could have (1) an association that is also an equal society; (2) an association that is also an unequal society; (3) a community that is also an unequal society; and (4) a community that is also an equal society. For purposes of the present discussion, the most significant of these are the third and fourth of these possibilities. I am interested in what Aristotle has to say about decision-making within non-state societies that are thought of as being communities, especially, but not only, those which are hierarchically ordered, containing individuals in positions of authority who administer their affairs.

IV

Aristotle's social theory and his ethics

We saw above that Aristotle recognizes the existence of a number of different types of small-scale society at a level intermediate between that of the household and the state narrowly conceived. In his view some of these societies are associated with various, different professions. They include, therefore, such people as doctors, architects, ship-builders and the like. In both the *Nicomachean Ethics* and the *Politics*, Aristotle expresses an interest in the different types of social relations that exist in these different types of, and especially, in the case of communities, in the ethical duties with which they are associated. In his discussion of friendship in the *Nicomachean Ethics* Aristotle argues that these ethical relationships will vary depending on the type of society. For example, he argues that a man 'does not seem to have the same duties to a friend, a stranger, a comrade, and a schoolfellow' (Aristotle 1984a, II, VIII, 12, 1162a30-33, 1836). Rather, 'the claims of justice differ' from society to society. Thus, he argues, 'the duties of parents to children and those of brothers to each other are not the same'. Nor are 'those of comrades and those of fellow citizens' (Aristotle 1984a: II, VIII, 9, 1159b32-1160a2, 1833). 'We ought', Aristotle concludes, 'to render different things to parents, brothers, comrades and benefactors' (Aristotle 1984a, IX, 2, 1165a16-17, 1841).

Of particular interest here is what Aristotle has to say about those ethical duties that have come variously to be called particular duties, relative duties or special obligations (Gert 2006: 77–98; Jeske 2014; Scheffler 1997). At least some of these relative duties can be associated with what Emile Durkheim refers to, in his *Professional Ethics and Civic Morals*, as professional ethics (Durkheim 1992 [1890–1900]); Durkheim 2002 [1902–1903]; also Oakley and Cocking 2001). Duties of this kind are usually contrasted with the duties in general, or the moral duties and obligations, which all human beings, persons or agents owe to one another (French 1977).

As an example of a corporate group that is both a community and an equal society, Aristotle refers to doctors or the medical profession. In this particular case, therefore, we are talking about medical ethics. When discussing this issue in the *Politics* Aristotle observes that 'he who can judge of the healing of a sick man' by a doctor is 'one who could himself heal his disease, and make him whole', that is to say a fellow doctor or 'a physician' (Aristotle 1984b: II, III, 11, 1281b39-1282a3, 2034). Aristotle goes on to draw the general conclusion that not only ought this to be the case with the medical profession but it ought also to be the case in all of the other 'professions and arts' in the Athenian society of his day. For, he argues, just as 'the physician ought to be called to account by physicians, so ought men in general to be called to account by their peers' (Aristotle 1984b: II, III, 11, 1281b39-1282a3, 2034).

Here Aristotle argues that the individual members of the medical profession are equals. Moreover, what connects them together as members of this particular society or corporate group is not the pursuit of temporal advantage or perceived short-term self-interest of a pecuniary nature. Rather, their connection to one another as well as to their patients is an ethical one. All of these individuals have relative ethical duties because they are members of the same profession. They have an ethical concern for the well-being of others, specifically their patients. Although it is an equal society, then, this particular society is also a community and not an association, in the sense in which Ferdinand Tönnies employs these terms. This raises the interesting further question of how the code of medical ethics to which Aristotle appears to be referring here was established. What were the decision-making or policy-making procedures that operated within this particular corporate society, given that it was an equal and not an unequal society? Unfortunately, Aristotle says nothing at all about this subject in the *Politics*.

I now turn to consider Aristotle's views regarding those other societies that are communities, but which, unlike the medical profession, are composed of unequals. Here we are talking about relationships of authority, or the ethical relationships that exist between superiors and their subordinates in societies that are ordered hierarchically. This is what I have in mind when I talk about 'institutions' or 'social institutions'. Societies of this kind rest upon the principle of that social division of labour which lies at the heart of both Plato's *Republic* and Aristotle's *Politics*.

The relationship that exists between the members of these hierarchical institutions is also an ethical one. What binds the members of such societies together are the ties of duty, albeit between unequals. Aristotle maintains that ethical relationships in societies of this type necessarily 'imply superiority of one party over the other', which is why, in his view, 'parents are honoured' (Aristotle 1984a, II, VIII, 11, 1161a18-22, 1835). Aristotle has a tendency to think of these relationships between unequals in terms of the notions of command and obedience, that is to say, authority. As examples Aristotle cites the relationship of 'father to son', of 'elder to younger', that of 'man to wife', and that of 'ruler to subject' in a *polis* (Aristotle 1984a: II, VIII, 7, 1158b12-24, 1831).

There has been relatively little discussion of Aristotle's views on the subject of authority. The most significant exception to this is the work of Andrés Rosler. However, Rosler focuses on Aristotle's views regarding the subject of political authority, narrowly conceived, which is not what is of interest to us here (Rosler 2005; but see also Keyt 2005). Rosler accepts that the concept of 'role-related duties' is a common one which 'surely exists in all forms of social organization'. He also accepts that Aristotle 'obviously recognizes that' (Rosler 2005: 117). His book, however, deals with what Aristotle has to say about the 'non-role-related sense of duty' that citizens have to obey the laws of the strictly political state (Rosler 2005: 118).

In his discussion of friendship in the *Nicomachean Ethics* Aristotle argues that the ethical duties that are associated with the dyadic relationships which exist within unequal societies are also varied. This is so for two reasons. In the first place, the specific nature of the relationships in question will be different, again depending on the type of unequal society under consideration. It is not, Aristotle says, exactly the same relationship 'that exists between parents and children and between rulers and subjects' (Aristotle 1984a, II, VIII, 7, 1158b12-24, 1831). In the second place, Aristotle argues that even within the dyadic relationship of a particular type of society, the rights and duties of the two parties concerned will also be different. Thus Aristotle argues that the relationship 'of father to son' is not 'the same as that of son to father', and the relationship of 'husband to wife' is not 'the same as that of wife to husband' (Aristotle 1984a, II, VIII, 7, 1158b12-24, 1831). Hence the specific character of the ethical ties that bind them together is 'different also' (Aristotle 1984a, II, VIII, 7, 1158b12-24, 1831). Aristotle maintains that, in consequence, 'the modes of rule' which are 'appropriate' to these 'different relations' in these different types of unequal society are again diverse (Aristotle 1984a, II, VIII, 10, 1160b23-1161a8, 1834).

When discussing ethical relationships within unequal societies, the general point that Aristotle wishes to make, in both the *Politics* and in the *Ethics*, is that 'we ought to render to each class what is appropriate and becoming' (Aristotle 1984a, II, IX, 2, 1165a17-18, 1841). One individual should 'always try to assign' to another 'what is appropriate' (Aristotle 1984a: II, IX, 2, 1165a31-32, 1841), or what is fitting, depending on the specific nature of the unequal relationship that exists between them. In Aristotle's view, however, this is in part a matter of their place or station in the particular society of which they are both members. J. W. Gough has rightly said of Plato that he 'presents us with an account of an organized society in which every man has his "station and its duties"' (Gough 1967 [1936]: 13). Sir Ernest Barker has also observed that for Plato, justice meant 'that a man should do his work in the station of life to which he was called by his capacities' (Barker 1959: 88; see also Alvin Gouldner 1965: 78-132). In my view, *pace* Richard Kraut, Aristotle's views here are the same as those of Plato (Kraut 2002: 151-2). He too endorses the principle of my station and its duties.

V

Aristotle's social theory and the idea of justice as reciprocity

Aristotle argues in Book VIII of the *Nicomachean Ethics* that ethical relationships in those unequal societies that are communities are reciprocal. He points out that within them both superiors and inferiors have respective rights and duties in relation to one another and that each can make legitimate claims on the other. It is entirely appropriate, therefore, to think of their relationship in terms of the notion of reciprocity. However, Aristotle also argues that their relationship is an asymmetrical one. He points out that the rights and duties of superiors are significantly different from those of their subordinates. This being so, he concludes, it follows that in general 'unequals must render' to their superiors 'what is in proportion to their superiority or inferiority'. In these unequal social relationships, 'each party' does not get 'the same from the other'. Nor, indeed, ought they 'to seek it' (Aristotle 1984a: II, VIII, 13, 1162a34-1162b4, 1837). Rather, each should render unto the other what is their due, again given the specific nature of the relationship of inequality that exists between them. In short, Aristotle argues here that the best way to think about the justice that exists in relationships between superiors and their subordinates in unequal societies is by reference to the notion of proportional reciprocity.

Aristotle argues that what he takes to be the Pythagorean view that justice is always and necessarily a matter of simple reciprocity 'cannot be' correct 'in relation to all persons', for 'the same thing is not just for a servant as for a freeman', or indeed for an 'official' and his prisoner, or for a father and his son, given that the individuals concerned are not equals at all, but unequals (Aristotle 1984c: II, I, 33, 1194a31-32, 1889; Aristotle 1984a, II, V, 5, 1132b28, 1787; Aristotle 1984a: II, VII, 6, 1149b7-13, 1816). It is important to note, however, that the conclusion that Aristotle draws from this is not that justice has nothing to do with reciprocity. It is, rather, that justice is not a matter of simple reciprocity. Aristotle accepts that justice and reciprocity are essentially the same thing, provided the reciprocity in question is proportional reciprocity.

VI

Aristotle and the idea of recognitive justice

Giorgio del Vecchio's reading of Aristotle is of particular interest, because it deploys the notion of 'recognitive justice' (del Vecchio 1956 [1924]: 88fn6, 90, 116). As del Vecchio understands it, this idea has an application to both equal societies and unequal ones. In words that echo Hegel's notion of 'reciprocal recognition' (Hegel 1977 [1807]: §184, 112; §188, 114), del Vecchio argues that for Aristotle, all relationships of justice are 'based on a mutual recognition of the being of each', at least within a particular 'defined sphere' (del Vecchio 1956 [1924]: 92). He maintains that for Aristotle, 'there is always and necessarily "a mutual recognition of several subjects"' del Vecchio 1956 [1924]: 116). He attributes to Aristotle the general view that justice is a matter 'of mutual respect', according to some standard or other 'of equality or proportion which we might call mathematical' (del Vecchio 1956 [1924]: 93). In the case of equal societies, this is a mutual or reciprocal recognition of one another as arithmetical equals, whereas in the case of an unequal society, it is a mutual or reciprocal recognition between unequals, or between superiors and subordinates. In short, it is a matter of geometrical equality and of proportional reciprocity.

Consider, for example, the society that is composed of the citizens of a *polis*, all of whom are recognized and recognize one another as equals who possess exactly the same rights and duties, at least in the sphere of corrective justice. When discussing this issue, del Vecchio argues that if we wish to understand Aristotle's views on this subject then it is necessary to admit a 'form of justice' called 'recognitive', that 'imposes the recognition of contraposited personalities according to a basic equality' (del Vecchio 1956 [1924]: 90). According to del Vecchio, Aristotle holds that every juridical 'subject', in this case every citizen of a *polis*, ought to be 'recognized (by others) for what he is worth'. Moreover, he also holds, in consequence of this, that 'to everyone shall be assigned (by others) what belongs to him', or what is due to him (del Vecchio 1956 [1924]: 85). Del Vecchio argues that this 'elementary notion of justice as balance and inter-subjective correlation', when applied within the sphere of rectificatory justice, resolves itself into the mutual claim to respect and the mutual possibility of preventing wrong, that is made by one citizen to another (del Vecchio 1956 [1924]: 105–6). He maintains that Aristotle provisionally accepts the Pythagorean view that within the sphere of rectificatory justice the principle that ought to apply, at least initially, is that of simple reciprocity. The basic principle of justice understood in this way, by Aristotle, is the 'juridical analogy of that moral concept', which del Vecchio claims can be found in 'the religions and philosophies' of a large variety of 'different peoples', namely, 'the Golden Rule', or the maxim: 'Do not that to another what thou would not have done to thyself' (del Vecchio 1956 [1924]: 87–8).

Let us now consider the application of the notion of recognitive justice to unequal societies or social institutions. The starting point here is the principle of my station and its duties. It will be recalled that unequal societies are based on a division of labour and on the existence of differential social roles within an ordered hierarchy. This hierarchy contains superiors, who occupy positions of authority, alongside of their subordinates.

Aristotle suggests that each of these roles is associated with a particular framework of reciprocal rights and duties. He emphasizes the importance of the fact that although they may be said to be reciprocal, nevertheless, the particular rights and duties of superiors are different from those of their subordinates. For example, those of a general are different from those of the soldiers under his command; those of the captain of a ship are different for those of the sailors who make up its crew; those of a master are different from those of a servant; those of a doctor are different from those of a patient; those of a judge or of an officer of a court are different from those of his prisoner; those of a father or a mother are different from those of a son or daughter; and those of a husband are different from those of a wife; and so on.

At the same time, however, it is clear that occupation of these different roles makes a significant contribution to the determination of the social identity of the individual concerned. Aristotle clearly implies, for example in his discussion of the case of the officer and his prisoner in Chapter 5 of Book V of the *Nicomachean Ethics* (Aristotle 1984a, II, V, 5, 1132b28-30, 1787), that the ethical duties of the individuals concerned depends on *who* they are. It is determined by their social identity, and this in turn depends on, or is at least greatly influenced by, their occupational role or function. It is at least in part established by their place or station in the particular society or social institution of which both superior and subordinate are members. Given this, it is not too surprising that when considering the thought of Aristotle from the standpoint of the notion of recognitive justice, del Vecchio observes that 'even the relation of inequality or subordination', that exists in unequal societies, all of which are assumed by Aristotle to be just, 'depends for its effective existence on a mutual recognition of superior and inferior' (del Vecchio 1956 [1924]: 54). For in the absence of such recognition, 'the authority of the superior would vanish' (del Vecchio 1956 [1924]: 54).

Conclusion

I have attempted to do two things. The first is to show how aspects of social theory, especially the Durkheimian tradition in the history of sociological thought, can shed light on our understanding of the politics of recognition. Of particular interest here are the views of Cillian McBride, who relies heavily on what Durkheim has to say about social institutions, differential social roles and the ethical rights and duties which are associated with them. The second is to connect a discussion of these issues to the writings of Aristotle, which seem to me to prefigure in a striking way some of the issues raised. Here there are numerous points of contact, not least a shared emphasis on the significance of the social division of labour and on the principle of my station and its duties. Given these similarities, it does not seem inappropriate to claim, as del Vecchio has done, that there is a clear recognitive dimension to Aristotle's thinking about justice in his *Ethics* and his *Politics*. One example of a contemporary thinker whose views make a contribution to an Aristotelian politics of recognition within social institutions is Alasdair MacIntyre. In order to address these issues, from a contemporary Aristotelian perspective, the distinction that is drawn by MacIntyre in *After Virtue* between the 'internal goods' of a 'practice' and the 'external goods' of an 'institution' seems to me to be especially significant (MacIntyre 2007 [1981]: 187–96, 222; Burns 2011). If we think of education as a practice, in MacIntyre's sense of the term, then we might turn our attention to the manner in which this practice has become institutionalized, for example in universities (MacIntyre 2009). This leads us to turn our attention to the question of the internal 'politics' of these social institutions, their structure and organization and the decision-making processes that operate within them. In the terminology of Grotius, which as we saw draws directly on Aristotle's *Politics*, we might ask whether they ought to be equal societies or unequal ones. These are not merely theoretical questions. They have a practical significance for all of those studying and working, in whatever capacity, in universities today.

Notes

1. For identity politics considered from the point of view of traditional sociological theory, see Berger and Luckmann 1975 [1966]: 45–8, 67–8, 84–5, 90–2, 108, 151–4, 158–9, 162, 185–93, 203–4; and Berger 1971 [1963]: 115–24, 140–1, 178.
2. Ross and Urmson translate *koinōnia* as 'community'. I have used 'society' throughout.
3. Jowett's translation of the *Politics* renders Aristotle's *koinōnia* as 'partnership'.

References

Abraham, J. H. (1973), 'Sociology in Ancient and Medieval Times', in *Origins and Growth of Sociology*, 21–43, Harmondsworth: Penguin.
Althusius, J. (1964 [1603]), *The Politics of Johannes Althusius*, abridged and translated by Frederick S. Carney, with a Preface by Carl J. Friedrich, Boston: Beacon Press.
Arendt, H. (1958), 'The Rise of the Social', *The Human Condition*, Chicago: University of Chicago Press, 38–49.
Aristotle (1984), *The Complete Works of Aristotle*, the revised Oxford translation, in 2 volumes, ed. J. Barnes, Princeton: Princeton University Press.
Aristotle (1984a), *Nicomachean Ethics*, trans. W. D. Ross, revised J. O. Urmson, in *The Complete Works of Aristotle*, Vol. 2, ed. J. Barnes, Princeton: Princeton University Press.
Aristotle (1984b), *Politics*, trans. B. Jowett, in *The Complete Works of Aristotle*, Vol. 2, ed. J. Barnes, Princeton: Princeton University Press.
Aristotle (1984c), *Magna Moralia*, trans. G. Stock, in *The Complete Works of Aristotle*, Vol. 2, ed. J. Barnes, Princeton: Princeton University Press.
Barker, E. (1959), *The Political Thought of Plato and Aristotle*, New York: Dover Publications.
Barker, E. (1960), 'Translator's Introduction', to Otto von Gierke, *Natural law and the Theory of Society: 1500 to 1800*, ix–xci, trans. Sir Ernest Barker, Boston: Beacon Press.
Barker, E. ([1951] 1961), *The Principles of Social and Political Theory*, Oxford: Oxford University Press.
Barnes, H. E. (1948), 'Ancient and Medieval Social Philosophy', in Harry Elmer Barnes (ed.), *An Introduction to the History of Sociology*, 3–28, Chicago: University of Chicago Press.

Berger, P. L. ([1963] 1971), *Invitation to Sociology: A Humanistic Perspective*, Harmondsworth: Penguin.

Berger, P. L. and T. Luckmann ([1966] 1975), *The Social Construction of Reality: A Treatise in the Sociology of Knowledge*, Harmondsworth: Penguin.

Burns, T. (2011), 'Revolutionary Aristotelianism? The Political Thought of Aristotle, Marx and MacIntyre', in P. Blackledge and K. Knight (eds.), *Virtue and Politics: Alasdair MacIntyre's Revolutionary Aristotelianism*, 35–53, Notre Dame, IN: University of Notre Dame Press, 2011.

Calhoun, C. ([1995] 2003), 'The Politics of Identity and Recognition', in *Critical Social Theory: Culture, History and the Challenge of Difference*, 197–8, Oxford: Blackwell.

Challenger, D. F. (1994), *Durkheim Through the Lens of Aristotle: Durkheimian, Postmodernist and Communitarian Responses to the Enlightenment*, Lanham, MD: Rowman & Littlefield.

del Vecchio, G. ([1921] 1956), *Justice: An Historical and Philosophical Essay*, Edinburgh: Edinburgh University Press.

Durkheim, E. ([1890–1900] 1992), *Professional Ethics and Civic Morals*, trans. C. Brookfield, London: Routledge.

Durkheim, E. ([1902–1903] 2002), *Moral Education*, trans. E. K. Wilson and H. Schnurer, New York: Dover Publications.

Ellwood, C. A. (1902), 'Aristotle as a Sociologist', *Annals of the American Academy*, 19: 63–74.

Figgis, J. N. (1960 [1907]), *Political Thought from Gerson to Grotius: 1414-1625*, Intro. Garrett Mattingly, New York: Harper Torchbooks.

French, P. (1977), 'Institutional and Moral Obligations (or Merels and Morals)', *The Journal of Philosophy*, 74 (10): 575–87.

Gert, B. (2006), 'Particular Moral Rules and Special Duties', in C. M. Culver and K. Danner Clouser (eds), *Bioethics: A Systematic Approach*, 77–98, Oxford: Oxford University Press.

Gough, J. W. ([1936] 1967) *The Social Contract: A Critical Study of Its Development*, 2nd ed., Clarendon Press.

Gouldner, A. W. (1965), *Enter Plato: Classical Greece and the Origins of Social Theory*, New York: Basic Books.

Grotius, H. ([1625] 2005), *The Rights of War and Peace*, in 3 Volumes, ed. R. Tuck, Indianapolis: Liberty Fund.

Hegel, G. W. F. ([1807] 1977), *Phenomenology of Spirit*, trans. A. V. Miller, Foreword J. N. Findlay, Oxford: Oxford University Press.

Hegel, G. W. F. ([1821] 1979), *Philosophy of Right*, trans. T. M. Knox, Oxford: Oxford University Press.

Hegel, G. W. F. ([1830] 1971), *Philosophy of Mind: Being Part Three of the Encyclopaedia of the Philosophical Sciences*, trans. W. Wallace, with *Zusatze* trans. by A. V. Miller, foreword by J. N. Findlay, Oxford: Clarendon Press.

Hegel, G. W. F. ([1831] 1953), *Reason in History: A General Introduction to the Philosophy of History*, trans. R. S. Hartmann, Minneapolis: Bobbs-Merrill.

Jeske, D. (2014), 'Special Obligations', *The Stanford Encyclopedia of Philosophy*, 2014 edn, ed. Ed N. Zalta. http://plato.stanford.edu/archives/spr2014/entries/special-obligations/.

Jones, N. F. (1999), *The Associations of Classical Athens: The Response to Democracy*, New York: Oxford University Press.

Keyt, D. (2005), 'Aristotle and Anarchism', in R. Kraut and S. Skultety (eds), *Aristotle's Politics: Critical Essays*, 203–22, Rowman & Littlefield.

Kraut, R. (2002), *Aristotle*, Oxford: Oxford University Press.
MacIntyre, A. ([1981] 2007), *After Virtue: A Study in Moral Theory*, 3rd edn, Notre Dame: Notre Dame University Press.
MacIntyre, A. (2009), 'The Very Idea of a University: Aristotle, Newman and Us', *British Journal of Educational Studies*, 57 (4): 347–62.
Marsilius of Padua ([1321] 1980), *Defensor Pacis*, trans. Alan Gewirth, Toronto: University of Toronto Press.
McBride, C. (2013), *Recognition*, Cambridge: Polity Press.
McCarthy, G. E. (2003), *Classical Horizons: The Origins of Sociology in Ancient Greece*, New York: SUNY Press.
Mulgan, R. G. ([1977] 2011), *Aristotle's Political Theory: An Introduction for Students of Political Theory*, Oxford University Press.
Oakley, J. and D. Cocking (2001), *Virtue Ethics and Professional Roles*, Cambridge: Cambridge University Press.
Rosler, A. (2005), *Political Authority and Obligation in Aristotle*, Oxford: Oxford University Press.
Ross, D. ([1923] 1964), *Aristotle*, London: Methuen.
Scheffler, S. (1997), 'Relationships and Responsibilities', *Philosophy and Public Affairs*, 26: 189–209.
Tönnies, F. ([1887] 1955), *Community and Association*, trans. C. P. Loomis, London: Routledge.
Zeitlin, I. M. (1993), *Plato's Vision: The Classical Origins of Social and Political Thought*, Englewood Cliffs, NJ: Prentice Hall.

13

Human flourishing and labour
Aristotle, MacIntyre and Marx

Egidijus Mardosas

Introduction

Aristotle's exclusion of workers from the ideal *polis* is well known to any student of Aristotle's ethical and political works. In order for Aristotelian considerations on human flourishing, as well as for any other philosophical approach as to what is conducive for human well-being, to have relevance for contemporary societies, the question of labour must be made central: most of us, after all, need to work to earn a living. Thus, Aristotle's views on the status of workers are not negligible when considering his ethical theory. In this chapter, my aim is not to reject or accept Aristotle's arguments, but to highlight the tension between human flourishing and labour, as it appears in Aristotle's works, and then to comment on two different attempts to deal with this tension: Alasdair MacIntyre's and Karl Marx's. I start with Aristotle's arguments of why workers cannot be citizens of the best *polis* and lead a flourishing life. I then turn to MacIntyre's attempt to make Aristotle's ethics more egalitarian and to reconnect virtue with work. Finally, I introduce Marx's considerations about freedom and labour to show that Marx retains and radicalizes some of Aristotle's arguments about human flourishing.

Aristotle on *banausoi*

Aristotle's *Nicomachean Ethics* (Aristotle 2009) and *Politics* (Aristotle 1998) form a continuous enquiry into the human good. It provides a detailed ethical exposition of the good life that culminates with a political account of the political order that would be most conducive to the human good. Unfortunately, Aristotle's theory is severely impaired by his restrictions as to who can lead a good life. Some people are natural slaves, argues Aristotle, and thus they are not capable of virtuous life; women are inferior to men, and the human good is out of their reach as well. Another case that Aristotle argues for continuously throughout *Politics* relates to the exclusion of workers. It receives much more attention in *Politics* than the question of slavery or gender inequalities, and is therefore more central to Aristotle's conception of the good life.

In Book 3 and then in Book 7 of *Politics*, we learn that the best kind of *polis*, that is, the *polis* that is dedicated to the cultivation of human excellence, will not grant citizenship to farmers, craftsmen or tradesmen. In other words, workers will not be allowed to share in the good life that the *polis* sustains:

> It evidently follows that in a city-state governed in the finest manner, possessing men who are unqualifiedly just (and not given certain assumptions), the citizens should not live the life of a vulgar craftsman or tradesman. For lives of these sorts are ignoble and inimical to virtue. Nor should those who are going to be citizens engage in farming, since leisure is needed both to develop virtue and to engage in political actions. (1328b36-1329a1)

Aristotle connects two points to argue his case against the inclusion of workers. First, he states that it is necessary to lead a life of leisure in order to cultivate virtues and rule the city. The second point is that productive activities in themselves, by their very nature, are inimical to the development of human excellence. The first argument is not sufficient in itself to ground the exclusion of workers, for one could argue that some workers could be educated to cultivate the necessary virtues and take part in the political life of a *polis*, provided that they have enough free time from work. But Aristotle's exclusion is absolute: in the best city-state, no citizen will work. This absolute interdiction is supported by the second point about the nature of work.

Aristotle ranks activities that are suitable for the free man (and it is always a man that Aristotle has in mind) and those that are not. He is concerned that his best citizens only engage in those activities that promote excellence of character and intellect. In Book II, Chapter 4 of the *Nicomachean Ethics*, for example, he argues that there is no relation between being good at certain *technē* (having the necessary skills to do the job well) and the development of virtue. One can be a good carpenter without being a good person. Skill and virtue are two different things. For this reason, people who spend their lives as workers cannot attain the kind of excellence attainable to those who dedicate all their time to cultivating virtues. Thus the best citizens must not work, must not preoccupy themselves with effort to secure material necessities, so they can dedicate their life completely to those actions and activities (which include governing the city) that befit the free and virtuous.

Throughout the *Politics*, Aristotle uses the term *banausoi* to describe those who work. It is a pejorative term to refer to various workers, and is usually translated as 'vulgar craftsmen'.[1] Although in Book 3 Aristotle notes that only a part of workers are *banausoi* (1277b1), implying that not all kinds of work are vulgar, in Book 8 of *Politics* he argues that, in light of the best *polis* and the best possible life for humans, everyone who needs to work for a living must be deemed vulgar:

> Any task, craft, or branch of learning should be considered vulgar (*banauson*) if it renders the body or mind of free people useless for the practices and activities of virtue. That is why the crafts that put the body into a worse condition and work

done for wages are called vulgar; for they debase the mind and deprive it of leisure. (1337b10-14)

That some kinds of work are damaging to both body and mind is not a controversial statement. But Aristotle's point is much stronger: everyone who works for a living does, in a certain sense, damage their mind. How so? Aristotle's theory of the good life rests heavily on his conception of reason and practical rationality. Virtues are of two kinds: moral and intellectual. Thus a good citizen will not only have good character but their reasoning will also be well ordered as well. Reason is central to Aristotle's conception of the human: the use of reason is a specifically human *ergon*, the human 'function' that separates humanity from the animal world. So the citizens of the best *polis* will cultivate their powers of rationality. As far as practical (and political) wisdom is concerned, citizens will need to reason and act in light of what is best in general, that is, in the way that furthers the human good (*Nicomachean Ethics* 1140a27). Aristotle's exclusions also derive from his ideas as to who can develop rational faculties in the right way. Natural slaves are bereft of reason entirely, while women's reasoning 'lacks authority', states Aristotle (1260a13). But what puts limits on the reasoning powers of workers is not their supposed nature, but their occupational activities. Aristotle does not devote much space to explaining why that is so, but as Richard Kraut shows (Kraut 2002: 215–17), Aristotle's underlying reasoning of why work limits workers' powers of reason is the following: those who need to work to earn a living become habituated to instrumental reasoning, which makes their rational faculties inadequate for considering the common good of the *polis*. They reason in terms of immediate gain, their minds are damaged by the necessity to secure a living. The minds of the best men should be free from these petty material and instrumental considerations, so they could reason and act in light of *the* human good, thus rising above individual interests. Thus Aristotle's statement (repeated several times in *Politics*) that 'it is impossible to engage in virtuous pursuits while living the life of a vulgar craftsman or a hired labourer' (1278a20-21) is central to his conception of the human good. Taken in absolute terms, the good life is life without work.

Freedom from work and life of leisure, of course, mean that the citizens will have to be materially secure. Aristotle is very clear about this and argues that property should be concentrated in the hands of the citizens:

> Moreover, the property should belong to them. For the citizens must be well supplied with resources, and these people are the citizens. For the class of vulgar craftsmen does not participate in the city-state, nor does any other class whose members are not 'craftsmen of virtue' (*tēs aretēs dēmiourgon*). (1329a17-20)

It is important to note that the line between citizen and non-citizen is drawn not on the basis of wealth; it is grounded in the distinction between life of leisure and life of labour. Aristotle notes that some craftsmen can and sometimes do become rich (1278a23), but in the ideal constitution, even rich craftsmen cannot have citizenship because of their occupation.

At several points in *Politics*, Aristotle contemplates the possibility of a more egalitarian society. Thus in Book 7 he asks whether it would be desirable to distribute equally the tasks necessary to sustain the *polis*:

> It remains to investigate whether everyone should share in all the tasks we mentioned (for it is possible for all the same people to be farmers, craftsmen, deliberators and judges), or whether different people should be assigned to each of them, or whether some tasks are necessarily specialized, whereas others can be shared by everyone. (1328b23-28)

A form of redistribution when 'everyone shares in everything' is characteristic of democracies, states Aristotle. But this equality cannot pertain to the best *polis*. Citizens of the best *polis* cannot dedicate even a fraction of their time to productive work, because they will be undertaking a task that is 'inimical to virtue', thus corrupting their lives with tasks unworthy of the virtuous man. In the best *polis*, citizens will cultivate the best life conceived in absolute terms. Thus, even when Aristotle entertains the possibility that citizenship could be extended to workers, he maintains that they would still remain 'second-class' citizens, for they will never be as virtuous as true citizens completely free from work:

> The best city-state will not confer citizenship on vulgar craftsmen, however; but if they too are citizens, then what we have characterized as a citizen's virtue cannot be ascribed to everyone, or even to all free people, but only to those who are freed from necessary tasks. (1278a7-12)

The passage about democracy reveals that Aristotle wants to draw the class line as sharp as possible. Workers did actually take part in the political life of Greek city-states and Aristotle here acknowledges that to be the case, but argues against it. Aristotle clearly prefers a highly unequal society, where a minority are completely liberated from work and free to cultivate human excellence, to a more equalitarian one based on collective sharing of work. Of course, given the prevailing forces of production at the time of Aristotle's writing, such redistribution, even if it were to be accomplished, would have meant that work necessary to sustain the *polis* would still have occupied the major part of citizens' lives. Aristotle does not explicitly reason in these terms, but we may presume that he was aware of it, especially given that the question of securing necessary goods was central to Aristotle's considerations about what geographical location is suitable for the best *polis*.

In another passage of *Politics*, Aristotle introduces a more extravagant line of speculation. Equality could be accomplished on the basis of technology: if technology allowed for full automation, that is, if human labour were no longer required to produce necessary goods and services, then hierarchical relations could be abandoned:

> For, if each tool could perform its task on command or by anticipating instructions, and if like the statues of Daedalus or the tripods of Hephaestus – which the poet describes as having 'entered the assembly of the gods of their own accord' – shuttles wove cloth by themselves, and picks played the lyre, a master craftsman would not need assistants, and masters would not need slaves. (1253b33-38)

Because such condition remained unreal for Aristotle's time – while we, on the other hand, live in the times of continuously increasing levels of automation – the argument serves only as a thought experiment. Unfortunately, Aristotle does not tell us whether everyone could potentially achieve *eudaimonia*, if such a condition were met. Clearly, the requirement of freedom from work would be satisfied. But other aspects of inequality would remain: both 'natural slaves' and women would, most probably, still remain excluded from citizenship. It seems, from these arguments, that the only way for those who work to share in the good life would be to eradicate work itself, that is, for workers to cease being workers.

Cary J. Nederman (2008) argues that Aristotle's exclusion of workers from citizenship could be rejected using Aristotle's own arguments. So an Aristotelian true to Aristotle's philosophy as a whole would be suspicious of or completely reject Aristotle's views on *banausoi*, as some medieval Aristotelians mentioned by Nedeman did. Aristotle acknowledges that some reasoning is involved in productive knowledge, and such knowledge contributes to the life of the *polis*, therefore workers must have a share in political life. Indeed, Aristotle does not contest that performing many productive tasks requires certain knowledge. But it would be difficult to sustain Nedeman's proposition, because Aristotle's exclusion of workers rests not on the statement that they make no use of reasoning powers, but on the idea that work corrupts practical reasoning and makes a worker unable to reason in terms of the human good, in addition to depriving him/her of leisure. It is important to remember that Aristotle does not argue that workers must be excluded from citizenship in every type of state, but only in the best possible one. Thus while they can be citizens in certain states, so Aristotle reasons, they must not be in the one that is dedicated to provide the best kind of life that humans could achieve.

These considerations shed light on the inequalities that underlie some otherwise egalitarian propositions Aristotle makes about the nature of the ideal *polis*. A city-state, argues Aristotle, 'is a community of equals, aiming at the best life possible' (1328a36-37). Citizenship, equality, community and the good life are, in the end, reserved only for the minority of rulers. The class line is sharp: on the one hand, the ruling men, owners of property who never work but dedicate all their time to cultivating moral and intellectual virtues; on the other, their subjects: women, slaves and all kinds of workers. Those whose work supports the *polis* have no part in the good life that the *polis* provides for their masters. In the end, Aristotle's ethical and political theory amounts to what could be called 'socialism for the ruling class': in Books 7 and 8, Aristotle argues that citizens (i.e. the ruling class) will have to rule in turn, that material inequality among them should be minimal and that the *polis* should provide communal education, as well as envisaging a variety of communal activities to keep the bonds of fellowship strong. But all this is accessible to the ruling class only.

MacIntyre's Aristotelianism of virtuous work

Alasdair MacIntyre presents his ethical and political theory as a modern version of Aristotelianism, injecting it with egalitarianism that Aristotle's own writings lacked.

Embracing Aristotle in *After Virtue* and subsequent works, MacIntyre acknowledges and seeks to rectify much of Aristotle's limitations concerning as to who can lead the good life. Some of Aristotle's views can be dismissed by insisting that they derive from prejudices of the time and are not central to his otherwise attractive ethical theory of virtues. This is one of the arguments in *After Virtue* (MacIntyre 2007: 159). MacIntyre makes an even stronger case by attempting to free Aristotle's ethics from his metaphysical assumptions about human nature, his 'metaphysical biology' (ibid., 162).

In *Whose Justice? Which Rationality?*, MacIntyre states that Aristotle's account of virtue is 'independent of any thesis about what kinds of persons are and are not capable of excellence' (MacIntyre 1988: 105). He argues that Aristotle's views that some groups of people are not capable of developing certain character traits (virtues) and leading a flourishing life demonstrate 'fallacious reasoning typical of ideologies of irrational domination' (ibid.). This fallacious reasoning damages Aristotle's conception of the best *polis*. Aristotle, according to MacIntyre, has failed to imagine how social and occupational roles could be restructured in order to conceive a more inclusive society: 'What Aristotle's invalid arguments direct our attention to is that in the best kind of *polis* the participation of women or of artisans would require a restructuring of their occupational and social roles of a kind inconceivable to Aristotle himself' (ibid.). But such a claim could hardly be sustained, because Aristotle, as quoted earlier, does consider the case where occupational roles could be distributed on egalitarian basis, that is, a society where 'everyone shares in everything'. Aristotle did conceive of a possibility of a more egalitarian society, but argued explicitly against it. His rejection of egalitarian distribution of work is grounded not only in an argument about the human nature but also in one about the nature of various activities: work done out of necessity, pursued for extrinsic reasons, distorts body and mind, deprives one of leisure and is not worthy of a free human being who undertakes only activities that 'produce virtue'.

Disconnecting Aristotle's account of virtues from his 'metaphysical biology' may be enough so far as slavery and gender inequalities are concerned. But the case for excluding workers is more significant and requires rethinking much of Aristotle's account of virtue. It remains necessary to reconceptualize the relation between virtue and work. MacIntyre's theory of practices does exactly that by situating the development of virtue in a variety of socially established cooperative activities that also include activities producing necessary goods to sustain the community. Some productive activities, such as farming, are given by MacIntyre in *After Virtue* as examples of practices, that is, activities through which virtues are developed and exercised (MacIntyre 2007: 187). But, clearly, the concept of practice leaves out many forms of actual work: workers working on an assembly line in a factory, for example, are not engaged in a practice. What matters is that MacIntyre's ethics envisages at least some kind of productive work that is ethically desirable or at least not destructive of virtues and the common good. This way, he establishes a possibility of virtuous work. Having reconnected virtue and work, MacIntyre can then argue that some important virtues are exercised through work:

> It is in and through our engagement in such laborious and productive activities as farming, construction work and the like that the number of virtues much needed

in our individual and communal lives are developed and exercised. (MacIntyre 2008: 275)

MacIntyre acknowledges that Aristotle's list of virtues can no longer be sustained in his own version of Aristotelianism. He proceeds, most famously in *Dependent Rational Animals* (1999), to envisage a set of virtues different from that of Aristotle in order to conceive virtuous communities that share work and its fruits on a more egalitarian basis. MacIntyre introduces 'the virtues of acknowledged dependence' that are needed to sustain networks of giving and receiving through which every member of a community secures best social conditions to lead a flourishing life. Such a flourishing community will engage in collective reasoning – and every member of the community will have access to institutions of collective deliberation – regarding the practices, goods and their ordering. Although Aristotle's ideal *polis* excluded the majority of the population from actual participation in its political life, Aristotelian conception of *polis* as a place to exercise powers of rationality retains its fascination for MacIntyre. From the MacIntyrean perspective, the process of shared deliberation must extend 'from the farm and the fishing fleet, the household and the craft workplace, to … political assemblies' (MacIntyre 1998a: 243).

Returning to the question of work, MacIntyre emphasizes that even unpleasant and tedious work can be meaningful and fulfilling, given right social circumstances:

> Most productive work is and cannot but be tedious, arduous, and fatiguing much of the time. What makes it worthwhile to work and to work well is threefold: that the work that we do has point and purpose, is productive of genuine goods; that the work that we do is and is recognized to be our work, our contribution, in which we are given and take responsibility for doing it and doing it well; and that we are rewarded for doing it in a way that enables us to achieve the goods of family and community. (MacIntyre 2011a: 323)

Thus MacIntyre's conception of inclusive and deliberative community provides a social context in which (at least some forms of) work is not destructive of well-being. Indeed, Aristotle's radical exclusion of workers from citizenship seems to leave them no incentive to work and work well, except for the bare need of survival. What is more, it is difficult to see how workers, excluded from the *polis*, would willingly give up the surplus of their production necessary to sustain the freedom of their rulers without some form of oppression. In MacIntyre's participative community that sustains networks of giving and receiving, everyone, irrespectively of occupation, would see their work as contributing to the common good that the community provides.

A turn to the local and the communal is central to MacIntyre's political thought. Already in *After Virtue*, as MacIntyre embraces Aristotle, he rejects the Marxist project, turns away from the politics of the organized working class, and states that he sees 'no tolerable alternative set of political and economic structures which could be brought into place to replace the structures of advanced capitalism' (MacIntyre 2007: 262). Seeing no progressive road forwards, MacIntyre focuses on local communities that could sustain the common good in face of adverse powers of capital and state. Thus

MacIntyre's attempt to reconnect work, virtue and human flourishing is marked by this context of communality. Approaching the question of economic life in a well-ordered community in his essay 'Politics, Philosophy and the Common Good', MacIntyre makes it clear that he has in mind communities of small producers, referring to family farm as an example of a morally desirable sort of production (MacIntyre 1998a: 249–250). Fishing communities are also invoked as another example (MacIntyre 1994; MacIntyre 2016: 179–80).

This fascination with the morals of fishing communities has a much wider cultural appeal – recall Luchino Visconti's masterful film *La Terra Trema* (1948). But the difference between Visconti and MacIntyre is that Visconti remained a dedicated communist and saw the struggles of fishermen as admirable, but eventually doomed outside the class struggle of the organized proletariat. MacIntyre, by contrast, wants to keep such communities, idealizing them as examples of virtuous communal life. A somewhat romantic understanding of communal life is clear in MacIntyre's reading of E. P. Thompson's description of pre-capitalist communities in *The Making of the English Working Class*. MacIntyre argues that the source of workers' radicalism was not their experience in factories, but recollection of the earlier life in the moral community (MacIntyre 1998b: 231–2). However, MacIntyre's approach departs from Thompson's in a similar way to how it differs from Visconti's. Thompson argues that the struggles of early proletariat against capitalist exploitation gave rise to a myth of the golden age of community (Thompson 1991: 254), warning, in a way, against idealizing pre-capitalist communal life. MacIntyre, on the other hand, wants to recreate such close-knit common-good communities as an alternative to the capitalist present.

It is significant that MacIntyre returns to Marx's critique of capitalism in his later works. He wants to retain several 'sets of truths' of Marx's in his Neo-Aristotelian virtue ethics. These truths concern the exploitative nature of the capitalist system, the commodification of labour, and the insight that capital movement has nothing to do with human needs (MacIntyre 2011b: 315). While retaining Marxist critique, he still rejects Marxist political project. It is important that, in his later work, MacIntyre provides a somewhat more progressive picture of anti-capitalist struggle by stressing the importance of conflict between various communities and forces of state and capital. In *Ethics in the Conflicts of Modernity*, MacIntyre returns to fishing communities, giving an example of fishing cooperatives in Denmark that struggle to sustain communal fishing in the face of the European Union policies that promote competition among independent fishers. MacIntyre's second example refers to struggles in the slums of Brazil to secure basic necessities like sanitation, sewage, education, healthcare, and so forth (MacIntyre 2016: 179–80). Important as they are, these struggles remain merely survival strategies against the destruction brought on by neoliberal capitalism. MacIntyre is still reluctant to place the struggle of those who work in capitalist enterprises at the very centre of his theory, focusing instead on the margins, cracks in the capitalist world where some sort of communal life still survives. Such communities, standing firm against capital and state, sustain various practices through which virtues are developed and practised.

MacIntyre's focus on the social relations that can make work worthwhile and fulfilling is, of course, important. But, I would suggest, he fails to fully recognize several important aspects. MacIntyre's emphasis on virtues of work in well-organized communities falls short of questioning more radically the nature of work and relations of production. Much of work can be and actually is inimical to human flourishing, debilitating and dangerous to one's health. And it remains so, even if we accept that it contributes to the good of the community. Second, discussion of technology is absent in MacIntyre's account of virtue and work. Technological change diminishes the necessary expenditure of human energy for various forms of productive work. Technology can make work less fatiguing and more productive. MacIntyre also fails to acknowledge that freedom from at least certain types of work is as important for human flourishing as work that is well-organized and purposeful. Freedom from work and access to leisure were central in Aristotle's reasoning about human flourishing, but MacIntyre seems to pay little attention to this issue. Aristotle's arguments against the inclusion of workers into his ideal citizenry were prejudiced, as MacIntyre points out, but there is a certain rationale to Aristotle's suspicion that necessities of production put important limits on human well-being.

Exclusive focus on virtuous communal work undermines the relevance of MacIntyre's virtue theory in significant ways. There remains the issue that most of us, citizens of contemporary capitalist societies, work neither in family farms, fishing communities or other forms of small-scale communal enterprise. Nor is it a very attractive, let alone feasible, perspective to return to small communal production as against the productive capabilities of big enterprises. Small communal production advocated by MacIntyre could hardly survive in the global market dominated by big producers and, in reality, would require much greater inputs of work to compete with them. Foxconn produces smart-phones and other gadgets on which our daily life depends in huge factory-cities with hundred thousand-strong armies of workers. It is difficult to see how MacIntyre's approach would apply in such a context. By focusing on communal resistance rather than state politics and organized labour struggles, MacIntyre is advocating a losing battle. Having these limitations in mind, I propose to turn to Marx's critique of capitalism, which retains a more optimistic approach to possibilities of freedom and well-being provided by capitalism and gives us a different interpretation of the relation between work and human flourishing.

Freedom and labour in Marx

Marx did not consider himself an Aristotelian, although he knew his Aristotle well. He attributed the distinction between use-value and exchange-value, on which his entire argument in *Capital* rests, to Aristotle. Although Marx's dismissal of moral philosophers is well documented, his own critique of capitalism is, of course, grounded in certain ethical ideals. Marx's theory retains, as I now will proceed to show, a tension between work and well-being, so characteristic of Aristotle, but reconceptualizes it from a revolutionary perspective.

Marx breaks the long tradition of equating 'being human' with 'using reason' that was central to Aristotle and, arguably, one of the sources of his prejudice against those who work for a living. Marx insists that production is a better description of 'characteristic human activity': we use tools, produce, interact with our environment and through this interaction form and reform our own conditions of existence. Such a point of departure does not in any way diminish or ignore the powers of reasoning, but avoids placing reason and labour in strict opposition. This puts labour at the very core of Marx's theory. Although Marx focuses on workers, he agrees with Aristotle that humans can truly flourish only when they are free from material necessities; as he states in *Economic and Philosophic Manuscripts of 1844*, animals 'produce only when immediate physical need compels them to do so, while man produces even when he is free from physical need and truly produces only in freedom from such need' (Marx 1992b: 329). Production here is a very broad category that includes all kinds of activity, be it physical work, intellectual labour or artistic creation.

Marx understands the historical and social importance of various kinds of work, its centrality for human well-being, but at the same time remains radically critical of how work is transformed under capitalism. It is not work itself that is inimical to human excellence, but the relations of production under capitalism that turn it into an alien and negative force. This is the central thesis of Marx's early theory of alienation. Under wage labour, when work is externalized and commodified, human beings do not engage in various activities in order to realize their powers and capabilities, but they sell their work in order to live; the worker 'does not confirm himself in his work, but denies himself' (Marx 1992b: 326). Forced to compete in the marketplace, people see each other only instrumentally, which destroys the bonds of shared humanity. Alienated labour, argues Marx, makes human life miserable. In this sense, work under capitalism is, for Marx, indeed *banauson*.

On the other hand, by turning his attention not to those who are free from work, as Aristotle did, but to those who work and struggle against capitalist exploitation, Marx discovers a possibility of humanist ethics. In *Philosophical and Economic Manuscripts*, *The Poverty of Theory* and other writings, we encounter outstanding passages about the dignity of workers in struggle. Embracing the Enlightenment's ideals of freedom and equality, Marx's political vision is that of liberating those who work from alienating and oppressive relations. Marx thus paints a complex picture where, on the one hand, capitalist exploitation turns work into a negative force, but on the other, struggle against exploitation can inspire visions of a better world and new ethics and politics. The shared struggle shapes a specific consciousness that breaks with the alienating character of capitalist social relations. Of course, this is not a spontaneous development, but required political organization of the workers and collective education into the nature of capitalist system and possible alternatives. Using the Aristotelian vocabulary, one can say that through this shared struggle moral and intellectual virtues are developed. Class consciousness is, for Marx, a foundation for a different society.

A firm believer in progress, Marx looks forwards without romanticizing pre-capitalist forms of community. Even if pre-capitalist producers were more in control of their work, even if they sustained relations conducive to the common good and community, even if their work was somehow more virtuous and dignified, capitalism and its technological possibilities had already made an entrance on the world stage.

Technological innovation under capitalism advances in historically unprecedented pace. Labour, organized under the control of capital, grows more and more productive; machines take over much of the tasks that previously required significant expenditures of human energy; less and less labour time is needed for social reproduction. Any theory of the possibilities for human flourishing in the contemporary world must rest on this new basis.

The central contradiction of capitalist economy for Marx is that the enormous potential for freedom (first of all, from work) is undermined by the predominant relations of production. Private ownership of the means of production results in chaotic production divorced from human needs and in enormous expansion of inequality under which a minority can live in unimaginable luxury while the rest are forced to spend most of their time working. But Marx's call is not to reject capitalism, but to take over the control of the forces of production and employ them for the improvement of humanity. In his view, the most important political demand is the democratization of production and the shortening of the working day. In the well-known passage from Volume 3 of *Capital*, Marx deals with an issue of freedom, human flourishing and material necessities. Here again, he invokes the same ethical ideal of freedom expounded in his early works: 'In fact, the realm of freedom actually begins only where labour which is determined by necessity and mundane considerations ceases' (Marx 1992a: 959). But freedom can be extended to the realm of necessity by democratizing production and correspondingly reducing the time and energy needed to produce the necessary goods:

> Freedom in this field [i.e. the realm of necessity] can only consist in socialised man, the associated producers, rationally regulating their interchange with Nature, bringing it under their common control, instead of being ruled by it as by the blind forces of Nature; and achieving this with the least expenditure of energy and under conditions most favourable to, and worthy of, their human nature. But it nonetheless still remains a realm of necessity. Beyond it begins that development of human energy which is an end in itself, the true realm of freedom, which, however, can blossom forth only with this realm of necessity as its basis. The shortening of the working day is its basic prerequisite. (ibid.)

With the shortening of the working day, people are left with more time to pursue other activities and develop their powers and capabilities, be they rational, artistic or something else. Marx invokes the same arguments that Aristotle uses to exclude workers from the best *polis* – and radicalizes them. So leisure is a necessary prerequisite, and the development of the forces of production, democratized relations of productions and the shortening of the working day offer the possibility of leisure on the basis of universal freedom and equality. Marx's early (and sometimes ridiculed) formulation of communism as a society that 'makes it possible for me to do one thing today and another tomorrow, to hunt in the morning, fish in the afternoon, rear cattle in the evening, criticise after dinner, just as I have a mind, without ever becoming hunter, fisherman, shepherd or critic' (Marx and Engels 1998: 53) recalls Aristotle's speculations about the possibility of democratic redistribution of tasks quoted in the first part of this chapter, the difference being that Marx takes it seriously as an achievable political ideal. Marx agrees with Aristotle that people flourish most fully when they engage in activities that allow them to express their human potential, and that such activities are most conducive to human flourishing when they are done for their own sake and not out of material necessity.

In Aristotle's view, political life was one of the best forms of life a human being can lead. Marx remains faithful to this ideal and again radicalizes it. Thus a self-governing political community is at the centre of Marx's political thought. Radical expansion of democracy means not only that production must be brought under collective democratic control but also that state functions must be thoroughly democratized. Marx explores this in his writings on the Paris Commune where he proposes that radical democratization of society, as experimented with by the Communards, is the political form that allows labour to be emancipated. Terry Eagleton comments, correctly, on this connection between the shortening of the working day and self-government: 'As Marx insists, socialism also requires a shortening of the working day – partly to provide men and women with the leisure for personal fulfilment, partly to create time for the business of political and economic self-government' (Eagleton 2011: 18). Collective political rule requires freedom from work, as Aristotle insisted. For Aristotle, this freedom should be absolute and those who rule must never work. For Marx, it does not have to be so, as the realm of production can itself be democratized, so that the same collective rule is extended in both realms. Marx's utopia is founded by workers, but one of the political tasks for these workers is to use the productive capabilities of modern industry to reduce necessary labour time to the minimum, thus coming closer and closer to the ideal of freedom from work.

Conclusion

Aristotle's arguments against citizenship for workers were partly based on his class prejudices, as revealed by his language, but they also contained a valid intuition that material necessities put important limits on human flourishing. Taken absolutely, the best possible life humans can lead is life without material considerations. The only realistic possibility that Aristotle saw for anyone to lead such a life was to construct a highly exclusive society where a small minority would be free from work to pursue human excellence. It is not surprising then that modern Aristotelians, like MacIntyre, are uneasy with this aspect of Aristotle's theory. MacIntyre proposes an Aristotelianism without Aristotle's view that human flourishing requires freedom from labour. Such Aristotelianism is grounded in a different conception of the *polis*: a community where everyone co-operates and contributes to the common good and the good life that this community sustains. To a significant degree, it is a community of work inspired by pre-capitalist forms of communal life. In this chapter, I have argued that Aristotle's views can be taken in another direction. Marx, who never thought of himself as an Aristotelian, points in a different political direction: a revolutionary radicalization of the argument that humans flourish when their actions are not guided by material considerations. The possibility for realizing such an ideal rests on the development of the forces of production and on workers' struggle to bring these forces under collective control in order to realize a utopia of freedom and equality. The choice is then between a more conservative approach of MacIntyre and a revolutionary utopianism of Marx.

Note

1 Although not all English translations stress the negative connotation. For example, Reeve always keeps 'vulgar' in his translation, while the Oxford edition of Aristotle's works is more neutral and, for example, renders *bios banausos* in 1278a20 as 'a life of manual toil'.

References

Aristotle (1998), *Politics*, trans. C. D. C. Reeve, Indianapolis, Cambridge: Hackett Publishing Company.
Aristotle (2009), *The Nicomachean Ethics*, trans. David Ross, Oxford: Oxford University Press.
Eagleton, T. (2011), *Why Marx Was Right*, London: Yale University Press.
Kraut, R. (2002), *Aristotle: Political Philosophy*, New York: Oxford University Press.
MacIntyre, A. (1988), *Whose Justice? Which Rationality?* Notre Dame: University of Notre Dame Press.
MacIntyre, A. (1994), 'A Partial Response to My Critics', in J. Horton and S. Mendus (eds), *After MacIntyre: Critical Perspectives on the Work of Alasdair MacIntyre*, Cambridge: Polity.
MacIntyre, A. (1998a), 'The Theses on Feuerbach: A Road Not Taken', in K. Knight (ed), *The MacIntyre Reader*, Notre Dame: University of Notre Dame Press.
MacIntyre, A. (1998b), 'Politics, Philosophy and the Common Good', in K. Knight (ed), *The MacIntyre Reader*, Notre Dame: University of Notre Dame Press.
MacIntyre, A. (1999), *Dependent Rational Animals: Why Human Beings Need Virtues*, Chicago and La Salle: Open Court.
MacIntyre, A. (2007), *After Virtue: A Study in Moral Theory*, 3rd edn, Notre Dame: University of Notre Dame Press.
MacIntyre, A. (2008), 'What More Needs to Be Said? A Beginning, Although Only a Beginning, at Saying It', in K. Knight and P. Blackledge (eds), *Revolutionary Aristotelianism: Ethics, Resistance and Utopia*, Stuttgart: Lucius & Lucius.
MacIntyre, A. (2011a), 'How Aristotelianism Can Become Revolutionary: Ethics, Resistance, and Utopia', in P. Blackledge and K. Knight (eds), *Virtue and Politics: Alasdair MacIntyre's Revolutionary Aristotelianism*, Notre Dame: University of Notre Dame Press.
MacIntyre, A. (2011b), 'Where We Were, Where We Are, Where We Need To Be', in P. Blackledge and K. Knight (eds), *Virtue and Politics: Alasdair MacIntyre's Revolutionary Aristotelianism*, Notre Dame: University of Notre Dame Press.

MacIntyre, A. (2016), *Ethics in the Conflicts of Modernity: An Essay on Desire, Practical Reasoning, and Narrative*, Cambridge: Cambridge University Press.
Marx, K. (1992a), *Capital: A Critique of Political Economy, Volume 3*, London: Penguin Books.
Marx, K. (1992b), 'Economic and Philosophic Manuscripts', in K. Marx, Early Writings, London: Penguin Books.
Marx, K. and F. Engels (1998), *The German Ideology*, Amherst: Prometheus Books.
Nederman, Cary J. (2008), 'Men at Work: *Poesis*, Politics and Labor in Aristotle and Some Aristotelians', in K. Knight and P. Blackledge (eds), *Revolutionary Aristotelianism: Ethics, Resistance and Utopia*, Stuttgart: Lucius & Lucius.
Thompson, E. P. (1991), *The Making of the English Working Class*, London: Penguin Books.

14

Alasdair MacIntyre's Aristotelianism

A Marxist critique

Paul Blackledge

Introduction

In two interesting engagements with Alasdair MacIntyre's mature ethics, Janet Coleman and David Miller have independently suggested that MacIntyre's Thomism does not cohere with his sociology of virtues. Coleman claims that whereas Thomas, like Aristotle before him, held to a transhistorical and universal conception of the good, MacIntyre's model of social practices points in the direction of a historically relativist ethics (Coleman 1994: 66). Relatedly, Miller submits that MacIntyre's embrace of Thomism in *Whose Justice? Which Rationality?* marks a retreat from the Neo-Aristotelian sociology of practices outlined in *After Virtue* (Miller 1994: 246). Clearly there is some truth to these charges. Indeed, so pronounced are the historically relativist implications of the sociological conception of practices outlined in *After Virtue* that, far from implying natural law theory, they form the rational core of the oft-repeated claim that MacIntyre is a communitarian thinker (Pettit 1994). Conversely, in *Dependent Rational Animals* MacIntyre explicitly embraced a naturalistic and seemingly universalistic account of the good that acts as a counterbalance to the implied relativism of his sociology, while simultaneously making it more consistent with a Thomistic conception of natural law (MacIntyre 1999: 78). Not that MacIntyre ever accepted either Miller's or Coleman's interpretation of his work. In a twofold response to Coleman's 1994 essay, he suggested, first, that he was in broad agreement with what she had written on Aristotle's and Aquinas's thought, and second, that his sociological claims were intended to illuminate those mechanisms through which these universal truths might be discovered and subsequently defended against competing traditions of enquiry. Certainly, he believed his sociology of virtues to be consistent with his Aristotelian Thomism:

> Both Aristotle and Aquinas recognize a distinction between those timeless truths about natural kinds, essential properties and the teleological ordering of things and persons in terms of which all true and justified explanations and understanding has to be framed, and the varyingly adequate attempts to formulate those truths which marked the history of enquiry. (MacIntyre 1994: 300)

The broadly critical realist understanding of the history of ethics suggested in this passage has the appeal of registering both continuity and change in human history (Turner 2003). Nevertheless, as formulated earlier, MacIntyre's approach to the history of ethics indicates a very simplistic model of this dialectic as a transitive history of ideas (and practices) above an intransitive human nature. This way of conceiving human history is not without merit. Against old fashioned biological racists on the one hand and contemporary postmodernist anti-essentialists on the other, MacIntyre is surely right to highlight a number of transhistorical needs and capacities that unite humans across the globe and through history as a species of an essentially similar genetic natural kind.

However, the fact that our human needs and capacities have evolved and have always been realized in specific cultural contexts arguably implies a much deeper conception of the transitive dimension of human history than is consistent with MacIntyre's response to Coleman. For while we may agree that all humans have certain basic needs, the multifarious contexts through which these needs have been met through history and the evolving capabilities through which humans have striven to meet them and in striving to meet them have developed new needs and capacities over time problematize any attempt to locate 'timeless truths' about humans as a natural kind. Indeed, the wide variety of communities in which humans have lived suggest that the concept of a 'timeless truth' either tends towards banality or, more insidiously, towards one or other form of apology for oppression – as, for instance, in Larry Arnhart's comments on women's oppression in a text approvingly cited by MacIntyre (Arnhart 1998: 139; MacIntyre 1999: 12, 125; cf. Blackledge 2018). The rational core of postmodern and postcolonial theory can be located in their resistance to the reactionary and oppressive implications of approaches that essentialize and then attempt to impose on Others particular ways of meeting our needs. If postmodernists have famously failed to realize the progressive implications of their critical frameworks, they have at least succeeded in exposing the untenability of the static essentialisms in the work of others. Interestingly, MacIntyre prefigured the negative success of postmodern theory at the conclusion of his journey through the Marxist left in the late 1960s: each existing morality was undermined, or so he had come to believe, by more or less obvious limitations with the model of human nature it assumed. As he wrote in the preface to the second edition of *A Short History of Ethics*:

> These philosophical attempts to present rationally justifiable universal claims to moral allegiance, claims upon human beings as such, claims about human nature as such, in the local and particular terms which each culture provides for its moral philosophers as their starting-point, had generated for each major moral philosophy its own particular difficulties and problems, difficulties and problems sometimes acknowledged and sometimes not. The subsequent history of each such moral philosophy revealed the extent to which each possessed or lacked the resources necessary to become aware of and to resolve those difficulties and problems – each by its own particular standards. And by *this* standard the major claimants in modern moral philosophy seemed to me then and seem to me now to fail. (MacIntyre 1998a: x)

Nonetheless, when he wrote *A Short History of Ethics*, MacIntyre was still, nominally at least, a Marxist. More to the point, for the Marxist account of human nature and morality to fail, it had to fail for different, if related, reasons to the reasons for the failures of competing liberal moralities. Concretely, liberal conceptions of morality, be they broadly deontological, utilitarian or whatever, fail for reasons related to their inability to understand the historicity of their own presumptions. These models of human nature tend to naturalize, in more or less sophisticated forms, modern capitalist social relations. If Bentham articulated one of the crudest variants of this failing – in Marx's words, 'with the dryest naïveté he assumes that the modern petty bourgeois, especially the English petty bourgeois, is the normal man' (Marx 1976: 759) – as MacIntyre suggested in a review of Rawls' *A Theory of Justice*, all forms of liberalism tend to share this general failing (MacIntyre 1972: 332–3). This failing is important because by transposing into the distant past the latest manifestation of human nature, modern (liberal) moral theory tends effectively to naturalize the modern capitalist context within which both it and egoistic individualism emerged (Ramsay 1997: 7–8, 12, 32–7). Milton Fisk argues that it is difficult to overstate the importance of this critique of liberalism. For, in satisfying personal rather than social interests, the capitalist market is a mechanism that forces actors to relate 'in a way that ignores any social links they may have'. Markets therefore tend to obscure the social aspect of human nature, and this limitation is carried over into liberalism's 'impoverished' model of human nature. One consequence of this facet of liberalism is that when liberals confront concrete ethical issues, they tend to explain these conflicts superficially in terms of personal interests and values without enquiring as to the social roots of these preferences and values. More generally, it is liberalism's impoverished theory of human nature that underpins the substantive relativism of contemporary moral discourse. By pointing to the social basis of liberalism, Fisk argues, Marx points beyond the seemingly intractable character of debates such as these within contemporary political philosophy (Fisk 1989: 275–88).

Long after his break with the revolutionary left, MacIntyre continued to argue that Marxism did not share liberalism's impoverished theory of human nature. Indeed, he famously argued that Marxism 'is the only secular post enlightenment doctrine to have' a 'metaphysical and moral scope' comparable to that of Christianity (MacIntyre 1995: vi). Marxism's failings sprang from quite different roots. Whereas Marx had been right, according to MacIntyre, to suggest that the ethical challenges posed by modernity could be overcome only on the basis of social practices rather than abstract moralities, he had misconstrued the potential agency of revolutionary change: workers' struggles so far from creating immanent tendencies to overcome the moral antinomies of modernity, had actually proved themselves to be trapped within these antinomies.

In his 1959 contribution to the British New Left's debate on socialist humanism, 'Notes from the Moral Wilderness', MacIntyre outlined a historical humanist Marxist ethics (Blackledge 2005; 2007a). He suggested that the concrete form taken by the universal human essence of freedom is always mediated by our practical engagement with nature to meet our needs. It is because this practice has a historical dimension that our essence tends to develop in a dialectical relationship with changes in both our needs and the productivity of labour. And as labour is a purposeful activity, these changes are registered through our ordering of changing desires. Labour, therefore, necessarily has an ethical dimension, and because it acts as the key medium linking the universal and the specific in human history, it provides a powerful basis from which to criticize both abstract universalist and simple historicist ethics. What universal moralities, which are abstracted from the concrete historical form of production, and historicist moralities, which are abstracted from the universal human essence, have in common is an inadequate, one-sided, model of human history. This characteristic of these theories undermines their competing claims to guide human practice. Neither abstract universalism nor historical relativism is able to provide a satisfactory account of practice as human behaviour, and consequently both fail as accounts of ethical life. It follows from this claim, that we should look for an ethical 'theory which treats what emerges in history as providing us with a basis for our standards, without making the historical process morally sovereign or its progress automatic' (MacIntyre 2008a: 57). To this end, MacIntyre claimed that Marxists should follow Aristotle specifically, and the Greeks more generally, in linking ethics to human desires: 'We make both individual deeds and social practices intelligible as human actions by showing how they connect with characteristically human desires, needs and the like' (MacIntyre 2008a: 58). He thus proposed to relate morality to needs and desires in a way that was radically at odds with Kant. For whereas, in Kant, 'the "ought" of morality is utterly divorced from the "is" of desire', MacIntyre insisted that to divorce ethics from activities which aim to satisfy needs and desires in this way 'is to make it unintelligible as a form of human action' (MacIntyre 2008a: 58). MacIntyre therefore sought to relate morality to human desires and needs in a way that radically historicized human nature without losing sight of its biological basis (MacIntyre 2008a: 63). The power of Marx's theory of history, or so he claimed, was rooted in his historicization of the human essence: for he refused to follow either Hobbes into a melancholic model of human needs and desires or Diderot into a utopian counter-position of the state of nature against contemporary social structures. Instead, Marx comprehended the limited historical truth of Hobbes's insight, but juxtaposed to it, not an abstract utopia, but the real collective movement of workers in struggle through which they realize that solidarity is a fundamental human desire. Marx, according to MacIntyre, understood both the deep historical and sociological content to this question when he suggested that 'the emergence of human nature is something to be comprehended only in terms of the history of class-struggle. Each age reveals a development of human potentiality which is specific to that form of social life and which is specifically limited by the class-structure of that society.' In particular, under advanced capitalism 'the growth of production makes it possible [for humans] to reappropriate [their] own nature'. This is true in two ways: first, the increasing productivity of labour produces the potential for us all to lead much richer lives, both morally and materially; and second, capitalism creates an agency – the proletariat – whose struggles for freedom begin to embody a new democratic spirit, through which individuals come to understand both that their needs and desires can best be satisfied through collective channels, and that they do in fact need and desire solidarity (MacIntyre 2008a: 64). Consequently, the proletariat, created objectively by the development of the forces of production, could begin in its struggles against capital, to match the potential inherent in its objective structure to create the conditions for the solution of the contemporary problems of morality: it begins to embody the practice which could overcome the 'rift between our conception of morality and our conception of desire' (MacIntyre 2008a, p. 63). By acting in this way, members of the proletariat come to realize that solidarity is not simply a useful means through which they struggle to meet their needs, but is in fact what they naturally desire (MacIntyre 2008a, 66). The political practice of socialists, who aim in the first instance to win majorities over to their view, is rooted in these new needs and desires. MacIntyre therefore understood the history of morality to be 'the history of men ceasing to see moral rules as the repression of desire and as something that men have made and accepted for themselves'. This process culminates in the socialist struggles of the proletariat against its alienation, and against reified ways of perceiving the world. Conversely, 'both the autonomy of ethics and utilitarianism are aspects of the consciousness of capitalism; both are forms of alienation rather than moral guides' (MacIntyre 2008a: 68). So, once the political left has rid itself of both the myth of the inevitable triumph of socialism and of the reification of socialism as some indefinite end that justifies any action taken in its name, then socialists will truly comprehend the interpenetration of means and ends through the history of class struggle, and will understand Marxist morality to be, as against the Stalinists, 'an assertion of moral absolutes' and 'as against the liberal critic of Stalinism it is an assertion of desire and history' (MacIntyre 2008a: 66).

In his most developed self-critique of this argument, 'The *Theses on Feuerbach*: A Road not Taken', MacIntyre argues that though workers may have embodied in their practice a revolutionary ethics of emancipation at certain moments in history, the process of proletarianization has confounded Marx's revolutionary hopes for the working class by simultaneously making resistance a necessary part of their lives while robbing it of its emancipatory potential. Proletarianization, contra Marx, 'tends to deprive workers of those forms of practice through which they can discover conceptions of a good and of virtues adequate to the moral needs of resistance' (MacIntyre 1998b: 232; Blackledge 2014a). It is this social fact that has led even the best of contemporary Marxisms to degenerate into one or other form of otherworldly utopianism. This development informed two distinct tendencies within Marxism. By creating an unbridgeable gulf between the real working class and the abstract idealized image of this class as it exists within Marxist theory, the 'moral impoverishment' of the working class has meant that Marxist theory tends to produce its 'own versions of the *Ubermensch*: Lukács's ideal proletarian, Leninism's ideal revolutionary' (MacIntyre 2007: 262). Conversely, even when led by well-meaning individuals, when nominally Marxist parties win or seriously challenge for power, they tend to reproduce all the failings of mainstream capitalist parties because they are not rooted in a politically conscious revolutionary class: 'As Marxists organize and move toward power they always do and have become Weberians in substance, even if they remain Marxists in rhetoric' (MacIntyre 2007: 109).

So, whereas liberalism embeds alienation in its constituent assumptions about human nature, Marxism through its attachment to the working class fails to extricate itself from alienated social relations. As early as 1962, MacIntyre wrote that in conditions of 'continually expanding investment and continually expanding consumption', the struggles of the working class, or at least part of it, had been 'institutionalised' (MacIntyre 2008b: 212). And though developments since the 1970s have tended to dash the idea of continually expanding investment and consumption, MacIntyre remains convinced that workers' struggles as such cannot offer a systematic ethical alternative to capitalism (Blackledge 2007b; 2008).

As is quietly suggested in the preface to the original edition of *After Virtue*, MacIntyre's mature ethics builds upon, and as he would portray it, critically deepens insights associated the interpretation of Marxism he articulated as an activist within the British New Left of the late 1950s (MacIntyre 2007: xvii–xviii). The key shift in his thought since the late 1950s stems from his rejection of his earlier Marxist claim that the anti-capitalist and socialist struggles of the working class could act as a potential practical foundation for a historically universal solution to the crisis of modern moral theory. By contrast with this claim, in what Kelvin Knight calls his mature 'post-Marxist' writings, MacIntyre has come to believe that working-class struggles, and with them Marxism as the, at its best, theoretical expression of these struggles, have become both practical and theoretical manifestations of this crisis. In effect, MacIntyre argues that while Marx had been right to recognize alienation as a defining characteristic of capitalism that precludes the formation of a practical conception of the common good, he erred in supposing that working-class struggles might systematically act as a practical alternative to this situation. In Knight's gloss on this argument, he claims that because 'Marx's sociology of capitalism was premised on the categories of labour and capital', far from being revolutionary, it remained trapped within the alienated standpoint of political economy (Knight 1999: 86). Whereas Marx, in his *Theses on Feuerbach*, had imagined himself to be authoring a 'new materialism' that transcended the limitations of liberalism's twin materialist and idealist faces, because the working class – labour in this diptych – was constituted through alienated relations, it proved itself incapable of performing the world-historic task Marx had asked of it. As MacIntyre put it in an important passage from *After Virtue*:

> One of the key moments in the creation of modernity occurs when production moves outside the household. So long as productive work occurs within the structure of households, it is easy and right to understand that work as part of the sustaining of the community of the household and of those wider forms of community which the household in turn sustains. As, and to the extent that, work moves outside the household and is put to the service of impersonal capital, the realm of work tends to become separated from everything but the service of biological survival and the reproduction of the labor force, on the one hand, and that of institutionalized acquisitiveness, on the other. Pleonexia, a vice in the Aristotelian scheme, is now the driving force of modem productive work. The means-end relationships embodied for the most part in such work – on a production line, for example – are necessarily external to the goods which those who work seek; such work too has consequently been expelled from the realm of practices with goods internal to themselves. (MacIntyre 2007: 227)

So, because modern capitalist labour is alienated labour, it cannot constitute an adequate standpoint for the critique of modern social relations. MacIntyre's subsequent articulation of a Neo-Aristotelian model of practices is best understood against this backdrop. In his mature thought, practices, by acting as the partial foundation for an ethical resistance to capitalist alienation, do at least some of the work that working-class struggles does in the Marxist schema.

MacIntyre famously defines practices as any

> coherent and complex form of socially established cooperative human activity through which goods internal to that form of activity are realized in the course of trying to achieve those standards of excellence which are appropriate to, and partially definitive of, that form of activity, with the result that human powers to achieve excellence, and human conceptions of the ends and goods involved, are systematically extended. (MacIntyre 2007: 187)

His hope has been that this conceptualization of social practices would help underpin a politics of self-defence against capitalist alienation: 'What is most urgently needed is a politics of self-defence for all those local societies that aspire to achieve some relatively self-sufficient and independent form of participatory practice-based community and that therefore need to protect themselves from the corrosive effects of capitalism and the depredations of the state' (MacIntyre 1995: xxvi; cf 1999: 129–46). It is in light of this claim that we can understand the power of Kelvin Knight's claim that MacIntyre's mature ethics is a form of 'revolutionary Aristotelianism' (Knight 2007: 224). However, it is somewhat idiosyncratic at best to describe as revolutionary a perspective that sees hope only for resistance (Blackledge 2009: 869). Indeed, while MacIntyre explicitly endorses Knight's characterization of his politics, he also writes that

> not only have I never offered remedies for the condition of liberal modernity, it has been part of my case that there are no remedies. The problem is not to reform the dominant order, but to find ways for local communities to survive by sustaining a life of the common good against the disintegrating forces of the nation-state and the market. (MacIntyre 1998c: 235)

Revolutionary or not, the power of MacIntyre's alternative to Marxism is somewhat mitigated by *After Virtue*'s one-sidedly sociological formulation of the good. Conceived thus, there was nothing in his original articulation of his mature ethics that disallowed the existence of 'evil' practices: the courage, for instance, of Nazi soldiers during the Second World War could be understood as a virtue despite the obviously evil aims of their actions (MacIntyre 2007: 180).

Clearly, to recognize the existence of evil practices implies a thoroughgoing moral relativism that tends to undermine MacIntyre's search for a sociological account of virtuous resistance to capitalist alienation. Equally clearly, any consistent solution to the problem of moral relativism generally, and evil practices more specifically, must include some conception of human nature as a standpoint for the critique of 'courageous Nazis' and the like. In *After Virtue*, MacIntyre seemed to conflate his rejection of 'Aristotle's metaphysical biology', which as a pre-Darwinian theory was plainly inadequate as a standpoint for such a critique, with a rejection of naturalism more generally because, as he wrote, any view of the virtues which sees them as fostering human flourishing must of necessity come into conflict with the reality that human history is characterized in part by 'deep conflicts over what human flourishing and well-being do consist in and the way in which rival and incompatible beliefs on that topic beget rival and incompatible tables of the virtues' (MacIntyre 2007: 148; 162; 196). Though this argument recalls the critique of regulative appeals to the concept of human nature found in *A Short History of Ethics*, MacIntyre was subsequently to claim that though he had not given 'an account of human nature in *After Virtue*, ... his account of teleology clearly presupposes that human beings, regardless of differences, share a common identity, a species-specific notion of flourishing, and a common teleological goal' (MacIntyre quoted in Lutz 2004: 134). And in the prologue to the third edition of *After Virtue*, he wrote that though he had been right to reject Aristotle's metaphysical biology, reading Aquinas had taught him that his sociological account of the reproduction of the virtues 'was bound to be inadequate until I had provided it with a metaphysical grounding' (MacIntyre 2007: xi). More concretely, in *Dependent Rational Animals* MacIntyre wrote:

> I now judge that I was in error in supposing an ethics independent of biology to be possible ... and this for two distinct, but related reasons. The first is that no account of the goods, rules and virtues that are definitive of our moral life can be adequate that does not explain – or at least point us towards an explanation-how that form of life is possible for beings who are biologically constituted as we are, by providing us with an account of our development towards and into that form of life. That development has as its starting point our initial animal condition. Secondly, a failure to understand that condition and the light thrown upon it by a comparison between humans and members of other intelligent animal species will obscure crucial features of that development. One such failure, of immense importance on its own account, is the nature and extent of human vulnerability and disability. And by not reckoning adequately with this central feature of human life I had necessarily failed to notice some other important aspects of the part that the virtues play in human life. (MacIntyre 1999: x)

According to Chris Lutz, MacIntyre's embrace of Aquinas marks the culmination of the process through which he solved the 'epistemological crisis' he had experienced from the late 1950s until the late 1970s (Lutz 2004: 21). After decades characterized by his inability to escape the parameters of moral relativism, by the late 1970s, MacIntyre had come to recognize that 'only a teleological ethical theory can serve to ground objective, exceptionless moral obligation, and that only the life of the culture and society as a whole can provide the *telos* for such an account' (Lutz 2004: 27). If MacIntyre's essay 'Can Medicine Dispense with a Theological Perspective on Human Nature' signalled his movement in this direction, *After Virtue* marked a decisive step in the process that culminated with MacIntyre's idiosyncratically brief embrace of Aquinas's conception of the unity of the virtues – 'I now, for example, think that my earlier criticism of Aquinas' thesis on the unity of the virtues was simply mistaken' – in *Whose Justice? Which Rationality?* and his deepening of this embrace through his comments on the natural law: 'The precepts of the natural law are those precepts promulgated by God through reason without conformity to which human beings cannot achieve their common good' (MacIntyre 1988: x; Lutz 2004: 74; MacIntyre 1999: 111).

However, while MacIntyre is right to claim that the problem of moral relativism and evil practices can only be overcome by reference to some conception of human nature, there is a very real problem imagining that Aquinas's understanding of natural law is adequate to this task.

In his 1953 study, *Marxism: An Interpretation*, MacIntyre wrote that, in Marx's critique, the 'essential mark of religion' was its 'otherworldliness' that 'places afar off the salvation that socialism brings near'. By contrast with this critique, he argued that 'the religion which is untouched by the Marxist critique is that which proclaims not the justification of every social order, but the inadequacy of every social order' (MacIntyre 1953: 80–3). MacIntyre's mature Thomism is, like the interpretation of religion he defended in 1953, a fundamentally critical doctrine; the content of which is less indebted to the fideism he once claimed set faith apart from philosophy and considerably more aligned to an interpretation of Thomism as a practically embodied tradition of opposition to capitalist and statist transgressions of natural law. According to MacIntyre, Aristotle's fundamental contribution to ethical theory is rooted in his articulation of the questions rational agents are compelled to confront as they seek to live their lives in the best possible way: 'What is my good qua member of a household, qua citizen, qua human being? What qualities of mind and character do I need to identify and order these goods correctly in my everyday practice so that I may function well as a human being?' (MacIntyre 2016: 86). Aquinas added to this approach a concern for the way 'plain persons' might through the precepts of natural law 'question the actions of those with authority and power' (MacIntyre 2016: 89).

Unfortunately, the rise of modernity has seen this conception of ethics very much on the defensive. In particular, modern (liberal) moral theorists have 'no place within their conceptual scheme for such Aristotelian and Thomistic notions as those of an end, a common good, or the natural law' (MacIntyre 2016: 98). In order to make sense of this turn of events he argues that Neo-Aristotelians need to learn from Marx how, through his conception of surplus value as the essence of the capitalist mode of production, 'individuals must think of themselves and of their social relationships, if they are to act as capitalism requires them to act' and of this explains 'why in capitalist societies individuals systematically misunderstand themselves and their social relationships' (MacIntyre 2016: 96). Thus, contemporary Aristotelians should read Marx to help explain why the common sense of plain persons is not that common in the modern world.

This is a powerful point, and is well made. But MacIntyre seems oblivious to its full implications. It is not simply that the rise of capitalism leads to the masking of our common goods, it is also that any modern 'Thomistic' account of the common good can only exist as an abstract shadow of a former, and long since passed, way of life. Lucien Goldmann has shown how the rise of capitalism, by fostering the rationalization (alienation) of social life, went hand-in-hand with the emergence of a bourgeois class whose life experiences became 'fundamentally irreligious'. This is not to say that this class was atheistic; far from it. Rather, religion became for the vast majority of its members an increasingly unimportant part of their lives (Goldmann 1968: 63). The development of an ever-more rationalistic and irreligious class meant not only the decline of the day-to-day power of the church but also a tension between the secular needs of this class and its nominal religious beliefs. In a context where the papacy had been, throughout the medieval period, not only an incredibly efficient force for the monopolization and centralization of God's grace but also a degenerate means of personal enrichment, it was only a matter of time before reasoned self-interest clashed with papal authority (Morton 1989: 151). This conflict took the form of a challenge to the natural law tradition because natural law, as articulated by Aquinas, had acted to legitimize religious authority over secular powers. For Aquinas, the existence of natural law 'presupposed', according to Ernst Bloch, 'a sinful, no-longer-just Adam'. And whereas *communis possessio* might have existed in the original state, 'Adam's sin justified the church's fall into sin, that is, its fall from the original Christian communism to the rules of the world'. Moreover, natural law criticisms of positive laws rested less on a disinterested conception of the good and more on the fact that the state's authority existed 'under the leadership of the church' (Bloch 1987: 25–6). In this context, the rational critique of the power of 'actually existing Christianity' articulated by representatives of the newly emergent bourgeoisie marked a progressive moment in the struggle for human liberation. Moreover, this process went hand-in-hand with contestation over the meaning of natural law itself: if the Anabaptists effectively developed natural law in the direction of eternal law (that is in the direction of prelapsarian communism), Luther's response to this revolutionary movement saw him interpret natural law in a way that freed the state from the authority of the church so that it could better repress Munster and his sinful comrades. The reactionary tendency within the natural law tradition was subsequently extended by Calvin on the one side and Leo XIII on the other, both of whom went beyond Aquinas to absolutize the reification of private property (Bloch 1987: 29–33; Brady 2008: 63; Curran 2002: 177).

When viewed in this light, Lutz's claim that MacIntyre's embrace of Aquinas's 'metaphysics of creation' solves the problems of relativism and evil practices is simply untenable (Lutz 2004: 123). It amounts to the utopian and reactionary demand that we revoke the second law of thermodynamics and rewind history to a point prior to the emergence of modern capitalist society, and in so doing, his argument merely adds another voice to the contemporary cacophony of incommensurable moral opinion. The simple fact is, as Goldmann writes, 'the "judgement of history" has passed Christianity by' (Goldmann 1968: 82). This is not to say that the further development of capitalism will give rise to increased and eventual triumphant secularization. On the contrary, as Engels wrote in *Anti-Dühring*, it should be expected that alienated relations will continue to provide the fertile ground for the reproduction of religious ideas: 'Religion can continue to exist as the immediate, that is, the sentimental form of men's relation to the alien, natural and social, forces which dominate them, so long as men remain under the control of these forces' (Engels 1987: 301; Blackledge 2019b).

But this type of religion is a modern phenomenon that can never recreate the conditions in which Aquinas's morality could have become a form of common sense for millions of people within a particular community. Does this fact mean that there is no ethical hope for us as creatures of the modern alienated world? Not if we accept the key strength of *After Virtue* that practices exist that underpin the ethical resistance to alienation. If it is also true both that the fundamental flaw of this text lies in its attempt to conceive these forms of resistance independent of biology, and that Aquinas' theorization of natural law is not adequate to the task of articulating the necessary complimentary biology, the problem remains of formulating a theory of human nature adequate to the task of biologically grounding a sociological account of the reproduction of the virtues.

Here it is apt that we return to Coleman's critique of MacIntyre's Thomism. Despite MacIntyre's protestations to the contrary, Coleman did illuminate a real problem regarding the relationship between the sociological and natural law aspects of his work, even if it is not quite the problem she suggests. The key weakness with attempts to ground modern virtue ethics in something like Aquinas' account of natural law is, contra James Daly (Daly 1996), that it entails a static view of the 'timeless truths' of human nature that sits uneasily with the deeply historical character of MacIntyre's sociology. MacIntyre's own answer to her criticisms somewhat sidestepped the issue. At its best, the problem that his work addresses is not primarily that of how the intransitive dimension of the human condition is to be captured in the transitive. Rather, it is of how the transitive nature of lives reflects changes in our very nature. MacIntyre recognized this fact in his Marxist phase, and nothing he has written since undermines this insight. The problem with the concept of essence in Aristotle and Aquinas is not simply that it is pre-Darwinian but also that it is pre-Marxist. And whereas Darwin's proof of the evolutionary (dynamic) unity of all life on earth fatally undermines any attempt to reify the functions of natural kinds, Marx's analysis of the evolutionary (dynamic) nature of the human essence through history similarly undermines any attempt to formulate 'timeless truths' about human nature. Joseph Margolis is wrong to argue that this claim entails a denial of essentialism (Margolis 1992). Rather, Marx is better understood as suggesting a reconstituted essentialism. His essentialism differs from Aristotle's in recognizing essences not as simple unities but rather as 'unities in contradiction' (Meikle 1985: 37). The socio-historical dimension of our essence is well captured by Terry Eagleton, who writes, 'It is not, as the historicists and postmodernists would have it, that the nature of humanity is culture, but that culture or history are of our nature—that there is that in our material nature which allows us to exceed and remake it, so that non-identity, for both good and ill, is thus part of what we are' (Eagleton 1999: 154). Marx expresses this dynamic model of human essence thus: humans are 'natural beings' or 'species being', but they are also '*active* natural beings' and this means that '*human* objects are not natural objects as they immediately present themselves' but rather they are historical beings: 'History is the true natural history of man' (Marx 1975: 389; 391). From this perspective, forms of practice through which conceptions of the common good emerge in the modern world are best understood also to be forms or practice through which our essence emerges from the egoism of the market place towards the socialism of the future.

As I have argued previously, as a Marxist, MacIntyre tended to understand the emergent nature of human essence in an undialectical and unpolitical way (Blackledge 2019a). After initially being too one-sidedly optimistic about the prospects for working-class socialism in the late 1950s, within a decade, he became too one-sidedly pessimistic. While nominally opposites, these two perspectives are best understood as flipsides of the same mistake. Whereas Marx understood that 'alienation has not only a negative but also a positive significance', MacIntyre tended to stress one side or the other of this contradiction, but not its unity (Marx 1975: 388). This weakness in his thought manifests itself in a contradiction between the essentialist dismissal of working-class struggles in his essay 'The *Theses on Feuerbach*: A Road Not Taken' and the recognition, in *Dependent Rational Animals* and elsewhere, that sometimes these struggles can underpin virtuous resistance to capitalism (Blackledge 2009; cf Lutz 2004: 28; Knight 1999: 86).

A more dialectical approach than is evident in MacIntyre's work would recognize the contradictory unity of struggles in and against capitalism. And rather than search simply for virtue forming practices that point to 'timeless truths', it is better to register that new social relations underpin novel forms of practice through which new needs and capacities are realized. Among these needs is the need for community in the decidedly modern form as expressed in Marx's vision of "an association, in which the free development of each is the condition for the free development of all" and through which the 'needs principle' might be realized: 'From each according to ability, to each according to need.' MacIntyre believes that relations between independent practical reasoners should satisfy this formula (MacIntyre 1999: 129–30). I think he is right, but this formulation is no transhistorical standard. Rather it emerged as an organic demand of Marx's 'new-fangled' working class (Blackledge 2012: 52; 60–1; 83). As such this principle itself reflects new needs and capacities, and thus a (potential) new nature that can only be realized politically through conflicts with the egoism reproduced by the market: this is the kind of political perspective that MacIntyre has unfortunately retreated from.

References

Arnhart, L. (1998), *Darwinian Natural Right*. New York: SUNY.
Blackledge, P. (2005), 'Freedom, Desire and Revolution: Alasdair MacIntyre's Early Marxist Ethics', *History of Political Thought*, 26 (4): 696–720.
Blackledge, P. (2007a), 'Morality and Revolution: Ethical Debates in the British New Left', *Critique*, 35 (2): 203–20.
Blackledge, P. (2007b), 'Alasdair MacIntyre: Marxism and Politics', *Studies in Marxism*, 11: 95–116.
Blackledge, P. (2008), 'Alasdair MacIntyre's Contribution to Marxism: A Road Not Taken', in P. Blackledge and K. Knight (eds), *Revolutionary Aristotelianism: Ethics, Resistance and Utopia*, 215–27. Stuttgart: Lucius and Lucius.
Blackledge, P. (2009), 'Alasdair MacIntyre: Social Practices, Marxism and Ethical Anti-Capitalism', *Political Studies*, 57 (4): 866–84.
Blackledge, P. (2012), *Marxism and Ethics*, New York: SUNY Press.
Blackledge, P. (2014a), 'Alasdair MacIntyre as a Marxist and as a critic of Marxism', *American Catholic Philosophical Quarterly*, 88 (4): 705–24.
Blackledge, P. (2018), 'Engels, Social Reproduction and the Problem of a Unitary Theory of Women's Oppression', *Social Theory and Practice*, 44 (3): 297–321.

Blackledge, P. (2019a), 'Utopias: Future, Present and Concrete in Alasdair MacIntyre and C.L.R. James', *International Critical Thought*, 9 (3): 420-35.
Blackledge, P. (2019b), *Friedrich Engels*, New York: SUNY Press.
Bloch, E. (1987), *Natural Law and Human Dignity*, Cambridge: MIT Press.
Brady, B. (2008), *Essential Catholic Social Thought*, New York: Orbis.
Coleman, J. (1994), 'MacIntyre and Aquinas', in John Horton and Susan Mendus (eds), *After MacIntyre: Critical Perspectives on the Work of Alasdair MacIntyre*, Notre Dame, IN: University of Notre Dame Press, 1994.
Curran, C. (2002), *Catholic Social Teaching*, Washington: Georgetown University Press.
Daly, J. (1996), *Marx, Justice and Dialectic*, Holywood: Priory Press.
Eagleton, T. (1999), 'Self-Realization, Ethics and Socialism', *New Left Review*, 237: 150-61.
Engels, F. (1987), 'Anti-Dühring', in *Marx and Engels Collected Works*, vol. 25, 5-309, Moscow: Progress Publishers.
Fisk, Milton (1989), *The State as Justice*, Cambridge: Cambridge University Press.
Goldmann, L. (1968), *The Philosophy of the Enlightenment*, London: Routledge and Kegan Paul.
Knight, K. (1999), 'The Ethical Post Marxism of Alasdair MacIntyre', in M. Cowling and P. Reynolds (eds), *Marxism, The Millennium and Beyond*, London: Palgrave.
Knight, K. (2007), *Aristotelian Philosophy: Ethics and Politics from Aristotle to MacIntyre*, Cambridge: Polity Press.
Lutz, C. (2004), *Tradition in the Ethics of Alasdair MacIntyre*, New York: Lexington Books.
MacIntyre, A. (1953), *Marxism: An Interpretation*, London: SCM Press.
MacIntyre, A. (1972), 'Justice: A New Theory and Some Old Questions' [Review of *A Theory of Justice* by John Rawls], *Boston University Law Review*, 52: 330-4.
MacIntyre, A. (1988), *Whose Justice? Whose Rationality?* London: Duckworth.
MacIntyre, A. (1994), 'A Partial Response to My Critics', in John Horton and Susan Mendus (eds), *After MacIntyre: Critical Perspectives on the Work of Alasdair MacIntyre*, 283-304, Notre Dame, IN: University of Notre Dame Press.
MacIntyre, A. (1995), *Marxism and Christianity*, London: Duckworth.
MacIntyre, A. (1998a), *A Short History of Ethics*, London: Routledge.
MacIntyre, A. (1998b), 'Theses on Feuerbach: A Road Not Taken', in K. Knight (ed.), *The MacIntyre Reader*, 223-34, Cambridge: Polity Press.
MacIntyre, A. (1998c), 'Politics, Philosophy and the Common Good', in K. Knight (ed.), *The MacIntyre Reader*, 235-52, Cambridge: Polity.
MacIntyre, A. (1999), *Dependent Rational Animals*, London: Duckworth.
MacIntyre, A. ([1981] 2007). *After Virtue: A Study in Moral Theory*, 3rd edn, Notre Dame: Notre Dame University Press.
MacIntyre, A. (2008a), 'Notes from the Moral Wilderness', in P. Blackledge and N. Davidson (eds), *Alasdair MacIntyre's Engagement with Marxism: Selected Writings 1953-1974*, Leiden: Brill.
MacIntyre, a. (2008b), 'The Sleepwalking Society: Britain in the Sixties', in P. Blackledge and N. Davidson (eds), *Alasdair MacIntyre's Engagement with Marxism: Selected Writings 1953-1974*, Leiden: Brill.
MacIntyre, A. (2016), *Ethics in the Conflicts of Modernity: An Essay on Desire, Practical Reasoning and Narrative*, Cambridge: Cambridge University Press.
Margolis, J. (1992), 'Praxis and Meaning', in G. McCarthy (ed.), *Marx and Aristotle*, Lanham, MD: Rowman & Littlefield.
Marx, K. (1975), 'Economic and Philosophical Manuscripts', in *Marx and Engels Collected Works*, vol. 3, 231-346, Moscow: Progress Publishers.

Marx, K. (1976), *Capital*, Vol. I, London: Penguin.
Meikle, S. (1985), *Essentialism in the Thought of Karl Marx*, La Salle: Open Court.
Miller, D. (1994), 'Virtues, Practices and Justice', in J. Horton and S. Mendus (eds), *After MacIntyre: Critical Perspectives on the Work of Alasdair MacIntyre*, Notre Dame, IN: University of Notre Dame Press.
Morton. A. L. (1989), *A People's History of England*, London: Lawrence and Wishart.
Pettitt, P. (1994), 'Liberal/Communitarian: MacIntyre's Mesmeric Dichotomy', in John Horton and Susan Mendus (eds), *After MacIntyre: Critical Perspectives on the Work of Alasdair MacIntyre*, Notre Dame, IN: University of Notre Dame Press.
Ramsay, Maureen (1997), *What's Wrong with Liberalism?* London: Leicester University Press.
Turner, S. (2003), 'MacIntyre in the Province of the Philosophy of Social Science', in Mark Murphy (ed.), *Alasdair MacIntyre*. Cambridge: Cambridge University Press.

Index

Ackrill, John Lloyd 74
acquisition 12, 19, 52–6, 65, 131, 140–1
action 2, 5, 15, 17, 19, 26, 45, 52, 59, 60, 62–7, 70–2, 78, 82–3, 85, 111–15, 119, 122, 130, 132, 135–6, 140, 144, 149–50, 153, 160, 171, 176, 177, 178, 182–3, 185, 193, 209, 220, 225, 226, 228, 230, *see also praxis* (πρᾶξις)
Adkins, A. W. H. 13, 14, 23
advantage 26, 84, 90, 100, 132–3, 198, 200
affection 3, 78, 82–5, 87–8, 89
agapē (ἀγάπη) 81, 103, 179, 180, 182, 185, 190
Alexander the Great 15, 25, 127
alliance (summachia/συμμαχία) 78, 82, 101, 137, 169
alochos (ἄλοχος) 41, 49, 55
Althusius, Johannes 198, 205
altruism 91
amicitia 81, 103
andreia (ἀνδρεία)/courage 17, 19, 33, 36–7, 44–5, 47, 72, 134, 144, 145, 176, 184–5, 228
animal, political (zōon politikon/ζῷον πολιτικόν) 6, 11, 14, 16, 29, 30, 33, 37, 40–1, 43–4, 48–51, 53–5, 57, 61, 68, 72–4, 76–7, 81, 93, 117, 121, 124, 137, 141–3, 145–6, 151, 153, 156–8, 160, 164, 172, 176–8, 184, 191, 210, 214, 217, 229
Annas, Julia 39
Anscombe, Elizabeth 1, 125, 127, 145
Anselm of Canterbury 101
antiquity 2, 95, 114
Apostoles, Michael 96
Aquinas, St Thomas vii, 1, 5, 11, 15–17, 23, 94–103, 105, 114, 119, 127, 159–60, 161, 184, 190, 191, 222, 229–32
  Thomism 5, 94, 98, 99, 101, 104, 120, 222, 230, 232

Arabatzis, George 102, 103, 105
Arendt, Hannah 40, 44–5, 186, 195
aretē (ἀρετή) 3, 13, 47–8, 50, 52, 56, 84, 88, 131–2, 183–4, 187, 210, *see also* excellence; virtue
aristocracy (ἀριστοκρατία) 48, 135, 138
Aristotle 1–7, 11–15, 17–23, 25–38, 40–56, 58–74, 76–91, 95–7, 99–104, 111–20, 123, 126–45, 148, 150–61, 164–5, 170, 175–8, 183–7, 189–90, 192–205, 208–14, 216–20, 222, 225, 228–30, 232
  Aristotelianism 1–2, 4–7, 18, 21, 94, 96, 97, 102, 104, 105, 113–14, 118–21, 123, 132, 147, 170, 186–7, 212, 214, 219, 228–9
  Aristotelian tradition 1, 4, 25, 119, 127, 145
Arnhart, Larry 223, 233
artefact 34, 41–2, 55, 149
aspiration 5, 98, 119, 160, 175, 178–9
association (koinōnia/κοινωνία) 26, 28–9, 38, 44, 47–8, 51, 54–6, 77, 82–5, 90–1, 180, 193–6, 198–200, 205–7, 233, *see also* community; society
Athens 11, 34, 36, 38, 52, 55, 57, 134–5, 141, 157, 193–6
Augustine, St 15, 96, 101, 112, 119, 120, 163, 181, 183, 190
Austin, J. L. 5, 111–23
authority 18, 20, 35, 48, 50, 55, 70, 96, 104, 194, 196–7, 199, 201, 203–4, 207, 210, 230, 231
automation (αὐτόματος) 40, 50, 54, 211, 212
autonomy 159, 160, 226

banausos (βάναυσος) 220
barbarian (βάρβαρος) 14, 29, 52, 104, 132
Barker, Ernest 39, 55, 57, 195–6, 202
Barlaam of Calabria 96, 97, 104

beauty 36, 129
Benakis, Linos G. 99, 105
benefactor 200
Bentham, Jeremy 5, 113, 118, 119, 122, 166, 224
Berlin, Isaiah 117, 119, 120, 123
Bernstein, Richard J. 165-6
Bessarion, Basilius 2, 94, 96, 97, 99, 104
Bielskis, Andrius vi, 6, 7, 40, 45, 46, 56, 90, 91
biology 37, 44, 48, 54, 121, 131-4, 142-3, 232
biology, metaphysical 129, 132, 213, 228-9
Blackburn, Simon 162, 169
Blackledge, Paul vi, 6, 223, 224, 226, 227, 228, 231, 232, 233
Bloch, Ernst 231
Blundell, Mary 81
Bodéüs, Richard 12
Borradori, Giovanna 163
Bradley, A. C. 21
Brisson, Luc 38
Broadie, Sarah 33, 78, 83, 84
Bryennius, Joseph 99, 103
Burns, Tony vi, 6, 192, 205
Byzantium 6, 94-6, 98-9, 101, 103, 106-7

Cabasilas, Nilus 99, 100
Calhoun, Craig 193
Callicles 50, 52, 56
capitalism 56, 214, 216-18, 225-8, 230-1, 233
Case, John 18, 19, 20, 23
Cassirer, Ernst 159
Cavell, Stanley 190
character 2, 27, 46, 48, 69, 78-9, 80, 83, 85-6, 88, 103, 116, 123, 127, 131-50, 159, 163, 176-7, 180-1, 184, 186-7, 195, 197, 199, 201, 209-10, 213, 217, 224, 230, 232
choice 25, 43, 63-6, 74, 87, 120, 152, 154, 157, 159-60, 220
Choumnos, Nikephoros 94
chrēmatistikē (χρηματιστική) 41, 53-4, 56
Christianity 120, 162, 176, 180-2, 184, 186-7, 190, 224, 231

chronos (χρόνος) 85, 87, 91, *see also* kairos; time
Chrysippus 159
Cicero, Marcus Tullius 81
citizen (politēs/πολίτης) 11-14, 22, 26-9, 32, 34-7, 44, 46-8, 69, 70-1, 73-4, 77, 81, 126-7, 129, 136, 138-41, 143, 157, 186, 192, 195, 197, 199-201, 203, 208-12, 216, 230
citizenship 11, 47, 209-12, 214, 219
city/city-state 5-6, 12, 15-16, 19, 21, 26-31, 33-8, 45-8, 55-6, 68, 77, 83, 92, 100, 126-9, 137-41, 195-6, 198, 209-12, *see also* polis (πόλις); society; state
Coleman, Janet 222-3, 232
Collingwood, R. G. 15, 163
communism 123, 192, 218, 231
communitarianism 126-8
communitarians 128-9, 136
community 3, 5-7, 26-7, 36, 44, 77, 91, 126-30, 134-7, 139-40, 143-4, 160, 195, 199-200, 205, 207, 212-17, 219, 227-8, 231, 233, *see also* association (koinōnia/κοινωνία); society
concord (homonoia/ὁμόνοια) 3, 83, 92
Connell, Sophia 55
Constant, Benjamin 2
constitution 14, 22, 30-3, 35-6, 38, 46-8, 59, 77, 83, 91, 98, 138-41, 193, 196, 210
contemplation 6, 62-3, 65, 68-74, 97, 152, 189
Cooper, John Madison 8, 38, 74, 80, 83, 161
Couloubaritsis, Lambros 87, 90, 91
Crete/Cretan 34, 36
Crisp, Roger 74
Cydones, Demetrius 5, 94-104

Daly, James 232
Darwin, Charles 228, 232
Del Vecchio, Giorgio 203, 204
Demetracopoulos, John A. 95
democracy (δημοκρατία) 4, 36, 46-7, 55, 138-9, 145, 206, 211, 219
deontology 1, 5, 122, 127

desire 11, 64–6, 81, 85, 89, 102, 115, 120, 122–3, 125, 141, 152, 156, 161, 172, 176–7, 180–3, 185, 187, 191–3, 221, 225–6
despotēs (δεσπότης) 41, 50, *see also* master
Diderot, Denis 225
dikaion (δίκαιον) 22
dikaiosunē (δικαιοσύνη) 83, *see also* justice
disposition/*hexis* (ἕξις) 3, 19, 31, 59, 87, 116, 131–2, 135–6, 145, 183
Doukas, Dimitrius 2
doulos (δοῦλος) 41, 45, 50–1, *see also* slave
Dreizehnter, Alois 56
Dunbabin, Jean 17
Dunne, Joseph vii, 6, 175
Durkheim, Émile 193, 194, 200, 204

Eagleton, Terry 183, 219, 232
education 5, 12, 17–20, 23–4, 30, 33, 37, 46, 49–50, 95, 100, 126–7, 140–1, 156–7, 198, 205–7, 212, 215, 217
egalitarianism 212
Elias, Norbert 188
emotivism 113, 115, 121, 165, 170, 171
energeia (ἐνέργεια) 59, 105
Engels, Friedirch 231
Enlightenment 2–3, 5, 113, 115, 119, 128, 148, 163–6, 168, 179, 190, 206, 217, 224
entelecheia (ἐντελέχεια) 42
equality/inequality 3, 40, 44–5, 49, 51, 188, 192–3, 199, 202–4, 211–12, 217–18, 220
erōs (ἔρως) 80–1, 89, 91, 92
eudaimonia (εὐδαιμονία) 2–3, 6, 13, 47, 58, 73–4, 77, 124, 130–2, 175, 212, *see also* happiness
eunoia (εὔνοια)/goodwill 52, 56, 84–5, 87–9, 90
eu zēn (εὖ ζῆν) 2, 45, 77
excellence 2–3, 7, 21, 45, 47–8, 57, 77, 83–90, 91, 113, 120–1, 128, 130–2, 134–6, 140, 184, 209, 211, 213, 217, 219, 228, *see also aretē*; virtue

Fisk, Milton 224
Foot, Philippa 1, 15, 176
Foucault, Michel 164, 168, 171, 188, 189
Frankfurt, Harry 162, 170
freedom 14, 40, 44–5, 70, 111, 114, 121, 123, 138–9, 148, 159–60, 208, 210, 212, 214, 216–20, 224–5, 233
Freud, Sigmund 162, 181
friendship 3, 6, 29, 46, 52, 76–93, 103, 129, 164, 176, 186, 194, 198, 200–1, *see also philia* (φιλία)
function/*ergon* (ἔργον) 14, 21, 30, 43–5, 47, 53, 58, 60–1, 63, 67, 131–2, 150–1, 176, 204, 210

Gadamer, Hans-Georg 1, 112, 163
Garlan, Yvon 52
Gazes, Theodore 96
Geach, Peter 1, 120, 123
Gerson, Lloyd 39
Gibbard, Alan 162
Glycofrydi-Leontsini, Athanasia vii, 5, 94, 99, 101, 102, 103, 104, 105
God/god (Θεός/θεός) 11, 33–4, 37, 72, 97–8, 100, 102, 105, 112, 120, 123, 137, 177–91, 199, 211, 230–1
Goldmann, Lucien 230, 231
good (*agathon/ἀγαθόν*) 3–6, 13–14, 16–20, 22, 28–37, 44, 47, 53, 55, 58–60, 62, 63–7, 69–71, 73–5, 77–9, 81–4, 86, 91, 111–23, 123, 124–5, 127–34, 137–44, 144, 145, 147–61, 161, 166, 175–88, 189, 191, 205, 208–11, 214, 216, 218, 222, 226, 228–9, 231
  common good 3, 12, 16, 19, 24, 40–50, 117, 120, 123, 136, 184, 215, 217, 219, 220, 227–8, 230, 232
  human good 6, 49, 58
good life 29, 77, 78, 86, 88–9, 122–3, 134, 212–13, *see also eudaimonia* (εὐδαιμονία); *eu zēn*
goodness 46, 52, 60
Gouldner, Alvin 194, 202
Greece 35, 38, 48, 57, 77, 81, 90, 92, 162, 206–7
Greek
  gospels 182
  imperialism 52
  intellectuals/scholars 96–7, 99, 104

language   5, 18, 20, 55, 94, 96, 99,
    100, 102–3, 113
  people   14, 45, 52, 81, 103, 132, 225
  philosophy   25, 91, 92, 102, 105–7, 181
  politics   25, 78
  studies   95
Green, T. H.   21, 116, 118
Gregoras, Nikephoros   94, 96, 97
Groff, Ruth   56
Grotius, Hugo   199, 205
Guthrie, W. K. C.   79

Hadot, Pierre   180, 189
Hampshire, Stuart   117, 119, 120, 123
happiness   6, 22, 45, 58–63, 66–75, 91,
    127–8, 130–2, 136–7, 145, 182–3,
    see also eudaimonia (εὐδαιμονία))
Hardie, W. F. R.   74
healthcare   215
health/*hugieia* (ὑγιεία)   26, 33, 36, 42,
    68–9, 129, 157, 177, 182, 216
Hegel, G. W. F.   117, 160, 170, 195, 196,
    197, 198, 203
Heidegger, Martin   112, 147, 159
Hellenistic schools   180–1
Hesychasm   96–7, 101, 105
historicity   164, 166, 224
history   3, 6, 15, 18, 23, 36, 92, 96, 104, 105,
    111–17, 119, 123–5, 128, 161, 163–5,
    170–2, 180–1, 183, 191, 193–4, 198,
    204–6, 222–6, 229, 231–3
Hobbes, Thomas   15, 42, 225
Homer   111, 184, 187
Hughes, Gerard J.   78, 92
humanism, Byzantine   95
  Italian   95
  socialist   224
Hume, David   121
Hursthouse, Rosalind   1, 176

institution   34, 36, 48–52, 115, 121–2,
    124, 144, 189, 190, 193, 196, 198,
    201, 203–5, 214
interaction   16, 38, 105, 152–3, 193,
    198–9, 217
interest/*sumphēron* (συμφέρον)   3–4,
    26, 40, 51–2, 69, 77–80, 82–4, 90,
    198–204
Irwin, Terrence   74

Jaspers, Karl   187, 190
Jones, Nicholas F.   196
justice   3, 6, 17, 19, 24–30, 36–7, 39,
    47, 52, 56–7, 60, 77, 83, 92, 102,
    119–20, 124, 126–8, 134, 136–9,
    141–2, 144–5, 157, 164, 166, 168–9,
    171–2, 176, 179, 185, 194, 199–200,
    202–4, 206, 213, see also dikaiosunē
    (δικαιοσύνη)

kairos (καιρός)   85, 87–90, 91, 92, see also
    time; *chronos* (χρόνος)
Kalekas, Manuel   99
Kallistos, Andronikos   2, 96
Kamariotes, Matthew   96
Kant, Immanuel   5, 43, 55, 78, 113, 120,
    121, 126, 157, 158, 159, 160, 164,
    166, 225
Kantianism/Kantian   43, 55, 111, 114,
    147, 159
kapilikē (καπηλική)   41, 53–4
Karamanolis, George   95, 96, 104
Keyt, David   75
Knight, Kelvin   viii, 5, 111, 122, 144, 227,
    228, 233
Konstan, David   80, 81
Korsgaard, Christine   43, 147, 158
Kraut, Richard   22, 41, 54, 55, 74, 202,
    210

labour   7, 45, 54, 140, 201, 203–4,
    208–11, 213, 215–19
language   25, 32, 49, 52, 56, 80, 100–1
Las Casas, Bartolomé de   18, 22
law   5, 12, 16–17, 19, 25–6, 34–9, 51–2,
    55–6, 77, 94, 102, 112–13, 121–5,
    140, 145, 161–2, 184, 195–6, 199,
    201, 205, 222, 230–2
  law ethics   102 (see also *nomos*
    (νόμος))
lawgiver   3, 36
Lawrence, D. H.   162
Lear, Jonathan   41
legislation   17, 28, 36–7, 126, 137, 141,
    159
Leontsini, Eleni   viii, 6, 76, 81, 85, 90
Levinas, Emmanuel   147, 151, 159, 160
liberalism   3–4, 118, 126–7, 168, 224,
    226–7

liberty 14, 21, 24, 27
Livanos, Christopher 96, 106
Lord, Carnes 21
Lubasz, Heinz 21
Lukács, György 226
Luther, Martin 231
Lutz, Christopher 229, 230, 231, 233

McBride, Cillian 193-4
McDowell, John 1, 133, 146
Machiavelli, Niccolò 18
MacIntyre, Alasdair viii, 1-2, 4-7, 11, 18, 19, 25, 30, 34-7, 40, 49, 55, 56, 103, 111-23, 126, 128-30, 132, 135, 136-45, 147-8, 153-61, 162-71, 176, 181, 183, 184, 189, 204-5, 208, 212-16, 219, 220, 222-33
Maggini, Golfo ix, 5, 162
Malakos, Apostolos ix, 5, 147
Mardosas, Egidijus ix, 6, 7, 208
Margolis, Joseph 232
Maritain, Jacques 120
Marsilius of Padua 196-7
Marx, Karl 7, 21, 45, 53-4, 56, 118-20, 123, 163, 169-70, 208, 215-20, 224-30, 232-3
master 6, 26, 40-1, 44, 50, 52, 102, 199, 204, 211-12, see also despotēs (δεσπότης)
Mayhew, Robert 39
medieval/Middle Ages 1-2, 17, 20-1, 23, 97, 103, 106, 127, 129, 194, 196, 205, 212, 231
Metochites, Theodore 94
Miller, David 222
Miller, Fred D. 4, 22-4, 39, 41, 57
Mitchell, Lynette G. 78, 92
modernity 1-4, 6, 21, 57, 111, 113, 120, 122-3, 125-7, 148, 161-3, 165, 168-72, 179, 189, 215, 221, 224, 227-8, 230
Montaigne, Michel de 88, 92
motivation 5, 88, 167, 171, 182
Mousourous, Marcus 2
Moutsopoulos, Evanghélos 91, 92, 94, 102, 104, 107
Mulgan, Richard G. 196, 207
Mulhall, Stephen 169, 171, 172, 190, 191
Murdoch, Iris 175, 189-91

Nagel, Thomas 147
nature 2, 6-7, 11, 15, 18, 22, 24-45, 48-57, 69, 71-2, 77, 80, 83, 90, 105, 111, 119, 126, 129, 131-9, 141, 143, 146, 148, 150-8, 160-1, 163, 170, 178, 180, 182-3, 187, 192, 194, 200-2, 209-10, 212-13, 215-18, 223-30, 232-3, see also phusis (φύσις)
Nederman, Cary J. 212, 221
Nehamas, Alexander 78, 92
Newton, Isaac 42
Nietzsche, Friedrich 5, 113, 115, 128, 160, 162-72, 187, 189
nomos (νόμος) 54
Nussbaum, Martha 4, 78, 92, 133, 134, 146, 162, 189, 191

oikonomia (οἰκονομία) 40-1, 44-5, 48, 53, 56
oikonomikē (οἰκονομική) 40, 53
oligarchy (ὀλιγαρχία) 19, 46-7, 138-9
Okin, Susan Moller 21, 22
Oresme, Nicole 17, 18, 23
organicism, political 45
Owen, G. E. L. 35, 36, 39

Pachymeres, Georgios 94
Pakaluk, Michael 78, 92
Palamas, Gregory 96-101, 104
Palamism 97-8, 100-1, 107
  anti-Palamites 99
Pascal, Blaise 179, 189
Péguy, Charles 187
philia (φιλία) 6, 46, 76, 78-92, see also friendship
phusis (φύσις) 32, 34, 38, 41-2, 48, 50-1, 54-5, see also nature
Piccolomini, Francesco 18-20, 23, 24
Planudes, Maximus 94
Plato 7, 12, 15, 25, 26, 28-30, 32-9, 43, 44, 46, 47, 50, 52, 56, 57, 90-2, 95-7, 99, 101, 104, 106, 111, 114, 117, 125, 131, 141, 161, 176, 180, 184, 192, 195, 196, 201, 202, 205-7
Plethon, Georgios Gemistos 94, 95, 104, 106, 107

polis (πόλις)   7, 11–13, 15, 19, 21, 25–6, 28–30, 40–1, 44–50, 76–8, 127, 137–40, 144, 145, 152, 161, 194–7, 199, 201, 203, 208–14, 218–19, *see also* city/city-state; society; state
politeia/polity (πολιτεία)   25, 46–8, 55, 145
Popper, Karl Raimund   117, 125
posis (πόσις)   41, 49, 55
practice   1–2, 6–7, 13, 19, 25, 28, 34, 38, 48–50, 53–4, 59, 68, 105, 112–13, 115–16, 119–21, 127–9, 135, 144, 151, 155, 157, 163, 166, 180–1, 189–91, 196, 205, 209, 213–15, 222–33
praxis (πρᾶξις)   41, 45, 59, 87
Price, Anthony   78, 80, 88, 92
Psellos, Michael   95

Rackham, H.   74, 75
Rapp, Christof   5, 146
Raptis, Buket Korkut   x, 6
Rawls, John   126, 224
recognition   64, 118, 142, 145, 164, 166, 182, 203, 204–7, 233
    recognition, politics of   6, 192–4, 204
Reeve, C. D. C.   56, 57, 220
Reinach, Adolf   122, 124, 125
renaissance   2, 11, 18–21, 23–4, 94–6, 99, 103, 163
Richardson Lear, Gabriel   62–7, 74, 75
Roche, Timothy   74, 75
Rosler, Andrés   201, 207
Ross, David   23, 56, 57, 90, 91, 116, 195, 205, 207, 220
Rowe, Christopher   38, 39, 74, 78, 83, 84, 92

Saunders, Trevor J.   38, 39
Schmitt, Charles B.   18, 23, 24
Schofield, Malcolm   39, 56, 57, 80, 92
Scholarios, Georgios Gennadios   95–7, 99, 100, 104–7
Scholasticism   98–9, 106
Schollmeier, Paul   78, 80, 92
Schopenhauer, Arthur   182, 183, 191
Searle, John   121, 122, 125
Sepúlveda, Juan Ginés de   18
Sherman, Nancy   78, 92

Skinner, Quentin   117, 125
slave   6, 14, 18, 29, 36, 40–1, 43–5, 48, 50–7, 81, 210–13, *see also doulos* (δοῦλος)
slavery/*douleia* (δουλεία)   45, 48, 50–2, 54, 56, 57, 209, 213
Slote, Michael   1
socialism   118, 212, 219, 226, 230, 232, 233
society   2–3, 16, 21, 25–30, 32, 36–7, 56, 70, 77, 83, 92–3, 107, 111, 113, 116, 118–20, 123, 125, 142, 159, 187–8, 192–205, 211, 213, 217–19, 225, 229, 231, *see also* association (koinōnia/κοινωνία); community
sōphrosunē (σωφροσύνη)   54
Sparshott, Francis   12, 24
Sparta   14, 34, 36, 138, 141
Springborg, Patricia   21, 24
Socrates   25–34, 36, 38, 50, 52, 56, 181, 188, 190
Sophocles   92, 115, 119
soul/*psuchē* (ψυχή)   26–7, 31–5, 37–8, 49, 58–63, 181, 184–5, 187
Stalley, Richard   6, 7, 29, 39, 55, 57, 90–2
state   3, 5, 20–1, 26, 35, 42–8, 54, 68–9, 78, 83, 92, 97, 115, 118, 122, 135–41, 163, 165, 176, 179–80, 182, 186–7, 195–201, 214–19, 225, 228, 231, *see also* association (koinōnia/κοινωνία); city/city-state, *polis* (πόλις); society
Stein, Edith   122, 124
Stern-Gillet, Suzanne   78, 81, 82, 93
Stevenson, Charles L.   169, 172
Strawson, Peter   112, 125
Swift, Jonathan   2

Tatakis, Basil   96, 107
Taylor, Charles   6, 162, 175–80, 182, 187–91
Telfer, Elizabeth   90, 93
Thomism, Aristotelian   222, 230
    pro-Thomists-anti-Thomists debate   97–8, 100
Thomism, Byzantine   5, 94, 98–9, 120
Thomism, MacIntyrean   222, 230, 232
Thrasymachus   31, 50, 52, 56

time 6–7, 11–13, 17, 27, 31, 41–2, 50, 76–89, 91, 100, 102, 113, 121, 135, 157, 160, 196, 209, 211–14, 218–19, *see also chronos* (χρόνος)
Tönnies, Ferdinand 194, 199, 200, 207
Trapezountios, George 96
Trotsky, Leon 165

Urmson, J. O. 78, 93, 124, 205
utilitarianism 1, 118, 226
utility 45, 82–6, 88, 95, 117–18

Venice 19–20, 77
Vico, Gianbattista 163
virtue 1–7, 12–20, 34, 36–7, 44, 46–8, 52, 56, 58–63, 65–73, 78, 81, 87–8, 93, 94, 102, 113–21, 123–46, 151–2, 161, 164–6, 168, 171–2, 175–7, 179, 183–7, 189, 190, 191, 205–17, 220, 222, 226–9, 232–3
Visconti, Luchino 215
Vitoria, Francisco de 18

Weber, Max 169, 194
Wilde, Oscar 162
William of Moerbeke 15
Williams, Bernard 5, 120, 123, 127, 133, 146, 148–54, 156–63, 170–2, 189
Witt, Charlotte 21
Wittgenstein, Ludwig 112, 121, 122, 124, 125

Yack, Bernard 90, 93